Protected Areas

and the

Regional Planning Imperative
in North America

Other books in the **Parks and Heritage** series:

Protected Areas

and the

Regional Planning Imperative in North America

Integrating Nature Conservation and Sustainable Development

J. G. Nelson,
J. C. Day,
and
Lucy Sportza,
editors,
with
Carlos Israel Vázquez,
and James Loucky

University of Calgary Press & Michigan State University Press

© 2003 J.G. Nelson, J.C. Day, Lucy Sportza, editors, with Carlos Israel Vázquez,
James Loucky. All rights reserved.

University of Calgary Press
2500 University Drive NW
Calgary, Alberta
Canada T2N 1N4
www.uofcpress.com

Michigan State University Press
1405 South Harrison Road
25 Manly Miles Building
East Lansing, MI 48823-5202
www.msupress.msu.edu

National Library of Canada Cataloguing in Publication Data

Main entry under title:

Protected areas and the regional planning imperative in North America : integrating nature conservation and
sustainable development / JG. Nelson, JC. Day, Lucy Sportza, editors, with Carlos Israel Vázquez,
James Loucky.

(Parks and heritage series, ISSN 1494-0426 ; 7)
(Henderson book series ; no. 30)
Papers from the conference, Regional Approaches to Parks and Protected Areas in North America,
held at Tijuana, Mexico, Mar. 2002.
Includes bibliographical references and index.
ISBN 1-55238-084-X University of Calgary Press
ISBN 0-87013-673-9 Michigan State University Press

1. Protected areas--North America--Congresses. 2. Natural
areas--North America--Congresses. 3. Nature conservation--North
America--Congresses. 4. Regional planning--North America--Congresses.
5. Sustainable development--North America--Congresses. I. Nelson, J. G.
(James Gordon), 1932- II. Day, John C. (John Chadwick), 1936- III.
Sportza, Lucy M. IV. Title: Regional approaches to parks and protected
areas in North America. V. Series. VI. Series.
QH77.N56P76 2003   333.78'16'097   C2002-910020-0

The Canada Council for the Arts
Le Conseil des Arts du Canada

We acknowledge the financial support of the Government of Canada through the Book Publishing Industry
Development Program (BPIDP) for our publishing activities.

The Henderson Book Series honours the kind and generous donation of Mrs. Arthur T. Henderson, who
made this series possible. The Canadian Parks and Wilderness Society gratefully acknowledges Mrs.
Henderson's support of our efforts to build public support for protecting Canada's wilderness areas.

The Canadian Parks and Wilderness Society (CPAWS) is Canada's grassroots voice for wilderness. Since our
founding in 1963, we have helped protect over 100 million acres of treasured wild places. We focus on
establishing new parks and on making sure nature comes first in their management. Call us at 1-800-333-
WILD for more information or to become members.

Printed and bound in Canada by AGMV Marquis
∞ This book is printed on acid-free paper.

Page, cover design, and typesetting by Mieka West.

A portion of the royalties from the sales of this book are contributed to Canadian Parks and Wilderness
Society to support wilderness protection.

To the nongovernmental organizations which have done so much to promote better understanding and appreciation of the vital roles of protected areas in regional conservation and sustainable development in Canada, the United States, and Mexico.

Contents

United States of America

The United States of Mexico

Retrospectives

Postscript

List of Figures

List of Tables

List of Boxes

List of Photographs

Foreword

Protected Areas and the Regional Planning Imperative in North America has at least five unique attributes. First, no comparable book is available on the role of protected areas in nature conservation and sustainable development in Canada, the United States, and Mexico. Second, the book links or integrates ecological, land use, economic, social, cultural, and institutional concerns about protected areas through regional planning at local, national, international, and continental scales. Only one earlier set of papers reflecting such a regional perspective seems to be available—*Conservation of Biodiversity and the New Regional Planning*—edited by R. E. Saunier and R. A. Meganck and published by IUCN-The World Conservation Union. Third, *Protected Areas and the Regional Planning Imperative in North America* takes a broad civic approach involving natural and social scientists, relevant government officials, nongovernment personnel, and citizens from all three countries. Fourth, the book includes relevant situations and examples from throughout North America, with some focus on the Baja California area in the case of Mexico. Fifth, the book reflects the influence of the North American Free Trade Agreement (NAFTA) which is forcing people in the three countries to think and plan more actively on international and continental scales.

In making the foregoing remarks, we are mindful of many cross-border international studies that have been done between Canada and the United States and Mexico over the years. However, it is primarily since the rise of international trade agreements, such as NAFTA, that comparative studies involving the three countries have become more salient and significant to research, public policy, and civic affairs.

In this respect, a few North American books could serve as companion pieces for this volume. Examples are Earle and Wirth's (1995) *Identities in North America: the Search for Community,* and Kiy and Wirth's (1998) *Environmental Management on North America's Borders.* The first volume deals in some depth with the historical, cultural, economic, and social differences among the three countries that arise rather frequently in *Protected Areas and the Regional Planning Imperative in North America.* The second volume is of special interest because it provides a picture of challenges and responses in other aspects of environmental planning, management, and decision making in the three countries; notably air and water quality. In our view, more comparative volumes like these are needed if we are to understand and respond effectively and equitably to the many challenges posed by the rapidly evolving new geography of North America in our time.

Gordon Nelson for the editors

References

Earle, Robet L. and John D. Wirth (eds). 1995. *Identities in North America: The Search for Community.* Stanford, CA: Stanford University Press.

Kiy, Richard and John D. Wirth (eds). 1998. *Environmental Management on North America's Borders*. College Station: Texas A&M University.

Saunier, Ricard E., and Richard A. Meganck (eds). 1995. *Conservation of Biodiversity and the New Regional Planning*. Gland, Switzerland: Organization of American States and IUCN–The World Conservation Union.

Preface

How shall we care for the North American landscape so that natural and human communities thrive? For me, this is the key question for our time.

We know that human activities are systematically reducing the life-supporting capacity of natural communities even as rising human populations and consumption make increasingly heavy demands on nature. We know that the current inventory of parks and protected areas are not enough to conserve nature; we are losing species in even the largest parks of North America. Encroaching industrial development around parks isolates wildlife populations, leaving them vulnerable to local extinction from natural catastrophe, genetic inbreeding, and human destruction.

Yet industrial developments prejudicial to sustaining nature enjoy priority as land uses, and often appear immune to land-use planning processes. Mining trumps all other uses in many North American jurisdictions, regardless of the wishes of local communities or property owners. Industrial logging under government-approved forest management plans usually overwhelms other more sustainable land uses enjoying community support. Oil and gas development under government-issued leases often does the same. If we care about nature conservation, such industrial and other development must be constrained and carefully regulated under regional planning frameworks.

So regional planning is imperative. Planning that is ecosystem-based, providing for ecological connections between protected wild places. Planning that realizes the potential of each parcel of land, whether privately or publicly owned, to contribute to the health of natural and human communities. Planning that is grounded in local communities and is not imposed by distant corporate enterprises or governments.

The Canadian Parks and Wilderness Society (CPAWS) was a leader in the Yukon to Yellowstone Conservation Initiative (Y2Y). It seeks to ensure that the wilderness, wildlife, and natural processes of this Rocky Mountain region continue to function as an interconnected web of life, capable of supporting its resident human and natural communities. Y2Y provides a big vision for regional planning that would allow ecological connections between protected areas to be maintained or renewed. The CPAWS-initiated Algonquin to Adirondacks Conservation Initiative (A2A), Baja California to Bering Sea Marine Conservation Initiative (B2B), and Boreal Forest Campaign all have similar objectives. This book reflects and builds on these and similar efforts of many other conservation organizations and individuals in Mexico, the United States, and Canada.

The book is a crucial contribution to understanding protected areas in the broader context of regional planning; in doing so it points the way forward to a cared-for North American landscape where natural and human communities will thrive.

Stephen Hazell, Executive Director
CANADIAN PARKS AND WILDERNESS SOCIETY
Ottawa, Ontario, Canada

Acknowledgments

This monograph is based on a workshop on Regional Approaches to Parks and Protected Areas in North America, held at Tijuana, Mexico, March 1999. Numerous people took part in, or presented a paper at, the workshop and we cannot thank them all specifically here. Many attendees covered their travel costs to the workshop and in preparing papers and we are grateful for this support. We recognize the organizational support of El Colegio de la Frontera Norte (COLEF), Western Washington University, and Simon Fraser University. These institutions entered into a joint program in environmental management in 1996 sponsored by the College and University Affiliations Program, U. S. Department of State. The principal workshop organizer was the Heritage Resources Centre, University of Waterloo in co-operation with these universities.

Funding support was critical to the success of the workshop and we thank the following for their contributions: Social Science and Humanities Research Council of Canada; Heritage Resources Centre, University of Waterloo; U.S. Information Agency; Simon Fraser University; North American Wetlands Conservation Council (Canada); Parks Canada; World Wildlife Fund-U.S.; Huxley College of Environmental Studies, Western Washington University; El Colegio de la Frontera Norte; and Canadian Parks and Wilderness Society. We especially thank Carlos Israel Vázquez of El Colegio de la Frontera Norte, who served as local arrangements coordinator and Jürgen Hoth, then of the Mexican Embassy, Ottawa. James Loucky provided important assistance in coordinating the workshop and arranging for papers for this volume. Lucy Sportza and Jim Porter helped in the preparation of the manuscript, Paul Degrace prepared the figures, Laurence Lee converted the photographs to tiff files and managed the photo collection, and Beth Dempster prepared the index. The editors also wish to acknowledge the Southwestern Research Station of the New York Museum of Natural History which provided a base and facilities to Gordon Nelson while editing this book. We also wish to thank University of Calgary Press staff for their guidance and advice, particularly Walter Hildebrandt, John King, Jean Llewellyn, and Mieka West. The Social Sciences and Humanities Research Council has supported the protected area and regional planning research of J. Gordon Nelson and his students in the Heritage Resources Centre at the University of Waterloo for more than a decade. It was this work which motivated the Tijuana workshop. Gordon Nelson took the photographs unless otherwise noted. Chad Day, Sabine Jessen, Marilyn Kazmers, Larry Lamb, Patrick Lawrence, and Southwest Parks and Monuments Association also contributed pictures. We are grateful for permission to include chapter 8 that was published previously in the *Natural Areas Journal*. Other chapters were also published previously in a special issue of *Environments*.

Overview of Protected Areas and the Regional Planning Imperative in North America: Integrating Nature Conservation and Sustainable Development

J. G. Nelson, J. C. Day, Lucy Sportza,
with Carlos Israel Vázquez and James Loucky

Widespread misunderstanding of socioeconomic, environmental, and institutional similarities and differences among Canada, the United States, and Mexico, is a fundamental challenge to nature conservation and sustainable development in North America. This failure to comprehend the broad setting for relevant planning, management, and decision-making, is a major barrier to building the awareness, and interaction essential to collaborative enterprises on a continental scale. And increased interaction and collaboration are absolutely vital to the individual, group, state, and international efforts required for effective nature conservation and sustainable development in North America (Ezcurra, Gatewood, and Williams and Nelson, this volume).

Nature conservation and sustainable development are essential requirements for the future well-being of human and other life on earth. Nowhere is this more apparent than in Canada, the United States, and Mexico. Our minds and our senses are assaulted each day by direct experiences with air and water pollution, and other environmental and social stresses. The press and other media raise evidence of, and concern about, degradation of the atmosphere, as well as the great grasslands, deserts, mountains, the Great Lakes heartland, and the coasts of the Arctic,

Photograph 1.1. Intensive erosion and land degradation in west central Mexico

Pacific, Atlantic, and Caribbean. On a daily basis we also engage in frequently fragmented and disjointed attempts to deal with these changes and their impacts on life, locally, nationally, and internationally. Seldom do we gather as people of different places, cultures, values, experiences, and lifestyles to compare notes on what is happening, what is being done about it, and whether we can do more together in our own and the common interest.

The papers in this volume arise from such a meeting—a scientific, professional, and civic workshop on protected areas and their role in nature conservation and sustainable development in Canada, the United States, and Mexico. The meeting was civic in the sense that it deliberately aimed to bring together people of different backgrounds and interests—notably ecologists and other natural scientists, economists and other social scientists, geographers, planners, and other bridge builders, government officials, staff of nongovernmental organizations (NGOs), educators, and citizens.

The focus of interest was the state of understanding and planning of national parks and protected areas in Canada, the United States, and Mexico, especially from a regional planning perspective. The meeting was held from 20 to 24 March 1999, at Tijuana, Mexico, and was attended by thirty to thirty-five participants, more or less equally representative of the three countries (appendix I). The meeting was organized by the Heritage Resources Centre, University of Waterloo; the Trinational University Consortium of Simon Fraser University, Canada, Western Washington University, U.S.A., and El Colegio de la Frontera Norte (COLEF), Mexico, that hosted the event.

Table 1.1. World Conservation Union (IUCN) Protected Area Categories [a]

I. Strict Nature Reserve/Wilderness Area
- areas of land and/or sea possessing some outstanding or representative ecosystems, geological or physiological features, and/or species
- large areas of unmodified or slightly modified land, and/or sea, which retain their natural character and influence
- primarily areas for scientific research and/or environmental monitoring
- areas without permanent or significant habitation
- protected and managed to preserve their natural condition

II. National Park
- areas managed mainly for ecosystem conservation and recreation
- areas designated to:
  - protect the ecological integrity of one or more ecosystems over the long term
  - exclude exploitation or incompatible occupation
  - provide a foundation for spiritual, scientific, education, recreational, and visitor opportunities, all of which must be environmentally and culturally compatible

III. National Monument
- areas managed mainly for conservation of specific features
- areas containing one or more specific natural or natural/cultural features which are of outstanding or unique value because of their inherent rarity, representative, or aesthetic qualities or cultural significance

IV. Habitat/Species Management Area
- areas managed mainly for conservation through management intervention
- areas of land and/or sea subject to active intervention for management purposes so as to ensure the maintenance of habitats and/or to meet the requirements of specific species

V. Protected Landscape/Seascape
- areas managed mainly for landscape/seascape conservation and recreation
- areas of land, with coasts and sea as appropriate, where the interaction of people and nature over time has produced an area of distinct character with significant aesthetic, cultural, and/or ecological value, and often with high biodiversity
- protection, maintenance, and evolution of the area requires conserving the integrity of the traditional interaction between people and nature

VI. Managed Resource Area
- areas managed mainly for the sustainable use of natural ecosystems
- areas containing predominantly unmodified natural systems, managed to ensure long-term protection and maintenance of biodiversity while providing for a sustainable flow of natural products and services to meet community needs

[a] McNeely 1994

A fundamental aim of the meeting was to build greater understanding of the essential roles that national parks and other types of protected areas play in nature conservation and sustainable development in the three countries. Many general roles are shown in the World Conservation Union Protected Area Categories (table 1.1), although a broader, more dynamic view is shown schematically in figure 1.1.

Figure 1.1 Land use and protected area spectrum: a schematic[a]

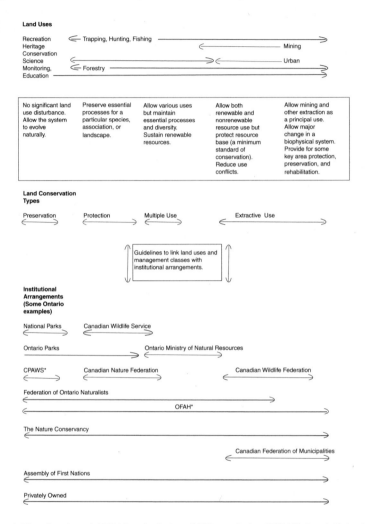

[a] amended from Bastedo et al. 1984. *Canadian Parks and Wilderness Society (CPAWS); Ontario Federation of Anglers and Hunters (OFAH).

The many vital ecological and socioeconomic services that protected areas offer to life in North America are still not sufficiently well recognized by scientists, scholars, professionals, citizens, and decision-makers. These fundamental services include: water, soil, plant, and animal conservation; improvements in environmental quality; environmental monitoring, assessment and research; historical and cultural understanding; beauty; recreation and renewal; tourism; education; and broad environmental and social learning. National parks and protected areas increasingly serve as lynchpins in comprehensive land use and regional planning. They play an essential role in cushioning development and providing for sustainability and restoration of the resources and environmental frameworks upon which all life ultimately depends.

It is also increasingly evident that, in cross-border situations, they can serve as a focus for building effective international working arrangements and as vehicles for peace. Concerned persons in all three countries have tended to focus on certain protected area services more than others; notably wildlife and biological conservation on one hand, and recreation and tourism on the other. Indeed the history of national parks and protected areas, at least in Canada and the United States, can be seen in terms of a struggle between these two kinds of services which are frequently incompatible with one another. In this context, the tendency since World War II has been to stress planning for large parks and protected areas located some distance from urban areas. The guiding vision has been one of an increasingly leisured public driving from the hurly-burly of cities to the peace of the hinterlands. Much more apt now, however, is a vision of protected areas as part of a comprehensive spectrum of different land uses, environmental conditions, and decision-making arrangements (fig. 1.1). This vision is one in which national parks and protected areas offer an array of essential services to cities, the rural countryside, and more remote wild lands and seas. In other words, national parks and protected areas play a variety of critical roles everywhere on the surface of the earth.

The previous remarks highlight some of the basic changes that have been taking place in understanding planning, managing, and deciding upon national parks and protected areas—especially since the 1982 and 1992 World Parks Congresses in Bali and Caracas respectively (McNeely 1992, McNeely and Miller 1982). Other major changes include moving away from viewing protected areas as "fortresses" more or less isolated from the surrounding areas and peoples, to seeing them as part of the broader regions in which they are located. This shift in thought and practice is based on a number of related changes. These include advances in scientific understanding, particularly in landscape ecology, biological conservation, and related fields (Sportza, this volume, Bastedo et al. 1984). These scientific advances indicate that protected areas are dependent for their biodiversity, ecological integrity, and environmental health

Photograph 1.2 .Multilaned Trans-Canada Highway fragmenting Banff National Park in the Bow River valley, Alberta, Canada

on corridors, buffers, and other connections with surrounding natural areas.

Another important force for change has been the need to recognize the significance of local participation, indigenous knowledge, and the economic and social needs of people living close to parks and protected areas (Forbes, et al., Jensen, and Martínez and Espejel, this volume). Increasingly, the support and interest of local people depend on their receiving economic benefits from protected areas. These ideas about benefits to, and involvement of, local people are inherent in newer concepts such as sustainable development and eco- and heritage tourism (Bringas and Ojeda, this volume).

Another important change is the growing interest in private stewardship, or a combination of public and private stewardship (Cox, and Nelson, et al., this volume). Public ownership and control of parks and protected areas are not sufficient to meet the formidable challenges posed by nature conservation and sustainable development, as they are increasingly understood today. For conservation to work effectively, people must see it as extending over large areas outside parks and protected areas, and so involving the emerging concepts of comanagement, shared management, and shared decision-making.

All the foregoing is associated with changing perspectives on parks and protected areas in the social or human sciences; for example, economics and planning. Ecological economics is relevant here with its interest in valuing the services of entire environments or ecosystems, as much or more than the trees, water, or other parts of the environment that we have seen and exploited as resources in the past (Fuentes and Vázquez, this volume).

In planning, the important shift has been away from an emphasis on corporate or rational approaches with their focus on the goals and objectives of a major industry, department, or corporation. This is being replaced by transactive, interactive, and adaptive civic planning and management, which attempt to deal with the goals, interests, and values of the many corporations, government agencies, and groups involved in society as a whole (Cox, Sportza, Nelson, et al., this volume).

All the foregoing changes are occurring in the face of a declining and changing role for governments in the protected area and related fields in North America (Gatewood, and Williams and Nelson, this volume). This move began in the 1980s and was justified initially by high government debt and diminishing financial and human resources. It continues today largely on ideological and political grounds. Cuts in the government role have led to a greater interest in, and commitment to, private stewardship and more effective cooperation among the increased number of nongovernmental organizations (NGOs) active in the protected areas field.

This volume focuses on our understanding of these and related changes, and their implications for the role of national parks and protected areas in linking or integrating nature conservation and sustainable development at local, state or provincial, national, and continental scales in North America. The volume consists largely of papers arising from the Tijuana workshop. The workshop involved participants from governments, nongovernment organizations, and universities, and followed a similar civic workshop and associated research and planning project undertaken previously in Krakow, Poland and nearby parts of Europe. The proceedings were published as *National Parks and Protected Areas: Keystones to Conservation and Sustainable Development* (Nelson and Serafin 1997). This workshop helped lead to a considerable amount of cooperative activity; for example, an international Carpathian Mountain Bioregion project led by World Wildlife Fund Europe. This workshop and associated activities suggest that Europeans have used collaborative cross-border and broadly regional planning approaches to nature conservation and sustainable development as effectively, if not more effectively, to date than North Americans.

European efforts largely arose from the establishment of the European Union (EU); a broad economic, social, and environmental agreement for collaboration unlike any available in North America. The North American Free Trade Agreement (NAFTA) offers a somewhat similar opportunity, but this agreement has been developed in a less inclusive way. NAFTA is focused on economics and trade. Other fields of concern, such as labor and environment, were left to sidebar agreements needed in order to achieve political support for the main enterprise. Nevertheless, NAFTA did provide the basis for the creation of international agreements, such as the Trinational University Consortium of COLEF, Simon Fraser University, and Western Washington University. This consortium, in turn, provided the framework for the meeting at Tijuana. The workshop also built upon some work carried out by the Commission for Environmental Cooperation (CEC), created with NAFTA; for example, its publication of *Ecological Regions of North America: Towards a Common Perspective* (1997). This report helps to highlight the interconnectedness of North American natural systems across the borders of Canada, the United States, and Mexico.

The Tijuana workshop produced many findings and recommendations, notably from a number of small working group sessions composed of mixes of participants from the three countries. The topics of the working group sessions were selected in open or plenary meetings of all workshop participants. The selected topics were: Bioregional Planning for Parks and Protected Areas in North America; Planning, Managing, and Deciding Upon Parks and Protected Areas in Local to Regional Context; Marine Protected Areas; and International Cooperation. The rich results of the working group sessions cannot be conveyed comprehensively here. However, each session prepared an "issues and vision" statement and these are presented in edited form as useful indicators of the challenges, needs, and opportunities involved in protected area planning, especially regional planning, in North America (boxes 1.1, 1.2, 1.3, 1.4). The group reports were prepared separately and often present different ideas and information. On the other hand, the reports sometimes come to similar conclusions, albeit from differing starting points or perspectives.

Box 1.1. Key Conclusions: Working Group on Bioregional Planning for Parks and Protected Areas

- It is critical to focus on conservation outside of protected areas as well as within them.

- Protected areas constitute a system or network of different types of protected areas, which can be linked effectively to different ecological and socioeconomic conditions and ways of life.

- Communities and populations inside and outside of protected areas can be more fully recognized in planning and management, especially in areas of poverty. One way of doing so is by transfer of benefits from those who gain to those who lose from conservation efforts.

- More recognition should be given to communal, traditional, or public rights to land, as for example in Mexican *ejidos*.

- Respect should be given to, and regular use made of, traditional or local knowledge as well as science and scholarship in planning, management, and decision-making.

- Civic approaches, involving a mix of research, government, nongovernment, business, and individual citizen involvement, should be applied to land use proposals that involve public and private as well as local, national, and international interests. Experiences with innovative approaches to planning such as shared decision-making (SDM) (Day et al., 1998) are useful and more equitable tools, although the frequently prolonged time commitment is a challenge to efficiency.

- Easements and other stewardship incentives can be used along with zoning, other regulations, and land purchase to facilitate conservation and sustainable development within, around, and among protected areas.

- Capacity building should be an ongoing part of planning, management, and decision making, if only because the players change over the years. Transparency should be a major criterion in reviewing conservation and development proposals, ideally yielding greater awareness and understanding of the values, interests, and needs of all stakeholders. Basic funding to permit stakeholder participation in planning should be required of proponents.

Box 1.2. Key Conclusions: Working Group on Planning, Managing, and Deciding Upon Parks and Protected Areas: In Local To Regional Context

- Protected area systems should be built upon strong scientific, scholarly, professional, and local knowledge. The ideal approach is multidisciplinary, multisectoral, interinstitutional, and broadly civic in nature. Regular communication among a variety of stakeholders should be promoted.

- Long-term research and education linkages should be built among protected area agencies, universities, colleges, and schools.

- Ideally monitoring, assessment, and research should be treated as land uses in protected areas in the same sense as campgrounds, access roads, and other recreational facilities have historically been seen as preeminent uses and given preference.

- Local and regional stakeholders should be involved systematically in protected area planning, management, and decision making; the process must; clarify roles, responsibilities, and expectations; provide for ongoing stakeholder learning and capacity building; and be based on language and communication procedures that reach all concerned parties.

- Regional approaches to protected areas should be undertaken at a variety of scales ranging from the park or local to district, state or provincial, national, international and continental levels.

- Protected area thinking and practice has been influenced by different natural and human histories, cultures, values, economies, and social and institutional arrangements in the three countries. Nature conservation has played a stronger role in Canada and the United States than in Mexico, and this will probably continue. As a developing country with a rapidly growing population, Mexico has and probably will remain more interested in multipurpose, interactive, and collaborative nature conservation measures such as biosphere reserves with their commitment to protection of the environment in association with careful land use, research, monitoring, and assessment.

Box 1.3. Key Conclusions: Working Group on Marine Protected Areas

- Marine protected are as important as terrestrial protected areas.

- The development of marine protected areas requires considerable attention in all three countries. The United States has the best developed system and this can be used as a general model by Canada and Mexico.

- The linkages between marine protected areas and coastal planning extend to concern for the conservation of streams and watersheds and relevant measures have been built into the coastal plans of many U.S. states. The U.S. *Wild and Scenic Rivers Act* provides a context for establishing protected areas along outstanding streams. The Canadian *Heritage Rivers* program is similar, although it seems to provide for a wider range of conservation and development activities. U.S. riparian conservation area laws provide for various kinds of resource use and conservation policies and activities along streams such as the San Pedro in Arizona. Similar approaches are developing in Mexico.

- Certain principles and processes should be considered consistently in planning, managing, and deciding upon marine and fluvial protected areas, including: ecosystem functions and processes; protected area benefits and costs; a broader geographic and socioeconomic context; and social, economic, and political systems at local to continental-scales, for example the Baja to Bering Sea proposal (Jessen and Lerch, this volume).

Box 1.4. Key Conclusions: Working Group on International Cooperation

- In Mexico, national parks and protected areas have not been as salient a public policy area as in Canada and the United States. National parks and protected areas have, however, frequently been set aside in Mexico for scenic, archaeological, historic, or cultural reasons and viewed mainly as tourism areas and sources of revenue for development.

- More recently, greater attention has been paid to establishing national parks and protected areas in Mexico on scientific grounds.

- Developing protected areas that complement rather than displace economic, social, and cultural values is of greater interest in Mexico.

- The varying values and approaches of the three countries are increasingly being recognized and involved in collaborative efforts, for example cross-border national parks and wildlife refuges.

- Future protected area planning, management, and decision-making in the three countries should include greater attention to:
  - Land use and regional planning across jurisdictions in line with ecosystem thinking and principles. Such collaboration must, however, be undertaken with appropriate care to the cultural, political, and other differences—the challenges of the human dimensions.
  - Regular means of civic communication and cooperation. Overall not enough is known about enterprises that are shifting the responsibility for interjurisdictional environmental management from federal to provincial, state, or municipal levels of governance. Research is needed on the strengths and weaknesses of these recent changes.
  - Analysis and assessment of multilateral interjurisdictional institutions such as biosphere reserves, the World Heritage Convention, the World Bank, and the World Conservation Union (IUCN).

Concluding Observations

In the light of the reports of the working groups, and review of the papers and discussion at the Tijuana workshop, the authors have reached some fundamental conclusions. These need to be highlighted and more widely recognized if national parks and protected areas are to attain their full potential in Canada, United States, Mexico, and elsewhere.

One

Conservation of plant and animal life and provision of recreational and tourism opportunities continue to be the major focus of interest in protected area planning, management and decision- making (Danemann, this volume). It is now time, however, to place much more emphasis on the many other ecological and social services provided by protected areas. Those currently of special interest are the conservation of air and water and associated monitoring and research. Also deserving of much greater emphasis are the land use, economic, cultural, and regional planning services offered by protected areas.

Two

In this context, protected areas need to be planned, managed, and decided upon as an integral part of overall land use and regional planning activities in the surrounding lands and waters (Ezcurra, Gatewood, and Martínez and Espejel, this volume). Focusing on land and waters within protected area boundaries is no longer sufficient for ecosystem, economic, social, and institutional reasons. Sediment, water, wildlife, air, tourism, goods, and people all continually cross borders. Protected areas can only be understood and dealt with by taking account of these local, regional, national, international, and continental flows. Corridors and buffers are a necessary but not a sufficient condition. These must be accompanied by consideration of broad regional activities that involve and affect any park and the natural and human systems of which it is a part.

Three

Regional planning for protected areas currently applies to a wide range of public and private land and is developing at several scales. The two best known scales are local or greater park ecosystem planning (Forbes et al., Nelson et al., Fuentes and Vázquez, this volume) and extensive national

Photograph 1.3. Smog and air pollution in the Pt. Pelee National Park area, north shore Lake Erie, Ontario, Canada

or international bioregional or landscape planning (Gatewood, Williams and Nelson, this volume). The first is usually driven by governments, and the second by nongovernmental conservation organizations. A third continental scale is now receiving greater recognition. Waterfowl and other birds, monarch butterflies, and other insects that annually migrate continentally or intercontinentally exemplify such protection programs (Cox, Jessen and Ban, Hermann, Hoth, and Nelson this volume). Effective programs will require large networks of protected areas, as well as careful stewardship of habitats on both public and private lands. These three scales of regional conservation planning need to be integrated with one another and with a broad public and private protected area system. Such a network would provide the framework or building blocks for effective stewardship in the surrounding lands and waters.

Four

Three types of systems need greater attention in multiscale regional planning for protected areas, nature conservation, and sustainable development. The first involves the seas and oceans and adjoining coastal lands and waters that have been long neglected in Canada and Mexico (Jessen and Ban, this volume). More progress has been made in the United States, but additional effort is still needed. The second system needing attention is watersheds, an integral part of planning for adjacent coasts and marine areas. Watershed planning has frequently been undertaken in Canada, the United States, and Mexico, but rarely has it involved the establishment of relevant protected area networks in a systematic way. We lack a model of an ideal watershed protected area system. The third system needing attention is parks and protected areas in urban regions that have traditionally been seen as major sources of environmental disturbance (Gosselin, and Roper et al., this volume). Urban areas have consequently been avoided in extensive bioregional and related conservation planning. However, it is now clear that protected areas are essential to the well-being of human and other life in cities. Urban protected area networks also have to be linked with those in the surrounding land and waters to conserve overall landscape health and sustainability.

Five

Recent advances in ecosystem theory and method have greatly strengthened planning for protected areas and nature conservation; however, further progress is needed (Vázquez-Domínguez, this volume). The focus of advances in thought, policy, and practice has been on wildlife and biological systems. What is needed now is greater attention to the wider atmospheric, geologic, hydrologic, and human dimensions of ecosystem planning, management, and decision-making. With the rise of water, air, and climate change problems, the need to expand the ecosystem concept in geologic, hydrologic, and atmospheric directions is growing. Specific types of protected areas are available to address these needs; for example, those for aquifers and for floodplains, or other hazard zones (Gosselin, this volume).

Six

The advances in ecological science which are driving planning to expand conservation policies and activities beyond protected area boundaries, also necessitate greater consideration of the human dimensions of protected areas and regional conservation planning (Danemann, Jensen, and Nelson, this volume). It is not enough to explain the science to people and tell them that they need to change their land use, economic, and social behavior patterns to comply with the dictates of science and nature conservation. Economic and social patterns and needs, and awareness of community, ethnic, and other values must all play a greater part in a broadly civic approach to protected areas, nature conservation, sustainable development, and quality of life.

Seven

In light of the foregoing, we need more assessments of how institutional and social systems operate in dealing with changes in protected area thought, policy, and practice in all three countries (Brennan and Miles, Castillo et al., Currie-Alder and Day, McNamee, and Miles, this volume). Examples include: impacts of recreational and tourism technology (Bringas and Ojeda, this volume); comparative experiences with biosphere reserves (Fuentes and Vázquez-Domínguez, this volume); public and private stewardship (Nelson, this volume); and broad landscape or regional conservation projects such as the *Yukon to Yellowstone*, the *Sky Islands*, and the *Chihuahuan Desert* (Gatewood, and Williams and Nelson, this volume). These regional conservation projects are especially interesting because they are mainly driven by nongovernmental organizations such as the World Wildlife Fund, the Canadian Parks and Wilderness Society, the Wildlands Project, and the Nature Conservancy. These organizations seem to work with one another and other groups in sometimes similar, and sometimes different, ways. We need assessments so we can learn from this varied experience. Are there, for example, differences in the ways that nongovernmental organizations have worked with one another and government agencies in Canada, the United States, Mexico, and other countries? If so, what are the implications and what can we learn from this history? The same sorts of questions apply from the standpoint of government agencies.

Eight

The final point is the importance of interjurisdictional communications at various regional scales (Ezcurra, and the *Retrospectives*, this volume). Regular communication is essential across park as well as urban, state, national, and continental boundaries. Such communication can take two basic forms. The first customary method involves scientists, professionals, and members of relevant nongovernmental organizations active in the protected area field. The second method cuts across these individuals and groups and involves a wider mix of scientific, government, and nongovernmental personnel as well as citizens. This last approach has been neglected in the past. It is, however, essential if more effective and equitable planning is to recognize the varying values, interests, and capacities of the numerous groups and individuals affected by protected areas, nature conservation, and sustainable development. This book is built upon such a civic approach which can be time consuming and messy. It is, however, one we need to learn how to use more effectively. This book demonstrates that the civic approach has the potential to make a definitive contribution to multiscaled planning for protected areas, nature conservation, sustainable development, and quality of life in North America.

Outline of the Book

The book begins with three papers that set the stage by briefly addressing the history, underlying values, current state, and general character of protected areas in Canada, the U.S., and Mexico respectively. Succeeding papers are organized into three sections, primarily according to the country of the lead author. Although they often focus on protected area experience in the country under title, many are comparative in approach and address local, national, international, and continental situations. Each section contains at least one paper referring to marine protected areas (Jessen and Lerch, Roper et al., Vázquez-Domínguez and Hermann et al.).

The papers in the Canadian and U.S. sections begin with those focusing on individual protected areas and build to the continental scale. The Mexican section, however, begins with a broad paper on nature conservation and sustainable development issues and trends in the greater Baja Region, an area of special interest in the Tijuana workshop. The following two papers focus first on the Northern Baja, and second on the Northern California Gulf and Colorado River Biosphere Reserve, which was visited in a one-day field trip by the workshop participants.

The Canadian, U.S., and Mexico sections of the book all contain at least one paper on a theme of wide relevance to protected areas and regional planning. For Canada, two such papers deal with *regional approaches to planning for protected areas and conservation* and *linking public and private stewardship* respectively. For the U.S., the relevant paper is on *environmental education*. The Mexican section contains three relevant papers on: *a multisectoral transdisciplanary approach*; *tourism*; and *phylogeography, historical patterns, and conservation of natural areas*.

Three papers involving relevant research that was underway but not tabled at the Tijuana workshop have been included because of the additional strength that they give to the book. The first of these is on planning for environmentally significant areas (ESAs) in the Waterloo urban region, Ontario, Canada (Gosselin). The second provides details on planning that links public and private stewardship in the Greater Sand Dunes National Monument region, Colorado, U.S.A. (Nelson). The third is an assessment of the effectiveness of planning for the Terminos Lagoon Protected Area, Campeche, Mexico (Currie-Alder and Day).

The book also includes three brief retrospectives on the Tijuana workshop. A participant from each of the three countries prepared these. Individually and collectively they highlight many of the fundamental conclusions made by the editors earlier in this overview. The retrospectives have a number of common elements, notably the need for a regional perspective and for more attention to community and to the human dimensions. Each retrospective also reflects some of the value differences that arise from national and personal experience.

Finally, a postscript includes two papers that were added after the Tijuana conference. These papers give insight into the work of the Commission for Environmental Co-operation (CEC). This commission was formed to monitor and respond to environmental challenges in Mexico, the U.S., and Canada following the North American Free Trade Agreement (NAFTA). Since the Tijuana conference in 1999, CEC has become increasingly active in protected areas and regional planning, notably at the North American scale. Indeed, the CEC has begun to address a number of the concluding observations of the conference, as set forth earlier in this overview. The work of the CEC is, therefore, highly relevant to protected areas and to regional planners, other professionals, and general readers of this book.

Values

Running through the papers and the book as a whole is a fundamental concern for values. This begins at the outset with the papers on protected areas systems in the three countries. The similarities and differences run deep and are apparent in many of the papers. At the risk of oversimplification, three general kinds of values are reflected to varying degrees in the papers. These can be labeled as environmental, developmental, and social values. Environmental values refer to various views on natural things including, for example, the right to life of all plants and animals, the need to protect nature for its own sake, and the importance of nature to human beings. The development values include views on progress as reflected, for example, in technical advancement, economic growth, and human artistic and cognitive evolution. The social values include views on social, cultural, and language rights, respect for different ways of life, and equity in general.

The authors of the papers tend to reflect their own and their national perspectives in dealing with such values. In general, they use regional planning as an implicit or explicit means of bringing together and reconciling the various values in order to reach more generally acceptable decisions at local, national, international, and continental scales. In doing so, they tell us something about the nature of the procedures they use, as well as about what they perceive to be successful or less successful approaches.

In these and other respects, the papers in this book constitute a valuable addition to our knowledge of how to conserve nature and achieve what has been referred to as sustainable development and quality of life. However, the papers leave questions about what these concepts and goals mean in different places, the ways they should be related to one another, the criteria that should be used to do so, and how a more detailed understanding of regional planning can help to answer such questions. In the end, then, the papers make a strong contribution to the understanding of protected areas and regional planning in North America and elsewhere. However, they also raise challenges that require further study and research as a basis for reconciling environmental, economic, and social values and associated policies and practices in the future.

The Regional Planning Imperative

For all the foregoing reasons, it is imperative that protected areas now be consistently planned and managed from a regional perspective where this includes the local, state and provincial, national, international, and continental scales referred to so often throughout this book. Some protected areas will be more sensitive than others to local economic, social, or environmental influences, although frequently these influences will reflect policies and practices at higher scales in the system. With their commitment to represent the natural diversity of surrounding regions and their openness to national and international tourism, national parks will have to be planned and managed in tune with economic, social, and environmental circumstances at the higher as much as at the local scales.

This regional planning imperative is reinforced by two ongoing changes in local to global environments that have not been addressed as much as they deserve in this book. These are air quality and climate change. These changes largely arise from industrial, transport, and other human activities, and have become apparent with the growth of population and economic development since World War II.

The changes in the level of atmospheric gases such as sulfur dioxide (SO_2), nitrogen oxides (NO_x), and ozone, as well as metallic particles such as lead, have caused declines in air quality in North America. Planners and managers of national parks and protected areas in the western U.S. or in the eastern Appalachians have had to deal with the damaging effects of these changes on vegetation, water quality, and other aspects of protected areas for some years. In doing so they have had to think in terms of pollution sources, ranging from local coal burning power plants to more distant urban areas such as Los Angeles. Some of the pollution sources lie across national boundaries; for example, in northern Mexico for the Big Bend National Park, Texas.

The effects of climate change on national parks and protected areas are not generally so well understood as declines in air quality. However, recent research on climate change and Canada's national parks reinforces the case for regional planning of protected areas. This research involves building climate change scenarios based on Global Change Models (GCMs), notably that of the Canadian Centre for Climate Modelling and Analysis (CCCMA). This is recognized as one of the most advanced and recent models involving the effects of doubling carbon dioxide (CO_2) levels (approximately A.D. 2050) and the moderating effect of sulfate aerosols (Scott and Suffling 2000). Table 1.2 is a summary of projected climate change impacts in national parks across Canada. All of the national parks, and the regions in which they are located, are seen as being affected to varying degrees.

Table 1.2. Projected Climate Change Impacts in Canadian National Park Areas by 2050 [b]

Atlantic Parks
    Cape Breton Islands
    Forillon
    Fundy
    Gros
    Morne
    Kejimkujik
    Kouchibouguac
    Mingan Archipelago
    Prince Edward Island
    Terra Nova
	• sea-level rise exacerbated by tectonic subsidence and greater storm intensity and frequency
	• increased coastal erosion and salt water intrusion
	• altered marine-terrestrial interface (dune systems, tidal pools, mudflats, salt marshes, and estuaries)
	• changes in ocean currents with a possible cooling influence for coastal water temperatures (expansion of cold-water species)
	• increased forest fire frequency
	• increased storm, fire, and pest disturbance (altering successional trajectories)
	• loss of boreal forest to temperate forest
	• reduction or isolated extirpation of arctic-alpine species and communities

Great Lakes-
St. Lawrence Basin Parks
    Bruce Peninsula
    Georgian Bay Islands
    La Maurice
    Point Pelee
    Pukaskwa
    Saint Lawrence Islands
	• lower average Great Lake water levels and summer stream flow
	• increased lake and stream water temperatures
	• reduced lake ice-cover and earlier spring freshet
	• loss of cold-water fish habitat and altered breeding/spawning and migration patterns
	• reduction of significant wetland areas
	• increased forest fire frequency and intensity
	• exacerbated acid rain stress
	• increased forest disease outbreak and insect infestations
	• altered successional trajectories and loss of mature forest habitat
	• loss of boreal forest to temperate forest
	• expansion of southern exotics

Prairie Parks
    Elk Island
    Grasslands
    Prince Albert
    Riding Mountain
    Wood Buffalo
	• altered seasonal hydrology (earlier and greater spring freshet, reduced base summer flows and warmer stream temperatures, reduced period of ice cover)
	• increased frequency and intensity of drought stress
	• reduced wetland area
	• altered waterfowl breeding and migration patterns and changed fish species composition (expansion of warm water species)
	• increased forest fire frequency and intensity
	• increased forest disease outbreak and insect infestations
	• loss of boreal forest to grassland and temperate forest
	• expansion of southern exotics

Western Cordillera Parks
    Banff
    Glacier & Revelstoke
    Jasper
    Kootenay
    Nahanni
    Waterton Lakes
    Yoho
	• altered seasonal hydrology (earlier and greater spring freshet, reduced period of ice cover)
	• increased snow pack and avalanche activity
	• variable mass balance of glaciers (low elevation glaciers projected to thin and retreat while those with higher accumulation zones may surge with increased winter precipitation)
	• possible temporary elevation of river toxins resulting from increased glacial melting
	• altered river ecology
	• latitudinal and elevational migration of ecozones
	• loss of some Alpine assemblages from mountain peaks
	• increased forest fire frequency and intensity
	• increased forest disease outbreak and insect infestations
	• increased wintering zone pressures and impaired migration of large animals

Pacific Parks
    Gwaii Haanas
    Kluane
    Pacific Rim
	• sea-level rise (moderated by ongoing isostatic rebound)
	• increased ocean surface temperatures
	• greater storm intensity and frequency
	• increased salt water intrusion
	• reduced nutrient upwelling and increased incidence of red tide blooms
	• reduced cold water habitat and expansion of southern fish species populations
	• altered seasonal hydrology (earlier and greater spring freshet)
	• altered spawning and migration patterns
	• loss of Alpine species from higher elevations
	• accelerated forest insect and disease cycles

Arctic Parks	
Aulavik	• northward expansion of the tree line (impaired soil conditions)
Auyuittuq	• increased permafrost active layer and thawing causing altered drainage patterns
Quttinirpaaq	
Ivvavik	• sea-level rise variably moderated by isostatic rebound or exacerbated by subsistence
Tuktut	• reduced sea and lake ice seasons and altered sea mammal distributions (polar bears, whales)
Nogait	
Vuntut	• increase snow pack and ice layers reducing browsing accessibility for ungulates
Wapusk	
	• altered migration patterns and diminished genetic exchange among arctic islands
	• potential for altered predator-prey relationships

[b]modified from Scott and Suffling 2000

The implications of these climate change scenarios are profound for national park planners, managers, policy makers, and citizens. They raise basic questions about current national park policies and practices. These questions apply to other types of protected areas as well. Of great interest from our perspective are the implications relating to regional planning. How well, for example, will each national park represent its natural region and the species and communities it is intended to protect, when the ecological character of the park and surrounding area are both shifting to outlying areas? If wildlife and other elements of park ecosystems migrate outside of current boundaries, will the park or the boundary be relocated, and what will be the reaction of people in the surrounding areas? Without going into any more detail, it is apparent that planning for the expected effects of air quality and climate change strongly support the regional planning imperative arising from the papers in this book.

At this point, as the reader prepares to move into the book, it must be apparent that parks and protected areas are complex and evolving institutions. Increasingly they are recognized as playing many different, but often complementary and essential roles in economic, social, and environmental well-being everywhere on earth. In consequence, they are of central interest to researchers, professionals, administrators, politicians, and also to citizens. The understanding and planning of protected areas, and the development of efficient, effective, and equitable policy and practice, necessarily involve drawing upon many fields of knowledge—indigenous and local as well as scientific and scholarly.

The understanding and planning of protected areas involves many specialties or disciplines such as geology, hydrology, biology, economics, sociology, anthropology, geography, law, and planning. This understanding also involves many broad perspectives or integrative approaches such as ecology, philosophy, landscape, history, land use, governance, human ecology, and traditional knowledge (Nelson and Serafin 1997).

Overall, the chapters reflect the theory and concepts of these many ways of knowing. They also reflect the many methods that are used to secure relevant information, including: analysis of historical and other documents; geographic information systems (GIS), remote sensing and other mapping methods; surveys and questionnaires; interviews; field observations; benefit-cost and other economic analysis; recent innovations in ecology such as gap analysis and study of DNA; workshops and consultations; cooperative cross-disciplinary research; and many more. Researchers, educators, students, planners, managers, and other decision-makers should be interested in these methods and their strengths and limitations, as also should concerned citizens whose understanding, participation, and ultimate benefit, will be strongly influenced by their awareness of these things.

References

Bastedo, J. D., J. G. Nelson, and J. B. Therberge. 1984. "Ecological Approach to Resource Survey and Planning for Environmentally Significant Areas: The ABC Method." *Environmental Management* 8(2): 125-134.

Commission for Environmental Cooperation. 1997. *Ecological Regions of North America: Towards a Common Perspective.* Montreal, Que.: Commission for Environmental Cooperation.

Day, J. C., P. W. Williams, and S. Litke. 1998. "Land and Water Planning in British Columbia in the 1990s." *Environments*—Special Issue 25(2&3).

McNeely, J. A., ed. 1992. *Parks for Life: Report of the IVth World Congress on National Parks and Protected Areas.* Gland, Switzerland: International Union for the Conservation of Nature and Natural Resources.

————. 1994. "Introduction: Protected Areas in the Modern World." pp. 5-28 *in* J. A. McNeely, J. Harrison, and P. Dingwall, eds. *Protecting Nature – Regional Reviews of Protected Areas.* Gland, Switzerland and Cambridge, England: IUCN.

McNeely, J. A., and K. R. Miller, eds. 1982. *National Parks, Conservation and Development. The Role of Protected Areas in Sustaining Society.* Proceedings of the World Congress on National Parks, Bali, Indonesia 11-12 October 1982. Washington, D.C.: Smithsonian Institution Press.

Nelson, J. G., and R. Serafin. 1997. *National Parks and Protected Areas: Keystones to Conservation and Sustainable Development.* NATO ASI Series. Berlin and Heidelberg: Springer-Verlag.

Scott, D., and R. Suffling, eds. 2000. *Climate Change and Canada's National Park System: A Screening Level Assessment.* Hull, Que.: Environment Canada and Parks Canada.

Country Overviews

Preserving Canada's Wilderness Legacy: A Perspective on Protected Areas

Kevin McNamee

Abstract

In November 1885, the Canadian federal government set aside a twenty-six square kilometer area in the Rocky Mountains, which was later expanded to become Banff National Park, a protected area of 6,641 square kilometers. Almost 115 years later, over 1.1 million square kilometers or 11 percent of Canada is conserved from development in almost eight thousand protected areas (World Wildlife Fund Canada 1999b, 2000).

This paper briefly summarizes the history behind the birth and growth of Canada's protected areas networks, examines some of the major events that helped develop the system, and presents some of the issues and opportunities to further expand and protect these areas. To provide an international perspective, this paper also makes several references to the impact of decisions of other nations, particularly the United States, on Canada's choices.

Introduction

At the outset, it is imperative to understand the role of government in Canada. With over 90 percent of the country being Crown, or government-owned land, governments, including those of First Nations, play a major role in allocating land to development or protected areas, and creating and enforcing legislation and policies that govern such decisions. Despite the fact that only 10 percent of Canada is private land, private stewardship is critical given that many of these private lands are found in the regions that are the most biologically diverse and among the most at risk.

There is some urgency to the situation, even for a country like Canada that has an abundant but shrinking wilderness land base. At the height of the recession in 1992, it was estimated that one square kilometer of wilderness was being lost every hour to logging, mining, oil and gas development, agriculture, urban development, and other consumptive practices. And while only 7 percent of Canada is allocated to wilderness or nature protection, fully 65 percent has been developed, or is allocated to development interests for future use.

New statistics demonstrate that 114 hectares of commercial forest is logged every hour in Canada. At this rate, an area the size of all of Banff National Park would be logged in just over six and a half years. In 1997, the area staked with new mineral land claims was 5,025 hectares. At this rate, it would take just fifty-five days to stake all of an area such as Banff National Park with mineral claims. In 1998, just over 7 percent of Canada was allocated to new mineral claims (World Wildlife Fund Canada 1999a).

Clearly, with only 7 percent of Canada protected from development, and over 65 percent developed, there is no balance when it comes to the conservation and development of the Canadian landscape. Canada constantly tells the world that we are a large country with a small population huddled up against the Canada-U.S. border. What we do not tell other nations is the extent to which our society has reached up into our near and far northern lands and altered the landscape to extract natural resources. These are destined for a largely urban-based population or international markets, particularly the United States, our largest trading partner.

What is at risk? Canada is the global steward of 20 percent of the planet's remaining wilderness. As we continue to lose these natural habitats, we put at risk (World Wildlife Fund Canada 1999a):

- 55 to 68 percent of the world's polar bear population
- 38 to 50 percent of the world's caribou population
- 42 percent of the world's bear population, and
- 33 to 40 percent of the world's wolf population

Early Natural Heritage Moments

When the federal government first considered protecting the hot springs at Banff, it looked to America's experience in administering the Arkansas Hot Springs. This area is significant in that, at the time, it was one of the few examples of government taking responsibility for a natural object and setting it aside as a reservation. The secretary of the Canadian Pacific Railway urged the deputy minister of the interior to follow the American example and take control of the Banff hot springs. The federal government did so in November 1885.

However, the operation of the Arkansas Hot Springs by private enterprise left the Canadians unimpressed. Two months after the Banff springs were protected, a federal civil servant visited Arkansas. Historian Fergus Lothian noted: "His report ... commented on the laxity of the management of the concessions, the obsolete plumbing and equipment, and the lack of control for reasons of health over the admission of patrons to the bath-houses" (Marty 1984:48). For that reason, the federal civil servant recommended absolute government control over the Banff reservation. The Canadian government found this too expensive an option, opting to lease one hot spring to private operators under strict regulations, and operating a second hot spring itself.

Two years later, the federal government passed legislation creating Rocky Mountain Dominion Park, which would later be named Banff National Park. The *Act's* statement of purpose used wording similar to legislation protecting Yellowstone. The *Yellowstone National Park Act* of 1872 states the area is "*dedicated* and set apart as a public park *or* pleasuring ground for the benefit and enjoyment of the people*." Passed on 23 June 1887, the *Rocky Mountains Park Act* stated that the area was "*reserved* and set apart as a public park *and* pleasure ground for the benefit, *advantage* and enjoyment of the people of Canada." The first regulations made under the *Act* were based largely on the regulations governing the Arkansas Hot Springs.

The early development of Canada's national park system had little to do with wilderness or environmental protection. The discovery of the hot springs was prompted by the construction of a transcontinental railway as its route was being pushed west of Calgary, Alberta, through the foothills and into the Rocky Mountains. The new reservation was seen as a means to attract tourists from central Canada to view the spectacular mountain scenery and hot springs and stay at new hotels constructed and owned by the Canadian Pacific Railway (Brown 1970).

But industrial development was not ruled out. The 1887 *Act* allowed for coal mining and logging within the park. As Marty (1984: 62) noted, "the government saw no contradiction between these activities and the enjoyment of the park by the public." Only a few members of Parliament objected to these activities. Said one: "If you intend to keep it as a park, you must shut out trade, traffic and mining." It was not until 1953 that the last coal mining operation was closed within the park.

In the nineteenth century, some of the provinces started to create their own forms of protected areas. In 1893, Ontario established Algonquin Park, as Canada's first provincial park, and Quebec soon followed, creating Laurentide Park in 1895. Both are similar to Adirondack State Park, New York, in that they exhibit leadership by a level of government below the federal level. They also are fairly large, designated for the purpose of protecting forests, wildlife, and water resources, but additionally allow some forms of development. For example, almost 80 percent of Algonquin remains open to logging. This practice is the subject of regular public disputes to this date.

The federal government used more than national parks to protect important natural areas. In 1887, Parliament created North America's first waterfowl refuge when it set aside one thousand hectares at Last Mountain Lake, Saskatchewan. After passing the *Migratory Birds Convention Act* in 1917, the federal government started establishing migratory bird sanctuaries to protect migratory birds and their habitats from physical disturbance and hunting. The *Canada Wildlife Act*, adopted in 1973, broadened the government's ability to protect wildlife other than migratory species. This *Act* enables the protection of wildlife and habitat through the establishment of national wildlife areas, similar to national wildlife refuges in the United States.

The largest protected area in Canada, the Queen Maude Migratory Bird Sanctuary, is 62,782 square kilometers in size. Located in northern Canada, it was established in 1961 and protects the nesting grounds of over 90 percent of the world's population of Ross's goose. To date, there are ninety-eight such sanctuaries that prohibit all disturbance, hunting, and collection of migratory birds and their eggs, when the birds are present. There are forty-eight national wildlife areas protecting about 3,500 square kilometers of wildlife habitat. Neither form of protected area absolutely forbids industrial development.

Expanding and Preserving Canada's National Parks System

While the United States was first to establish a national park, Canada was the first to create a bureaucracy to manage the parks. In 1911, five years before the U.S. National Park Service was created, the Dominion Parks Branch was established for the purpose of administering the six areas that were the founding parks of the national park system. Its first director, James Bernard Harkin, left an indelible imprint: he expanded the national park system from its western base into Central Canada, Ontario, and Atlantic Canada, tripling the number of national parks from five to sixteen, and putting an end to resource extraction within the parks.

Harkin was partly influenced by American wilderness advocate John Muir. Wildlife historian Janet Foster reports that Harkin "shared the philosophy of John Muir that sunshine, scenery, and fresh air could strengthen the body and rejuvenate the spirit." She also writes that Harkin "paid tribute to Muir for having clarified the purpose of national parks and frequently quoted the American author in his departmental reports on the need for park reservations." In short, Foster (1978: 80) observed, "Harkin's belief in the parks and wilderness values frequently border on the mystical."

In 1930, this belief was translated into the passage of the *National Parks Act*. For Canadian national parks, this *Act* is critical. While American national parks draw their direction both from the *Organic Act* of 1916 that created the National Park Service and separate legislation that is passed by Congress for each park, Canada relies solely on this *Act*. Agreements creating all new national parks must conform to the *Act*. It allows for very few nonconforming uses, which are generally focused on allowing local people to maintain traditional resource subsistence activities. It also prohibits industrial development in the parks. Any attempt to delete a national park, or to change its boundaries, requires the approval of the Canadian Parliament. This is unlike most other Canadian protected areas, which can be eliminated at the stroke of a pen.

Again, Canada turned to the U.S. for some inspiration in wording the *Act*. Its purpose statement asserts that the national "parks are hereby dedicated to the people of Canada for their benefit, education and enjoyment ... and such parks shall be maintained and made use of so as to leave them unimpaired for the enjoyment of future generations." The latter phrase—"to leave them unimpaired for the enjoyment of future gen-

Photograph 2.1. Rundle Mountain and the Vermillion Lakes in Banff National Park, Alberta, Canada

erations" is taken directly from Public Law No. 235, which created the U.S. National Park Service. This is also a phrase first suggested by the architect Fredrick Law Olmstead, who designed both New York's Central Park and Montreal's Mont Royal Park.

The Canadian National Park System

In 1968, the Canadian federal Cabinet decided to expand the national park system, in part to respond to growing public concern over the health of the world's environment. The minister in charge of the national park system, the Honorable Jean Chrétien, now prime minister, declared that in order to represent Canada's natural heritage, between forty and sixty new national parks were required.

To direct this expansion program in a systematic fashion, Parks Canada adopted a *National Park System Plan* that divides Canada into thirty-nine distinct natural regions (figure 2.1). The goal is to establish at least one national park in each region that captures and protects the geological, biological, and geographical features of the natural region in which it is located. For almost thirty years, this plan has guided the national park establishment process. Currently, Canada still needs fourteen new national parks to complete this system.

While efforts to expand the national park system were based on strong social concerns over the environment, some initial efforts crashed on the rocks of growing social opposition to governments telling people what to do. The creation of a number of new national parks in the 1960s and 1970s was achieved through expropriation of land from local people. For example, to create Forillon—the first national park in Quebec—over two hundred families were forced from their land. In response to growing resistance to such actions, federal policy was changed in 1979 to exclude the use of expropriation programs. Now, designation of new national parks does not proceed unless there is local support for protection of a specific area.

In 1978, the federal government used the system plan to respond to the nation's growing concern over the future of the Canadian wilderness in northern Canada. Concerns were centered on accelerating industrial development. The government launched public consultations for five proposed national parks that would represent five northern natural regions in the system. Not all of these sites were immediately protected—because of the lack of local support from Aboriginal communities—and remain priority candidates for new national parks.

When the federal government attempted to legislate the boundaries of the first northern national parks, it ran into unexpected opposition from Aboriginal people. Government and environmental groups assumed, incorrectly, that Aboriginal groups would welcome the protection of natural areas and wildlife that they use to sustain their ways of life. However, for them the creation of new national parks was a form of expropriation. Having never signed a treaty, or given up their rights to these lands, they opposed the new parks.

In response, the government amended the *National Parks Act* in 1976 to ensure that the right of Aboriginal people to continue to pursue fishing, trapping, and hunting for subsistence purposes was upheld. In addition, where the government proposed a national park on northern lands for which there was an unresolved Aboriginal land claim—if native people agreed—the area was declared a national park reserve. In essence, lands were held in reserve for a national park pending the successful negotiation of a land claim agreement.

In 1984, Ivvavik National Park on the north slope of the Yukon became the first Canadian national park established directly through the settlement of a land claim agreement with the Inuvialuit of the western Arctic. Their land claim agreement established the park to protect the calving grounds of the Porcupine caribou herd from industrial development.

Photograph 2.2. Lake Waterton in Waterton National Park, Canada, part of the International Peace Park with Glacier National Park in the U.S.A.

However, the park and its caribou population remain at risk as long as the potential exists that the U.S. government will open up the coastal plain in the Arctic National Wildlife Refuge to oil development.

Perhaps the creation of Ivvavik National Park was the realization of American Indian painter George Catlin's call for a *nation's park*, which some credit as the birth of the national park idea. Concerned about the impending extinction of the bison and Indian, he suggested that government take action and protect them in "a magnificent park." Continuing, he wrote: "A nation's Park, containing man and beast, in all the wild[ness] and freshness of their nature's beauty!" (Nash 1982:101). This is the essence of Ivvavik—protecting habitat and wildlife—upon which Aboriginal people depend.

In addition to pursuing new national parks in the north, the federal government was interested in diversifying its protected area tool chest. In 1978, the minister in charge of national parks, the Honorable Hugh Faulkner, called for the development of a wild rivers program and the establishment of national landmarks to protect small natural features of Canadian significance (Faulkner 1978). These were to emulate the U.S. *Wild and Scenic Rivers Act* and national monument program. The Canadian Heritage Rivers System was subsequently created. Designation under the program does not provide any legal protection to rivers, relying instead on moral persuasion. The national landmarks proposal faltered because the federal and provincial governments could not reach agreement on how to implement it.

What Has Canada Protected?

As of March 1, 1999, Canada has established 7,968 protected areas, plus over 1,150 private land initiatives, protecting over 1,059,405 square kilometers or almost 10.6 percent of Canada. Some of this total is within strictly protected areas, while the rest allows some form of development (World Wildlife Fund Canada 1999b) (table 2.1). By Canada Day, 2000, the total amount of protected land had increased to over 10.8 percent of the nation.

When this total is broken down, all Canadian jurisdictions have protected 6.8 percent of the land and water from industrial development since Banff was established as the first national park in 1885. Half of this total was designated during the last decade. The 683,277 square kilometers of protected wilderness this represents is in almost 3,250 protected areas that include: thirty-nine national parks as well as numerous provincial and territorial parks; wilderness and wildlife reserves; ecological reserves; and other types of protected areas.

The federal government, through Canada's national park system, contributes more than one-third of this total. Almost 244,540 square kilometers, or 2.5 percent of Canada, is protected in the thirty-nine national parks (fig. 2.1). Some of these are huge. At 44,000 square kilometers, Wood Buffalo National Park is Canada's largest and is the size of Switzerland. Others, such as Point Pelee, are quite small, but no less important. Point Pelee, the second smallest national park in Canada, contains the most endangered species of any national park and is one of the last remnants of the disappearing Carolinian forest.

An additional 4 percent, or 400,713 square kilometers, of Canada is in other kinds of protected areas. A major portion of this total is the 146 national wildlife areas and migratory bird sanctuaries that—while protected—could allow forestry, timber, and oil and gas development through a ministerial permit.

Another way to count progress is the degree to which a protected areas network represents a nation's natural regions. This is a goal espoused by the *World Conservation Strategy* (1980), the Brundtland Commission (1987), and the *Convention on Biodiversity Conservation* (1992), as well as by both the 1982 and 1992 *World Congress on National Parks and Protected Areas*. During the 1990s, all of Canada's senior governments were committed to representing all of their natural regions within a protected areas network free of industrial development.

Photograph 2.3. The French, a Canadian Heritage River, Ontario, Canada

In Canada, the federal and provincial governments have defined 486 distinct natural regions. In the summer of 2000, World Wildlife Fund Canada concluded an assessment of how well governments were meeting their commitments to adequately represent all of Canada's natural regions.

Of the 486 natural regions (World Wildlife Fund Canada 1999c),

- 43 natural regions were judged to be *adequately* represented (8.8%)
- 90 natural regions were judged to be *moderately* represented (18.5%)
- 150 natural regions were judged to be *partially* represented (30.9%), and
- 203 natural regions were judged to have *little* or *no* representation (41.8%)

Such assessments have been done on an annual basis since 1995. They indicate that between 1995 and 2000:

- adequately represented regions increased from 4 to 9 percent
- somewhat represented regions increased from 42 to 49 percent, and
- regions with little or no representation decreased from 54 to 43 percent

Table 2.1. Types of Canadian Protected Areas[a]

Type of Protected Area	Number	Total Size (km²)	Endangered Spaces Standard (km²)
National Parks	39	246,926	246,926
National Wildlife Areas	48	3,500	2,677
Migratory Bird Sanctuaries	98	112,000	
Canadian Landmarks	1	7	
Provincial Parks	1,789	210,652	197,434
Territorial Parks	56	3,650	875
Wildlife Management Areas	365	159,939	57,982
Wilderness Areas and Parks	17	33,957	33,896
Ecological or Nature Reserves	356	10,801	8,151
Forest Reserves	85	25,338	2,801
Private Reserves	395	453	452
Natural Areas	401	14,762	7,813
Conservation Reserves	304	15,938	15,938
Community Pastures	22	9,150	
Conservation Authorities	233	1,574	174
Stewardship Agreements	2,070	4,255	
Recreation Areas	681	17,182	353
Critical Wildlife Habitat	727	52,212	13,760
Private Land Initiatives	542	1,163	15
Aboriginal Conservation Lands	2	8,954	8,954
Others	157	126,592	59,969
Total	8,388	1,059,005	658,170

[a] World Wildlife Fund Canada 1999b

In signing the *Biodiversity Convention*, Canada made a global commitment to represent its natural regions within a protected areas network. The statistics above indicate that Canada has achieved less than 10 percent of the convention's target, although it has also reduced the number of natural regions with no representation by 12 percent. More critically, over 40 percent of the natural regions have virtually no representation. These gaps in Canada's protected areas network are throughout the boreal forest and subarctic regions of Quebec, Labrador, and the Central Barrens of the Northwest Territories, as well as throughout Nunavut and the grassland plains of southeastern Alberta.

Figure 2.1 National parks of Canada

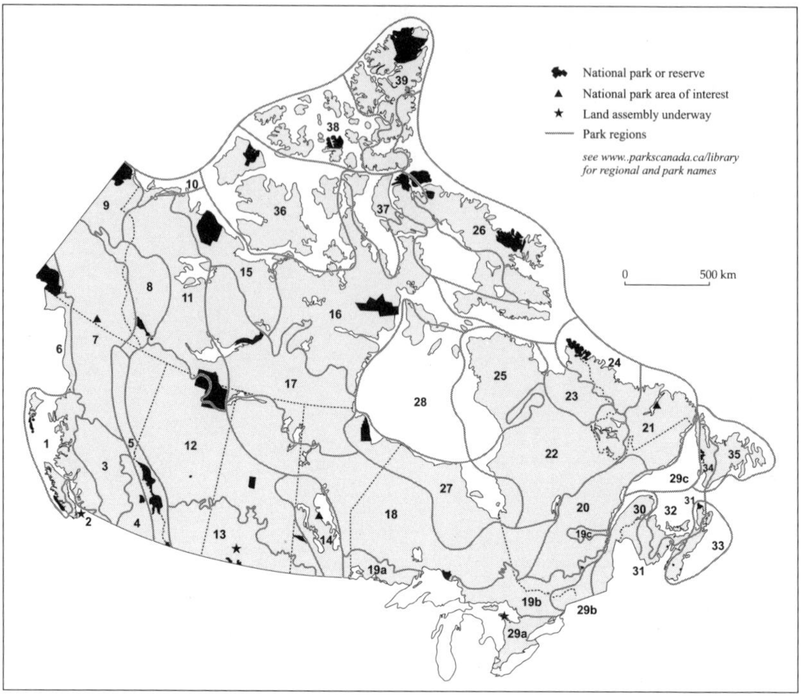

It is also worth noting that despite governments having made a national commitment on a number of occasions to completing a representative protected areas network, it is the nongovernmental sector that provides the only ongoing assessment of how governments are progressing. Over the past decade, World Wildlife Fund Canada—working with a number of national and regional conservation organizations, the Canadian Council on Ecological Areas, and a number of conservation biologists—has developed the in-house scientific and technical capability to produce annual assessments that were made public every spring until the year 2000.

Endangered Spaces Campaign

A key factor in the recent expansion of Canada's protected areas networks has been the *Endangered Spaces Campaign*. Launched by World Wildlife Fund Canada in 1989, this ten-year initiative secured the commitment of all of Canada's senior governments to completing a national network of protected areas free of industrial development by the year 2000. The campaign succeeded in putting protected areas and wilderness protection on the public and political agenda to varying degrees across Canada.

When the campaign started in September 1989, 3.2 percent of Canada was protected in a wilderness state with no logging, mining, hydroelectric projects, or oil and gas development permitted. By July 2000, that figure increased to 6.84 percent. Thus, from the time land was first set aside for Banff National Park to the launch of the *Spaces Campaign*, it took 104 years to protect 3.6 percent of Canada. It took just over nine years to double that figure by adding another 3.2 percent to the protected wilderness category. Between 1989 and 2000, the amount of protected wilderness in Canada grew from 323,750 to 683,277 square kilometers.

The campaign represents an important shift in how environmental nongovernmental organizations (ENGOs) have approached wilderness issues. Prior to the campaign, most ENGOs engaged in a site-by-site, valley-by-valley approach, with much of their resources directed towards one specific site, such as South Moresby, Temagami, or the Stein Valley. There was no national strategy or campaign aimed at the whole country. Rather, it was the more controversial issues, with most focused on old-growth forest and temperate rain forest, which drew the attention of conservation groups across the country.

Several factors prompted a more comprehensive approach. First, in 1987, a federal Task Force on Park Establishment (Canada 1987) warned that if Canadians did not act by the year 2000 to protect its wilderness heritage, many critical areas would be lost or allocated to development. Environmentalists seized on this warning, urging governments to take action.

Second, the arrest of seventy-two Aboriginal people of the Haida nation, including elders, gave national and international prominence to threatened temperate rainforest of South Moresby wilderness archipelago on the Queen Charlotte Islands. In essence, South Moresby served as Canada's national wake up call to take action to protect its disappearing wilderness. In 1992, the area was designated as Gwaii Haanas National Park Reserve and Haida Heritage Site.

Third, in 1983, the Ontario government made an unprecedented decision to establish 155 new provincial parks, dramatically increasing the province's protected areas network. The government and conservation groups used a natural regions framework to identify candidate sites, allowing them to defend protection on both scientific and natural heritage grounds. This success demonstrated that a natural regions framework could serve as an effective lobbying tool to achieve the protection of a large number of sites at once, as opposed to focusing on one.

Finally, there was a growing international consensus and calls for governments to complete protected area networks by representing their major natural regions. The 1987 landmark report of the World Commission on Environment and Development recommended such action as a component of a larger sustainable development strategy. Many Canadian institutions rushed to embrace the concept of sustainable development, providing environmentalists with a platform to urge institutions to embrace and support protected areas as part of a sustainable future.

It was against this background that the *Endangered Spaces Campaign* was launched in 1989. In essence, it was a national campaign aimed at governments, urging them to complete the very protected area systems that many of them had already identified. Many governments, including the federal, were already working to varying degrees on completing a protected area network within their jurisdiction. Some were making progress, like Ontario; others had the framework, but were doing nothing with it. What the campaign was able to do was rally public support behind the idea of completing these networks by a target date—the year 2000—and getting political commitments to complete the task by a set date.

Government and industry support for the goal came quickly. In 1992, all of Canada's ministers of environment, parks, and wildlife endorsed the *Tri-Council Statement of Commitment on Protected Areas*, agreeing to complete their protected area networks by the year 2000. Similar commitments were given by the forestry and mining sectors. On paper, at least, no longer was the question "should Canada establish protected areas?" but "how?" and "where?"

Provinces such as British Columbia, Nova Scotia, and Manitoba made steady progress during the campaign. British Columbia established over two hundred new protected areas, and Nova Scotia protected almost 20 percent of its Crown land from industrial development in thirty-one new protected areas. The federal government has made some progress since 1989, creating five new national parks and providing interim protection for another two proposed national parks in the Northwest Territories. Early in the campaign, Quebec reserved almost thirty thousand square kilometers of land for future parks. Manitoba established four new large wilderness parks, and Newfoundland created its second major wilderness reserve.

As the campaign draws to a close, a number of governments have made some important last minute contributions. In early 1999, the Ontario government announced the creation of 333 new protected areas and the expansion of forty-five existing protected areas, bringing some form of security to over 2.4 million hectares. However, sport hunting and mineral activity may be permitted in some of the parks. Working with First Nations, as well as the mining and environmental community, the Manitoba government has approved twenty new protected areas for consultation.

Land claim agreements between First Nations and governments have increasingly delivered new national parks and protected areas, many of which will contribute to protecting both representative landscapes and areas important to maintaining traditional ways of life. First Nations and park agencies will comanage many of these new parks. The last five national parks to be designated—Aulavik (1992), Vuntut (1993), Wapusk (1996), Tuktut Nogait (1998), and Sirmilik (1999)—are all products of successful federal negotiations with Aboriginal communities. This trend will be continued for all future national parks.

A number of protected terrestrial and marine parks were made possible because of the cooperation of industry. For example, West Fraser Timber Ltd. gave up its timber rights in the Kitlope Valley, enabling the creation of the largest protected temperate rain forest area in the world. Mineral and oil rights were given up by industry to allow for the creation of Grasslands, Vuntut, and Tuktut Nogait National Parks, as well as for the new Northern Rockies protected area in northwestern B.C. Major oil companies surrendered their rights to potential oil and gas fields within the South Moresby Archipelago, making it possible for the federal government to make progress on the Gwaii Haanas National Marine Conservation Area Reserve.

Growing Contribution of Environmental Groups

During the life of the Endangered Spaces Campaign, Canada, like many nations, has seen the decline in the ability of governments to control the agenda, and to spend their way out of various issues that plague society. In many jurisdictions, progress on establishing new protected lands was based on the need to demonstrate, to varying degrees, some form of consensus around protected areas. This process may benefit these areas in the long run, with communities having had some stake in their protection.

It has also forced the environmental community to broaden its discussions to include representatives of First Nations, industry, and other stakeholders. During the 1990s, Canada experienced a growing presence and participation by both Canadian and American foundations in encouraging and funding the work of conservation groups. This allowed groups to break their reliance on government funding, to steadily improve their technical, scientific, and advocacy capabilities, and simply to achieve more on-the-ground conservation gains. Parliament further amended the *Act* in the fall of 2000 to make the restoration and maintenance of ecological integrity the first priority in all national park management decisions.

Conservation groups also made important contributions to the management of national parks. In 1988, they convinced Parliament to amend the *National Parks Act* to make ecological integrity the priority consideration in park management. Parliament directed Parks Canada to make the maintenance of ecological integrity the priority in developing park management plans, park zoning, and visitor use programs. This amendment resulted in a dramatic change in how Parks Canada approaches the management of protected areas, and has become a public and political foundation for decision-making.

Groups also led the way in making Parks Canada more publicly accountable for the health of the national park system. Through another amendment, Parks Canada must now table a *State of the Parks Report* in Parliament every two years. The 1997 report (Canada) is the most comprehensive statement ever produced on the health of Canada's national park system. It clearly indicates that many national parks are under serious ecological stress from a number of human activities originating both inside and outside the parks.

In March 2000, the minister of Canadian Heritage released the report of the Panel on the Ecological Integrity in Canada's National Parks along with her action plan. Calling upon the government to devote $328 million in new spending over a five-year period, the panel identified over one hundred actions; from strengthening Parks Canada's legislative mandate for conservation, to designating portions of national parks as legally protected wilderness areas, to significantly enhancing Parks Canada's science capacity, to working more aggressively with adjacent landowners. In releasing the report, the minister committed to implementing recommendations in the report where humanly and legally possible.

Conservation groups are also turning to the courts for assistance in protecting national parks. For example, the Canadian Parks and Wilderness Society succeeded in using the federal Court in 1992 to put an end to the last commercial timber operation in Canada's national park system. In the process, Parks Canada agreed that logging in Wood Buffalo National Park was contrary to its legislation. In another example, the federal court ordered the reopening of environmental assessment hearings on the proposed Cheviot open pit coal mine adjacent to Jasper National Park after five organizations, including the Canadian Nature Federation, Canadian Parks and Wilderness Society, and Alberta Wilderness Association took the government to court.

Unfortunately, the Cheviot case also revealed that global conservation agreements, such as the World Heritage Convention, mean little to decision makers. The approval of the Cheviot coal mine on lands adjacent to Jasper National Park, a World Heritage Site, was in clear violation of the spirit and intent of the conventions. Yet, in meetings with federal officials and in the federal government's Cabinet decision, it was clear that these agreements were irrelevant. This is a continuing trend as Canada simply signs such agreements and does virtually nothing to implement them. For their part, conservation groups have done little to prepare a comprehensive overview of Canada's failure to live up to such agreements.

Where to Now?

So what is the future conservation agenda in Canada for protected areas? This author suggests three points: (1) continuing the process of creating new protected areas that help protect the nation's biological diversity; (2) maintaining and improving the ecological viability of the existing protected areas; and (3) inciting governments, industry, First Nations, local communities, and other Canadians to promote and take action to preserve a representative portion of the Canadian landscape from industrial development.

The target date of 2000 for completing Canada's protected areas networks is past. With the only assessment of progress indicating that there are still 203 of 486 natural regions with little or no representation, much remains to be done. With the impending end of the Endangered Spaces Campaign, two questions remain unanswered: Will governments simply abandon progress on this front as the target date passes? Will the conservation lobby that has pushed for new protected areas dissipate? And beyond the terrestrial national parks and protected areas that are the focus of this paper, there are continuing struggles to establish an effective marine parks or marine conservation areas policy and a system of such areas in Canada.

On the federal scene, action to establish new national parks is stalled mainly because of the lack of federal funds. However, in its 2001 election platform and *Speech from the Throne*, the current Liberal government pledged to devote at least $100 million to the creation of new national parks and the maintenance of ecological integrity. As well, a number of foundations have indicated their commitment to funding the lobbying initiative of the Canadian Nature Federation to encourage the federal government to establish the necessary fourteen new representative areas to complete the national parks system.

If national parks and protected areas are to be maintained as government financing shrinks, the conservation community will have to raise more external financing. The question that must be debated is: What is the appropriate role and mix of government, private sector, academic, and nongovernmental organizations in the delivery of protected area programs? It is no longer sufficient to simply reject the notion of private sector involvement in park programs. It is clear that even the concept of privatization is very poorly understood. A focused approach by academia on the philosophical and practical challenges of more nongovernmental involvement in park programs is essential.

A major impediment to establishing more protected areas continues to be the annual allowable cut allocated through timber licenses, and the issuance of mineral prospecting and exploration permits. In the case of timber supply, producing timber from Canada's forests is a legal requirement while the creation of new parks from the forest base is largely a policy consideration with little political commitment. As a former Ontario civil servant put it: "The forest industry staff start from the premise that they were there first and therefore have priority. Any Johnny-come-lately park is therefore a withdrawal from land that was committed to timber operations" (Clark 1995: 6).

Conclusion

In doubling its network of national parks and protected areas over the last decade, Canada has gained a tremendous amount of insight, expertise, and practice in the art of making new protected areas. It has also greatly diversified the range of institutions involved in the negotiations, establishment, and management of protected areas. Thus, it is absolutely critical in looking ahead to the next decade, that all involved not only continue to make on-the-ground progress, but reflect on the experience of the last decade to plot a course of action for the next.

Editorial note: Prime Minister, Jean Chrétien, announced ten new national parks and five marine conservation areas in late 2002.

References

Brown, Robert Craig. 1970. "The Doctrine of Usefulness: Natural Resource and National Park Policy in Canada, 1887-1914," pp. 46-62. In *Canadian Parks in Perspective*, ed. J. G. Nelson and R. C. Scace. Montreal, Que.: Harvest House. Nelson, 1970.

Canada. Task Force on Park Establishment. 1987. *Our Parks: Vision for the 21st Century.* Ottawa: Environment Canada.

Canada. Parks Canada. 1997. *State of the Parks Report: 1997.* Ottawa: Minister of Supply and Services Canada.

Clark, T. 1995. *Timber Supply and Endangered Spaces.* Toronto: World Wildlife Fund Canada.

Faulkner, H. 1978. "The Opening Address," pp. 3-14. In *The Canadian National Parks: Today and Tomorrow—Conference II,* ed. J. G. Nelson, R. D. Needham, S. H. Nelson, and R. C. Scace. Waterloo, Ont.: University of Waterloo.

Foster, J. 1978. *Working for Wildlife: The Beginning of Preservation in Canada.* Toronto: University of Toronto Press.

Hummel, M. 1995. *Protecting Canada's Endangered Spaces: An Owner's Manual.* Toronto: Key Porter Books.

Lothian, W. F. 1976. *History of Canada's National Parks.* Volumes 1 and 2. Ottawa: Minister of Indian Affairs and Northern Development.

Marty, S. 1984. *A Grand and Fabulous Notion: The First Century of Canada's Parks.* Toronto: NC Press.

McNamee, K. 1993. "From Wild Places to Endangered Spaces: A History of Canada's National Parks", pp. 17-41. In *Parks and Protected Areas in Canada,* ed. P. Dearden and R. Rollins. Toronto: Oxford University Press.

_____.1994. *The National Parks of Canada.* Toronto: Key Porter Books.

McNeely, J. A., ed. 1992. *Parks for Life: Report of the IVth World Congress on National Parks and Protected Areas.* Gland, Switzerland: International Union for the Conservation of Nature and Natural Resources.

McNeely, J. A., and K. R. Miller, eds. 1982. *National Parks, Conservation and Development: The Role of Protected Areas in Sustaining Society.* Proceedings of the World Congress on National Parks, Bali, Indonesia, 11–12 October 1982. Washington, D.C.: Smithsonian Institution Press.

Nash, R. 1982. *Wilderness and the American Mind.* New Haven: Yale University Press.

Nelson, J. G., ed. 1970. *Canadian Parks in Perspective.* Montreal: Harvest House.

World Commission on Environment and Development. 1987. *Our Common Future.* New York: Oxford University Press.

World Wildlife Fund Canada. 2000. *Endangered Spaces: The Wilderness Campaign that Changed the Canadian Landscape.* Toronto: World Wildlife Fund Canada. 28 pp.

_____. 1999a. *Backgrounder* for Media Event held on 30 November 1999. Toronto.

_____. 1999b. *Conservation Lands in Canada* [March 1999]: *1998/1999 Endangered Spaces Report.* Toronto. 3 pp.

_____. 1999c. *Status of Canada's Terrestrial Protected Areas System* [26 April 1999]: *1998/1999. Endangered Spaces Progress Report.* Toronto. 4 pp.

NATIONAL PARKS, WILDERNESS, AND PROTECTED AREAS IN THE UNITED STATES

Scott Brennan and John C. Miles

Abstract

Core elements of the United States' efforts to protect its natural legacy are the National Park System and the National Wilderness Preservation System. These systems currently protect over 100 million acres of federal wild lands. The American system of conservation and preservation is the product of its unique history, resulting in a system increasingly viewed as inadequate to address such recent concerns as the conservation of biological diversity. Federal protection efforts are complemented by activities at the state level and by private sector initiatives. Growing pressure for recreational and resource development uses currently challenge all land protection in the United States, and additional lands are advocated for the future.

Origins

The concept of a national park began the process of land protection in the United States. The first well-documented call for a "nation's park" on the North American continent is apparent in the writings of an inveterate traveler and accomplished painter, George Catlin (Miles 1995, Mackintosh 1984). In 1832, while traveling through what is now North and South Dakota, he advocated the preservation of wildlife, intact landscape, and native cultures by calling for "some great protecting policy

Photograph 3.1. Yosemite National Park, California, U.S.A.

of government in a magnificent park. A nation's park, containing man and beast, in all the wild[ness] and freshness of their nature's beauty" (Mackintosh 1984:10).

Catlin was well ahead of his contemporaries in his thinking. The idea of parks for the American people gradually emerged in the decades following his initial expression of this idea. As the nation expanded westward, and places of exceptional beauty and curiosity were encountered, a movement to protect some of them appeared. Congress first established Yosemite Park in 1864 to protect the sublime features of that valley, and ceded it to the new state of California. This was followed in 1872 by a decision to create a park around the geysers and other curiosities of the upper Yellowstone River region, resulting in the first truly national park. Congress could not cede this park to a state, since Wyoming was still a territory, so the precedent of a protected area under federal jurisdiction was set. Protection was minimal at this early stage, consisting principally of the area being withdrawn from public entry under federal land laws. Many other national parks have been created in the more than 130 years since the creation of Yellowstone. The National Park System now includes 378 areas of various categories (table 3.1) intended to preserve the natural and cultural legacies of American society while at the same time meeting some of the recreation needs of this nation of 278 million people (U.S. NPS 2001).

Table 3.1 National Park System Designations (Nov. 1998)[a]

Designation	No. of Units
International Historic Site	1
National Battlefields	11
National Battlefield Parks	3
National Battlefield Site	1
National Historic Sites	77
National Historical Parks	38
National Lakeshores	4
National Memorials	28
National Military Parks	9
National Monuments	73
National Parks	54
National Parkways	4
National Preserves	16
National Recreation Areas	19
National Reserve	2
National Rivers	6
National Scenic Trails	3
National Seashores	10
National Wild and Scenic Rivers	9
Parks (other)	11
Total:	378 units, 83.3 million acres

[a] US 1997a.

Over the decades, the National Park Service has had a penchant to develop part of its domain for recreation, thereby contributing to the growth of a movement to create a higher level of protection than that offered by designation as a national park. This came to be called the "wilderness movement" and resulted, in 1964, in congressional passage of the *Wilderness Act*. This *Act* established 9.1 million acres of wilderness in national forests, and directed the Forest Service, the National Park Service, as well as other federal agencies, such as the Fish and Wildlife Service, to study lands they administered for their suitability for inclusion in the National Wilderness Preservation System. They would recommend to Congress areas that should be designated as wilderness, and Congress might then consider such designation. A fourth federal agency, the Bureau of Land Management, joined the process in 1976: As of 2002 the National Wilderness Preservation System consists of approximately 105 million acres.

Photograph 3.2. Portal, Arizona, East entrance to the Chiricahua Mountains and
Colorado National Forest, site of a U.S. Forest Service Primitive or Wilderness Area

How, one might ask, did so many agencies become involved in management of the National Wilderness Preservation System? The public
lands of the United States were divided among four major land management agencies following congressional passage of the *General Revision Act
of 1891*. With this measure, Congress authorized the president to
"reserve" portions of public forestland when they were judged by him as
too valuable to transfer to private ownership for lumbering or other
exploitive purposes. The principal value Congress was concerned about
in the 1890s was the role that forests played in maintenance and protection of water quantity and quality (Williams 1989 393-424.) Ultimately
these "forest reserves" became national forests. In 1905, Congress established the United States Forest Service as the agency of the federal government to manage these lands.

Over the years, Congress retained its powers to create national parks
individually through specific legislation. In 1906, however, Congress
granted power to the president to proclaim as protected national monuments those public lands which were of special antiquarian or scientific
value. Numerous national monuments were established by the middle of
the second decade of the twentieth century, some administered by the
Forest Service and some by other entities (Rothman 1989). The growing
array of national parks and monuments needing consistent and coordinated management resulted in creation by Congress of the National Park

Service, which will be explained in more detail below. Another nineteenth century crisis of conservation involved wildlife, and led to establishment of the Bureau of the Biological Survey that was created to coordinate a national research program on America's wildlife. The bureau gradually acquired the responsibility of enforcing the nation's interstate wildlife laws and managing a growing number of wildlife refuges. In 1939 the agency was involved in government reorganization and renamed the Fish and Wildlife Service. Under its jurisdiction, the national wildlife refuge system continued to grow, and when Congress passed the *Wilderness Act*, it required the agency to review its refuge system for lands that might meet the requirements set for inclusion in the National Wilderness Preservation System.

The fourth agency that became involved in wilderness was the Bureau of Land Management. This agency was created in 1946 when the General Land Office, which had administered public lands since the beginnings of the United States, and the National Grazing Service, were combined. The new agency was named the Bureau of Land Management. The land it administered was essentially all of the public land left over after Congress had dedicated portions of it to the status of national forest, national park and monument, or national wildlife refuge. This oversimplifies a complex system, but is the essence of the situation. The bureau was not mandated in1964 to undertake a wilderness review, as were the other three agencies; But in 1976 Congress passed legislation giving the bureau a clearer management mandate and it began a wilderness review.

When the *Wilderness Act* was being debated in Congress in the late 1950s and early 1960s, one issue was whether a new system of public land, with yet another management agency, would be the best way to proceed. Advocates of the legislation realized that a new system and a new agency would be strongly opposed by the existing agencies and their supporters in Congress, and would work against passage of any wilderness legislation. Early in the process they decided that if and when an area under the jurisdiction of the Forest Service, National Parks Service, or Fish and Wildlife Service was recommended for wilderness, it would be administered as such by its current management agency. Thus the National Wilderness Preservation System became an interagency system with no special management cadre dedicated specifically to it.

The federal government has undertaken most land protection in the United States. However states have protected portions of their land base in state parks, natural resource conservation areas, and other protected categories. A survey in 1983 found that nine states had wilderness preservation programs involving more that 1.3 million acres (Hendee, Stankey, and Lucas 1990, 172). Some states have established programs to protect undisturbed natural areas. New York led the way when, back in 1885, it established the Adirondack Forest Preserve to be "forever kept as wild forest lands". The Forest Preserve of 2.6 million acres is the core of a six-million-acre park that is a unique mixture of public and private land, protected area, and working landscape. In the West, Washington State has a Natural Area Preserve Program, and a system of national resource conservation areas. Programs such as these offer a measure of protection, on a relatively small scale, for unaltered natural systems in many states.

The private sector has also achieved significant levels of protection for natural areas, though on a smaller scale than on government lands. An example is the Nature Conservancy, an organization that emerged in 1951 from a professional association of ecologists who wished to work for conservation. While it operates worldwide, in the United States it offers protection in 2002 for 12,621,000 acres, its reserves ranging in size from a few acres to many thousands. Most land that it manages is open to public use on terms it sets for each area.

Natural area protection in the United States is thus a diverse enterprise. The emphasis in this paper is upon national parks and wilderness areas, but they are only part of the story. The pressures on the land and its communities arising from growing human population and its ever-expanding search for resources have led, over the century and a half of land preservation, to an increasing effort to protect remaining wild and natural areas.

The National Park System

National parks in the United States were established for many reasons. Often the primary purpose was the preservation of scenery or assurance of a "pleasuring ground" for city folk. Some parks became havens for wildlife, but this was seldom the goal. According to national park historian Alfred Runte (1979), rationales for protected park and wilderness areas in the U.S. fall into four categories:

Photograph 3.3. Grand Canyon National Park, Arizona, U.S.A.

1. Monumentalism: the belief that enormous, beautiful, or otherwise unusual features such as the Grand Canyon, Mount Rainier, and Yellowstone's exotic caldera should be protected .
2. The absence of valued resources: when a proposed park holds little of economic value, it is easy to set aside because no one wants to buy or sell it.
3. Utility: a protected watershed will assure cities and towns of clean, plentiful drinking water, and fewer floods.
4. The recreational value of protected land.

The consequence of such rationales was that park boundaries were seldom established with any natural values in mind. Politics and economics dictated where the boundaries would be, rather than geography or ecology. The protection of natural values—such as wildlife and ecological services—from park and wilderness designations, thus, is much less today than it might have been had other resource values been emphasized.

In 1916, President Woodrow Wilson signed the *National Park Service Act*, creating the National Park Service. The service replaced the U.S. Army as caretaker of Yellowstone and other national parks. The service, arguably an improvement over the army, caused many problems and failed to solve others it had inherited. The nature of some of these problems in Yellowstone and other parks was evident in the direction given the service (United States 1916).

> The service ... shall promote and regulate the use of ... parks, monuments and reservations ... to conserve the scenery and natural and historic objects and wildlife therein, and to provide for the enjoyment of the same in such manner and by such means as will leave them unimpaired for the enjoyment of future generations.

> The Park Service was to protect scenery, nature, history, and wildlife "unimpaired" while allowing the greatest number of people to enjoy these amenities. These conflicting responsibilities have been the source of many troubles for the Park Service and the National Park System. How should the service balance preservation and use? This question has plagued park managers since the first days of the service, and, in the face of growing pressures for both more use and more resource protection, continues be a challenge for it to the present.

One issue for national park managers was that the American people wanted to enjoy their national parks, and politicians wanted them to be able to do so, yet they must remain "unimpaired." In most cases a new park was wild, and development was necessary to make it accessible to visitors. The Park Service needed to build its constituency in order to survive threats from rival agencies and compete in the struggle for budget, so it accommodated visitors. The service did not, in the view of some critics, seem to be giving its protection mission adequate priority, and this was one motive for citizen activists to begin a campaign for a new class of legal protection for landscapes of concern.

The principal rival federal land management agency of the National Park Service was the Forest Service, and in the 1920s this rivalry took a turn of importance to the protection of wilderness. The Forest Service embraced outdoor recreation as one of its functions at this time and, thus, was in direct competition with the Park Service. Furthermore, since the Park Service was coming under fire for its development of national parks, the Forest Service launched a campaign to convince the public that it could preserve wild nature more effectively than could the Park Service. Aldo Leopold was a Forest Service official who suggested that wilderness might, in some cases, be the "highest use" to which portions of the national forests could be dedicated (Leopold 1921, 78). This was controversial with many of his Forest Service colleagues but, inspired by Leopold's writings and the need to fend off an aggressive Park Service (most new national parks were carved out of national forests), the Forest Service administratively dedicated its first wilderness in 1924. A new protective category was born.

But how protective was this Forest Service wilderness? It was not, as it turned out, very much so. Over the next several decades the Forest Service established "primitive," "wild," and "wilderness" areas, but as often changed them and invaded them for logging or other resource development. At the same time, criticism of the Park Service's development of wild parks continued, and all of this led to a push for de jure wilderness that would be beyond the reach of dueling bureaucrats.

After WWII, a pent-up demand for timber resulted in invasion of many road-less areas in national forests. At the same time, visitation to national parks rose rapidly, and the National Park Service launched a major campaign, called MISSION 66, to improve park infrastructure. These perceived threats to wilderness protection in both national forests and national parks led to the campaign for de jure protection of wilderness that resulted in the *Wilderness Act* of 1964 (Miles 1996, 187-194).

The National Wilderness Preservation System

The *Wilderness Act* provides the highest degree of protection available to significant landscapes in the U.S. The *Act* defines wilderness (United States 1964).

> A wilderness, in contrast with those areas where man and his works dominate the landscape, is hereby recognized as an area where the earth and its community of life are untrammeled by man, where man himself is a visitor who does not remain. An area of wilderness is further defined to mean an area of undeveloped federal land retaining its primeval character and influence, without permanent improvements or human habitation, which is protected and managed so as to preserve its natural conditions and which (1) generally appears to have been affected primarily by the forces of nature, with the imprint of man substantially unnoticeable; (2) has outstanding opportunities for solitude or a primitive and unconfined type of recreation; (3) has at least five thousand acres of land or is of sufficient size as to make practicable its preservation and use in an unimpaired condition; and (4) may contain ecological,

geological, or other features of scientific, educational, scenic, or historical value.

This definition offered latitude for interpretation but, in the decades since its passage, the *Wilderness Act* has proven to be a vehicle for preservation on a scale beyond the expectations of its 1960s proponents. It does not provide complete protection since, for instance, mining claims could be filed until 1983, and those claims can still be worked. Aircraft may access some areas. Yet the *Act* still offers a high level of protection. Managers in the agencies administering lands within the system have developed wilderness management principles and protocols that sharply limit the changes human activity can make in the wild landscape (Hendee, Stankey, and Lucas 1990).

The 1964 *Act* designated 9.1million acres of national forest wilderness. Additions to the National Wilderness Preservation System came slowly at first with agencies dragging their feet on road-less area reviews, largely because they were searching for ways to minimize the impact of the *Act* upon their administrative discretion over their lands. The system grew dramatically with passage of the *Alaska National Interest Land and Conservation Act* (ANILCA) in 1980. The largest wilderness area, at 8.7 million acres, is within Wrangell-St. Elias National Park in Alaska, and more than half of all wildernesses in the U.S. are in Alaska (The Wilderness Society 1999). In April 2002 the system included 104,739,168 acres (Wilderness.net)(table 3.2).

Table 3.2. The National Wilderness Preservation System, 2002

Agency	Units	Federal Acres	Percent of NWPS Acres
Entire NWPS			
BLM	133	5,237,800	5.0%
Forest Service	400	34,766,995	33.2%
F&W Service	71	20,686,134	19.8%
National Park Service	44	44,048,239	42.1%
TOTAL	648	104,739,168	
NWPS excluding Alaska			
BLM	133	5,237,800	11.3%
Forest Service	381	29,014,774	62.3%
F&W Service	50	2,009,222	4.3%
National Park Service	36	10,295,156	22.1%
TOTAL	600	46,556,952	
NWPS in Alaska			
Forest Service	19	5,752,221	9.9%
F&W Service	21	18,676,912	32.1%
National Park Service	8	33,753,083	58.0%
TOTAL	48	58,182,216	

Figure 3.1 National parks of the United States

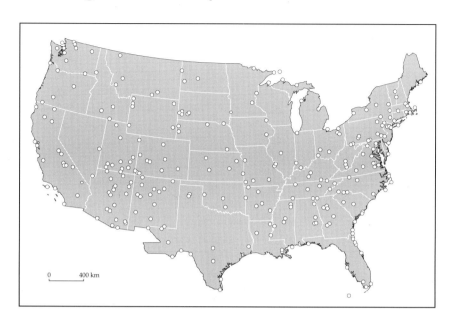

These numbers reveal that, while the National Wilderness Preservation System total is a very impressive number, over half the system is in Alaska. Writing in 1994, Gorte noted that, at that time, a total of 132.9 million acres of the 2.271 billion acres of the U.S. landmass had been designated or recommended for wilderness. Land so designated in Alaska accounted for twenty-eight percent of the land in that state. The other 64.6 million acres were distributed among forty-five states. The total area designated or recommended for wilderness at that time was nearly six percent of the total of all land in the U.S., less than four percent of the land outside of Alaska. It comprised more than twenty percent of all federal land (Gorte 1994).

If one looks at the national park and national wilderness preservation systems on maps of the United States (figs. 3.1 and 3.2), their units are scattered widely across the land, concentrated in the West, with fewer units east of the Mississippi River. This is an artifact of history, of course, as is the occurrence of such large wilderness units in Alaska. The park and wilderness preservation efforts occurred recently in the history of the United States, and the lands available for protection lay in the arid and remote regions of the West. Protection was provided where federal land was present and development pressures still relatively light. There has

Figure 3.2 National wilderness preservation system of the United States

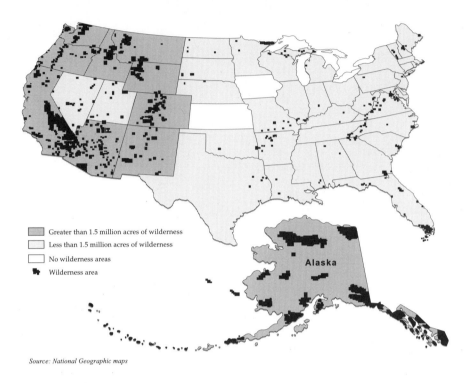

Greater than 1.5 million acres of wilderness

Less than 1.5 million acres of wilderness

No wilderness areas

Wilderness area

Alaska

Source: National Geographic maps

been little attempt to protect ecosystems or biodiversity in the establishment of these systems.

Challenges of the Future

For a century, the conservation movement in the United States aimed to protect natural resources from destruction or depletion. Forests were reserved in order to assure water supplies. Scenic and scientifically unique and interesting areas were protected from those who might degrade them or deprive the American people from access for the enjoyment of them. However, outdoor recreation grew rapidly in popularity and people flocked to the hinterlands, needing roads to get them there and accommodations when they arrived. As a result of growing recreational and tourism pressures, the National Parks Service developed new kinds of reserve designations to meet changing needs. These designations cannot be discussed in detail here. More information can be obtained from the U.S. National Parks Service (2001). Wild places continued to be threatened and a prolonged effort was made to protect some of them so that future generations would be able to enjoy a wilderness experience. Boundaries were drawn around park and wilderness areas as political expedience allowed.

The 1960s "age of environmentalism," informed by the emerging science of ecology, led to review of the purpose of the national park system in the U.S. A committee of wildlife biologists, led by A. Starker Leopold, was convened in 1963 to advise the Department of the Interior as to what should guide its management of the National Park System. This committee recommended that the primary goal of national park management be to restore national parks to "the conditions which prevailed when the areas was first visited by the white man:" a "vignette of primitive America" (Leopold et al. 1963). The Park Service attempted to follow these recommendations, but found it difficult. What were these conditions, and how could they be restored? Were conditions at the time of arrival of Caucasians static and somehow ideal? Was such a goal feasible when even the largest national parks, at least in the contiguous states, were small islands or relatively undisturbed lands?

Recently the Park Service has shifted its goals and its management from restoration of "vignettes" toward what has been described as a "moving picture" of the landscape and its community of life (Agee and Johnson 1988). This approach brings problems of its own: disturbances outside park and wilderness boundaries threaten and interfere with restoration efforts inside the boundaries; laws aimed at other goals constrain management options; and the public is unwilling to accept change, as in public outrage at the "destruction" caused by wildfire in national parks like Yellowstone. Park and wilderness management has come to be seen by managers as an experiment. An ever growing number of visitors travel to parks with preconceptions of what their experience should be. Often their expectations cannot be met.

Yet current national parks and other protected areas are being asked to play new roles. Once considered primarily, if not exclusively, from an anthropocentric perspective involving inspiration and recreation, they are now being considered by some as of central importance for the maintenance of biological diversity (Noss and Cooperrider 1994, 129-177). If the goals of park and protected area management continue to shift, as they have since the 1960s in the United States–from provision of the park and wilderness experience for visitors to protection of systems for the maintenance of their biological diversity–the constantly growing throng of visitors may increasingly be denied access. They will be regulated, and this may lead to protest and lack of support for park and wilderness protection. There will be a difficult and growing supply and demand problem in outdoor recreation.

To counter this, there is renewed effort in the conservation community to see that more land is protected as wilderness. The rich and extensive system of parks and protected areas in the United States can, activists believe, be considerably enlarged. Much of the land under the management of the Bureau of Land Management may qualify for addition to the National Wilderness Preservation System. Many areas in national parks, reviewed and recommended for wilderness status by the National Park Service in the 1960s and 1970s, await designation by Congress as parts of the system. Millions of road-less acres remain in the national forests outside of any designated protected status. Portions of these might be added to the system. The prospect that the National Wilderness Preservation System may grow by many tens of millions of acres is quite good.

At the same time, private sector efforts to protect smaller increments of nature have been increasing. The land trust movement has been growing. Creative approaches to land saving have been developing, such as the recent protection of 25,000 acres of the Loomis Forest in north-central Washington. In this case a coalition raised funds to compensate the Common School Trust for loss of projected timber revenue from the transfer of prime lynx habitat to natural resource conservation area status. Flush with this success, a coalition with some of the same players is striving to raise $125 million in private and public funds to bring 75,000 acres of mostly industrial timberland into public ownership. If this can be done, it will increase connectivity between two large ecosystems at the core of the Washington Cascades, in an area of great potential for restoration and maintenance of a diverse natural community. A century of preservation has yielded over 2.5 million acres of national parks and wilderness in this region. Yet the 75,000 acres of timber industrial timberland impedes essential connectivity (Friedman 2001). The current system of reserves needs, here and elsewhere, to be supplemented if the emergent goal of protecting biological diversity is to be addressed.

Photograph 3.4 Arctic tundra and wilderness on the Yukon and Alaska north coasts near the border of Yukon National Park, Canada, and the Arctic Wildlife Range, U.S.A.

The challenges are great, but the history of park, wilderness, and other categories of protected areas in the United States suggests that additional land protection is achievable. A 1994 assessment of endangered ecosystems in the United States revealed the urgency of the challenge (Noss, LaRoe, and Scott 1994). The world has changed greatly since the first national park was created at Yellowstone. At that time, many in Congress felt that Yellowstone was so remote that a park there would never be of consequence one way or the other. Some held similar views about remote and little-visited Alaskan park, wilderness, and wildlife refuge areas at the time of the establishment of this system in 1980. Yet today, growing numbers of visitors have spread the word about their high natural values. Any additions to the U.S. national park and wilderness system now would very likely be viewed in a similarly positive way in future.

References

Agee, J. K., and D. R. Johnson. 1988. *Ecosystem Management for Parks and Wilderness.* Seattle: University of Washington Press.

Friedman, M. 2001. "A Checkerboard Conundrum: A Conservation Partnership Raises Funds to Link the Cascades," *Wild Earth* 11(2)(Summer 2001): 33-37.

Gorte, R. W. 1994. *Wilderness: Overview and Statistics.* Report for Congress, #94-976, ENR. Washington: Congressional Research Service.

Hendee, J. C., G. H. Stankey, and R. C. Lucas. 1990. *Wilderness Management.* 2d ed. Golden, Colo.: North American Press.

Leopold, A. S., S. A. Cain, C. M. Cottam, I. N. Gabrielson, and T. Kimball. 1963. "Study of Wildlife Problems in National Parks: Wildlife Management in National Parks," pp. 28–45. In *Transactions of the North American Wildlife and Natural Resources Conference.* Washington: North American Wildlife and Natural Resources Society.

Leopold, A. 1921. "The Wilderness and Its Place in Forest Recreation Policy." 1991. In *The River of the Mother of God and Other Essays,* ed. S. Flader and J. B. Callicott. Madison: University of Wisconsin Press.

Mackintosh, B. 1984. *The National Parks: Shaping the System.* Washington, D.C.: U.S. National Park Service.

Miles, J. C. 1995. *Guardians of the Parks: A History of the National Parks and Conservation Association.* Washington, D.C.: Taylor and Francis.

Noss, R. F., and A. Y. Cooperrider. 1994. *Saving Nature's Legacy: Protecting and Restoring Biodiversity.* Washington, D.C.: Island Press.

Noss, R. F., E. T. LaRoe, and J. M. Scott. 1994. Endangered Ecosystems of the United States: A Preliminary Assessment of Loss and Degradation. U.S. Fish and Wildlife Service Report, Washington, D.C.

Rothman, H. 1989. *America's National Monuments: The Politics of Preservation.* Lawrence: The University of Kansas.

Runte, A. 1987. *National Parks: The American Experience.* 2d ed., rev. Lincoln: University of Nebraska Press.

The Wilderness Society. 1999. *About the Wilderness Society.* Accessed online 2 May 99. url: www.wilderness.org/abouttws.

United States. Sixty-fourth Congress, First Session, 25 August 1916. U.S. Statutes at Large. 39, 535. *National Park Service Act.* Washington, D.C.: U.S. Congress.

———. Eighty-eighth Congress, Second Session, 3 September 1964. U.S. Statutes at Large 78 (1964): 890. *Wilderness Act.* Washington, D.C.: U.S. Congress.

United States. National Park Service. 2001. *The National Parks: Index 1999–2001.* Washington, D.C.: Department of the Interior.

Williams, M. 1989. *Americans and Their Forests: A Historical Geography.* Cambridge: Cambridge University Press.

The Mexican Park and Protected Area System

*Carlos Castillo S., Bruce A. B. Currie-Alder,
and J. C. Day*

Abstract

This brief history of the Mexican parks system focuses on recent challenges to protected areas and responses to them. Reference is made to the 1995 to 2000 *National Development Plan* and the programs that it supports. A number of strategies are also presented to advance the state of Mexican national parks and protected areas including: enlargement of the scope and representation of the protected area system; financing, public participation, and social comanagement; opportunities for regional development; institutional coordination; and education and training. Recently, considerable emphasis has been placed on the conservation of biodiversity, which is higher in Mexico than other parts of the world.

Introduction

Mexico's federal system of protected areas began in 1876 with the establishment of *Desierto de los Leones* near Mexico City. This area was reclassified in 1917 and became the country's first national park. Protected areas were a low priority until the late 1930s and 1940s when over thirty national parks were established during the administration of President Lazaro Cardenas; a legacy that represents a third of the present protected area system. With the beginning of the global environmental movement, and the first IUCN World Conservation Congress, a second

Photograph 4.1. Sea of Cortez coast near Northern Gulf of California and
Colorado River Delta Biosphere Reserve, Mexico

boom in conservation started in the 1970s. Under the influence of
international conservation agencies, Mexico diversified its protected area
system to include new categories such as biosphere reserves. Over half of
Mexico's protected areas were established in the 1980s and 1990s
(México, INE 2000). Mexico's present system currently includes over a
hundred protected areas (fig. 4.1, table 4.1).

Mexico's present system of protected areas is defined in the biodiversity
chapter of the *Federal Environmental Law* (México, *Diario Oficial* 1988,
1996), and a *Protected Area Regulation* (México, *Diario Oficial* 2000). The
law describes protected area categories and provides a legal framework
for the protected area system. A primary reason for establishing protected
areas is to conserve habitat for species listed in the *Endangered Species
Rule*, but the rule does not provide for government intervention on private lands (México, *Diario Oficial* 1994). Responsibility for the federal
system of protected areas lies with the National Institute of Ecology
(INE—*Instituto Nacional de Ecología*). This government agency is part of
the federal environmental department, previously known as SEMAR-
NAP (*Secretaría de Medio Ambiente, Recursos Naturales y Pesca*). When fishery responsibilities were transferred to the federal agricultural department
in December 2000, the federal environmental department changed its
name to the Secretariat of Environment and Natural Resources
(SEMARNAT- *Secretaría de Medio Ambiente y Recursos Naturales*).

Figure 4.1 Marine and terrestrial priority areas and natural protected areas of Mexico

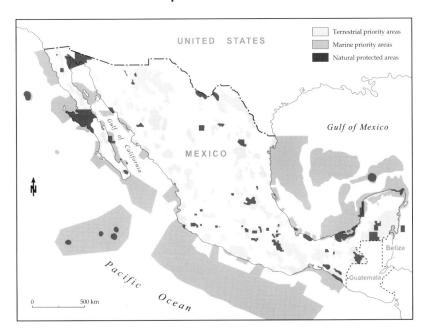

Table 4.1. Mexico's federal system of protected areas*

Category	Number of Parks	Total Area (000's ha)
Biosphere Reserve	26	8,821
National Park	64	1,396
Natural Monument	4	13
Protected Area for Natural Resources	5	281
Protected Area for Flora and Fauna	11	1,661
Sanctuary	7	518
TOTAL	117	12,690

*Mexican biosphere reserves are similar to, but independent of, protected areas included in the UNESCO Man and Biosphere Program. Biosphere reserves in Mexico are intended to contain core areas that are subject to strict conservation, and surrounding buffer zones in which land and resource use are managed for nature conservation and sustainability. (Sources: México, INE 2000, Ghimire and Pimbert 1998,10; México, Diario Oficial 1988, 1996)

The process of establishing a federal protected area begins with a presidential decree (*decreto*) that is published in the legal gazette of the Mexican government (*Diario Oficial de la República*). While this legal document creates the protected area, the decree simply justifies the reasons for establishing the area, its boundaries, and designates a protected area category. Establishment of protected areas in Mexico seldom changes existing land tenure, and Mexican protected areas often include a mixture of state property, private lands, and communal or *ejida*[1] lands. Preexisting landowners continue to hold and retain title to their lands. The government only owns lands assigned to it by law, regardless of protected area designation (Currie-Alder 2001).

In Mexico, property rights are dispersed among many landowners and the role of government is to coordinate the activities of these landowners. Not surprisingly, Mexico faces a difficult challenge in implementing protected area policies as landowners also have a right not to cooperate with the plans of government agencies and many centrally managed protected areas have experienced degradation (Gómez-Pompa and Kaus 1999).

Prior to changes made in the *Federal Environmental Law* in 1996, the federal government was the main player in environmental management. The changes allowed state and local governments to develop their own environmental legislation and to declare their own protected areas independent of the federal system. The administration of federally designated protected areas remains with that government, although there is an understanding that its activities will be coordinated with state and local governments. Such coordination occurs through an informal relationship between these governments and a local office that the federal government establishes within each protected area. Additionally, the *Federal Protected Areas Program* (México, SEMARNAP 1996) provided the opportunity for contract-based collaboration, whereby certain manage-

---

1.   *Ejidos* were created during the agrarian reform at the end of the Mexican revolution in the 1930s. The government expropriated large, single-owner *latifundos* land holdings, and converted them into *ejidos* for landless peasants. Officially, ejidos were state property, but use and possession rights were given to a group of individuals known as *ejidatarios*. Each *ejidatario* possessed a small, individual "parcel" of land within an *ejido*. An *ejidatario* was essentially autonomous for decisions regarding his parcel, but decisions regarding an *ejido* as a whole had to be made in assemblies of all member *ejidatarios*. The *ejido* ceased to exist following modification of article 27 of the national constitution in 1992. New *ejidos* can no longer be created and existing ones are being converted to private property, jointly owned by the *ejidatarios*. Nevertheless, land redistribution remains a powerful idea and symbol in Mexican society and many parks and protected areas have been created on *ejidal* lands. The Mexican Ministry for Agrarian Reform has the detailed story on its website (www.sra.gob.mx).

Photograph 4.2 Pressure on forest ecosystems in the coastal mountains of Sonora, Mexico

ment responsibilities may be transferred from the federal government to other actors (México, SEMARNAP 1996:103).

Challenge and Response

In recent years, the extraordinary ecological and biological wealth of Mexico has been extensively documented. Scientific understanding of the important goods and ecological services provided by biodiversity and natural areas has also increased. Natural areas are considered strategic assets for Mexico as the country attempts to move toward environmentally sustainable development.

Since the establishment of the *National Development Plan: 1995-2000* (México, SEGOB 1996), a hierarchical structure has been in place for the establishment and management of protected areas (*áreas naturales protegidas*). The *National Plan* places special emphasis on addressing environmental degradation that occurs as a consequence of increased population concentration and urban sprawl. Other causes of degradation include: contamination of ecosystems; waste generation; deforestation; inappropriate land use practices; contamination and increasing scarcity of aquatic resources; and unsustainable harvest of certain species. One strategy put forward in the *National Plan* to address degradation is increased conservation of biodiversity through the creation of new protected areas, as well as decentralizing administration and restoring existing national parks.

In this context, the objectives of the *Protected Areas Program: (Programa de areas naturales protegidas de México* 1995-2000) are twofold. First, expand the coverage of the national system of protected natural areas. Second, consolidate and promote appropriate planning and management, both through more efficient management mechanisms and more effective institutions. These objectives seek opportunities to involve new actors in the administration and management of protected areas in order to extend the commitment and responsibility for conservation and strengthen local communities. The *Protected Areas Program* also aims to use protected areas as a basic element in new regional development plans to achieve sustainability (México, SEMARNAP 1996).

The government of Mexico relies on a variety of instruments including the Mexican legal framework, public administrative system, and social incentives to achieve these objectives. These instruments include declarations, covenants, and agreements for participation. As well, intergovernmental agreements are included on coordination, fiscal financing, and international financing. Other instruments include volunteer exchanges, international covenants, management programs and systems, research, information, education and communication, regulation, and protection of wildlife. These instruments aim to conserve protected areas through such means as ecological zoning and other measures.

These instruments are laid out as strategies in the *Protected Areas Program* and involve the following major policy initiatives (appendix 1 of this paper):

- Consolidating management systems
- Expanding the protected area system
- Decentralizing and restoring existing national parks
- Developing organizational structures and local institutions
- Financing
- Promoting public participation and comanagement
- Creating opportunities for regional development
- Increasing interinstitutional coordination
- Developing information systems

For the federal government, the *Protected Areas Program* constitutes the cornerstone for conserving biodiversity and biological resources. The program represents a means of reconciling ecological integrity and the needs of ecosystems with institutional and management arrangements solidly based in federal legislation.

The amount of land dedicated to parks and protected areas in Mexico covers more than 12 million hectares and seems considerable in absolute terms (table 4.1). Yet this amount is disproportionately small and scarcely representative of the biological diversity of Mexico. At 6.5 percent of the country's landmass, the proportion of territory under legal protection in Mexico is precariously inadequate in comparison to other nations.

The small size of many Mexican protected areas threatens the survival of populations of many critical species. As a result, the Mexican government is committed to increasing the amount of territory under legal protection. Other relevant government actions involve consolidating the administration, and management of existing protected areas. Given the shortage of financial resources, efforts have been concentrated in a limited number of protected areas that cover the largest land area. These areas represent most of the country's major ecosystems, and encompass a large proportion of the country's biodiversity. These efforts often focus on areas of international importance. These programs will be expanded in the future to other areas by means of self-financing and contributions from multilateral agencies.

Each protected area is to develop a management plan and an operation plan. A management plan is a general framework describing conservation goals, restrictions on the human use of the area, and the responsibilities of each government agency involved in its management. Management plans are often valid for periods of five years or more, and may also include a zoning map. Operation plans describe how management plans are to be implemented, including constructing infrastructure, acquiring new equipment, establishing new programs and research. Operation plans are often valid for one year. Management and operation plans are developed and implemented when personnel, finances and other considerations permit.

In the early 1990s, the Global Environmental Facility donated $25 million to the Mexican government for improving the federal protected area system. However, after almost three years, the money had not been used due to bureaucratic complications. Even though the exercise was extremely inefficient due to the large number of procedures required to access the funds, ten protected areas received new funding. The number of protected areas benefiting from international funding increased to twenty-five in 1996, and thirty-four in 1999. These thirty-four areas include a total protected surface of almost ten million hectares. Work is currently underway to arrange funding for another twenty protected areas. The government's goal is obtain international funding for a total of forty-eight additional protected areas.

Where appropriate, protected area management plans are associated with outreach programs to increase coordination between protected areas and local communities, all levels of government, academic institutions, and the private sector. Many protected areas now possess advisory bodies called technical advisory committees (CTA—*Comités Técnicos Asesores*). These committees include the local municipal presidents and state governors, and offer the potential for integrating government policy within and outside a protected area. A CTA may also include other stakeholders, such as nongovernmental organizations, resource user groups, or indigenous groups. Through their involvement, CTAs provide new opportunities for public participation into protected area management.

Conclusion

Prior to the 1990s, Mexico's protected area system was haphazard and disorganized. Many protected areas were too small to achieve their conservation goals, and management practices differed widely between areas. The system represented historical interest in conservation rather than the country's true wealth of biodiversity.

Over the past decade, Mexico has begun a process of increasing the efficiency of its protected area system through new legislation and new initiatives included in the National Development Plan and Protected Areas Program. While much work remains to be done, Mexico has taken significant steps to standardize management practices and expand the protected area system to include ecosystems that were previously under-represented. Strategic use of international financing has been key to recent developments in Mexico's protected area system.

In the twenty-first century, Mexico's system seeks to increase the efficiency and effectiveness of protected area management by establishing creative partnerships with other stakeholders, and creating new opportunities for public participation. Management within Mexican protected areas is increasingly transparent and moving beyond park boundaries to become an integral part of sustainable regional development.

References

Currie-Alder, B. 2001. "Collaborative management of the Mexican Coast: Public participation and the oil industry in the Terminos Lagoon Protected Area". Master's thesis. Burnaby, British Columbia: School of Resource and Environmental Management, Simon Fraser University.

Ghimire, K. B., and M. P. Pimbert. 1998. *Social change and conservation: environmental politics and impacts of national parks and protected areas.* London, England: UNRISD and Earthscan Publications.

Gómez-Pompa, A., and A. Kaus. 1999. "From pre-Hispanic to future conservation alternatives: lessons from Mexico." *Proceeding of the National Academy of Sciences* 96: 5982-5986.

México. Diario Oficial de la Federación. 30 Nov. 2000. *Reglamento de la Ley General del Equilibrio Ecológico y la Protección al Ambiente en Materia de Areas Naturales Protegidas.*

_____. 16 May 1994. *Que determina las especies de flora y fauna silvestre terrestres y acuáticas en peligro de extinción, amenzadas, raras y las sujetas a protección especial, y que establece especificaciones para su protección.* Norma Oficial Mexicana NOM-059-ECOL-1994.

_____. 28 Jan. 1988. *Ley General del Equilibrio Ecológico y la Protección al Ambiente.* (revised 13 Dec. 1996).

_____. Instituto Nacional de Ecología. 2000. *Listado de Áreas Naturales Protegidas en México.* D.F., México: INE. Web document accessed 13 June 2000 from: www.ine.gob.mx/ucanp/listaanpcate.php3.

_____. Secretaría de Gobernación. 1996. *Plan Nacional de Desarollo: 1995-2000.* D.F., México: SEGOB.

_____. 1998. *Programa de Manejo de la Reserva de la Biosfera de El Pinacate y Gran Desierto de Altar 1998-2002*: Rev. ed. D.F., México: SEMARNAP.

_____. Secretaría de Medio Ambiente, Recursos Naturales y Pesca. 1996. *Programa de areas naturales protegidas de México 1995-2000.* D.F., México: SEMARNAP.

_____. Secretaría de Medio Ambiente, Recursos Naturales y Pesca.1995. *Programa de Manejo 2: Reserva de la Biosfera de El Pinacate y Gran Desierto de Altar.* D.F., México: SEMARNAP.

Appendix 1

Protected Area Program Strategies: 1995-2000

The *Protected Area Program* proposed a number of strategies (México, SEMARNAP 1996). These strategies are often constrained by limited government budgets, yet all have been at least partially implemented. The National Institute of Ecology (INE) will likely continue these strategies in the future. A new *Protected Areas Program* for the period 2001to 2006 is expected shortly, but was not yet available at the time of publication.

Consolidating Management Systems

INE will standardize management practices among Mexican protected areas by formalizing land tenure and property rights. The key reason for establishing protected areas is to protect rare and endangered species.

Experiments with new administration systems will be conducted through pilot areas, and linking of sister parks, to combine administration and reduce management costs. This strategy also includes establishing biological stations and ecotourism development, new infrastructure and equipment, and expanding antipoaching programs.

Expanding the Protected Area System

INE will expand the protected area system in order to protect sensitive ecosystems and increase the representation of coastal and marine ecosystems. Existing protected area decrees, management plans, and operation plans will be updated and new ones developed. INE also supports the Mesoamerican Biological Corridor—an international initiative to establish a continuous chain of protected areas from Mexico to Panama.

Decentralizing and Restoring Existing National Parks

Park administration is to be decentralized away from Mexico City to local offices established at the park level. Where possible, efforts will be undertaken to restore protected areas that have experienced degradation. Protected area decrees will be revised to correct differences between actual boundaries and those that are legally defined in the decree. Outdated decrees will be retired, and protected areas belonging to categories no longer supported by the *Federal Environmental Law* will be redefined to match existing classification system.

Developing Organizational Structures and Local Institutions

Advisory committees will be established for all protected areas to include other stakeholders in protected area management. Local organizations and local trusts will be fostered in order to increase local skills and financial self-sufficiency in park management.

Financing

INE will continue to provide fiscal financing and seek opportunities for international financing. A national trust for protected areas will be established, while individual protected areas will be encouraged to seek financial self-sufficiency through such means as ecotourism.

Promoting Public Participation and Comanagement

INE will promote the involvement of other stakeholders by establishing a national council for the protected areas program, involving the private sector in conservation projects, and developing research agreements with universities. Where appropriate, INE may also develop partnerships with state or municipal governments, and nongovernmental organizations to provide a role for these stakeholders in protected area management. INE will also support and formalize initiatives by the private sector and civil society that are complementary to conservation goals.

Creating Opportunities for Regional Development

In partnership with other stakeholders, INE will prompt the sustainable use of soil, water, and wildlife by developing regional maps of land use suitability. INE will also develop regional programs for the use of such resources as fisheries and forestry.

Increasing Interinstitutional Coordination

INE commits to coordinate its activities with other government agencies.

Developing Information System

INE aims to improve information regarding protected areas by expanding the use of geographical information systems within protected areas, developing biodiversity inventories, and developing information systems for each protected area. This strategy also encourages new publications regarding Mexican protected areas, and includes programs for community and public awareness.

Canada

REGIONAL APPROACHES TO PLANNING FOR PROTECTED AREAS AND CONSERVATION [1]

Lucy M. Sportza

Abstract

The perceived roles of protected areas have evolved over time, and now include conservation of biodiversity, enhancing quality of human life, and playing a key role in sustainability. In this context, setting aside individual parks, the traditional approach is limited for a number of reasons. In brief, protected areas are often too small, too isolated, and too fragmented to protect the values for which they were originally designated. Regional and other newer approaches to planning are required if protected areas are to fulfill their potential.

Developments in a number of bodies of knowledge offer insight into how and why we should consider planning for protected areas over more regional scales. Landscape ecology and conservation biology are providing new insights into protected areas planning for biodiversity conservation and ecological integrity. Regional and bioregional planning, common property theory, stewardship, and ecosystem management all have important contributions to make to new frameworks for conservation planning. Some of these bodies of knowledge are examined here in an attempt to provide direction for regional conservation planning. Important considerations include: using both ecological and

---

1.   This paper was presented at the Regional Approaches to Parks and Protected Areas Workshop in Tijuana, B.C., and published in *Environments* 27, no.3.

human factors to define the planning region; determining the scale or hierarchical context of conservation initiatives; developing appropriate goals; understanding the social, economic, and cultural, as well as the ecological context; and using a participative planning framework and alternative property regimes.

Introduction

The overall context for this paper is the role of parks and protected areas in conservation. In the sense used here, conservation deals with the appropriate balance of different types of land and water use, ranging from preservation to intense exploitation (Nelson 1987). The goal of conservation is to maintain, restore, and enhance ecosystem integrity, health, and sustainability, over the long term.

A number of bodies of knowledge were reviewed in preparing this paper. Their contributions to regional planning for protected areas and conservation are summarized in table 5.1. Some brief notes on the different bodies of knowledge are offered below. However, the focus of this paper is on integrating the ideas to develop some preliminary criteria for the creation of regional planning approaches for protected areas and conservation.

A common theme that the bodies of knowledge share is a need for major changes in the way planning, management, and decision-making are undertaken to help address complex goals such as conservation and sustainability. Writers in bioregionalism (Sale 1985) and conservation biology (Noss and Cooperrider 1994), noted that the approach they proposed was significantly different than traditional paradigms; for example, resource management. Ecosystem management, when considered in its more biocentric[2] form, implies a focus on, or concern about, all living beings and it is used in ecosystem management. Its antonym is anthropocentric or human-centered. A biocentric emphasis represents a major revision in traditional planning and management approaches. The shift from more traditional, natural resource management approaches to more recent ideas of ecosystem management includes:

- a world view that is more comprehensive and holistic

---

2.   Biocentric means focused on, or concerned about, all living beings, not just humans. It is used to highlight a difference in focus from most traditional approaches to environmental management that are anthropocentric, or human centered.

- a more complex array of goals including sustainability, conservation, and equity
- an expanded focus on community, collaboration, cooperation, and coordination
- living within ecological limits
- interdisciplinary and transdisciplinary study compared to traditional disciplines
- incorporation of socioeconomic and ecological factors and the use of local or traditional knowledge, and
- an expanded scale of study from local to global, short- to long-term

Table 5.1. Selected Contribution to Regional Planning for Protected Areas and Conservation

Theory	Contribution to Regional Planning for Protected Areas and Conservation
Ecological Science/ Conservation Biology	• large, buffered, connected reserve network required to meet conservation goals such as biodiversity conservation, maintaining ecological and evolutionary processes • upwards of 25 to 75 percent of any given area may require some degree of protection • surrounding areas, not just core reserves, must be considered in planning and management
Regional Planning & Bioregional Planning	• wilderness is an essential element of the regional mosaic • importance given to human/nature relationship, and balance between ecology and socioeconomic factors • regional approaches help to address problems which • impact beyond their source
Ecological Economics	• for long-term sustainability and intergenerational equity, should protect complete ecosystems, keeping ecological and evolutionary processes intact
Participative Planning	• development of approaches to improve planning and decision making in complex environments such as when planning for sustainability and ecological integrity
Common Property & Stewardship	• understanding cultural capital—how societies interact with, and manage, their environments • alternative approaches that may help complement and support traditional protected areas, such as extending conservation activities outside of protected area boundaries
Ecosystem Management	• process of managing and understanding the interaction of biophysical and socioeconomic environments within regional systems—of understanding the humannature relationship • emphasizes the need to focus on large-scale, system-wide perspectives to achieve goals such as ecological integrity, biodiversity conservation, and sustainability

These ideas were incorporated in the civics model proposed by Nelson and Serafin (1996). The civics approach was created with a pluralistic spirit in mind. The central theme of the approach was an emphasis on involving a wide range of people and groups in understanding and taking responsibility for their impacts on the world around them—the ecosystems, human activities, and institutions that interact to form society.

Ecological Sciences

Island biogeography (MacArthur and Wilson 1967) and associated theory such as landscape ecology (Forman and Godron 1986) and conservation biology (Soulé 1980) were critical in turning attention to what were relatively neglected topics, such as reserve size, design, minimum viable population size, patch dynamics, and connectivity among protected areas (Shafer 1990). From ecological science, a general theme for protected area design emerges: Protected areas should be large, buffered, and connected by corridors. A well-designed system of protected areas is increasingly seen as vital to protect biodiversity over the long-term, with not only protected areas in need of attention, but also the regions or context in which they are located: It is no longer seen as feasible to plan only for individual parks (Meffe and Carroll 1997, Mosquin, Whiting, and McAllister 1995, Noss, O'Connell, and Murphy 1997, Schonewald-Cox et al. 1992, among others). Models that incorporated these themes included biosphere reserves (UNESCO 1996), multiple-use modules (MUMs) (Harris 1984, Noss and Harris 1986), reserve networks (Noss 1987), and greater park ecosystems (Grumbine 1990).

Regional Planning

Regional planning has a long history, dating back at least to the mid- to late-nineteenth century in Europe and North America (Friedmann and Weaver 1977; Hodge 1994, 1998; Robinson and Hodge 1998). One key contribution of this early work was the introduction, by the Regional Planning Association of America (1923-1933) and members such as Mumford and MacKaye, of wilderness as an essential element of the regional mosaic (Weaver 1984).

  Bioregionalism may offer a starting point for revitalizing regional planning (Hodge 1994), as may the development of regional governance and more collaborative approaches (Saunier and Meganck 1995, Wallis 1994, Wight 1996, 1998).

Bioregional Planning

Miller (1996:1) suggested that bioregional planning and management offer an answer to the question: "How can the elements of wild nature

... be maintained in landscapes that also need to produce material goods, environmental services and the many cultural, aesthetic, and spiritual benefits that people everywhere want?" In this sense, the aim of bioregional planning is to enhance biodiversity conservation by addressing the social and economic needs of people living either in, or near, protected areas (Miller 1996). Hodge (1998) noted that introducing bioregional concepts into planning would require a re-examination of the central elements of concern to planning, from the conventional focus on land use and economic development to ecology and community.

Ecological Economics

The goal of ecological economics is to develop a greater understanding of the linkages between ecological and economic systems, and to use this understanding to develop effective policies that will help guide us towards sustainability (Costanza 1996). In terms of habitat protection and biodiversity, one point of ecological economics is that in selecting a stock of natural capital—nonrenewable and renewable resources and environmental services—to pass along to future generations and to maintain long-term sustainability, emphasis should be given to resources such as living ecosystems. These are rich in biodiversity and capable of supporting the ecological and evolutionary processes essential to adapting to human-induced and natural change over the long-term (Costanza et al. 1997). In this regard, large, intact, self-sustaining ecosystems should be one focus of planning, management, and decision-making.

Participative Approaches to Planning

Tomalty et al. (1994) suggested that participative or collaborative approaches are needed when planning seeks to change human attitudes, structures and behaviors, such as in planning for sustainability. Day, Williams, and Litke (1996) noted that changing societal values, and associated interactions and conflicts among groups, were resulting in a growing demand for more participatory forms of decision-making. Others have also found participative approaches to be effective at incorporating difficult issues relating to human/nature interactions and environmental complexity (Briassoulis 1989, Hudson 1979).

Many benefits of participative planning approaches have been identi-fied, and there is a growing body of examples and lessons. British Columbia, through the Commission on Resources and Environment

(CORE), used shared decision-making as a conflict management strategy (for an overview see Day, Williams, and Litke 1998; Roseland, Duffy, and Gunton 1996). Innes (1996) discussed several successful collaborative planning exercises in California that dealt with a variety of social and environmental issues. Others have discussed these approaches in terms of specific resources; for example, coral reefs (White et al. 1994), and wetlands and wildlife (Porter and Salvesen 1995).

Challenges facing participative or collaborative planning approaches include: being time and resource intensive and uncertain; issues of governance; process design and management; time commitment; stakeholder involvement; and power distribution (Day, Williams, and Litke 1998, Porter and Salvesen 1995). Nonetheless, these approaches are valuable, especially in instances where controversial and complex matters must be addressed.

Common Property Theory

Common property theory examines property rights; that is, private, state, and common property regimes, and how these may be applied for more efficient use and management of the natural environment and resources (Hanna, Folke, and Muler 1996). Conventional wisdom has held that common property regimes would result in overexploitation; for example, Hardin's *Tragedy of the Commons*. Research has shown that this is not necessarily so (Berkes et al. 1989, Berkes and Folke 1998, Fenney et al. 1990). Instead, communities dependent on common property resources have often adopted various institutional arrangements to manage them. Useful mechanisms for successful common property regimes include (Folke, Berkes, and Colding 1998):
  • using management practices based on local ecological knowledge
  • designing management systems that *flow with nature*
  • enhancing social mechanisms for building resilience
  • promoting conditions for self-organization and institutional learning
  • rediscovering adaptive management
  • developing values consistent with resilient and sustainable socioecological systems

Stewardship

Stewardship may be defined as efforts to create, nurture, and enable responsibility in land, and resource owners and users to manage and protect land and natural resources (Mitchell and Brown 1998). It can aid biodiversity conservation by: extending conservation practices beyond the boundaries of protected areas; providing buffers or linkages between public lands; responding to social interests; and engaging local people in improving conservation practices (Mitchell and Brown 1998). Experience has shown that people are willing to practice land stewardship when they are encouraged but not coerced (Wright 1992).

Stewardship includes a wide variety of techniques such as education, written or verbal agreements, management agreements, transfer of development rights, conservation easements, and acquisition (Hilts, Kirk, and Reid 1986, Mitchell and Brown 1998). Land trusts and use of conservation easements have grown tremendously in recent years, particularly in regions with low federal land ownership, such as the New England States and the Atlantic Provinces of Canada (Endicott 1993, Mitchell and Brown 1998).

Ecosystem Management

Ecosystem management is a holistic approach to planning and management, providing a greater understanding of the human/nature relationship (Grumbine 1994, Meffe and Carroll 1997, Tomalty et al. 1994). It has developed at least partly because of the perceived failure of past approaches to balance environmental conservation and socioeconomic needs (Slocombe 1993b).

Commonalities among definitions of ecosystem management include (Meffe and Carroll 1997):

- emphasis on large-scale, system-wide perspectives
- focus on composition and processes of ecological systems and their complexities
- recognition of the need for integration across multiple scales as well as ecological, economic, and cultural fields of concern
- long-term sustainability of the ecosystem

Meffe and Carroll (1997) defined ecosystem management as:

> … an approach to maintaining or restoring the composition, structure and function of natural and modified ecosystems for the goal of long-term sustainability. It is based on a collaboratively developed vision of desired future conditions that integrates ecological, socio-economic, and institutional

perspectives, applied within a geographic framework defined primarily by natural ecological boundaries.

In short, ecosystem management is a process of managing and understanding the interaction of the biophysical and socioeconomic environments within regional or larger systems (Slocombe 1998b). As such, it can provide a new opportunity to describe, understand, and integrate humans and nature (Stankey 1994). Adaptive management (Holling 1978, Lee 1993, Gunderson, Holling, and Light 1995) is an important element of ecosystem management.

Although ecosystem management holds promise, there are obstacles to be overcome (Meffe and Carroll 1997, Slocombe 1993a, 1993b, 1998b, Vogt et al. 1997). These include difficulties defining the management unit, attempting to deal with the interdisciplinary nature of ecosystem management, and creating appropriate planning and management frameworks. Appropriate goal development is also a key barrier to ecosystem management (Slocombe 1998a). Institutional change is another constraint. Agencies often must overcome historic competition and conflicting mandates to work cooperatively to implement newer goals and mandates such as biodiversity conservation. Grumbine (1991) provided a discussion of the United States Forest Service and National Park Service in this regard.

Criteria for Regional Planning for Protected Areas and Conservation

Some preliminary thoughts can be offered at this point on criteria or components that appear to be important for regional conservation planning, focusing on protected areas. These criteria emerge from the bodies of knowledge reviewed for this paper and may tend more towards the ideal rather than practical. They are presented in no particular order.

Defining the Region

A region should be defined, preferably based on natural features. The central theme for the regional planning process should be ecology and human communities, and these factors should be recognized in the definition of the region. Regional boundaries should be flexible and adaptable, to accommodate new information and understanding, and respond to changing issues and concerns.

Scale or Hierarchical Context

It is critical to be explicitly aware of the scale or hierarchical context of a region. For example, what are the larger and smaller spatial contexts in which a region is placed? What approaches or planning exercises are occurring at the various spatial and temporal scales? All regional plans should be as compatible as possible with those at different scales, and certainly not contradictory. For example, the goals developed at any one scale should not preclude the fulfillment of goals developed for larger or smaller scale units. Reserve networks developed at one scale should fit into larger scale reserve networks, enhancing or complementing them.

Goals

Goals should be both substantive and procedural, as outlined by Slocombe (1998a). Goals should be interdisciplinary, and should be part of a hierarchy of goals, objectives, and criteria. General goals, such as *biodiversity* or *sustainability*, should be complemented by more specific goals or objectives reflective of a particular region.

Using Ecological Principles

The ecological information that is used should include both scientific and local ecological knowledge. Where data are lacking, the cost of acquisition is prohibitive, or uncertainty abounds, an adaptive or flexible approach should be used following the precepts of the precautionary principle (Myers 1993).

A reserve system, based on ecological criteria, should be designed to include core protected areas, buffers, and linkages. The idea is to develop a system of land use categories, ranging from areas for protection or preservation, to areas for built environments, and for restoration (Nelson 1987). The system should link land uses to the degree of protection required to fulfill goals and objectives, or alternately, the degree of human use and intervention that can be accommodated, based on the precautionary principle. Implementing and refining the reserve network "on the ground" should involve both further ecological science, and socioeconomic and cultural concerns and factors.

Mapping techniques, such as gap analysis (Kavanagh and Iacobelli 1995, Scott et al. 1993) and the ABC resource survey (Bastedo, Nelson, and Theberge 1984), can be helpful in designing a system of protected area. Both methods, roughly speaking, attempt to find the most important and appropriate locations for future protection. Macroecology can also help by presenting a "big picture" and using a more interdisciplinary approach than traditional ecological disciplines (Brown 1995). Macroecology can provide critical answers regarding biodiversity faster and more efficiently than traditional disciplinary studies. Biodiversity frameworks, such as that developed by Peck (1998), are also useful for determining the ecological limits within which planning must occur.

The Social, Economic, and Cultural Context

This includes the values, concerns, issues, and needs of local communities, as well as understanding of the institutions and forms of governance, both formal and informal, in the region. For example, what are the policies, agencies, and levels of government involved? Who are the key actors in the region? What is the economic base of the community/communities?

Shared Decision-Making

All stakeholders should be involved throughout the planning process. Penrose, Day, and Roseland (1998) outlined a useful framework for designing and evaluating collaborative processes (table 5.2). The focus on participative planning is valuable for a number of reasons, and is especially useful to address issues that are controversial and complex, or where conflict prevails. In less confrontational circumstances, different planning approaches may be useful.

Learning

Several different types of learning should be included. Lee (1993) spoke of learning as a key to sustainability. This includes learning about the relationship between humans and nature and among people, as well as learning from experimentation in policy and action. Learning is also important in the sense of developing greater understanding of the ecological and socioeconomic and cultural contexts, and how to work within an inter- or transdisciplinary environment. Learning is not just important at the level of government or agency policy and action, but also for other actions, such as those that might develop as common property regimes or local stewardship initiatives. Public education would be included under this principle.

Table 5.2. Design and Evaluative Criteria for Shared Decision-Making Processes[a]

Support for Process
- Participant support
- Government support

Representation and Resources
- Inclusive representation of interests
- Effective representation of interests
- Sufficient resources for participants
- Effective process management

Negotiation Design
- Clear terms of reference and realistic scope
- Participatory design
- Comprehensive and effective procedural framework
- Structured and integrative decision-making framework

[a] adapted from Penrose et al. 1998

Alternative Property Regimes

An understanding of the types of common property regimes and stewardship arrangements in the region is necessary; for example, as part of understanding the social and cultural context of planning. It is also important to understand the potential roles of the different types and combinations of state, private, and communal property regimes in the region, and how each can work best towards fulfilling regional goals. There will be cases where it may be best to have state acquisition and control of a key area, but there are also likely to be instances where it is possible or advisable to embrace a common property regime or stewardship approach. In these instances, it is important to understand how these approaches can be fostered, supported, and enhanced.

Concluding Remarks

A number of theories and issues have been briefly reviewed in an effort to formulate some preliminary thought about regional planning for protected areas and conservation. Given current understanding in ecological science, regional planning, ecological economics, participative planning, common property theory, and stewardship and ecosystem management, eight preliminary criteria were introduced.

Human-needs centered conservation approaches, such as single-species management and sustained yield, have not worked. It is equally likely that biocentric approaches will ultimately fail because of their strong emphasis on the needs of nonhuman species. What is needed, rather, are approaches that emphasize developing, promoting, and enhancing the human/nature relationship and building understanding of the vital roles of protected areas in nature conservation and human development. Communication is critical in this regard. It must be recognized that participative approaches and developing a greater understanding of the human/nature relationship require large amounts of time, money, and other resources. Growing experience in participative decision-making for conservation and resources management are showing that the time and effort is worthwhile, however, and can result in more broadly accepted decisions and reduced conflict.

The papers in this volume illustrate attempts to conduct regional planning for conservation and protected areas at different scales in North America. No one scale is the "best" for regional conservation planning. Scales are illustrated ranging from local, regional or greater park ecosystem, to transcontinental. The papers also highlight the different methods or approaches taken to begin to integrate conservation needs with human needs such as economic and social development. Ultimately, understanding the successes and failures of theory and case studies such as those presented in this volume will provide invaluable insight into the kinds of planning, management, and decision-making approaches that will best serve the needs of nature conservation, protected areas, and human development. To this end further research focusing on understanding, assessing, and comparing regional planning approaches is required.

References

Bastedo, J.D., J.G. Nelson, and J.B. Theberge. 1984. "Ecological Approach to Resource Survey and Planning for Environmentally Significant Areas: The ABC Method." *Environmental Management* 8(2): 125-134.

Berkes, F., and C. Folke. 1998. "Linking Social and Ecological Systems for Resilience and Sustainability," pp. 1-25. In *Linking Social and Ecological Systems: Management Practices and Social Mechanisms for Building Resilience,* ed. F. Berkes and C. Folke.. Cambridge, England and New York: Cambridge University Press.

Berkes, F., D. Feeny, B.J. McCay, and J.M. Acheson. 1989. "The Benefits of the Commons." *Nature* 340: 91-93.

Briassoulis, H. 1989. "Theoretical Orientations in Environmental Planning: An Inquiry into Alternative Approaches." *Environmental Management* 13(4): 381-392.

Brown, J. H. 1995. *Macroecology.* Chicago: University of Chicago Press.

Costanza, R. 1996. "Ecological Economics: Reintegrating the Study of Humans and Nature." *Ecological Applications* 6(4): 978-990.

Costanza, R., J. Cumberland, H. Daly, R. Goodland, and R. Norgaard. 1997. *An Introduction to Ecological Economics.* Boca Raton, Fla.: St. Lucie Press.

Day, J. C., P. W. Williams, and S. Litke, eds. 1998. "Land and Water Planning in British Columbia in the 1990s." Special Issue. *Environments* 25(2-3).

Endicott, E., ed. 1993. *Land Conservation Through Public/Private Partnerships.* Washington, DC and Covelo, Calif.: Island Press.

Feeney, D., F. Berkes, B. J. McCay, and J. M. Acheson. 1990. "The Tragedy of the Commons: Twenty-Two Years Later." *Human Ecology* 18(1): 1-19.

Folke, C., F. Berkes, and J. Colding. 1998. "Ecological Practices and Social Mechanisms for Building Resilience and Sustainability," pp., 414-436 In *Linking Social and Ecological Systems: Management Practices and Social Mechanisms for Building Resilience.* F. Berkes and C. Folke, eds. Cambridge, England and New York: Cambridge University Press.

Friedmann, J., and C. Weaver. 1977. *Territory and Function: The Evolution of Regional Planning Doctrine.* Berkley, Calif.: University of California Press.

Grumbine, R. E. 1990. "Protecting Biological Diversity through the Greater Ecosystem Concept." *Natural Areas Journal* 10(3): 114-120.

_____. 1991. "Cooperation or Conflict? Interagency Relationships and the Future of Biodiversity for U.S. Parks and Forests." *Environmental Management* 15(1): 27-37.

_____. 1994. "What is Ecosystem Management?" *Conservation Biology* 8(1): 27-38.

Gunderson, L. H., C. S. Holling, and S. S. Light. 1995. "Barriers Broken and Bridges Built: A Synthesis," pp. 489- 532. In *Barriers and Bridges to the Renewal of Ecosystems and Institutions,* ed. L. H. Gunderson, C. S. Holling, and S. S. Light. New York: Columbia University Press.

Hanna, S.S., C. Folke, and K-G. Muler, eds. 1996. *Rights to Nature: Ecological, Economic, Cultural, and Political Principles of Institutions for the Environment.* Washington, D.C. and Covelo, Calif.: Island Press.

Hardin, G. 1968. "The Tragedy of the Commons." *Science* 162: 1243-1248.

Harris, L. D. 1984. *The Fragmented Forest: Island Biogeography Theory and the Preservation of Biotic Diversity.* Chicago and London: The University of Chicago Press.

Hilts, S., M. Kirk, and R. Reid. 1986. *Islands of Green: Natural Heritage Protection in Ontario.* Toronto: Ontario Heritage Foundation.

Hodge, G. 1994. "Regional Planning: The Cinderella Discipline." *Plan Canada* 34 (July): 35-39, 42-49.

_____. 1998. *Planning Canadian Communities: An Introduction to the Principles, Practice and Participants.* 3rd ed. Toronto: ITP Nelson.

Holling, C. S., ed. 1978. *Adaptive Environmental Assessment and Management.* Chichester, England: John Wiley.

Hudson, B. M. 1979. "Comparison of Current Planning Theories: Counterparts and Contradictions." *American Planning Association Journal* 35: 387-398.

Innes, J. E. 1996. "Planning Through Consensus Building: A New View of the Comprehensive Planning Ideal." *Journal of the American Planning Association* 62(4): 460-472.

Kavanagh, K., and T. Iacobelli. 1995. *Protected Areas Gap Analysis Methodology.* Toronto: WWF - Endangered Spaces Campaign, World Wildlife Fund Canada.

Lee, K. N. 1993. *Compass and Gyroscope: Integrating Science and Politics for the Environment.* Washington D.C. and Covelo, Calif.: Island Press.

MacArthur, R. H., and E. O. Wilson. 1967. *The Theory of Island Biogeography.* Princeton, N.J.: Princeton University Press.

Meffe, G. K., and C. R. Carroll, eds. 1997. *Principles of Conservation Biology.* Sunderland, Mass.: Sinauer Associates, Inc.

Miller, K., W. Reid, and J. McNeely. 1989. "A Global Strategy for Conserving Biodiversity." *Endangered Species UPDATE* 6(3): 1-8.

Mitchell, B., and J. Brown. 1996. "Stewardship: A Working Definition." *Environments* 26(1): 8-17.

Mosquin, T., P. G. Whiting, and D. E. McAllister. 1995. *Canada's Biodiversity: The Variety of Life, its Status, Economic Benefits, Conservation Costs, and Unmet Needs.* Ottawa, Ont.: Canadian Centre for Biodiversity, Canadian Museum of Nature.

Myers, N. 1993. "Biodiversity and the Precautionary Principle." *Ambio* 22(2-3): 74-79.

Nelson, J. G. 1987. "National Parks and Protected Areas, National Conservation Strategies and Sustainable Development." *GeoForum* 18(3): 291-319.

Nelson, J. G., and R. Serafin. 1996. "Environmental and Resource Planning and Decision Making in Canada: A Human Ecological and a Civics Approach", pp. 1-25. *Canada in Transition: Results of Environmental and Human Geographical Research*, ed. R. Vogelsang. Bochum: Universittsverlag Dr. N. Brockmeyer.

———. 1997. "Keys to Life: Contributions of National Parks and Protected Areas to Heritage Conservation, Tourism and Sustainable Development", pp. 2-10. *National Parks and Protected Areas: Keystones to Conservation and Sustainable Development*, ed. J. G. Nelson and R. Serafin. Berlin and Heidelberg: Springer-Verlag.

———. 1997. *National Parks and Protected Areas: Keystones to Conservation and Sustainable Development*. Berlin and Heidelberg: Springer-Verlag.

Noss, R. F. 1987. "Protecting Natural Areas in Fragmented Landscapes." *Natural Areas Journal* 7(1): 2-13.

Noss, R. F., and A. Y. Cooperrider. 1994. *Saving Nature's Legacy: Protecting and Restoring Biodiversity.* Washington, D.C. and Covelo, Calif.: Island Press.

Noss, R. F., and L. D. Harris. 1986. "Nodes, Networks, and MUMs: Preserving Diversity at All Scales." *Environmental Management* 10:299-309.

Noss, R. F., M. A. O'Connell, and D. D. Murphy. 1997. *The Science of Conservation Planning: Habitat Conservation Under the Endangered Species Act.* Washington, D.C. and Covelo, Calif.: Island Press.

Peck, S. 1997. *Planning for Biodiversity: Issues and Examples.* Washington, D.C. and Covelo, Calif.: Island Press.

Penrose, R. W., J. C. Day, and M. Roseland. 1998. "Shared Decision-Making in Public Land Planning: An Evaluation of the Cariboo-Chilcotin CORE Process." *Environments* 25 (2-3): 27-47.

Porter, D. R., and D. A. Salvesen. 1995. *Collaborative Planning for Wetlands and Wildlife: Issues and Examples.* Washington, D.C. and Covelo, Calif.: Island Press.

Robinson, I., and G. Hodge. 1998. "Canadian Regional Planning at 50: Growing Pains." *Plan Canada* 38(3): 10-15.

Roseland, M., D. M. Duffy, and T. I. Gunton, eds. 1996. "Shared Decision-Making and Natural Resource Planning: Canadian Insights." *Environments* Special Issue 23(2).

Sale, K. 1985. *Dwellers in the Land: The Bioregional Vision.* San Francisco: Sierra Club Books.

Saunier, R. E., and R. A. Meganck. 1995. "Introduction," pp. 1-6. *Conservation of Biodiversity and the New Regional Planning.* R. E. Saunier and R. A. Meganck, eds. Gland, Switzerland: IUCN-The World Conservation Union.

Schonewald-Cox, C., M. Buechner, R. Sauvajot, and B. A. Wilcox. 1992. "Cross-boundary Management between National Parks and Surrounding Lands: A Review and Discussion." *Environmental Management* 16(2): 273-282.

Scott, J. M., F. Davis, B. Csuti, R. Noss, B. Butterfield, C. Groves, H. Anderson, S. Caicco, F. D'Erchia, T. C. Edwards, Jr., J. Ulliman, and R. G. Wright. 1993. "Gap Analysis: A Geographic Approach to Protection of Biological Diversity." Wildlife Monographs no. 123. Supplement to *Journal of Wildlife Management* 571.

Shafer, C. L. 1990. *Nature Reserves: Island Theory and Conservation Practice.* Washington D.C.: Smithsonian Institutional Press.

Slocombe, D. S. 1993a. "Environmental Planning, Ecosystem Science, and Ecosystem Approaches for Integrating Environment and Development." *Environmental Management* 17(3): 289-303.

———. 1993b. "Implementing Ecosystem-based Management." *BioScience* 43(9): 612-622.

———. 1998a. "Defining Goals and Criteria for Ecosystem-based Management." *Environmental Management* 22(4): 483-493.

———. 1998b. "Lessons from Experience with Ecosystem-based Management." *Landscape and Urban Planning* 40: 31-39.

Stanley Jr., T. R. 1995. "Ecosystem Management and the Arrogance of Humanism." *Conservation Biology* 9(2): 255-262.

Tomalty, R., R. B. Gibson, D. H. M. Alexander, and J. Fisher. 1994. *Ecosystem Planning for Canadian Urban Regions.* Toronto: ICURR Publications.

UNESCO. 1996. *Biosphere Reserves: The Seville Strategy and the Statutory Framework of the World Network.* Paris, France: UNESCO.

Vogt, K. A., J. C. Gordon, J. P. Wargo, D. J. Vogt, H. Asbjornsen, P. A. Palmiotto, H. J. Clark, J. L. O'Hara, W. S. Keaton, T. Patel-Weynand, and E. Witten. 1997. *Ecosystems: Balancing Science with Management*. New York: Springer.

Wallis, A. D. 1994. "Inventing Regionalism: A Two-phase Approach." *National Civic Review 83(4):* 447-468.

Weaver, C. 1984. *Regional Development and the Local Community: Planning, Politics and the Social Context*. Toronto: John Wiley & Sons.

White, A. T., L. Zeitlin Hale, Y. Renard, and L. Cortesi. 1994. *Collaborative and Community-based Management of Coral Reefs*. West Hartford, Conn.: Kumarian Press.

Wight, I. 1996. "Framing the New Urbanism with a New Eco-regionalism." *Plan Canada* 36(1): 21-23.

———. 1998. "Canada's Macro-Metros: Suspect Regions or Incipient Citistates?" *Plan Canada* 38(3): 29-37.

Wright, J. B. 1992. "Land Trusts in the USA." *Land Use Policy* 13:83-86.

Natural Area Policies, Regional Municipality of Waterloo, 1973 to 2001 and Beyond

Christopher Gosselin

Abstract

For the past quarter century, the Regional Municipality of Waterloo has been a leader in Canada in the conservation of significant natural heritage. Over the years, the focus has expanded from protecting "islands of green" during the development process, to the conservation of biodiversity of the regional landscape. This evolution has been aided by widespread public and political support for these initiatives, a professional technically qualified ecological and environmental advisory committee, new computing capabilities, technical guidance by the Province of Ontario—such as policy statements—and a Natural Heritage Information Centre. Also helpful were the inauguration of conservation easements in the province and dissemination of insights from the emerging discipline of landscape ecology. A greater challenge for the future is disseminating this information to landholders and motivating them to manage natural landscape areas in a holistic and sustainable fashion. The Waterloo region experience should be of value to planners, educators, academics, politicians, and citizens as to what a midsize municipality can accomplish toward the protection of its biodiversity and natural resources.

Introduction

The Regional Municipality of Waterloo encompasses 1,382 square kilometers in the middle of the Grand River Watershed in southwestern Ontario (fig. 6.1). The Grand River flows through the middle of the region and is joined by the Conestoga and Speed Rivers. Another tributary, the Nith, traverses the western and southwestern extremities of the region. The local topography bears witness to an eventful geological history. The Waterloo, Galt, and Paris Moraines run parallel to the Grand River and its tributaries and determine their courses. Elsewhere, outwash plains, melt water channels, till plains, kames, kettles, and eskers characterized the landscape.

The region's comparatively rich biodiversity is, in part, due to its varied topography, and, in part, to the fact that it straddles the transition zone between the Great Lakes—St. Lawrence and "Carolinian"[1] life zones. The remnant natural areas in the region comprise: maple-beech forests, conifer swamps, sphagnum bogs, oak-hickory forest, oak savannas, fens, silver maple swamps, tall-grass prairies, floodplain meadows, limestone cliffs, and even a meromictic lake.

The region's population and economy are as diverse as its natural features. While the Old Order Mennonite and Amish communities in the north of the region live a lifestyle that outwardly has changed little since the late nineteenth century, the high-tech community around the University of Waterloo is developing the technological innovations of the early twenty-first century. Within the population of approximately 460,000, descendants of settlers who arrived nearly two hundred years ago live and work among migrants from across Canada and around the world, who are attracted by a diverse and rapidly growing economy, excellent educational institutions, and a community with rich cultural and recreational amenities.

Early Development of Waterloo Region's Environmental Policies

In 1973, the former County of Waterloo[2] was reorganized into the Regional Municipality of Waterloo, a two-tier municipality consisting of

---

1.   Or Eastern Deciduous Forest.

2.   The county was established in 1853.

Figure 6.1 Environmentally sensitive policy areas in the Waterloo Region, Ontario

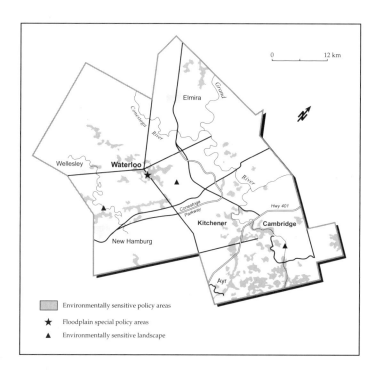

seven area municipalities—cities of Cambridge, Kitchener, and Waterloo, and townships of North Dumfries, Wellesley, Wilmot, and Woolwich. Influenced by the Faculty of Environmental Studies at the University of Waterloo, the new regional government embarked on groundbreaking environmental initiatives. In 1973, it appointed the first Ecological and Environmental Advisory Committee (EEAC) in Canada. Now a well-established part of the region's development approval process, and an active participant in the ongoing evolution of the region's environmental policies, EEAC has served as a model for similar environmental advisory committees across the province. In 1976, the region adopted its first *Regional Official Policies Plan*, and, in the process, designated sixty-nine environmentally sensitive policy areas (ESPAs); the first municipally designated environmentally sensitive areas in Ontario.

From the outset, the region's ESPA policies were—and are—a balance between respect for landowners' property rights, and the general public interest in conserving environmentally significant features and functions, while developing land for human use. The right to apply for development approval within or "contiguous to"[3] an ESPA is recognized, but an applicant may be required to submit an environmental impact statement in support of the application. If the EEAC is of the opinion that a proposed development poses no "serious adverse environmental impact"[4] to an ESPA, the application may be approved.

Criteria for ESPA Designation

Successive regional official policies and plans (ROPPs) have contained scientific criteria for the identification of ESPAs. The criteria of the 1976 and 1985 ROPPs did not explicitly weight or rank the criteria. In practice, however, precedence tended to be given to the presence of regionally significant species of plants and animals. In the third ROPP (Region, 1995, 1996b), the criteria were reworked to emphasize the quality, and rarity of habitat, rather than the mere presence of species deemed "significant" (table 6.1). Moreover, although all ESPAs are treated equally from a policy perspective, there is an implicit hierarchy for ranking. An area designated by the province as a provincially significant life science area of natural and scientific interest (ANSI), is automatically designated an ESPA. The second tier of ESPAs is designated on the basis of habitat considerations related to quality, rarity, or sustaining significant species. The third tier of ESPAs may manifest a lower level of habitat quality, but exhibit some special feature or function such as: hydrology, migration, diversity, or unusual landform (table 6.1). The *Regional Official Policies Plan* (Regional Municipality of Waterloo 1985) also provides for natural areas, not fulfilling sufficient criteria for

---

3.   The ROPP avoids the "cookie-cutter" approach of an arbitrarily determined area of concern around a natural feature. The stated definition of *contiguous* allows the region to determine the applicability of the policies on a case-by-case basis. The definition reads: "lands adjoining an Environmental Protection Area or Environmentally Sensitive Policy Area which are situated in sufficiently close proximity that development could reasonably be expected to produce one or more of the following impacts: alterations to existing hydrological or hydrogeological regimes, clearing of existing vegetation, erosion or sedimentation into the Environmental Protection Area or Environmentally Sensitive Policy Area; or producing a substantial disruption of existing natural linkages or the habitat of a significant species known to inhabit the Environmental Protection Area or Environmentally Sensitive Policy Area."

4.   In 1998, the ROPP was amended to include a comprehensive definition of *adverse environmental impacts.* The definition includes a list of examples of such impacts that is used as a checklist in evaluating development proposals.

designation as ESPAs by the region to be designated as locally significant natural areas by local municipalities.

Table 6.1. Original and Revised Criteria for the Designation of ESPAs

1985 Criteria (7.11)			1995 Criteria (4.3.2)	
A	the occurrence of significant, rare, or endangered indigenous species within a designated area	a)	be identified by the province as a regionally significant life science area of natural and scientific interest, or a provincially significant earth science area of natural and scientific interest; or fulfil at least two of the following criteria:	
B	the identification of plant and/or animal associations and/or landforms which are unusual or of high quality regionally, provincially, or nationally	b)	i) comprise ecological communities deemed unusual, of outstanding quality, or particularly representative regionally, provincially, or nationally	
C	the classification of an area as one that is large and undisturbed, thereby potentially affording a habitat to species which are intolerant of human disturbance		ii) contain critical habitats which are uncommon or remnants of once extensive habitats such as old growth forest, forest interior habitat, Carolinian forest, prairie-savannas, bogs, fens, marl meadows, and cold water streams	
D	the classification of an area as one which is unique with limited representation in the region, or a small remnant of once larger habitats which have virtually disappeared		iii) provide a large area of natural habitat of at least twenty hectares which affords habitat to species intolerant of human intrusion; or	
E	the classification of an area as one containing an unusual diversity of plant and animal communities due to a variety of geomorphologic features, soils, water, and micro-climatic effects		iv) provide habitat for organisms indigenous to a region recognized as nationally, provincially, or regionally significant; or prairie-savanna, bogs, fens, marl meadows, and cold water streams;	
F	the identification of an area as one which provides a linking system of undisturbed forest, or other natural refuge, for the movement of wildlife over a considerable distance		vi) provide a large area of natural habitat of at least twenty hectares which affords habitat to species intolerant of human intrusion; or	
G	the performance of an area in serving a vital ecological function such as maintaining the hydrological balance over a wide area acting as a natural water storage or recharge area, or		vii) provide habitat for organisms indigenous to a region recognized as nationally, provincially, or regionally significant; or	
H	the recognition of an area as one demonstrating any of the above qualities, but suffering from a minor reduction of its uniqueness or rareness by intrusion of human activities	c)	fulfil one of the criteria in b) above and any two of the following: i) contain an unusual diversity of native life forms due to varied topography, microclimates, soils, and/or drainage regimes ii) perform a vital ecological function such as maintaining the hydrological balance over a widespread area by acting as a natural water storage, discharge, or recharge area ii) provide a linking system of relatively undisturbed forest or other natural habitat for the movement of wildlife over a considerable distance iv) serve as major migratory stop-over, or v) contain landforms deemed unusual or particularly representative at the regional scale	

Identification and Designation of ESPAs

The first sixty-nine ESPAs were designated in 1976, after an extensive three-year program involving: university staff, field naturalists, and staff of the region and other agencies with a conservation mandate. Within a decade, however, it was evident that areas of equal or greater ecological significance had been overlooked; ten new ESPAs were designated in 1991. The current ROPP takes a more systematic approach to the identification of new ESPAs. A stated area of regional interest in watershed studies is the identification of potential new ESPAs. The first ESPA identified in this manner was designated in 1995 and, at present, seven other areas are in the designation process.

The actual process of designation has also become more systematic. The initial designations in 1976 were a pioneering effort, and occurred after long discussions with affected landowners. Astonishingly, no objections were received from the hundreds of landowners involved. The second round of designations in 1988 to 1991 had to contend with numerous objections. At the direction of the Regional Planning and Development Committee, the lands of objecting landowners were removed from the proposed designations. By 1995, however, the province had issued a policy statement requiring the protection of significant natural heritage features in a manner similar to what had been the case in the region for nearly twenty years. This direction from the province implied that such features would be identified in some fashion, and thereby strengthened the region's position with respect to objecting landowners. In late 1996, regional council endorsed a formal procedure for the designation of new ESPAs that includes directions for addressing landowners' objections.[5]

Stewardship of ESPAs

The *Regional Official Policies Plan* is most relevant to the conservation of ESPAs when a development application is made for contiguous lands pursuant to the *Ontario Planning Act*. Other than that, the policies can do no more than encourage good stewardship. As most of the land in ESPAs continues to be privately owned, stewardship depends upon the respective landowners; as a result, it varies considerably from property to property, or on a given property, as the land changes hands. Policies in an official plan cannot address such potentially damaging practices as grazing in woodlands, draining wetlands, or using recreational vehicles in natural areas. At best, environmentally destructive land stewardship can be prevented, or minimized, by conservation authority regulations that

---

5.   PC-96-032 Implementation of Section 4.3.4 of the Waterloo Regional Official Policies Plan: *Procedure for the Identification and Designation of New Environmentally Sensitive Policy Areas*.

prohibit alterations to watercourses or wetlands, or the region's Tree By-law that outlaws the most unsustainable tree harvesting practices.

Public ownership has traditionally been viewed as the most effective means of assuring informed stewardship over the long term. As lands adjoining ESPAs are developed for urban use, municipal parks departments acquired the natural areas as passive open space. This, then, leads to the development of a comprehensive trail network within an ESPA, as well as a consistent approach to management. In some areas, where ESPA lands have not been acquired by a public authority, the region or a lower tier municipality have negotiated conservation easements to protect portions of ESPAs on private property.

Conservation Easements and Land Trusts

Conservation easements are a relatively new legal tool for conserving ecological values on privately owned land in Ontario. At present, five conservation easements are in place—or pending—as a result of development applications affecting ESPAs, and two more have been negotiated as a means of effecting woodland restoration following serious contraventions of the regional Tree By-law.

In the Village of Branchton, a group of concerned residents worked with the Nature Conservancy of Canada and a local land developer to acquire a nine-acre woodland in ESPA 67 through the creation of a locally based private conservation land trust. Discussions occur sporadically about the establishment of a more broadly based land trust, to own land or hold conservation easements on other ecologically significant properties.

Future Directions

Elaboration of the Natural Habitat Network

The original approach to ESPAs in Waterloo Region was to identify and protect "islands of green" which harbored significant species or highly specialized habitats. With the adoption of the third ROPP in 1995, this approach had evolved into a Natural Habitat Network, consisting of a variety of natural features, in which ESPAs were only the most prominent part. Studies are to be undertaken to develop criteria for, and then identify, significant woodlands, valley lands, natural corridors, and wildlife habitat. As this work is completed in the coming years, it is expected that a more coherent landscape-based environmental planning context will be articulated.

Tracking Regional Biodiversity

Some valuable new tools will enable the region and other conservation bodies to improve their biodiversity conservation initiatives. In 1996 the Grand River Conservation Authority published the *Atlas to the Ecoregions of the Grand River Watershed*, which divides the Grand River Watershed into ecoregions. Nine are wholly or partially represented within the Region of Waterloo. The traditional categorization of the region as Great Lakes—St. Lawrence north of Highway 401, and "Carolinian" south of the 401—is now moving to a higher level of resolution as sites are identified within specific ecoregions. In 1998, Ontario issued its Ecological Land Classification system that will allow the identification and mapping of specific types of ecological communities (Ontario, Ministry of Natural Resources 1998). This could permit regional policy to widen its concern from such highly specialized ecosystems as sphagnum bogs and tall grass prairie remnants to habitats such as mud flats or mature plantations that, in the past, were overlooked. Indeed, these may sustain significant biota, and be poorly represented within the region. These habitats may also be viewed in the context of their respective ecoregion rather than the region as a whole. GIS, that was first applied to ESPA mapping in 1994, combined with high-resolution digital aerial imagery in April 2000, are now facilitating development of a geo-referenced habitat database.

The recent adaptation of the Coefficient of Conservatism, by the province's Natural Heritage Information Centre, now makes it possible to quantify the conservatism of ecological communities. In future, it may support policies which explicitly afford a greater degree of protection to more conservative and, hence, less replaceable, habitats.

The region has maintained a listing of significant species for the purpose of ESPA designation since the 1970s. This listing of vascular plants, birds, mammals, and herpetofauna, adopted in 1986, has been undergoing systematic review by panels of experts convened by the region. *Revised Breeding Bird* (Region 1996a) and *Vascular Plant* (Region 1999) lists now assist in the identification of ESPAs. As resources permit, the region plans to review the mammal and herpetofauna lists, and develop new lists for fish and butterflies. In future, it is hoped that expanding knowledge of the region's biodiversity will facilitate the development of listings of bryophytes, fungi, insects, and other invertebrates. The Waterloo Region Ecological Database, which now holds over 25,000 observations of mostly vascular plants and birds, will then be expanded to hold observations of these species, so that up-to-date species lists may be produced for specific natural areas and, ultimately, for their component ecological communities. It is also expected that species data will be interpreted by ecoregion so that "significance" will come to be interpreted subregionally as well as nationally, provincially, and regionally, as is now the case.

Monitoring

To date, the monitoring of ESPAs has been done sporadically, either by retaining summer students or by observing developer compliance with conditions of approval. In 1993, a summer monitoring effort to confirm the validity of some existing designations revealed that one ESPA no longer fulfilled sufficient criteria for designation; it was subsequently de-designated.

As its west side develops rapidly around ESPAs 18, 19, and 80, the City of Waterloo has made a substantial commitment to continually monitoring natural areas: predevelopment, during development, and postdevelopment. This is providing an invaluable stream of empirical data about ecological change in urbanizing areas. Clearly, there is a challenge to institute some form of monitoring throughout the natural habitat network. The development of new curriculum packages may facilitate at least some of this work currently being undertaken by school groups.

Future Challenges

Through nearly a quarter century, Waterloo region's natural heritage policies have protected its most significant natural areas, as adjacent lands were subdivided, mined for aggregate, or developed to accommodate public infrastructure. In the process, many of these areas were brought into public ownership. The challenge of the future is two-fold: reconnecting the fragmented natural landscape; and ensuring wise stewardship of natural heritage resources.

Two centuries of European settlement have left the landscape of Southern Ontario highly fragmented. While fragmentation made way for the farms, urban areas, and transportation infrastructure that sustain a high standard of living, it left remnant natural areas and natural resources vulnerable to ecological degradation. The current natural heritage system approach, embodied in provincial policy and the ROPP policies should, over time, lead to efforts to strengthen, and even recreate natural corridors and linkages, which tie together core natural features. At present, this is being accomplished in newly developing areas, where stream corridors are being preserved from development, pursuant to conservation authority regulatory setbacks. Increasingly, such stream corridors are being revegetated with native plant species, and, in some cases, also developed for community trails by local municipalities. Quite apart from the development process, some rural landowners are voluntarily restoring stream corridors with funding from the Region of Waterloo's innovative *Rural Water Quality Program* (Region 2000); and practical assistance from the Grand River Conservation Authority, and community volunteer organizations, such as the Woolwich Clean Waterways Group.

In 2000, the region's vital groundwater resources were afforded new protection through the wellhead protection policies that restrict certain high risk industrial land uses in the vicinity of municipal well fields. In future, the challenge will be to motivate public and private landowners to devote land and resources to: reconnecting stream corridors, wetlands, and woodlands across the landscape; conserving the habitat of native species of plants and animals; and ceasing activities that imperil groundwater.

At the root of good stewardship is landowner education. This applies no less to the general public who collectively own parkland, than to private landowners seeking to optimize economic returns from natural resources. As society increasingly appreciates the contributions of natural features and functions to human well-being in all its dimensions, greater support will be devoted to protecting and enhancing environmental stewardship. Society will have to: foster sustainable woodland management in the face of historically high timber prices; protect surface and groundwater resources from intensive agricultural operations, and urban expansion; restrict certain kinds of recreational activities within natural areas; and combat the spread of ecologically destructive nonnative plants, insects, and pathogens. There is limited scope for land use policy to achieve these goals, and so other types of public policy, and public-private partnerships need to be developed.

References

Grand River Conservation Authority. 1996. *Atlas to the Ecoregions of the Grand River Watershed.* Cambridge, Ont.: Grand River Conservation Authority.

Ontario. Ministry of Natural Resources. 1998. *Ecological Land Classification System for Southern Ontario: First Approximation and its Application.* SCSS Technical Manual ELC-005, 19 June 1998. London, Ont.: Ministry of Natural Resources.

Regional Municipality of Waterloo. 1985. *Regional Official Policies Plan.* March 1993 Consolidation. Kitchener, Ont.: Regional Municipality of Waterloo.

———. 1993. *Listing of Trees and Shrubs Native to the Regional Municipality of Waterloo and Invasive Alien Herbaceous Species.* Kitchener, Ont.: Regional Municipality of Waterloo.

———. 1995. *Regional Official Policies Plan: Revision of Criteria for Environmentally Sensitive Policy Areas in Rotation to Natural Heritage Policy. Statements.* Report PC-EEAC-95-007, Dec. 1998 consolidation. Kitchener, Ont.: Regional Municipality of Waterloo.

———. 1996a. *Revisions to Waterloo, Region's Significant Species List: Breeding Bird Component.* Report PC-96-02. Kitchener, Ont.: Regional Municipality of Waterloo.

———. 1996b. *Implementation of Section 4.3.4 of the Regional Official Policies Plan: Procedure for the Identification and Designation of New Environmentally Sensitive Policy Areas.* Report PC-96-023. Kitchener, Ont.: Regional Municipality of Waterloo.

———. 1996. *Atlas to the Ecoregions of the Grand River Watershed.* Cambridge, Ont.: Grand River Conservation Authority.

———. 1999. *Revisions to Waterloo Region's Significant Species List: Native Vascular Plant Component.* Report PC-99-028 1. Kitchener, Ont.: Regional Municipality of Waterloo.

———. 2000. *Report PC-00-131/E-00-106. Regional Official Policies Plan Amendments to Protected Municipal Groundwater Supplies— New Designations Permitting Non-residential Uses.* Kitchener, Ont.: Regional Municipality of Waterloo.

———. 2000. *Report PC-131.1. Regional Official Policies Plan Amendment—Water Resources Protection Strategy.* Kitchener, Ont.: Regional Municipality of Waterloo.

Riley, J. L., and P. Mohr. 1994. *The Natural Heritage of Southern Ontario's Settled Landscapes.* Toronto and Peterborough, Ont.: Ministry of Natural Resources.

Making Ecosystem-Based Science into Guidelines for Ecosystem-Based Management: The Greater Fundy Ecosystem Experience [1]

Graham Forbes, Stephen Woodley, and Bill Freedman

Abstract

The Greater Fundy Ecosystem (GFE) project is an attempt to design and implement a plan to manage a landscape on an ecologically sustainable basis. The overall aim is to protect ecological structures, functions, and processes while providing sustainable flows of goods and services for people. A key element of the GFE project is the integration of a protected area into its regional landscape as a single greater ecosystem. At the core of the GFE project is Fundy National Park (FNP), a small (206 km^2) national park located on the upper Bay of Fundy in New Brunswick, Canada. The landscape surrounding the park is managed mainly for industrial forestry, often to the park boundary. The contrast between the park and adjacent landscape led to concerns that the ecological integrity of FNP was being affected and that these stresses should be defined and, if needed, mitigated. During our research and the development of guidelines related to the maintenance of forest biodiversity, it became apparent that successful implementation of an

---

1.   This paper was presented at the Regional Approaches to Parks and Protected Areas Workshop in Tijuana, B.C., and published in *Environments* 27, no. 3.

ecologically sustainable landscape relies on several key things. These include: a landscape-level appreciation of ecological process; stand-scale application of best-management practices; a political climate that supports change in forest management practices; and a vehicle for stakeholders to work for change.

The Fundy Model Forest, one of ten such sites in Canada, was the vehicle that allowed partners to reach a comfortable balance of objectives with values for the environment and economy. Fundy National Park represented a benchmark for conducting comparative research of the impact of industrial forestry and "natural" forest. In our work we found that the large protected area was instrumental in distributing the perceived costs of biodiversity over an ecologically defined forestry operation. Industrial forest managers were more willing to adopt objective-based guidelines than restrictive practice-based rules. The process of making science into guidelines requires recognition of the limitations of science and the stage when that science must be replaced by professional judgment.

Introduction

The Greater Fundy Ecosystem (GFE) project was established in 1991 (fig. 7.1). From the beginning, the project was conceived as a research and monitoring effort to provide the scientific support necessary to manage an ecologically sustainable landscape. This early research focus was essential to bring all parties together under a common, nonthreatening agenda. The project was conceived as multidisciplinary, with members from industry, government, and academia. The aim of the GFE project has been to be inclusive, and not to be seen as aligned with the aspirations of a particular group or agency.

The Greater Fundy Ecosystem (GFE) project grew out of concerns, mainly from park managers and academics, that managing the park in isolation from surrounding lands was not adequately protecting the ecological values of the park. The GFE intensive study area (1,049 km^2) contains the federally owned park (19.6%), "Crown" or provincially owned land (43.6%), privately owned land managed by a forestry company (16.1%), and individual land holdings (20.7%). The landscape outside FNP is dominated by the results of intensive forestry practices on mixed hardwood or softwood forest, managed mainly with clear-cut forestry and plantations. In the last few years, however, there has been

Figure 7.1 Greater Fundy Region

intensive management of hardwood forests. Road density in a ten kilometer radius surrounding FNP is 1.27 kilometers road/square kilometer, and logging roads define two of FNP's boundaries.

A study of the ecological integrity of the park (Woodley, 1993) documented a history of losses of native species, invasions by exotic species, habitat fragmentation and conversion, and significant doubts that species associated with old-growth coniferous forests, such as American Marten (*Martes americana*), would survive in the area. The high road density, concurrent forest fragmentation, and decline in age class distribution created a younger forest, and a landscape possibly more restrictive to movement of habitat-sensitive species. The goals for the GFE project were established as follows.

1. To identify strategies to maintain viable populations of native species within the Greater Fundy Ecosystem by focusing on species whose population levels are perceived to be at risk
2. To quantify species-habitat relationships for select species in the Greater Fundy Ecosystem so that the information can be used in land management decisions
3. To examine environmental stresses in the GFE and understand how they affect valued resources
4. To identify operational management options that may ensure the ongoing sustainability of the Greater Fundy Ecosystem

Research Agenda and Guidelines

The GFE Research Group (GFERG) identified a number of research projects that would be needed to apply ecosystem-based management. Research projects were designed around a stress-response framework for several levels in the ecological hierarchy (Rapport, Heiger, and Thorpe 1981). These levels included gene, organism, population, community, and landscape. The GFE research agenda is based upon (1) a fundamental need to first characterize the ecosystem, (2) a stress-response framework that accounts for specific stressors—such as stand conversion or forestry roads—so that the impacts can be avoided or mitigated, and (3) the need to design a research program that accounts for the inherent scales or hierarchical nature of ecosystems. Table 7.1 lists many of the projects used to develop biodiversity guidelines by the GFERG (1998).

We believe that it is impossible to plan for the conservation of biodiversity on a species-by-species basis. There are simply too many species and we do not know nearly enough about each one. Thus, to conserve native biodiversity, the GFERG took a combined top-down (coarse-filter) and bottom-up (fine-filter) approach (table 7.2). The coarse-filter approach allows for planning of larger scale arrangements of communities, including their composition, size, adjacency, and age class distribution (Haufler, Mehl, and Roloff 1996). The hypothesis is that in creating a viable landscape, the needs of the vast majority of native species may be accommodated, and the need for single-species management is lessened. However, to counter that species are missed by the coarse-filter approach, we also examined the specific requirements of species that are likely to become vulnerable, given the significant changes that result from modern forest management. The basic guidelines are outlined in table 7.2 and the full guidelines are available online at: http://www.unb.ca/web/forestry/centers/cwru/opening.htm.

Table 7.1 Projects Used by the GFERG to Develop Biodiversity Guidelines[a]

Historical Context	Forest Harvest within Buffer Strips
• Disturbance regimes • Fire scar project (Kendrick) • Colonial era Forest Reconstruction (Lutz and Loo)	• Hydrochemistry (Pomeroy) • Small mammals (Parker) • Breeding birds (Hache) • Cavity-nesters (Doucette) • Fish (Chiasson)
Landscape Pattern of Forest Harvest • Influence of fragmentation on interior sensitive species—Ovenbird (*Seiurus aurocapillus*) Project (Sabine, UNB) • Influence of connectivity on flow of forest-associated species—Northern Flying Squirrel (*Glaucomys sabrinus*) Project (Bourgeois)	Specific Ecological Requirements to Support Viable Populations Associated with Mature or Old-Growth Forests • Pileated Woodpecker (*Dryocopus pileatus*) Project (Flemming) • American Marten (*Martes americana*) Project (Bourgeois)
Effect of Different Disturbance Regimes on Nutrient Cycling • Carbon storage and dynamics in natural versus silvicultural forests—Coarse Woody Debris Project (Flemming) • Stream ecology (O'Brien) • Sediment flow (Coles and Clay)	Selected Species at Risk • Road access impact on game species Black Bear (*Ursus americana*) Project (Forbes) • Salamanders and clear cuts (Waldick) • Cavity-nesting birds and plantations (Woodley and Freedman) • Bird diversity and plantations (Johnson) • Plant diversity and plantations (Roberts and Veinotte)

[a]Publications from these projects and other research activities are listed online at http://www.unb.ca/web/forestry/centers/gfe.htm

Table 7.2 Components of a Coarse and Fine-Filter Strategy for Maintaining Forest Biodiversity

Coarse filter

Ecological Land Classification
+
Natural Disturbance Regime
+
12% In Mature Patches
+
Connectivity
+
Silviculture By Disturbance
+
Protected Areas
+
Road Density Limit

Fine filter

Special Status Species
(Rare, keystone, economic)
+
Snag And Cavity Tree Retention
+
Coarse Woody Debris
=
GFE Biodiversity Strategy

Objectives vs. Rules

Forest managers prefer to incorporate quantified objectives for modeling future forests and their values (Erdle 1998). A specific objective can be tracked through long-range planning forecasts. By contrast, a rule that is applied to every stand limits the different interventions available to foresters and, more importantly, implies that all land should be managed for the same values (Erdle and Sullivan 1998). In the GFE exercise, the emphasis and objective was on creating a landscape that would support native processes and species. The means of creating that landscape were generally undefined. The coarse-scale approach fits well with the current natural disturbance paradigm in forestry. Disturbances such as fire and insect outbreaks create landscapes that, conceivably, can be mimicked by forestry operations (Patch 1997). Though the avoidance of restrictive rules fostered support from landowners, we note potential risk to biodiversity since different practices can produce the same result, but some practices are more detrimental to nontimber values.

Importance of a Vehicle

The GFE project was one of twenty partners that applied for a "Model Forest" grant from the government of Canada. The *Model Forest* program is a large national and international effort by Canada to promote research and demonstrate sustainable forestry. The other partners include forest companies, private woodlot owners, federal and provincial government agencies, universities, and nongovernment agencies such as environmental groups and clubs. The area of the Fundy Model Forest (FMF) extends north and west of Fundy National Park to encompass approximately 0.5 million hectares (fig. 7.1).

Implementation of change, particularly when involving holistic concepts typical of ecosystem management, requires that those in control of the resource are willing to listen and act. Implementation of the GFE guidelines was strongly dependent upon the willingness of the forestry company, the provincial government, and the small, private woodlot owners in the FMF to indicate what components of the guidelines would be applied on their land. To a large extent, this willingness was supported by an agenda of the private forest company and the woodlot association to become externally certified as a sustainable forest. The private woodlots were seeking certification under the Canadian Standards Association Program for Sustainable Forest Management while the industrial partner was seeking certification under the Forest Stewardship Council Program. Both programs recognize many of the principles outlined in the GFE guidelines, and ecosystem management in general.

The FMF partnership adopted a modified set of the GFE Guidelines for a case study in sustainable forest management. A smaller area, approximately 20 percent of the FMF, was planned with multiple objectives for timber, biodiversity, and recreation, and to give an indication of the impact of the guidelines and their ease of implementation. Landowners then chose which guidelines they would implement on their own holdings.

Overall, landowners accepted many of the concepts. However, in numerous cases the details were not accepted. For example, one GFE objective is for 12 percent of stand-replaced forest communities to be in mature-overmature condition of 300-hectare patches. The magnitude component, that is 12 percent of the forest in the ecoregion will be maintained in the mature-overmature class, was accepted. But that this 12 percent should be in minimum patch sizes of 300 hectares was not accepted, mainly because it restricts numerous modeling options. In another example, the GFE objective to alter existing proportions of community types to reflect the historical precolonial forest, instead led to the willingness of landowners to change silvicultural practices and foster, for example, an increase in cedar (*Thuja occidentalis*) forest. But they would not adopt an explicit quantity, that is 8 percent of the total forest.

Role of Protected Areas

Parks and other protected areas must be managed at the extreme preservation end of the conservation gradient, and should not be compromised by other land uses. Moreover, all land uses external to protected areas must be compatible or the protection role will not be possible. At the heart of the GFE project is a core-protected area; Fundy National Park. The GFE project aims to ensure that management actions on the surrounding landscape are compatible with the protection of the ecological values of the park.

The existence of Fundy National Park was instrumental to the development of ecosystem-based management in numerous ways. First, the park provided a benchmark for comparisons of relatively natural processes and conditions with those on adjacent intensively managed forestland. Fundy's status as a park attracts scientists who wish to conduct long-term

Photograph 7.1 Three of four boundaries of Fundy National Park are demarcated by logging roads, creating a striking contrast in the contiguous forest landscape and resource management practices. Photo credit: Graham Forbes

research, knowing the site will remain in a natural condition. These researchers then create the mass of information and energy required to contemplate management of ecosystems.

The presence of the park also assisted in implementation of the guidelines. The GFE emphasized the coarse scale as a strategy for maintaining biodiversity; objectives can be applied over large blocks of land, as compared to strict rules applied to all land. An existing park can offset the impact of new biodiversity objectives on timber supply if it already contains, for example, 62 percent of the objective for mature cedar forest in that ecodistrict. In regions such as New Brunswick, where the wood supply is maximized and any removal of timber is seen as a loss in jobs, implementation of biodiversity guidelines is more likely to succeed if foresters can consider existing protected areas as part of the sustainable forest. This recognition could lead to a new cooperative era between extractive industries and protected area managers. Planning could be based more on ecological boundaries and less on administrative ones.

Professional Judgment and Hard Science

A concern many ecologists have is that we do not know enough to manage ecosystems well (Galindo-Leal and Bunnell 1995). Science will always lag behind resource management practices. For example, much of

Photograph 7.2 Fundy National Park to the left of the road, private forest land on the right. Photo credit: Graham Forbes

the GFE research compared plantations to natural forests, in many cases indicating substantial differences in plant and animal diversity, productivity, and structure (Freedman et al. 1996). Because time negated the luxury of monitoring a single plantation for thirty years, we resorted to using a chronosequence design to compare ten-, twenty- and thirty-year old plantations. But, since ecosystems are complex, research is difficult. Do uncertainties regarding site-to-site uniqueness or other factors negate comparison of sites for species diversity, and so warrant rejection or just caution? We found certain results were readily accepted; however, in more problematic issues, managers raised uncertainties in design, and the results were quickly dismissed.

If the science is always reacting to the practice, then can adaptive management be the answer? From our experience we believe that if ecosystem-based management is to meet its goal of maintaining ecological integrity, and if we recognize that our ignorance will continue for the foreseeable future, then the only prudent strategy is one of adaptation and precautionary principles. The onus should be on showing that activities that are evidently different from natural processes are benign before they are implemented. When data are lacking, professional judgment, tempered by consensus, should be given standing in lieu of fact. Biodiversity guidelines and ecosystem-based management will never succeed if society waits for all of the science.

References

Erdle, T., and M. Sullivan. 1998. "Progress Towards Sustainable Forest Management: Insight from the New Brunswick Experience." *Forestry Chronicle* 74: 378-384.
_____. 1998. "Forest Management Design for Contemporary Forestry." *Forestry Chronicle* 74: 83-90.
Freedman, B., V. Zelazny, D. Beaudette, T. Fleming, S. Flemming, G. Forbes, S. Gerrow, G. Johnson, and S. Woodley. 1996. "Biodiversity Implications of Changes in the Quantity of Dead Organic Matter in Managed Forests." *Environmental Reviews* 4: 238-265.
Galindo-Leal, C., and F. Bunnell. 1995. "Ecosystem Management: Implications and Opportunities of a New Paradigm." *Forestry Chronicle* 71: 601-606.
Greater Fundy Ecosystem Research Group. 1998. *State of the Greater Fundy Ecosystem,* ed. S. Woodley, G. Forbes, and A. Skibicki. Accessed online: http://www.unb.ca/web/forestry/centers/cwru/state.htm.
Haufler, J., C. Mehl, and G. Roloff. 1996. "Using a Coarse-filter Approach with Species Assessment for Ecosystem Management." *Wildlife Society Bulletin* 24: 200-208.
Patch, J. 1997. "Solving the Biodiversity Conundrum Using the Natural Disturbance Paradigm," pp. 75-80. In *Proceedings Ecological Landscape Management Workshop.* Montreal, Que.: Canadian Woodlands Forum.
Rapport, D. J., H. A. Regier, and C. Thorpe. 1981. "Diagnosis, Prognosis, and Treatment of Ecosystems Under Stress," pp. 269-280. In *Stress Effects on Natural Ecosystems,* ed. G. Barrett and R. Rosenberg. Chichester, England and Toronto: Wiley Press.
Woodley, S. 1993. *Assessing and Monitoring Ecological Integrity in Parks and Protected Areas.* Unpublished Ph.D. Thesis. Faculty of Environmental Studies, University of Waterloo, Waterloo, Ont., Canada.
Woodley, S., and G. Forbes. 1997. *Forest Management Guidelines to Protect Native Biodiversity in the Fundy Model Forest.* University of New Brunswick, Fredericton, N.B.: New Brunswick Cooperative Fish and Wildlife Research Unit. Accessed online: http://ww.unb.ca/web/forestry/centers/cwru/open.htm.

Assessing Ecosystem Conservation Plans for Canadian National Parks [1]

J. G. Nelson, Patrick Lawrence, and Heather Black

Abstract

Since the conservation of ecological integrity was introduced as the prime mandate of Canadian national parks in 1988, ecosystem conservation plans (ECPs) have been developing as a major method of controlling land use pressures in and around national parks. Such plans are now required for all Canadian national parks. Many have been prepared, or are in preparation, across the country, although no information on the overall status of national park ecosystem conservation planning is known to be available at this time. This preliminary analysis and assessment is based, largely, on experience with ecosystem conservation planning at Georgian Bay Islands, Bruce Peninsula and St. Lawrence Islands National Parks in Ontario, and Fundy National Park in New Brunswick, Canada. The study should be of value to all those concerned with ecosystem-based planning, in Canada and other countries. The results show that ecosystem conservation planning involves many contextual, historical, social, economic, and planning factors, other than ecosystem science. Of special importance are: the unique natural and human circumstances that apply to each national park and its region; the need for a communication strategy to inform and bring together the many agencies, groups, and individuals normally

---

1.   This paper was published previously in the *Natural Areas Journal* 20(3). A shortened version was presented at the Regional Approaches to Parks and Protected Areas Workshop in Tijuana, B.C., 1999.

involved both inside and outside the parks; and a long-term interactive and adaptive planning approach. Details on these important considerations in ecosystem conservation planning are outlined in the paper, which is prepared in such a manner that it offers some general guidelines based on our experience to date.

Introduction

Land and resource use pressures on Canadian national parks have increased to the point where they now pose major threats to the natural values that protected areas are intended to conserve (Parks Canada 1998). Canadian national parks are subject to intensifying recreational, tourism, and related pressures within, and forestry, mining, and other land use pressures outside their boundaries (Canada 1998). Parks Canada has used several major methods to deal with these pressures. The main one is the park management plan and zoning system. A second major method is environmental impact assessment (EIA). Both these methods focus on development effects within the park. The third major method—the ecosystem conservation plan, or ECP—is a more recent addition to the planning kit. It is concerned with development pressures both within and outside national parks (Zorn, Stephenson, and Grigoriew 1997).

Ecological or ecosystem approaches to planning and management of national parks have been underway since at least the first Canadian National Park Conference in 1968 (Nelson and Scace 1969). Interest in such approaches to planning began to rise markedly with the pioneering work on the Yellowstone Greater Parks Ecosystem, and with advances in landscape ecology, conservation biology, and other branches of ecosystem science in the 1980s (Woodley, Kay, and Francis 1993, Grumbine 1994, Halvorson and Davis 1996, Lertzman, Spies, and Swanson 1997). Planning for national parks in a broader ecosystems framework was reinforced by the rise of deep ecology and bioregional thinking among ecologists, professionals, and concerned citizens during this time (Lertzman, Spies, and Swanson 1997).

Interest in the application of ecosystem approaches to Canadian national parks accelerated after the 1988 amendments to the *National Parks Act*, when ecological integrity was introduced as the basic guiding concept and prime mandate for Canadian national parks (Canada 1992, Zorn, Stephenson, and Grigoriew 1997). Ecosystem conservation plans were to link land and resource uses to ecological processes, conditions, and changes—both inside and outside of national parks—in recognition of the fact that these parks occupy only part of the ecosystem, or ecosystems, in which they are located (Canada 1992, Zorn, Stephenson, and Grigoriew 1997).

Table 8.1 Brief Description of the Canadian National Parks in this Study

	Bruce Peninsula National Park	Georgian Bay Islands National Park	St. Lawrence Islands National Park[a]	Fundy National Park
Established	1987	1929	1914	1948
Location	Terrestrial park 154 km² in size; on western shoreline of Georgian Bay, Ontario	Collection of 59 islands totaling 26 km²; on the southeastern shoreline of Georgian Bay, Ontario	Collection of 21 islands totaling 9 km²; in the St. Lawrence River, eastern Ontario	Terrestrial park 206 km² in size; on the Bay of Fundy, New Brunswick
Natural Character	Sedimentary bedrock with steep cliffs, shorelines, wetlands, and forests	Islands of Canadian shield, and adjoining Paleozoic sediments, which provide habitat for many rare and threatened species	Collection of islands consisting of Precambrian bedrock, and with significant fish and wildlife habitat	Forest uplands and coastal regions
Major Land and Resource Use in the Park	Camping, hiking, cliff climbing	Camping, hiking, boating	Camping, boating, hiking	Camping, hiking, golf course
Major Land and Resource Uses outside the Park	Tourism, cottages, logging	Tourism, boating, cottages	Tourism, boating, cottages	Logging, tourism
Status of ECP	In progress (b)	Completed 1997	Completed 1995	Completed 1997

[a]Information from: *St. Lawrence Islands National Park 1995, Nelson and Skibicki 1997, Parks Canada 1997, Nelson 1998.*

[b] A preparatory report for the ECP for Bruce Peninsula National Park and adjacent Fathom Five National Marine Park (FFMNP) was completed in 1998 (Nelson, 1998). An ECP was completed by National Park staff in 2002.

In this paper we describe a preliminary analysis and assessment of ecosystem conservation planning for Canadian National Parks, focusing on Georgian Bay, St. Lawrence Islands, and Bruce Peninsula National Parks in Ontario, and Fundy National Park in New Brunswick, Canada (fig. 8.1 and table 8.1). We have been directly involved in ecosystem conservation planning for Georgian Bay and Bruce Peninsula National Parks (Nelson and Skibicki 1997, Nelson 1998). We were also involved in the early stages of ecosystem conservation for the St. Lawrence Islands and have since followed this work (Canada 1995). We have also closely tracked the planning for Fundy National Park (Canada 1997, Stephenson and Zorn 1998). The analysis and assessment in this paper is based upon this detailed experience, and upon the review of many relevant docu-

Figure 8.1 Canadian national parks discussed in this study

ments, papers, and reports, as well as numerous discussions with park staff and other concerned parties. The senior author is also a member of the Park Advisory Committee for Bruce Peninsula National Park and neighboring Fathom Five National Marine Park (Photographs 8.1, 8.2). The senior author and students have regularly attended the annual meeting of the Georgian Bay Association; a group of cottage associations that convenes a yearly forum, and review of land use, recreational, and other activities in the Georgian Bay National Park area.

All of the foregoing experience is drawn upon to some degree in this analysis, which is intended to be broadly strategic in nature. It suggests a method that could assist in ecosystem conservation planning in national parks in Canada, or elsewhere. This work is organized around a set of criteria that are derived from our study and experience. These include: context; goals, vision or objectives; sources of information; plan preparation procedures and methods; implementation; and other considerations (table 8.2).

Photograph 8.1. Fathom Five National Marine Park, Georgian Bay shoreline and islands. Photo credit: Patrick Lawrence

Table 8.2. Criteria for Analyzing and Assessing Ecosystem Conservation Plans (ECPs)

Context

The geographical setting of the park; the natural, socioeconomic, land use history, and current state of the park and surrounding area; sense of place and apparent regional boundaries; the major agencies, actors, and interest groups, their values, preferences, and concerns; means of interaction, communication, and decision making; and similar information relevant to an ECP.

Goals, Visions, Objectives

The ways in which the purposes and directions of ECPs are set forth, and any principal assumptions or special considerations relating thereto, recognizing that the ECPs reflect the interests and values not only of national parks staff, but of other agencies, groups, and people involved in the park and region.

Sources of Information

Information used in preparing the ECPs, including existing reports or documents of scientific, scholarly, local, or related nature; consultations among staff and officials of parks, and other agencies and professional groups; meetings and workshops with local people, visitors, and other concerned parties; field work and related observations; and new research.

Plan Preparation Procedures and Methods

Procedures used in securing information and preparing the plan. Focal points, key concepts, and organizational and planning approaches. Identifying and addressing key issues such as boundaries for the plan area, and who should be involved. Means and scope of consultations. Applicable scientific and professional staff, budget, and other available resources. Use of consultants, time for preparation of the plan.

Implementation

Ways of carrying out the plan and any follow-up to learn what has happened as a result of the planning. Monitoring the results and adapting accordingly.

Other Considerations

Other considerations affecting the plan; for example, changes in key personnel, changes in budget and staff, changes in economic, social, or political circumstances.

The environmental, socioeconomic, historical, institutional, political, and other aspects of a study such as this—and of ecosystem planning itself—are enormous. The foregoing criteria are intended to provide a broad organizational framework for thinking about, analyzing, and assessing information and findings. These criteria, and the associated analytical and assessment framework, are considered to be a working approach which could be improved in the future. The criteria focus on the planning process, and its implications, rather than on the effects of ecosystem conservation planning on land use and the ecological integrity of the parks. These effects will be more apparent with time, given appropriate monitoring, assessment, and review. Ecosystem conservation planning in terms of the Canadian experience will now be reviewed and assessed on the basis of these criteria.

Context

In our experience, ecosystem conservation plans for Canadian national parks do not give many details on the broad context in which the plans have been prepared. Yet the historical, socioeconomic, and political context of such planning can be very important; for example, in terms of the response of the local community to the preparation of the plan. Georgian Bay Islands is an older national park, generally well accepted in the region in which it has been located since the 1920s. Bruce Peninsula National Park is a more recent one, established and developed since the mid-1980s, in an atmosphere of tension and controversy—notably among local people, Parks Canada, and supporting conservation groups. The reaction of local people to the preparation of an ecosystem conservation plan for lands and waters outside the park boundaries differed in these two cases. The reaction of park officials also differed; the Georgian Bay National Park personnel tended to see the ecosystem conservation plan as an opportunity to build upon outreach and cooperative activities already underway. The Bruce Peninsula National Park staff was more uncertain about outside consultation and involvement in the plan in light of the local challenges.

Photograph 8.2. Steep cliffs of Niagara Escarpment at Overhanging Point, on Georgian Bay shore, Bruce Peninsula National Park. Photo credit: Larry Lamb

The foregoing examples illustrate the importance of preliminary scoping, communication, and consultation, prior to beginning the actual planning process. There is in these, and undoubtedly in other, cases a need to understand the context, and help park staff, local people, and other concerned groups prepare to work with one another on such plans (Nelson 1998). Park staff and any consultants retained to do a plan will

Photograph 8.3. The Grotto, a wave-washed cave in limestone, Bruce Peninsula
National Park. Photo credit: Larry Lamb

benefit from having designated time available to gain an understanding of
the context in which the plan will be prepared, and any special challenges or needs that might arise under the circumstances. Park staff,
members of the local community, and other concerned groups also will
benefit from the opportunity to understand one another and the ecosystem planning exercise that they are about to embark upon.

Goals, Visions, Objectives

Parks Canada's planning initiatives often involve ideas such as ecological
integrity and biodiversity; concepts whose meaning may be, more or less,
understood by those accustomed to using them, but not by people who
normally work in other fields. Goals, visions, objectives, values,
preferences, and language often differ among local people, business
people, tourists, government officials, politicians, and others involved; as
well as among park staff, depending on their responsibilities and
background in the agency. Review of ecosystem conservation planning
for all four of the Canadian national parks focused upon in this study,
shows that the audience, or market, for the plans was not generally well
thought out and specified in terms of the foregoing challenges, and the
short- to long-term means of addressing them. Relatively little attention
has been paid as to how to inform and involve concerned groups and
individuals on the ongoing and interactive basis that is needed for the

Photograph 8.4. Mixed deciduous and coniferous forest and pocket beach, Bruce Peninsula National Park. Photo credit: Larry Lamb

intra- and intergroup learning necessary for ecosystem conservation planning.

Parks Canada has tended to focus ecosystem conservation planning on the identification of problems, issues, and concerns (PICs). In this respect, the conservation plans are usually oriented to the needs of Parks Canada staff and programs–notably staff in the natural resources field. Examples are the ecosystem conservation plans for St. Lawrence Islands and Fundy National Parks. The Fundy plan does, however, include an innovative ecological integrity statement, which lays out a vision and broad goals for the park, as well as some specific objectives to be addressed in the plan. The main product of the ecosystem conservation plans, with which we have some familiarity, has usually been to identify research needs for ecosystem conservation planning and to establish a budget, timetable, and work plan for staff to meet these needs over three- to five-years. Such research needs generally do not include much on the socioeconomic or human dimensions of ecosystem conservation planning, especially in terms of the needs and activities of local people and their effects on the parks. For decades, scientists and planners have stressed the need for national parks to consider and contribute to the needs and well being of the local community, in return for their support and cooperation in conserving nature in the parks (Nelson 1987).

Sources of Information

Ecosystem conservation plans are generally prepared on the basis of information available in the offices of national park and related agencies, and from knowledgeable groups and individuals in universities or similar organizations. Information can be scattered among the various departments, sections, and individuals in a national park office, as well as among agencies and sources located outside a park. It is often difficult to get a good grasp of the available information and its relevance to ecosystem planning in the time available to prepare the plan. Many national parks are in the process of developing inventories of completed research and of research needs. They also are using geographical information systems (GIS) to collect and organize data. Such information systems generally contain much more ecological than socioeconomic information and mapping.

Information can also be out of date, uneven in coverage, and focused on the national park, with relatively little comparable information available on the surrounding lands and waters. Examples of this situation are Bruce Peninsula and St. Lawrence Islands National Parks, although ongoing research is gradually closing the information gaps. It would be helpful to park staff—and to consultants preparing ecosystem conservation plans—to have the time and opportunity to survey and assess the available research and information as part of the scoping phase at the beginning of national park conservation planning.

Plan Preparation Procedures and Methods

Personnel

Parks Canada staff as well as consultants—including private companies and universities—have prepared ecosystem conservation plans. The national park staff is generally warden service members who may have some university or college training, considerable field knowledge of the national park, and a high commitment to nature conservation, as well as the safety and well-being of park visitors. Consultants can bring a broad range of theoretical, technical, and planning experience to the task, yet may lack detailed field knowledge, and the time and resources to do the job in the manner wished for by the national park staff. Planning can also be complicated by differences in views among park staff; for example, at the park, the region, district, and national levels. The traditional knowledge of First Nations or of local people is generally not called upon or used to any significant degree. In our experience, involvement of both national park staff and consultants in ongoing, collaborative, and mutually reinforcing work on ecosystem conservation planning is uncommon. Fundy National Park is somewhat of an exception for reasons that are not well understood at this time (Canada 1997).

Budget, Time, and Resources

The resources used in preparing ecosystem conservation plans are often not specified, nor are details given on the way plans were prepared. Examples are St. Lawrence Islands National Park and Fundy National Park. Budgets seem to vary considerably, as do time horizons and resources committed to planning. Bruce Peninsula National Park had a budget for consultants of approximately fifty-two thousand dollars Canadian for about eighteen months. This also included work on an ecosystem conservation plan for adjacent Fathom Five National Marine Park. About fifty-five thousand dollars Canadian was available to consultants to prepare the ecosystem conservation plan for Georgian Bay Islands National Park in approximately a two-year period. In the foregoing cases, a national park liaison officer was available on a part-time basis and national park staff gave some assistance. In contrast, Fundy National Park had a budget of perhaps two hundred thousand to three hundred thousand dollars Canadian for three- to five-years of work leading to an ecosystem conservation plan as well as a recent state of the environment report for the national park. Differences in budget, timing, and resources can seriously affect the scope and usefulness of the ecosystem conservation plans; moreover, the quality of the plans can also vary considerably as a result.

Boundaries and Planning Area

One early challenge in preparing ecosystem conservation plans is to decide on the greater park ecosystem, or the extent of the surrounding lands and waters that will be covered in the planning. In theory, this region would be defined in natural or ecosystem terms. In practice, this is difficult to do for several reasons. One is that air masses, rivers and waters, wildlife, and other elements that move over vast distances, well beyond park boundaries, influence most parks. An outstanding example in the four Canadian national parks on which we focus in this paper is songbirds; their populations in the national parks often include numerous transcontinental migrants from Central and South America. Another is the difficulty in defining the region or study area in natural or ecosystem terms, where past logging or other human activities have changed the species, communities, and landscapes in and especially around the parks in fundamental ways. It is, therefore, often challenging to map precisely a natural region, or regions, with strong links to the parks.

Approaches to the park region—or greater park ecosystem—therefore vary considerably. In the case of St. Lawrence Islands National Park, relevant areas or regions around the park have been identified at several scales, including the "Algonquin to Adirondack" bioregion traversing Ontario and New York State (Stephenson and Zorn 1998). In the case of Georgian Bay Island National Park, the boundary was drawn by agreement among park officials, local people, and consultants. The boundary follows natural features for part of its length; otherwise it follows roads and other cultural features. The Fundy National Park ecosystem conservation plan does not provide a single scientific boundary. Here the greater park ecosystem is considered to be "an area of interest" defined according to the species, communities, or challenges involved at the time (Canada 1997). Letting the management and planning challenges or concerns define the greater park ecosystem or region seems to be a practicable approach, given the conceptual and information difficulties that often arise in determining a boundary on a scientific or ecological basis.

Planning Theory and Method

With respect to planning theory, Parks Canada favors a corporate, rational, or synoptic approach (Hudson 1979). In this context the focus is on the goals, values, and objectives of Parks Canada and on the regulation and control of land and resource uses within, and so far as possible outside, the national parks. In the plans for the four parks of principal interest here, little reference is made to other planning methods, including interactive and adaptive or transactive planning, public and private stewardship, landowner contacts, economic incentives, easements and other agreements (Nelson 1991). An exception is the preparatory report for the ecosystem conservation plan for Bruce Peninsula National Park (Nelson 1998). In this report such methods were suggested not only for the area around the park, but also for the close to

40 percent of the land area within park boundaries that is still in private ownership and being slowly acquired on a willing seller and willing buyer basis.

Communication and Cooperation

A communication strategy can help broaden and deepen the work on ecosystem conservation planning as shown in the cases of Georgian Bay Islands and Bruce Peninsula National Parks. The aim of such a strategy is to identify who should be involved, how, and what values, information, and assistance they can bring to the table in preparing ecosystem conservation plans. Communication strategies can bring knowledge from sources outside of an national park and can provide information on the values, goals, and objectives of a range of interested groups and individuals living in the vicinity of, as well as some distance away from, the park (Nelson and Skibicki 1997).

Communication strategies can provide opportunities for concerned people to work together with Parks Canada on ecosystem conservation planning from the very early or scoping stage. Links can be made with related provincial, municipal, or private planning and management efforts, to the potential benefit of all concerned. Communication strategies can also assist in explaining the numerous uses, roles, and functions of national parks to citizens who, often, are unaware of the wide range of wildlife, water, and soil conservation, research, environmental monitoring, education, recreational, tourism, and other services that national parks can offer to communities and societies. Communication strategies offer a two-way exchange in which park staff can come to a better understanding of local communities and their needs, as well as the ways they might contribute to, and benefit from, national parks.

In the four national parks of principal interest here, the best example of a strong communications approach is Georgian Bay Islands National Park. Although a communication strategy was completed and used as part of the ecosystem conservation plan, work on improving communications had already begun through the efforts of park staff before the ecosystem planning process actually got underway. Consultants were retained and workshops held to delimit the area, or greater park ecosystem, that was to provide the framework for dealing with growing external resource and land use pressures on this park. This initial work was beneficial to the completion of the ecosystem conservation plan, which contains strong recommendations to strengthen communications through mechanisms such as a consultation committee and an annual forum (Nelson and Skibicki 1997). Recently, independent cottage organizations—belonging to the Georgian Bay Association—have become involved in improving communication and cooperation for nature conservation by working with Parks Canada and other concerned groups on establishing a UNESCO World Biosphere Reserve for much of the eastern islands and shores of Georgian Bay.

Implementation

Parks Canada is involved in several major types of park plans in addition to the ecosystem conservation plan. The different types of plans seem to have grown along with attempts to introduce ecosystem science into management, and with attempts to put Canadian national parks on a more commercial and economically self-sustaining basis. The national park management plan has been the principal guiding document since well before the advances in ecosystem science and the economic cutbacks experienced in Canada since the 1980s. Other major plans for each national park include a monitoring plan and a visitor services plan. Specific plans may also be prepared for areas or topics of particular concern, such as shorelines or trail systems. All these documents are linked in one way or another to the new requirement for a national park business plan, which seems to be the plan of greatest operational significance in Canadian national parks today. Plans and projects that are incorporated into the business plan are the ones that can expect to receive funding and other support. Approval for the national park business plans occurs at higher administrative levels and is, to some degree, a competitive process for a limited amount of funding. Interest in costs and commercial benefits is part of the judgment process, along with ecological integrity, visitor safety, and other considerations. Given these circumstances, the implementation of ecosystem planning seems to be an uncertain and uneven process.

An ecological integrity panel—consisting of knowledgeable people from government, university, recreational, tourism, conservation, First Nations, and other groups—has reviewed progress and problems with planning and managing for ecological integrity in Canadian National Parks. It submitted a report to the responsible minister in December

1999. The report addresses some of the circumstances and uncertainties relating to ecosystem planning and its implementation.[2]

Little time has passed since completion of the first ecosystem conservation plans for national parks in Canada; thus, it is difficult to assess their full effects. Some positive results have occurred in Fundy and Georgian Bay Island National Parks. Cooperative planning among government agencies and other concerned groups is underway, and Parks Canada and other agencies and groups are sharing in the development of geographical information systems (GIS). In the Georgian Bay National Park area, Parks Canada staff is assisting local governments with the development of a scientific framework for planning a municipal system of environmentally significant areas. These areas can be linked to one another and the national park via a nodes and corridors approach. Progress in the case of the Bruce Peninsula National Park ecosystem conservation plan is more uncertain. At least two attempts have been made to develop a plan, but these have not come to fruition. The last effort resulted in a report which is being worked on by Parks Canada staff and which may be linked to the monitoring plan already in place for this park (Nelson 1998). Developments in regard to the St. Lawrence Islands National Park ecosystem conservation plan are not well known to us at this time.

An important part of the planning and implementation of ecosystem conservation plans is provision for monitoring and reporting. These activities are part of the ecosystem conservation plans for all four national parks of particular interest here, especially in regard to the natural, as opposed to human, dimensions of the ecosystem management challenge. More attention needs to be paid to the human dimensions, as they are an integral part of ecosystem planning. Monitoring and assessment of ecosystem conservation plans should include indicators of success in contributing to the goals, visions, and objectives of other government agencies and private groups involved in cooperative planning for national parks, and for sustainable development in the surrounding lands and waters (Nelson 1987). Equity should be a significant consideration as ecosystem conservation plans can have substantial effects on the interests of groups other than Parks Canada—especially in terms of use of the surrounding lands and waters.

---

2.   The Ecological Integrity Panel report was released in spring 2000 and is available online at www.pch.gc.ca.

Important elements in the implementation of ecosystem conservation are awareness, understanding, and commitment among park staff and other concerned persons. Within Parks Canada, planning and operations continue to be organized along departmental, or sectoral, lines so that people in one part of the agency may not be familiar with the concepts, plans, and operations underway in other parts. In Bruce Peninsula National Park, for example, a communication strategy was prepared as part of the ecosystem conservation planning process. Another is now being prepared for Bruce Peninsula National Park visitor services, without much apparent linkage with the communication strategy for ecosystem conservation planning. More intra-agency interaction is needed in dealing with a holistic and integrative process such as ecosystem planning. Linkages need to be built for regular exchange of information within, and among, Parks Canada and other agencies and groups. This can be done through internal workshops or through regular forums, which could be used by Parks Canada in cooperation with others. One example is the Georgian Bay Association, with its annual September meeting, or forum for the eastern Georgian Bay area.

We have done some preliminary follow-up on the ecosystem conservation plan for the Georgian Bay Island National Park and found some positive developments. These include:

- Recommendations to monitor the environmental effects of snowmobiling have been addressed, with the intent of assessing implications for continuation of this activity in the national park by the next scheduled park management plan review in 2000.
- As recommended in the plan, two new staff—one for implementation of a GIS and another for related ecological and outreach work—have been assigned ecosystem planning duties at least on a short-term basis
- In accordance with the plan, a cooperative GIS is being developed by Parks Canada with other federal, provincial, and local government agencies.
- A park consultative group, originally convened by the park superintendent, continues its work. This group includes some private citizens as well as staff from senior and local governments having major responsibilities and programs in relation to the plan.
- The scientific basis for a natural nodes and corridors system, previously identified for lands around the national park by the park consultative group, is being refined with the assistance of

park staff. This work is associated with an official plan review for the adjacent municipality; the District of Muskoka. It is also associated with easements, land acquisitions, and other work by private heritage conservation foundations in the area.

- No meeting has been called for the Greater Park Ecosystem Forum, which was recommended in the plan, although yearly meetings of the Georgian Bay Association perform a somewhat similar function. The Greater Park Ecosystem Forum was intended to be a place where the public at large could become informed about, and learn to participate in, ecosystem planning, management, and decision-making. In this respect, the forum was to serve as a capacity building event for all concerned.

- Finally, the preparation of the plan has been associated with a rising interest in improved environmental management in the eastern Georgian Bay island area. Much of the leadership, in proposals for the establishment of a world biosphere reserve for the region, has come from the Georgian Bay Association.

Other Considerations

In the course of their preparation and implementation, many factors can influence ecosystem conservation plans, in addition to those discussed above. Examples include: reductions in government funding for national parks; cuts in the budgets of other concerned federal and provincial agencies; the amalgamation, reorganization, and refinancing of local municipal governments, as occurred recently in Ontario; changes in park personnel; elections and ensuing changes in policies, programs, and the people involved; and so forth. Such considerations have affected ecosystem conservation planning for all four of the national parks examined in this study. These changes are becoming more common and make it increasingly difficult to use a corporate or rational planning approach in which certain objectives are envisioned as being accomplished, and problems solved, within a particular planning period, or by a specific target date. Rather, ecosystem conservation planning should be seen as more of an ongoing adaptive planning, management, and decision-making process among the changing agencies, groups, and individuals involved. This strategy or process should relate not only to ecological concerns, but also to economic and social challenges faced by concerned agencies, groups, and individuals in the vicinity of a park and beyond.

In this context, the scientific or professional style and language of the plans makes them difficult for many agencies, groups, and individuals to understand and use. Greater effort should be placed on user-friendly brochures, videos, interpretation programs, consultative committees, civic forums, workshops, and regular networking. These tools are an important means of promoting the communication, understanding, and involvement required to achieve ecological integrity in national parks, and environmental health and sustainable development in the surrounding lands and waters.

Viewed from this perspective, ecosystem conservation planning is a multidisciplinary, multi-interest process that relies on ecosystem science, yet has considerable human dimensions. The implications of this—and of the outreach rather than the fortress outlook associated with ecosystem conservation planning—are that ecologists, geographers, land use planners, and others with varied backgrounds all need to be involved. The broad human dimensions of planning need to receive as much careful attention from park and other planners as the science involved in ecosystem conservation planning. These requirements have implications for the type of staff Parks Canada and other concerned agencies will need in the future.

Conclusions

Ecosystem conservation planning is a proactive and integrative process, which, on one hand can work against unanticipated programs, projects, or events that may adversely affect the ecological integrity of national parks. On the other hand, ECP can also facilitate environmentally sensitive developments of value to people in surrounding regions. This vision of the fundamental role of ecosystem conservation planning is, however, one that does not yet seem to be shared widely by senior people in Parks Canada, or other relevant agencies and organizations. Ecosystem conservation plans are signed and approved by Parks Canada officials at various levels of seniority and responsibility. This, and the inequitable funding and other support provided for ecosystem conservation planning, indicate that its potential contribution to the ecological integrity of national parks and to sustainable development in surrounding regions is insufficiently appreciated by many of those concerned with its development in Canada's national parks. In this regard, serious consideration should be given to making ecosystem conservation planning an integral part of the park management plan, which has been the basic guiding document for the management of national parks for many years.

Acknowledgments

The authors wish to thank the Social Sciences and Humanities Research Council of Canada and Parks Canada for grants in support of this research. Results of work on ecosystem conservation plans for Parks Canada also contributed to this paper. We appreciate comments provided by reviewers on an earlier draft of this paper. We are also grateful to many people who discussed ecosystem conservation planning with us and gave us an opportunity to discuss preliminary findings and ideas in meetings and seminars.

References

Canada. Parks Canada. 1992. 'Ecosystem Conservation Plan,' pp. 7.1-13. In *Natural Resource Management Process Manual*. Cornwall, Ont.

_____. 1994. *Guiding Principles and Operational Policies*. Ottawa, Ont.

_____. 1997. *Ecosystem Conservation Plan, Fundy National Park*. NP: Parks Canada Southern New Brunswick Field Unit. 115 p.

_____. 1998. *State of the Parks Report: 1997*. Canadian Heritage. Ottawa, Ont. 190 p.

Canada. Parks Canada. St. Lawrence Islands National Park. 1995. *Ecosystem Conservation Plan for St. Lawrence Islands National Park*. Mallorytown, Ont. 60 p.

Grumbine, R. E. 1994. "What is Ecosystem Management?" *Conservation Biology* 8(1): 27-38.

Halvorson, W. L., and E. Davis. 1996. *Science and Ecosystem Management in the National Parks*. Tucson, Ariz.: University of Arizona Press. 362 p.

Hudson, B. M. 1979. "Comparison of Current Planning Theories: Counterparts and Contradictions." *American Planning Association Journal* October: 387-398.

Lertzman, K., T. Spies, and F. Swanson. 1997. "From Ecosystem Dynamics to Ecosystem Management," pp.361-382. In *The Rainforests of Home: Profile on a North American Bioregion,* ed. P. K. von Hagen, B. Schoomaker, and E. C. Wolf. Washington. D.C.: Island Press.

Nelson, J. G. 1987. "National Parks and Protected Areas, National Conservation Strategies and Sustainable Development." *Geoforum* 18(3): 291-319.

_____. 1991. "Beyond Parks and Protected Areas: From Public and Private Stewardship to Landscape Planning and Management." *Environments* 21(1): 23-34.

_____. 1998. *Preparing for an Ecosystem Conservation Plan for Bruce Peninsula National Park*. Report for Parks Canada, Ontario Region, Cornwall, Ont. Waterloo, Ont.: Heritage Resources Centre, University of Waterloo. 80 p.

Nelson, J. G., and R. C. Scace. 1969. *The Canadian National Parks: Today and Tomorrow*. Studies in Land Use History and Landscape Change no. 3. Calgary, AB: University of Calgary. 1027 p.

Nelson, J. G., and A. J. Skibicki. 1997. *Georgian Bay Islands National Park Ecosystem Conservation Plan: Planning for Nature Conservation in the Georgian Bay Island National Park Region.* Waterloo, Ont.: Heritage Resources Centre, University of Waterloo. 66 p.

Stephenson, B., and P. Zorn. 1998. "Assessing the Ecosystem Management Program of St. Lawrence Islands National Park, Ontario, Canada." *The George Wright Forum* 14(4): 51-64.

Woodley, S., J. Kay, and G. Francis. 1993. *Ecological Integrity and the Management of Ecosystems.* Boca Raton, Fla.: St. Lucie Press. 217 p.

Zorn, P., B. Stephenson, and P. Grigoriew. 1997. *Ecosystem Management Program and Assessment Process.* Cornwall, Ont.: Parks Canada. 20 p.

Linking Public and Private Stewardship: Planning for the Great Sand Dunes National Monument Area, Colorado, and Its Implications for Canada

J. G. Nelson

Abstract

Within the southern Rocky Mountains lies a large basin known as the San Luis Valley of Colorado (fig. 9.1). This basin forms the northern part of the Rio Grande that eventually flows through the states of New Mexico and Texas, as well as Mexico, into the Caribbean Sea. On the eastern flank of the valley is a large complex of sand dunes managed by the U.S. National Park Service in a national monument created by President Hoover in 1932. In recent years, the professional and general view of the dunes has changed, from a focus on their unique geography and landforms, to recognition that the dunes are part of a diverse ecosystem that extends well beyond the boundaries of the monument. This recognition by the U.S. National Park Service, a private organization, The Nature Conservancy, and other agencies and organizations, as well as politicians, and citizens has led to the creation of innovative new conservation arrangements centering on a proposed national park. These arrangements and related planning approaches are the prime interest in this paper that should be of value to relevant government agencies, nongovernmental organizations, and participant individuals in Canada, and other countries.

Figure 9.1 San Luis Valley, Colorado

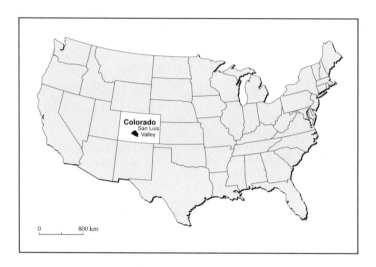

The Context

The great sand dunes and the monument cover about 103.6 square kilometers (forty square miles), and in places attain a vertical relief of about two hundred and fifty meters (seven hundred and fifty feet) (fig. 9.2). The dunes are a result of erosion and transport by prevailing winds blowing over glacial and postglacial silts and sands laid down centuries ago in the Rio Grande basin to the west. The winds have unloaded the silts and sands against the eastern barrier of the Sangre de Cristo Mountains before passing over the relatively low Medano Pass onto the foothills and plains of central, and eastern Colorado. The dunes are stunning and remarkably beautiful landforms that are visited by approximately three hundred thousand people annually. The major reason that concerned agencies, organizations, and citizens have taken a wider view of the dunes and the monument is water. The National Park Service recognizes that the sustainability of the dunes depends on the maintenance of water levels in the system. Decline in water levels could lead to desiccation and erosion of the dunes. In this respect, the upper watershed of the dunes system lies east of the monument on U.S.

Photograph 9.1. Great Sand Dunes National Monument, Colorado, looking east towards the Sangre de Cristo Mountains, U.S.A. Photo credit: Southwest Parks and Monuments Association

National Forest Service wilderness lands in the adjoining Sangre de Cristo Mountains. This federal agency has a different mission than the National Park Service, including industrial logging, and other multiple-purpose uses. Any forest or other disturbances from such activities can affect water flow, erosion, and other processes that, ultimately, could affect the dunes. Potential threats also lie to the west, where water withdrawals for long-standing irrigation projects on ranch and settled lands are believed to be lowering the water table and stressing small lakes and wetlands in the dunes region. These wetlands provide prime habitat for sandhill crane, waterfowl, and other migratory birds, including the occasional whooping crane.

Of major concern have been proposals for the mining and export over the mountains—to Denver and other growing foothills urban areas—of large quantities of groundwater, deposited over the centuries in the deep deposits of the San Luis Valley. The Baca Ranch, located immediately west and north of the monument, is of particular interest. Private investors, interested in exploiting the groundwater supplies, purchased this ranch some years ago.

In the 1990s, the Colorado Nature Conservancy, a major nongovernmental conservation organization in the state, developed a strong interest in the sand dunes area for the foregoing reasons. The conservancy was

Figure 9.2 Schematic origin of Great Sand Dune National Park area

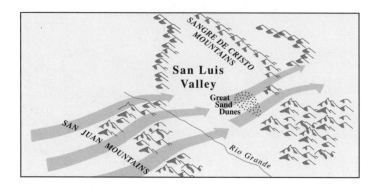

also apprehensive because inventories and assessments led to the identification of the San Luis Valley as a significant target for its biodiversity protection programs in the state. At that time about 40,479 hectares (one hundred thousand acres) of the Medano-Zapata Ranch, to the west and south of the monument, came up for sale and were purchased by The Nature Conservancy.

The valued features of the monument region now include: alpine tundra; the Sangre de Cristo Mountains; extensive pine forests; alpine lakes; large stands of Aspen and Cottonwood; massive sand dunes and grasslands; as well as nearby lowland lakes and wetlands which offer valuable habitat to migratory birds and other animals. Wildlife is diverse, including Rocky Mountain species such as elk, bighorn sheep, black bear, pika, and ptarmigan. Desert species embrace kangaroo rats, short-horned lizards, and six to eight thousand insects indigenous to the sand dunes. Grassland species consist of pronghorn antelope, prairie dogs, jack rabbits, and badgers (fig. 9.2). Wetland species include sandhill crabs, leopard frogs, beavers, avocets, pelicans, and white-faced ibis. Archeological remains also attest to the human presence thousands of years ago.

The recognition of this wide-ranging ecological diversity, and especially the threat of water shortages and export, caused numerous federal, state, and local organizations other than the conservancy and the U.S. National Park Service, to take an increasing interest in the conservation

Photograph 9.2. Pronghorn in Sand Dunes National Monument Area, Colorado, U.S.A. Photo credit: Southwest Parks and Monuments Association

of the sand dunes and adjoining lands in the 1990s. Local, state, and federal politicians and concerned citizens developed the idea of expanding the monument into the surrounding lands and waters and creating a national park. This designation would conserve the full range of biologic and hydrologic features of the region, as well as the geology and landforms protected by the national monument. Following various political bipartisan meetings, a bill was passed by Congress in November 2000, and proclaimed by the president, creating new conservation arrangements for the Sand Dunes National Monument area. These arrangements reflect numerous consultations, adaptations, and compromises made by concerned agencies, nongovernmental organizations, and other groups and individuals to reach an agreement that was, so far as possible, in their own as well as the general interest.

The New Arrangements

The framework for the new arrangements is set forth in the *Great Sand Dunes Monument and Preserve Act* (U.S. 2000). It is not possible to discuss the *Act* in detail here. The official highlights are given in table 9.1 and figures 9.3 and 9.4. This table summarizes the major features of the *Act* and associated interaction, planning, and adaptation among concerned agencies, organizations, and individuals. To this official summary should be added reference to an important section of the *Act* which states that when:

> ... the Secretary (of the Interior) determines that sufficient land having a sufficient diversity of resources has been acquired to warrant designation of the land as a National Park, the Secretary shall establish the Great Sand Dunes National Park in the state of Colorado ... (U.S. 2000, sec. 4)

Provision for continued interaction, planning, and adaptation among concerned parties is, therefore, built specifically into the legislation.

Figure 9.3 shows the proposed framework for the national park as seen primarily, from a federal government perspective. Figure 9.4 reveals the complex set of land tenure arrangements from which the foregoing framework must be created (personal correspondence, Chaney, March 2001). The figure does not show, however, one of the key adaptations that made the arrangements possible. This is the inclusion of The Nature Conservancy's Medano-Zapata Ranch as a major private in-holding within the boundaries of the proposed national park. In this context, the conservation goals of the National Park Service and the conservancy are, generally, compatible, centering in both cases on protection of biodiversity and water.

Table 9.1. *Great Sand Dunes National Park and Preserve Act* of 2000

- Expands the boundary of the existing monument by about 28,300 hectares (70,000 acres), 26,700 hectares (66,000 acres) of which are privately and/or state owned. The secretary of the interior is authorized to designate the area as a "National Park" when sufficient area (generally considered to mean the Baca Ranch) is acquired.
- Authorizes government acquisition (from willing sellers) of all private and state lands, mineral interests, and water rights within this new boundary.
- Creates a new NPS unit called the "Great Sand Dunes National Preserve" where hunting would be allowed, by transferring about 17,000 hectares (42,000 acres) of USFS lands (dunes watershed) to the NPS
- Authorizes the secretary of the interior to establish the 37,000 hectares (92,000 acre) "Baca National Wildlife Refuge" when sufficient lands have been acquired. The refuge is to be formed from the western 1/3 of the Baca Ranch and NW 1/4 of the Medano/Zapata Ranch.
- Expands the Rio Grande National Forest by about 5,600 hectares (14,000 acres) consisting of the northeast corner of Baca Ranch, which includes the 4,317 meters (14,165 foot) Kit Carson Peak.
- Authorizes the continuation of existing grazing leases by The Nature Conservancy on federal and acquired lands that are incorporated in the national monument/park.
- Preserves all existing federal water rights and wilderness designations.
- Does not create a "federal reserved water right" and requires the United States to follow procedures established by the state of Colorado in obtaining water rights for the protection of the new park.
- Requires the establishment of a 10 member advisory council to work with the NPS on development of a management plan for the park and preserve (From Official Summary of Great Sands Dunes National Park and Preserve Act, 2000). (Source: U.S. National Park Service)

Figure 9.3 Proposed land management for the Great Sand Dunes National Park expansion

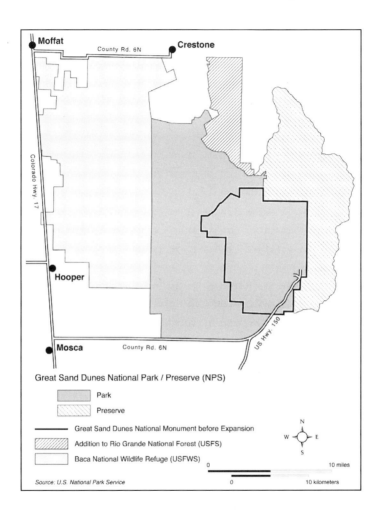

The agreement also is somewhat unusual in that it provides not only for protection of elk and other wildlife, but also allows for grazing by cattle and bison, which have been herded domestically for many years. Domestic stock is not normally considered consistent with the official preference for indigenous wildlife populations in U.S. national parks. The agreement recognizes that grazing has traditionally been a natural feature of this landscape. It is being used as a land management and conservation tool by the conservancy, as well as a potential source of income.

Another significant adaptation to the planning challenges posed by Great Sand Dunes Monument involved the creation of a national preserve in the headwaters in the Sangre de Cristo Mountains (personal correspondence, Chaney, March 2001; Gibson, March 2001). The U.S. Forest Service, the owner of the lands, wished to protect the interests of hunters who have harvested mountain sheep and other animals in this area for many years. Hunting groups, tourism, and other agencies and concerned individuals also supported the continuation of a hunt. Hunting is, however, generally prohibited in national parks. The solution to this challenge was the establishment of a national preserve which allows for regulated hunting, but can be used to prohibit logging and other activities which could disturb the water regime and the Great Sand Dunes area to a significant degree. The national preserve was originally created as a U.S. protected area category in the late 1970s in Alaska. The need there, also, was for a high level of conservation while providing for long standing hunting by local people, primarily for subsistence purposes.

Another adaptation to the planning challenges of the Great Sand Dunes Monument situation is the proposed purchase and resale by The Nature Conservancy of the Baca Ranch, west and north of the monument. As noted previously, the current owners are primarily interested in developing underlying groundwater resources for export to the eastern slope. They have, however, encountered major local, state, and national opposition, and are considering a sale. The current asking price is about thirty million dollars for approximately 40,479 hectares (one hundred thousand acres); a price that is beyond the immediate resources of the federal government (personal correspondence, Gibson, March 2001). The government has been able to appropriate about $8.5 million since the passage of the new legislation in fall 2000. The Nature Conservancy secured a credit of twenty-two million dollars to cover the expected purchase price. The conservancy expects to resell the land to the federal government and recover its investment in the next few years.

The Baca Ranch land would be divided among three federal agencies (figs. 9.3 and 9.4): the U.S. National Park Service, the U.S. Forest Service, and the U.S. Fish and Wildlife Service. This agreement would result in strict conservation arrangements for the national park lands, and more flexible conservation and land use arrangements for the wildlife refuge and U.S. Forest Service lands. The completion of the purchase and resale

Figure 9.4 Land forms and land tenure arrangements for Great Sand Dunes National Monument, Colorado

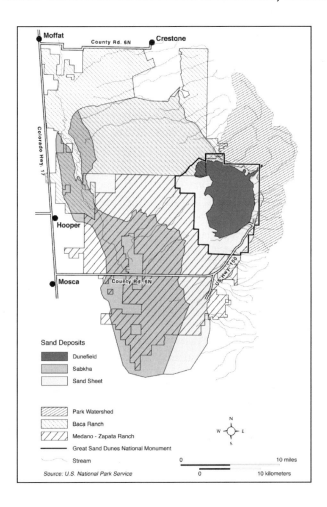

would trigger the creation of the Great Sand Dunes National Park from the current monument and national preserve. The Nature Conservancy is also contributing to the completion of the new conservation arrangements through its proposed purchase of state lands, located to the west and south of the monument, that are within the Medano-Zapata Ranch. This block of land will become a major in-holding in the proposed new national park. An estimated three- to four-million dollars are being raised by the conservancy for these purchases in the Medano–Zapata (personal correspondence, Gibson, March 2001).

Conclusions

Enough details have been given to make it possible to highlight the major innovative characteristics of the new conservation arrangements for the Great Sand Dunes Monument area. These include:

- *Bringing together an array of different types of protected areas to meet the more specific objectives of the National Park Service, The Nature Conservancy, and other national, state, and local organizations.* These arrangements also satisfy the more general objectives required for conservation, and sustainable use of the ecosystem as a whole. The result is a, more or less, mutually supportive set of protected areas—a protected area mosaic of the kind recommended for parts of the Yukon in the early 1980s (Nelson and Theberge 1986), or as a multiple use module (MUM) in the U.S. in recent years (Noss 1987). The new arrangements for the Great Sand Dunes Monument can also be seen as an example of effective public and private stewardship, or comprehensive landscape planning (Brown and Mitchell 1997).

- *Creating the new protected area mosaic in stages over time.* The numerous interactions and adaptations involved are in line with such theoretical approaches as adaptive management (Gunderson, Holling, and Light 1995, Lee 1993), mixed scanning (Etzioni 1967), and transactive or interactive and adaptive planning (Friedmann 1973, Cardinal and Day 1998, Nelson and Sportza 1999, Sportza this volume).

- *Multidisciplinary and cross-sectoral planning, management, and decision-making that are broadly inclusive and civic in nature.* Much of the interaction and adaptation is built on regular communication, monitoring, and assessment, and is informal rather more than formal in character. To date, for example, no memorandum of understanding or other formal agreements have been made between the U.S. National Park Service and The Nature Conservancy for the Sand Dune National Monument region.

- *Planning, management, and decision-making that stress social and political processes, and careful consideration of the different values, interests, and objectives of the various concerned parties. Negotiations and planning for a mix of different types of protected areas;* these, reflect the

Figure 9.5 Colorado priority conservation sites

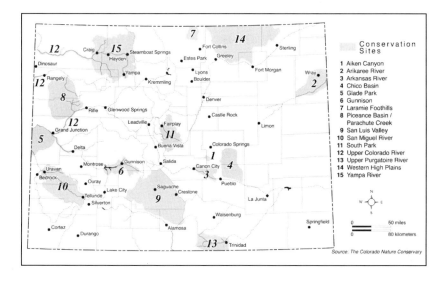

values and interests of different user groups, and government agencies. They are built upon scientific and scholarly ideas and methods, notably ecosystem science.

- *Planning at various overlapping and interacting scales.* For example, the conservancy has been, and is, planning for the Great Sand Dunes area: strategically at a broad ecoregional or state level (fig. 9.5); regionally at the San Luis Valley level; and also at the site level in the context of the Medano-Zapata Ranch. At each scale, targets are identified after inventory and analysis reveal biologic, hydrologic, and other significant areas vital to the diversity and integrity of the area of interest. Subsequently, conservation plans, and management plans are developed as a framework that drives the conservancy's efforts (personal correspondence, Gibson, March 2001).

- *The taking up by private organizations, such as by the Nature Conservancy, of increasingly strong roles in protected area, and regional conservation planning.* This arises, in part, because of the decline of government funding and involvement, and in part because extensive landscape-scale planning and management are often beyond the jurisdictions of government, and traditional federal and state-protected area agencies. The efforts of NGOs can, in these situations, be facilitated through the regulatory and legislative frameworks of federal, state, and local government. This is evident in the Great Sand Dunes area where initiatives of The Nature Conservancy have been complemented by the U.S. National Park Service, the U.S. Forest Service, the federal Fish and Wildlife Service, and state agencies.

In conclusion, as the Great Sand Dunes case shows, the U.S. federal government agencies can bring an array of potentially complementary types of protected areas together to address and adapt to challenges, including national monuments, national parks, national preserves, fish and wildlife refuges, and Forest Service wilderness areas. Although this option is not so evident in the Great Sand Dunes case, the varied federal tool kit can also include federal Bureau of Reclamation lands. The interactive efforts of these federal and state agencies, and the various institutional arrangements available to them, can be increasingly applied to building corridors and connections among various natural areas, and land uses involved in conserving and sustaining valued ecosystems.

Some Implications from a Canadian Perspective

Canada does not effectively use an array of protected area types at the federal level. The main Canadian federal protected area type is the national park. We do have arrangements for Canadian wildlife areas, but these have been greatly weakened, notably, since major budget cuts of the Mulroney government in the 1980s. A plan for Canadian landmarks, comparable to U.S. national monuments, was instituted in the late 1970s, but curtailed severely to the point of disappearance in the 1980s. Responsibility for forest, wildlife, and other resources lies mainly at the provincial level in Canada, although the federally supported Model Forest Program has been associated with some apparently effective regional stewardship programs; for example, in the Fundy National Park area, New Brunswick (Forbes, Woodley, and Freedman this volume).

In the Canadian situation, arrangements like those designed for the Sand Dunes Monument area would be hindered by limitations of the federal protected area tool kit, and would have to involve much more federal-provincial interaction and cooperation than in the U.S. Such cooperation has been difficult to achieve in the past, although the cooperative Canadian Heritage Rivers program suggests that this is by no means impossible. We need evaluations of the process and the results involved in federal-provincial cooperative efforts such as those for heritage rivers. These might provide evidence on how interaction and cooperation could proceed more effectively elsewhere in future.

Some examples are emerging, however, which show that interactive use of protected areas, and land use planning and management, can provide the basis for extensive landscape or regional conservation planning among provincial agencies and NGOs. An outstanding example is British Columbia's Muskwa-Kechika area, where a blend of protected areas and special management zones was established over a total of sixty-three thousand square kilometers in the Northern Rockies (Anonymous 2001). The Canadian Parks and Wilderness Society (CPAWS), and First Nations people played a strong lead role in this initiative. A somewhat comparable provincial example would be the provincial *Lands for Life* process undertaken recently in Ontario.

In my view, a major lesson to be learned from the Great Sand Dunes, and other similar cases in the U.S., is the catalytic role that the monument or landmark type of protected area can play in interactive public and private conservation stewardship efforts. A monument or landmark generally provides protection for some specific geologic, hydrologic, archaeological, or comparable feature. Once in place, it can provide the focus for development of various kinds of interaction among government agencies and nongovernmental organizations, leading to much broader conservation programs. Monuments and landmarks seemingly could be especially helpful with the interactive public and private stewardship efforts needed for the success of regional conservation and sustainable use planning in more highly settled areas.

A second major lesson for Canadians from the Great Sand Dunes case is the potential value of a more flexible approach to ownership of land within national parks. The goal of ultimately having complete Crown ownership of all land within national park boundaries is desirable, but frequently costly, difficult, and time-consuming to achieve. Inclusion within national park boundaries of large private in-holdings, even where held by compatible private conservation organizations, may be stretching Canadian taste. But easements and other agreements could be attempted for blocks of private land like those, for example, in Bruce Peninsula National Park, Ontario. Such easements and agreements could deter development damaging or destructive to national park goals and objectives, at least until a time when fee-simple acquisition may be possible.

From the broad perspective of ecosystem theory, and current efforts at extensive landscape planning through public and private stewardship, the use of more flexible planning, management, and decision-making arrangements seems desirable, as the Great Sand Dunes case illustrates.

References and Sources of Information

This paper is based on field research, consultations, and interviews in the Great Sand Dunes National Monument area in March 2000 and 2001. Of particular value were interviews with Steve W. Chaney, Superintendent, Great Sand Dunes National Monument, (Mosca, Col., 81146-9798), and Mike Gibson, Director of Community Based Conservation Programs, San Luis Valley, The Nature Conservancy of Colorado, (Mosca, Col., 81146). I am very grateful for their assistance and for the opportunity to have informal discussions with other people in the Great Sand Dunes National Monument area. The people who helped me are, of course, free of responsibility for the information and interpretations presented in this paper, which are my own.

Anonymous. Spring 2001. "Setting a Wild Example," pp. 1. *Wilderness Activist*. Canadian Parks and Wilderness Society/CPAWS, National Newsletter, Ottawa.

Brown, J., and B. Mitchell. 1997. "Extending the Reach of National Parks and Protected Areas: Local Stewardship Initiatives," pp. 103-116. In: *National Parks and Protected Areas: Keystones to Conservation and Sustainable Development,* eds. J. G. Nelson and R. Serafin. NATO ASI Series, vol. G 40. Berlin and Heidelberg: Springer-Verlag.

Cardinall, D., and J. C. Day. 1998. "Embracing Value and Uncertainty in Environmental Management and Planning: A Heuristic Model." *Environments* 25(2-3): 110-125.

Etzioni, A. 1967. "Mixed-Scanning: A 'Third' Approach to Decision-Making." *Public Administration Review* 27: 385-392.

Forbes, G., S. Woodley, and B. Freedman. 1999. "Making Ecosystem-based Science into Guidelines for Ecosystem-based Management: The Greater Fundy Ecosystem Experience." *Environments* 27(3): 15-23.

Friedmann, J. 1973. *Retracking America: A Theory of Transactive Planning.* Garden City, N.J.: Anchor Press/Doubleday.

Gunderson, L. H., C. S. Holling, and S.S. Light, eds. 1995. *Barriers and Bridges to the Renewal of Ecosystems and Institutions.* New York: Columbia University Press.

Lee, K. 1993. *Compass and Gyroscope: Integrating Science and Politics for the Environment.* Washington, D.C. and Covelo, Calif.: Island Press.

Nelson, Gordon. 2002. "Some Perspectives on the Human Dimensions of Park and Protected Area Research and Ecosystem-Based Planning, Management and Decision-Making," pp. 692-710. In *Managing Protected Areas in a Changing World*, ed. Soren Bondrup-Nielsen and Neil W. P. Munro. Proceedings of the Fourth International Conference of Science and Management of Protected Areas, 14–19 May 2000. Canada: SAMPAA.

Nelson, J. G., and L. M. Sportza, eds. 1999. "Special Issue: Regional Approaches to Parks and Protected Areas in North America." *Environments* 27(3): 1-15.

Nelson, J. G., and J. B. Theberge. 1986. *Aishihik Lake Resource Survey: Institutional Aspects. Environmentally Significant Area Series.* Report 5, Committee on Northern Studies. Waterloo, Ont.: University of Waterloo, Canada.

Noss, R. F. 1987. "Protecting Natural Areas in Fragmented Landscapes." *Natural Areas Journal* 7(1): 2-13.

Sportza, L. M. 1999. "Regional Approaches to Planning for Protected Areas and Conservation." *Environments* 27(3): 1-14, and this volume.

U.S. Congress. 2000. *Great Sand Dunes National Park and Preserve Act.* Washington, D.C.

WINGS ACROSS THE BORDER [1]

Kenneth W. Cox

Introduction

The *North American Waterfowl Management Plan* (*NAWMP*) is a success story about managing ducks, geese, and swans. It is also a success story about: international cooperation and coordination; creative funding; adapting biological goals to habitat requirements; building multilevel partnerships; the power of voluntary approaches; and planning, implementing, and evaluating on a landscape level. Such landscape level programming necessitates the inclusion of private, corporate, and common and public lands including parks and protected areas.

This paper will outline NAWMP, where it has been, and where it is going. It will highlight the basis of the *Plan's* three visions, based on a biological foundation, a landscape approach, and building partnerships. It will also present some suggestions on the *Plan's* applicability for the management of other migratory wildlife, and its applicability to other biodiversity and endangered species recovery programs. Not forgotten in the paper will be comment on the challenges of dealing with three federal

1.   This paper is not a "stand alone" document. It was prepared as part of a submission on the North American Waterfowl Management Plan to the Workshop on Regional Approaches to Parks and Protected Areas in North America, El Colegio de La Frontera Norte, Tijuana, Mexico in March 1999. It was published in *Environments* 27, no. 3. Portions of the paper are adapted from the document: Canada. Minister of the Environment. March 1999. *Expanding the Vision: North American Waterfowl Management Plan, 1998 Update.* Ottawa, Ont.: Environment Canada.

Photograph 10.1. Ephemeral lake basin in west central Mexico of the type used by waterfowl in winter

governments, many state, provincial, and municipal governments, three different languages, many different cultures, different disciplines, managing species throughout their life cycles and the varying habitats they require, as well as perpetuating a successful program.

While the *North American Waterfowl Management Plan (NAWMP)* (Canada 1986) does not have any direct objectives linked to the creation or perpetuation of government parks or protected area systems, it is a major contributor to the protection of wetland and associated upland habitats across much of North America. As well, the delivery of this program in Mexico has mainly been adjacent to, or on, parks or protected lands; in Canada and the United States, this is not the case. For millennia, ducks, geese, and swans have migrated across North America's landscapes in an annual ritual that evokes a sense of wonder at the forces, mysterious yet consistent, that send millions of birds the length of a continent and back again. Yet among conservationists, the mystery of migration is accompanied by the certain knowledge that waterfowl are dependent upon a complex, and increasingly vulnerable, chain of habitats extending across international borders . Underlying the spectacle of migration is a challenge of unprecedented proportions—the conservation of a migratory resource on a continental scale (Photographs 10.1 and 10.2).

The conservation of these migratory birds is dependent upon a wide range of initiatives that transcend international borders, sectors of the economy, academic disciplines, environmental funding traditions, and management of North American landscapes, to name but a few.

North American Waterfowl Management Plan

The *North American Waterfowl Management Plan* (*Plan*) is the most ambitious continental wildlife conservation initiative ever attempted. It seeks to restore waterfowl populations in Canada, the United States, and Mexico to the levels recorded during the 1970s, a benchmark decade for waterfowl. Numerous pressures during the latter decades of the twentieth century resulted in a severe drop in waterfowl populations. The *Plan* responds to the challenge of revitalizing those populations, in perpetuity, during average environmental conditions.

The *Plan* recognizes that land-use practices and policies on extensive areas across the continent must be altered. Conservation efforts have to move beyond the limits of public natural resource lands to deal with whole landscapes, including private and common lands. Partners venture beyond the security of long-established wildlife programs and relation-ships; to embrace programs and policies that most directly affect the eco-logical health of the landscape, and to benefit not only wildlife but people as well.

The legacy established by the *Plan* in its first thirteen years—imple-menting biologically based conservation across priority landscapes through innovative partnerships—has changed the approach to conserva-tion as it pertains to all wildlife, not just waterfowl. Thousands of partners representing diverse interests in three countries worked to conserve over five-million acres of wetland ecosystems.

Between 1986 and 1997, *Plan* partners invested over one and a half bil-lion dollars U.S. to: secure, protect, restore, enhance, and manage wet-lands and associated uplands in priority landscapes; to conduct research and monitor specific waterfowl populations; and to provide environmen-tal education and conservation planning with community involvement. *Plan* partners cooperated within each country and internationally to influence agriculture, forestry, water, and trade policies that almost cer-tainly indirectly affected a much larger portion of the continent's land-scapes than direct conservation projects themselves. To live up to the

Photograph 10.2. Luther Lake and marsh: a wildlife and water conservation area managed cooperatively by the Grand River Conservation Authority, Ontario, Canada and other agencies

legacy established by the *Plan,* and to expand the vision, three areas of emphasis have been identified for future action.

Strengthening the Biological Foundation

The Vision

Plan partners enhance the capability of landscapes to support waterfowl and other wetland-associated species by ensuring that *Plan* implementation is guided by biologically based planning, which in turn is refined through ongoing evaluation. The biological foundation logically links the *Plan's* continental population goals to its regional conservation strategies and, therefore, depends upon knowledge of how landscape conditions affect waterfowl abundance.

The *Plan's* biological foundation can be strengthened through a systematic process of strategic planning, implementation, and evaluation, where

- planning relies on management objectives and the anticipated effects of management actions to evaluate alternative conservation strategies
- implementation proceeds in accordance with the preferred conservation strategy, recognizing constraints on conservation actions and limits to biological understanding

- evaluation measures progress toward management objectives and provide a basis for refined strategies in future planning efforts

In this context, the justification for biological planning is to ensure successful conservation strategies, while the rationale for evaluation is to improve the effectiveness of that planning.

Toward Landscape Conservation

Plan partners define the landscape conditions needed to sustain waterfowl, benefit other wetland-associated species, and participate in the development of conservation, economic, and social policies and programs that most affect the ecological health of these landscapes.

Effective delivery of the *Plan* requires an understanding of the landscape context in which conservation efforts are undertaken. While public lands provide critical habitat and refuge for waterfowl and other migratory birds, most areas used by these species are on landscapes that are also used to produce economic returns—working landscapes that sustain communities through such activities as agriculture, mining, fishing, and forestry. Across the continent, these important landscapes include wetlands, aquatic systems, grasslands, forests, riparian areas, and near-shore seascapes.

A landscape approach to habitat management seeks to balance conservation and socioeconomic objectives within a region. To achieve *Plan* population goals, a myriad of habitats must be conserved, most of which exist in working landscapes. The interests of the people who share these landscapes with wildlife must be considered if *Plan* goals are to be achieved. The *Plan* provides the institutional framework for all conservationists to work with these interests to achieve mutual benefits across the continent's landscapes.

Broadening the Scope of Partnerships

Plan partners collaborate with other conservation efforts, particularly migratory bird initiatives, and reach out to other sectors and communities to forge broader alliances in a collective search for sustainable uses of landscapes. The drafters of the 1986 *Plan* realized that restoring waterfowl populations would require more than federal intervention on federal lands with federal dollars. Waterfowl conservation may have its roots in international treaties, but the resources to support it must come from the private, state, provincial, and federal sectors.

Figure 10.1 Important waterfowl habitat areas in North America

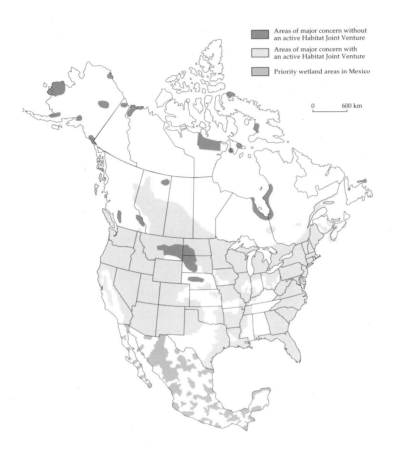

This new approach to conservation helped stimulate passage of the *North American Wetlands Conservation Act* by the U.S. Congress in 1989 (U.S. 1989). This *Act* created a funding mechanism for wetlands projects conducted under the *Plan*. Today, the concepts of pooling, matching, and sharing resources have been replicated so often by *Plan* partners that the business of waterfowl conservation has undergone a fundamental and enduring change. In some regions, these partnerships or joint ventures have expanded beyond waterfowl to include soil and water conservationists, land and water resource development interests, and most importantly, private and community landowners (fig. 10.1).

Integrating Migratory Bird Management

The *Plan* has always promoted an ecological approach; one that encompasses as full a range of biodiversity conservation as is possible under its goals. It has been, and remains, a waterfowl focused initiative. But with each update of the *Plan,* and because of other developments in North America, more emphasis was placed on the conservation of North America's rich biological diversity in the *1998 Update* (Canada 1998). It will continue to secure, restore, protect, and improve habitats not only for other species of migratory birds, but also amphibians, fish, mammals, and plants.

In 1986, the first year of the *Plan,* waterfowl conservation on an international level was largely synonymous with migratory bird conservation; formal international partnerships aimed at nongame migratory birds were only beginning to emerge. The *Western Hemisphere Shorebird Reserve Network* (WHSRN) was less than one-year old, and it would be nearly five years before *Partners In Flight* (PIF) would begin to address the other nearly 800 species of nongame migratory birds. More recently, a coalition of interested partners began to consider a conservation plan for colonial waterbirds. Inspired by the success of the *Plan,* these international efforts are now engaged in conservation planning on a continental scale, thus broadening the scope and vitality of migratory bird conservation in North America. In addition, a broad coalition of government, nongovernmental organizations, and academia is considering how best to coordinate and integrate these bird conservation plans. The Commission for Environmental Cooperation is facilitating this effort through its North American Bird Conservation Initiative (NABCI).

Part of the vision of the *1998 Update* (Canada 1998) is strengthening and expanding partnerships. A conscious and concerted effort will be made by *Plan* partners to facilitate other bird conservation efforts, as well as building other species conservation initiatives into waterfowl projects.

This brief overview of the *Plan*[2] outlines some of the past and present activities associated with this thirteen-year program. While the past and present represent exciting developments in continental cooperation, wetland and migratory bird conservation and resource management approaches, the future appears even brighter.

---

2.   See full document: *Expanding the Vision: North America Waterfowl Management Plan, 1998 Update* for more detail.

Underlying Principles and Lessons Learned

The following section outlines the parameters associated with *NAWMP* and provides some comment on their importance. While not all-encompassing, the discussion provides on-the-ground reflections and insights into *NAWMP,* and the critical role it plays in protecting, enhancing, and managing wetland and associated upland habitats, migratory birds, and wetland-related species in North America.

International Aspects

Ecoregions or physiographic features on the landscape seldom conform to political boundaries. Neither do the habits nor habitats of migratory birds. Canada, the United States, and Mexico have cooperated for most of the twentieth century in the management of migratory birds. Thus, there was some history of cooperation between these three countries before the farsighted and complex *NAWMP* program was initiated in the mid-1980s. Planning, developing, managing, and administering a conservation program over an extended time-space continuum is challenging in itself. Undertaking that activity among three countries that stretch three-quarters of the way between the Equator and the North Pole, provides an even greater obstacle. But that is the challenge that the professionals who, initially, conceived a continental approach to the management of ducks, geese, and swans—*NAWMP*—had to envisage and then address.

Planning for the program started before talks about the *North American Free Trade Agreement (NAFTA)* began to take shape. Yet the design of, and goals outlined for, the program fit well as an example of tripartite environmental cooperation under this international trade agreement. Through concept design, objective setting, and written words, care must be taken to express views and programs from the aspect of standing in the north looking south, standing on the U.S. Great Plains looking both north and south, or standing in Mexico looking north. Only in this way can success be achieved.

Cultural Diversity

As birds wing their way north or south, east or west, across the continent, they are observed by, and reside with a multitude of different cultures, cultures varied in language, dialect, religious practice, and social mores. Some of these cultures manage wildlife from arms length trying to make them fit into the infrastructure already established within their culture and political system. Others work intimately with the migratory resource, interacting or using it daily for their survival. Any plan to manage a species for its entire lifecycle across the numerous habitats it uses throughout the year, must take into consideration both the methods of management and the acceptability to these diverse cultures conserving such a resource. While some cultures see migratory birds only for their beauty, others also see them as food on the table. While some are willing to spend considerable time and money on migratory bird management for the sheer pleasure and preservation of the species, others see such birds as agricultural or fisheries pests to be severely restricted. While some agencies or administrations will develop a program for migratory bird conservation unilaterally, other conservation plans must be integrated into a multipurpose plan to enhance agriculture, forestry, fisheries, and tourism.

Biological Integrity, Evaluation, and Monitoring

Above all else, the *Plan*'s purpose is to restore the migrating numbers of ducks, geese, and swans in North America with a fall flight of 100 million birds and a spring flight of sixty-two million birds. Many individual species' goals are included in that overall figure. These bird numbers are to be sustainable over time, during periods of average environmental conditions. To do so, it is critical to remember that the objective is to secure, enhance, and manage wetlands and wetland-related habitats to produce a continuing population of birds. One success of the *Plan* has been the partners' continuing observation of that objective. One critical aspect of maintaining this biological integrity is the establishment of monitoring systems and an evaluation process. These allow concerned people to relate increases or decreases of waterfowl to additions, deletions, or changes in waterfowl habitat, so that modification of programming can take place to reach the original population objective.

Landscape Approach and Management

Managing wildlife resources on a landscape basis is not something that is practiced in many parts of the world. Certainly, North America has not been known for being on the leading edge of this type of ecosystem management. However, with the first update in 1994 (Canada 1994), it became obvious that this was the approach that must be taken to accomplish our objectives. This is not meant to suggest that the *Plan* and the programs upon which it is based are a model of the landscape approach and landscape management. But with the *1998 Update* (Canada 1998), it is now a firmly established objective of the *Plan*. Part of our traditional management on a species-by-species or a site-by-site basis, stems partly from the educational system of the past fifty years in North America, and partly from the difficulty of managing on an ecosystem basis. The existing political and administrative infrastructure that has been established across most of the continent has not been supportive of such binational and trinational coordination and cooperation.

Partnerships

In the last two decades of the twentieth century, partnerships have become so important that one could arguably state that any meaningful kind of species conservation would be impossible without such arrangements. Partnerships have been one of the underlying reasons for moving toward the landscape approach to wildlife management. Part of this realization stems from the fact that the partnerships formed with government, nongovernmental, corporate, and community sectors were created with partners that do not have wildlife conservation as their reason for being. Many of these agencies are involved in forestry, agriculture, mining, or industrial development. Indeed, planned and developed properly, cross-sectoral planning for wildlife can make a major contribution to making development sustainable across a healthy landscape and within a healthy economy.

It is important to point out that there is one other critical partner, the private landowner, upon whom the great bulk of the Canadian part of *NAWMP* is based. Becoming a *Plan* partner is a 100 percent voluntary initiative. The *Plan*'s success in many areas of North America, particularly the Prairie and Great Plains, is because private landowners and *NAWMP* partners have been able to reach win–win solutions for sustainable income at the "farm gate," as well as for wetland conservation.

Funding

While the soul of the *Plan* is biological integrity, there is no doubt that the heart of the *Plan* is money. Although some small local programs can be accomplished with a minimum of cash and a maximum of community and individual input, a program the size of *NAWMP* can only be accomplished with annual major infusions of money. The dedication of the agencies and individuals in those agencies is paramount, but without the monetary commitment of each partner, such a major undertaking would be fruitless.

Few realize that when the *Plan* was agreed to between the nations, there was no money attached to it. A full two years went by before the U.S. Congress (1989) passed the *North American Wetlands Conservation Act* (*NAWCA*) and provided a creative funding source, one which could not only be used in the U.S., but also in Mexico and Canada. The brilliance of this funding decision lies in the fact that the U.S. federal government establishes yearly, a base amount of money that can be accessed only by matching the amount of money a proponent requests. In Canada, at the time of the last authorization, every federal dollar invested in the program resulted in an additional seven Canadian dollars being injected into the *Plan* through a system of partner matches. And, for every federal U.S. dollar committed to Canada, twenty-three Canadian dollars are also committed.

Administrative Control

If the International Plan Committee had mapped out the administrative hoops that must be negotiated to get project approval and funding, both in one country and across jurisdictions, it never would have proceeded with the design of the *Plan*. However, the goals were ecological and biological in nature and the feeling was that if the money could be found to drive the system, methods could be found to make the administrative controls workable. Suffice it to say, in the ten years of funding for the *Plan*, some one and a half billion dollars U.S. have been expended at the ground level. It could be argued that *NAWMP* was a major catalyst in not only defining a new method for funding programs, but also one which helped define cross-sectoral cooperation, at both the governmental and nongovernmental levels. That is to say, the *Plan* demands that being a partner forces various governmental levels and departments to share money, share authority, and share credit with other departments and other government levels. *NAWMP* provides an example of how this can be achieved through a very positive process.

Migratory Birds and Other Species

The *Plan* has also been a catalyst to move ahead and probably accelerated the design of, and planning for, a number of other continental migratory bird strategies. These strategies include: *Partners in Flight* (PIF) (land birds); *Western Hemisphere Shorebird Reserve Network* (WHSRN), now referred to in some regions as the *Continental Shorebird Program*; the *Colonial Waterbird Program*; and, the *North American Bird Conservation Initiative* (NABCI). As well, there have been continental plans suggested for bats, butterflies, moths, and dragonflies. Because of the longevity of the *Plan* and its successful administrative infrastructure, interest has been expressed by other migratory wildlife initiatives in being partners with those involved in the *North American Waterfowl Management Plan*. The *Plan*, in its *1998 Update*, invited discussions with other migratory wildlife efforts regarding how *Plan* partners might help one another.

It is also important to make clear that the *Plan* has been involved with the conservation of amphibian, reptile, fish, and other wildlife species. This has been accomplished through a multispecies design of many of the *Plan*'s projects. This integration of species conservation has been useful in a couple of ways including a greater understanding of species interaction and greater capability to deliver all species objectives within a wetland-associated upland system. This history of building nonwaterfowl benefits into the *Plan* will continue and strengthen.

Communication and Education

Both communication and education are critical to the implementation and perpetuation of such a major program. Communicating failures and successes, and educating the people involved both in the *Plan* and outside the *Plan,* are daunting tasks. These challenges arise not only because of differences in languages and dialects, differences in climate and species associated with particular ecoregions, and differences in the methods used to communicate, but also because the bulk of money available to the *Plan* is spent on habitat. In an effort to minimize administrative costs, communication and education activities have been funded at, what some would consider, inadequate levels. There appears to be an effort at this point in time to enhance communications, particularly at the national and international levels. An example of one of the better communications media is a successful newsletter in English, French, and Spanish entitled "*Waterfowl 2000.*" It is published three times a year and is the major vehicle for partners to understand the different components of the continental *Plan*.

Celebration

In some cultures, mothers impress on children that the two most important words in their vocabulary are "thank you." This is an important message to convey, especially if program longevity is to be expected. *Plan* partners have been generous with their appreciation of other partners' efforts and funding available to *NAWMP*. The International Plan Committee that is the senior planning authority for *NAWMP* provides two awards annually that are given to individuals or agencies that have made significant contributions to the program. In Canada, because considerable funding for the Canadian program comes from both the U.S. federal and state governments, as well as Ducks Unlimited Inc., partners have been exemplary in recognition of these contributions through what are commonly called Canada Nights. In addition the three countries celebrated the ten-year anniversary of the *Plan* in 1996.

Retaining Success

No other continental habitat or species-based conservation program has survived ten years, let alone thirteen, with an approved *Plan* for a further five years. Thus, unlike other major conservation programs, *NAWMP* has maintained its authority and momentum. There are many reasons why major programs fail. These include improper design, insufficient planning, a lack of vision, administrative chaos, and the inability to accomplish the objectives. So perhaps the largest challenge of all, for both the *Plan* and its partners, is the continuation, refinement, and expansion of the *North American Waterfowl Management Plan*. This is easier said than done. Time tends to have a numbing effect on existing programs. When programs are new, everyone wants to be involved; when programs are old and reliable, they tend to be forgotten and with this often comes neglect and eventually inoperability. It is no accident that the *North American Waterfowl Management Plan* has survived thirteen years and it should not be surprising if it survives another ten. If this occurs, it will be because of dedication to the task and the continued ability of the partners to work together, to plan for the future, and to execute the plan as a team.

References

Canada. Canadian Wildlife Service. 1986. *North American Waterfowl Management Plan: A Strategy for Cooperation*. Ottawa, Ont.: Canadian Wildlife Service, Environment Canada.

Canada. Canadian Wildlife Service, U.S. Fish and Wildlife Service, and Mexico. Secretaría de Desarrollo. 1998. *1998 Update to the North American Waterfowl Management Plan: Expanding the Vision*. Ottawa, Ont.: Environment Canada, Canadian Wildlife Service, Washington D.C.: United States Fish and Wildlife Service, and Mexico: SEMARNAP.

_____. 1994. *1994 Update to the North American Waterfowl Management Plan: Expanding the Commitment*. Ottawa, Ontario: Environment Canada, Canadian Wildlife Service, Washington, D.C.: United States Fish and Wildlife Service, and Mexico: Secretaría de Desarrollo Social (SEDESOL).

Cox, K. W. 1993. *Wetlands: A Celebration of Life. Final Report of the Canadian Wetlands Conservation Task Force*. Sustaining Wetlands Issues Paper no. 1993-1. Ottawa, Ont.: North American Wetlands Conservation Council (Canada).

Lynch-Stewart, P., I. Kessel-Taylor, and C. Rubec. 1991. *Wetlands and Government: Policy and Legislation for Wetland Conservation in Canada*. No. 1999-1. Ottawa, Ont.: Environment Canada and Ducks Unlimited Canada.

Lynch-Stewart, P., C. D. A. Rubec, K. W. Cox, and J. H. Patterson. 1993. *A Coming of Age: Policy for Wetland Conservation in Canada*. Report no. 93-1. Ottawa, Ont.: Canadian Wildlife Service, Environment Canada.

U.S. Congress. 1989. *North American Wetlands Conservation Act*. Public Law 101-233 as amended 16 USC 4401, et seq.

Baja California to the Bering Sea:
A North American Marine Conservation Initiative[1]

Sabine Jessen and Natalie Ban

Abstract

The Pacific region off the coast of North America has undergone dramatic changes over the past fifty years. These include: declines in Steller sea lion and sea otter populations in Alaska; decreases in salmon populations in British Columbia and Washington State; increased populations of fish such as Pollock in the Bering Sea; changes in food supply for sea birds; and changes in the migration of gray whales. Although the causes of these changes are not fully understood, they are forcing scientists to think about the need to move beyond the current focus on economically important species to a marine management approach.

For a number of years, marine protected areas (MPAs) have been advocated by some scientists and conservationists as a tool which can contribute to better management of the marine environment through a holistic ecosystem approach, in contrast to traditional species-by-species management. While some steps have been taken to establish MPAs in the Baja to Bering Sea region, the current system is considered to be inadequate

---

1.   This paper was presented at the Regional Approaches to Parks and Protected Areas Workshop in Tijuana, B.C., and published in *Environments* 27, no. 3.

Figure 11.1 Baja to Bering Sea surface currents

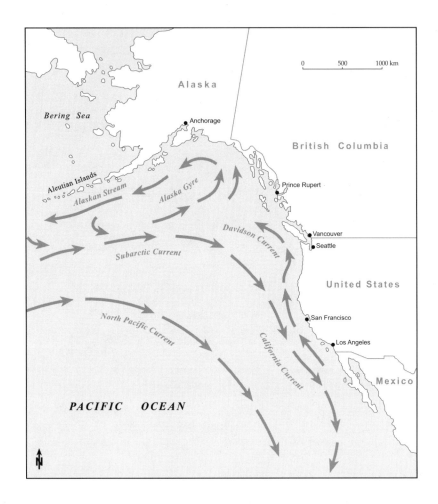

(IUCN 1995), and much work remains to be done. Marine protected areas are only one part of the equation if we are to succeed in ensuring the long term integrity of marine ecosystems. We will need to consider how we use the areas outside marine protected areas, and how we can ensure that critical ecosystem connections are maintained, allowing the core protected areas to truly protect biodiversity.

In addressing challenges to marine conservation in the Pacific waters stretching from the Baja Peninsula, Mexico, to the Bering Sea, Alaska, we begin with a review of the physical, oceanographic, and biological properties of Pacific waters—from the Baja to the Bering Sea—and demonstrate the connected ecosystem nature of this region. This is followed by a description of some of the potential focal species which could be used to develop a marine conservation strategy. Human influences and environmental trends in the region along this coast are then discussed, prior to a summary of the existing marine protected area networks in each country. The paper ends with a discussion of how we can learn from the *Yellowstone to Yukon Conservation Initiative*, and develop a conservation strategy for the Baja to Bering Sea region. In sum, this paper explores the rapidly developing field of conservation biology and how it can guide a new approach to the conservation of marine life on the Pacific Coast of North America.

Regional Overview

Physical Environment

Geology : The basic geological features of the North American coastal region began to form about 200 million years ago when the southwest flowing continent of North America slowly, but forcefully, met the northward moving floor of the Pacific Ocean. The prolonged impact continues today. It has caused the heavy sea floor to sink gradually into the planet's hot interior and rugged mountains to rise steeply along the continent's edge. About 150 million years ago, a great marine trench began to form that stretches four thousand kilometers from California to Alaska, seaward of the Continental Shelf. Created by combinations of glaciation, sinking land, silting, and wave action, the continental shelf creates a relatively shallow sea floor that skirts the coast north to south. Although some stretches of the shelf are flat, most are very rugged, much like the corresponding land areas, modified only by erosion and deposits of sediment (Cannings, Cannings, and de Jong Westman 1999).

Oceanography : Oceanic currents are parts of huge gyres—immense eddies of water driven by prevailing winds and Coriolis forces. The general current patterns on the North Pacific are shown in fig. 11.1. Of particular interest is the Subarctic Boundary located north of the North Pacific currents. North of this boundary, precipitation matches evaporation. South of the Subarctic Boundary, evaporation removes water from the surface faster than precipitation can replace it. Since the salts are retained, the surface water becomes more saline. North of the boundary, precipitation adds water to the solution, diluting it and lowering the salinity. This abrupt change in salinity at the Subarctic Boundary creates a barrier to fish movements between the northern and southern marine domains. For example, tuna prefer the warm waters in the south and salmon the cold, rich waters in the north (Cannings, Cannings, and de Jong Westman 1999).

Large-scale upwelling occurs along the Pacific coast of North America each summer, driven by the northwest winds. These winds create drift currents down the coast. The Coriolis effect caused by the earth's rotation, in turn, deflects these currents offshore. As the surface water moves away from the coast, cold bottom water rises to replace it. Phosphates, nitrates, and other nutrients from the deep ocean are pushed up to the surface by these upwellings. At the surface, more nutrients are added by runoff from rivers. The result is that the waters above the continental shelf are so rich in nutrients that they support an abundance of microscopic green algae, or phytoplankton. On the Pacific Shelf, the diverse topography, rich nutrient supplies, and cold temperatures result in a high diversity of marine life.

Biogeographic Provinces in the Baja California to Bering Sea Region

Development of a marine classification framework is the first step in identifying gaps in representation of marine natural regions in a protected areas system, and in identifying new sites that will contribute to a representative system of marine protected areas. IUCN (1995) suggested eight biogeographic provinces for the Baja California to Bering Sea Region (fig. 11.2). From north to south they are: Beringian; Aleutian; West Coast Fjords; Oregonian; Montereyan; San Diegan; Cortezian; and Mexican. Further ecological classification work is required below the broad level of marine province. The British Columbia government completed this for the Pacific Region of Canada (Zacharias, Harper, and Wainwright 1998) World Wildlife Fund Canada developed a hierarchical marine classification framework for Canada, which should be applied to the Baja California to Bering Sea region.

Figure 11.2 Baja to Bering Sea biogeographic zones

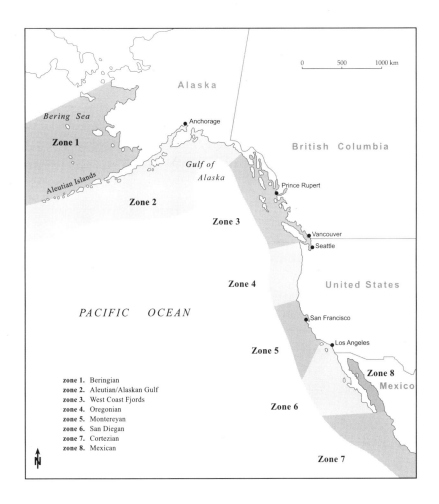

The Science: Conservation Biology

Work on developing science and principles for conservation in terrestrial systems could be adapted to the marine environment. Noss (1997:23), for example, developed a number of principles and goals for maintaining the ecological health or integrity of both terrestrial and marine systems. These include

- representing all kinds of ecosystems, across their natural range of variation, in protected areas
- maintaining viable populations of all native species in natural patterns of abundance and distribution
- sustaining ecological and evolutionary processes within their natural ranges of variability, and
- building a conservation network that is adaptable to environmental change

To achieve these goals, ecological structure, diversity, and resilience have to be maintained through strict, large-scale protection of entire ecosystems. Terrestrial conservation biology indicates that, where crucial processes such as predation are distorted or absent, ecological systems often collapse with the loss of large numbers of species. Therefore, in order to be effective, biological conservation must be planned and implemented on large spatial scales (Soulé and Terborgh, 1999). In the marine environment this seems to be the case as well. Sea otters, as one example, are an indication of this. When sea otters are removed, sea urchin populations expand rapidly, devouring and destroying the kelp forest (Estes and Carr, n.d.).

A number of important considerations must be addressed in order to maintain ecological structure, diversity, and resilience. First, a system of core protected areas representative of the variety of marine habitats in the region must be established. Second, focal species' requirements must be identified and considered. Third, connectivity among protected areas, based on ecological processes and habitat requirements of focal species, must be taken into account. Fourth, management regimes are required both inside and outside the core reserves to ensure long-term ecological integrity of the reserves and the broader marine environment.

In contrast to terrestrial environments, closed ecosystems rarely exist in the oceans. Many free-swimming species have large spatial ranges, and water currents carry the genetic material of sedentary or territorial species over long distances, often hundreds of kilometers (IUCN 1992). Therefore, "the minimum size of an MPA necessary for viability is likely to be many times larger than the minimum viable size of a terrestrial reserve" (IUCN 1992: 14).

An Ecosystem Representation Approach

Establishing a system of protected areas representative of ecosystems is one step towards conserving biodiversity and ensuring that we do not allow our inadequate knowledge to delay action (Noss 1995). In order to be truly representative, the reserve network must represent all habitats, communities, species, and other natural features (Noss 1995). World Wildlife Fund Canada's Endangered Spaces Campaign was based on this approach. Protecting a diversity of geologic or physiographic types—"enduring features"—would also preserve a diversity of biological communities (Recchia and Broadhead 1995:12).

In addition to protecting the various life stages of many marine species—including highly mobile ones such as fish and whales—protecting representative examples of different marine habitats also compensates for our lack of knowledge about critical marine species and ecological processes. According to Recchia and Broadhead (1995), assuming all habitat types are equally worthy of protection means that we do not have to rely on human judgment as to which habitats and species are most important.

The Need for Connectivity

Connectivity is essential for many species, especially large animals, which cannot maintain viable populations in small, isolated areas. In the terrestrial realm, ensuring corridors and linkages between protected areas is crucial to maintaining biological diversity. In the sea, there is a much higher degree of connectivity, which has both positive and negative implications for marine protected areas. Such areas can serve as sources of larval fish and invertebrates for surrounding areas of the ocean but they are also vulnerable to downstream effects, for example from pollution that originates hundreds or even thousands of kilometers away.

Marine Reserve Design and Management Considerations

Some marine conservation biologists are developing the scientific underpinnings for the design of marine protected area networks. These networks will help protect species against petroleum development pollution, and other effects of human activity. Much of this work is focused on the need to establish some reserves where all fishing activity is prohibited. This focus arises from a concern about the rate at which humans are depleting marine populations and degrading marine ecosystems (Murray et al. in press). Another concern is that we have a poor appreciation of mechanisms at work in the marine environment. We need to apply the precautionary principle and protect marine environments despite our incomplete knowledge of them.

Although marine protected areas (MPAs) represent a precautionary approach to human use and management of the ocean environment, it is important to ensure that fishing effort is not simply displaced to areas outside the protected areas. Otherwise the overall benefits of MPAs may result in outside unprotected areas being even more degraded. In this respect, overall conservation of fish and other species will, in many cases, require reductions in fishing effort as well as substantial marine protected areas. These areas are required for sedentary organisms such as abalone and other invertebrates, fishes such as rockfishes and local herring stocks and many other species (Pauly, Pitcher, and Preikshot 1998). MPAs will also provide refuges for migratory marine animals. Corridors connecting MPAs could prove immensely beneficial for the survival of such migratory animals.

A Focal Species Approach

Considerable work has been done on terrestrial reserve networks (Soulé and Terborgh, 1999). A fundamental concept in this work is the need to consider focal species in the planning and management of protected areas systems because their requirements for survival represent factors important to maintaining ecologically healthy conditions overall. Four main types of focal species have been identified:

- *keystone species* that enrich ecosystem function disproportionate to their numerical abundance
- *umbrella species* that cover large areas in their daily or seasonal movements
- *flagship species* that are charismatic creatures that have wide appeal and, thus, draw attention to a conservation objective
- *indicator species* that are tightly linked to specific biological elements, processes, or qualities, are sensitive to ecological changes, and are useful in monitoring habitat quality

Photograph 11.1. Gray whale mother and calf migrating from breeding lagoons in Baja California to feeding grounds in Alaska. Photo credit: Marilyn Kazmers

In selecting focal species for a regional conservation initiative, a list of ecologically threatened, economically important, and endemic organisms should be compiled for the target area.

Potential Focal Species of the Baja California to Bering Marine Region

The following preliminary list of focal species can be used to illustrate protection needs in the northeast Pacific Ocean. The range of some of these species can be found in figure 11.3.

Gray Whales

The gray whale, an umbrella and flagship species, has long been the icon species of the northeastern Pacific. The public are fascinated with its annual ten-thousand kilometer migration from calving lagoons in Baja California to its feeding areas in the Bering Sea, and with its return from the brink of extinction. More than twenty thousand gray whales migrate each year between Baja California and the Bering Sea. Beginning in late February, small groups begin moving north along the coast, never more than a kilometer from land. Beginning in September, the return migration to the lagoons of Baja California begins, ending in December. The ten thousand-kilometer trip takes six to eight weeks, and is the longest known migration of any species of mammal (Gordon and Baldridge 1991).

Kelp Forests

Various kinds of kelp plants form a framework or forest for the marine community where they grow. In a kelp forest, the water depth, rocky outcrops, sandy patches, and seaweeds of various heights establish the structural layers. Giant and bull kelp need sunny spots, and create the uppermost layer of the forest. Their canopies shade the plants below, such as winged kelp and other shrub-like kelps. The multiple layers in a kelp forest offer many different kinds of habitats, promoting a diversity of inhabitants (Connor and Baxter 1989). Kelp are keystone and indicator species because they provide habitat for a large number of marine organisms.

Sea Otters

Sea otters are an important keystone predator in kelp ecosystems because they control sea urchin populations. Unchecked, a horde of hungry urchins will eat everything in reach, leaving barren rocks where a kelp forest once stood. Sea otters were once abundant across the rim of the North Pacific, from northern Japan to the Alaska Peninsula, and along

Figure 11.3 Range of selected potential focal species in the Baja to Bering Sea Region

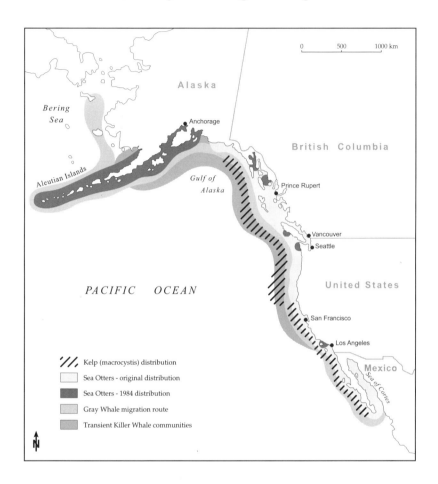

the Pacific coast of North America to Baja California. Widespread commercial hunting that began in the mid-1700s led to the near-extinction of the species (Riedman 1997), and to the destruction of many areas of extensive kelp beds from Alaska to California (Thorne-Miller 1999). Since the early 1900s, the worldwide sea otter population has gradually increased as otters have recolonized their former range. Today, an estimated 100,000 to 150,000 sea otters occupy most of their historical range in Russia and Alaska. However, only small groups of transplanted Alaska otters now occur off Washington, British Columbia, and southeast Alaska, and only one native southern sea otter population survives off the central California coast.

Rockfish

Rockfish are a fascinating group of species that give birth to live young (viviparous) and are some of the longest-lived of all fishes. The rougheye rockfish, common from the Bering Sea to Oregon, lives at least 140 years, while the shortraker rockfish lives to 120 years, and the yelloweye to 118 years. Generally species of colder regions live the longest. Rockfish, or *Sebastes*, are a genus of great diversity with about 100 species worldwide. Most rockfishes, about 71 species, live in the eastern Pacific, from the Bering Sea to the Gulf of California (Bloeser 1999). Substantial declines can be seen in the estimates of current total and spawning biomass levels for black, yellowtail, widow, Pacific Ocean perch, and canary rockfish (Pacific Marine Conservation Council 1999). Rockfish have several life-history characteristics, including being long-lived, increasing fecundity with age, and high site fidelity that make them good candidates for responding favorably to marine refugia (PMCC 1999). Because rockfish are long-lived, they are an indicator species of the fishing pressures exerted on their habitat.

Sea Lions

Sea lions live along the entire north Pacific coast. California sea lions are distributed from northern Mexico to British Columbia, while Steller sea lions range from California to Alaska. Steller sea lions are endangered in Alaska, while California sea lion populations are increasing. The number of Steller sea lions in most areas has shown a continuous decline, from about 300,000 individuals to less than 100,000 since the 1970s. This continuing decline led the U. S. National Marine Fisheries Service to list the Steller sea lion as threatened under the *Endangered Species Act* in April 1990 (U.S., NOAA 1999). While the reasons for this decline remain unsolved, possible causes include: increased incidence of parasites and disease; predation by killer whales; nutritional stress through competition with humans and other species for food; and nutritional stress caused by natural or human-induced changes in the abundance, quality, and distribution of prey (North Pacific Universities Marine Mammal Research Consortium 1998). Sea lions are flagship species because of their charisma and public appeal. They are also indicator species as they are highly sensitive to human disturbances.

Black Oystercatchers

The Black Oystercatcher is an important member of rocky intertidal communities along the west coast of North America. It is entirely dependent on marine shorelines for food and nesting. During breeding, black oystercatcher pairs establish well-defined territories where there is abundant intertidal prey, which they tend to occupy each year. Because predation by oystercatchers—primarily on mussels and limpets (Andres and Falxa 1995)—strongly influences the abundance and species composition of intertidal plants (Estes and Carr, unpublished), these birds are an important keystone species. The most significant impacts on populations of black oystercatchers come from human and mammalian disturbances. This sensitivity also makes them a good indicator species of coastal ecosystem health. Breeding pairs were extirpated on the small islands off the coast of Baja California by scientific collecting, human disturbance, and mammalian predation.

Human Influences and Trends

Human impacts on the ocean environment and its occupants have increased in the last 200 years. Major changes in the abundance of seals, whales, and sea birds are evident in the North Pacific in recent decades. In Alaska, harbor seals are greatly reduced in number, northern fur seals are depleted, and Steller sea lions have been declared endangered in parts of their range. Similar declines have been reported in some seabird breeding colonies. In British Columbia, Steller sea lion numbers appear stable, and harbor seal populations are increasing rapidly. Further south, striking increases are being observed in the range and abundance of elephant seals and California sea lions (North Pacific Universities Marine Mammal Research Consortium 1998).

In the eighteenth century, the Steller's sea cow was hunted to extinction in the Aleutian Islands within twenty-seven years of being discovered. Closely related to dugong and manatees, the Steller's sea cow had a very small population and lived exclusively in this region (Pitcher 1998). Because sea cows fed on shallow-water and surface canopy kelps, their absence undoubtedly had a great effect on kelp forest ecosystems. We can only guess about the important ecological relationships that probably existed between sea cows, sea otters, and kelp forest communities.

Fur Trade

The sea otter fur trade, which began in 1741 when a Russian expedition discovered sea otters on the Commander Islands, had monumental historical and biological consequences in the North Pacific. Within fifty years, the Alaskan otter population had been nearly exterminated, leading the Russians to move south to California. By the early 1900s, sea otters were nearly extinct all along the Pacific Coast. Only 1,000–2,000 otters survived throughout their range. When the *International Fur Seal Treaty* of 1911 (Riedman 1997) established protection for sea otters, only thirteen small otter colonies persisted from the Kamchatka Peninsula south to Mexico. In 1968, the British Columbia government began a program to reintroduce sea otters. Some were taken from Amchitka Island in the Aleutian chain, and from Prince William Sound, and released in a remote part of northwestern Vancouver Island. Currently sea otters are considered threatened in the United States and Canada.

Whaling

Indigenous people along the Pacific coast started hunting whales about 6,000 years ago (Spalding 1998). In the far north, the Inuit of Alaska and the Canadian Arctic still are whale hunters. The commercial whale hunt along the Pacific coast started with whale sightings by early explorers such as Captain Cook. The Pacific soon turned into a major destination for whalers (Spalding 1998). Scammon's Lagoon in Mexico—a critical part of gray whale habitat—was the site of a sea of slaughter as hunters attacked whales of all sizes, driving gray whales to the brink of extinction (Earle 1995). Humpback whales, along with right and sperm whales, also suffered from overexploitation and showed signs of serious depletion by the mid-1800s.

Whale hunting reached its peak in the 1950s and 1960s, when the industry was killing more than 50,000 animals per year. Whaling continues today at a reduced level. The harvest of whales in the North Pacific released a substantial amount of biomass to other consumers, and reduced predation pressure on certain species. Some species, such as pollock, stood to benefit from the increase in prey resources. Along with large changes resulting from the removal of herring, yellow fin sole, and Pacific Ocean perch, the whale harvest could have contributed to changes such as: the development of a less diverse community and food web structure; and an increased sensitivity of the community to variability in the physical environment. Another hypothesis under consideration is that ecosystem change resulted from variability in patterns of weather and climate. In 1985, the International Whaling Commission (IWC) declared a moratorium on commercial whaling, but several nations declined to accept it. Norway, Japan, Russia, and Iceland have all violated the moratorium (Thorne-Miller 1999, Earle 1995).

Fishing

More than 25 percent of the world's fish populations are considered overexploited or depleted, and 40 percent heavily to fully exploited (Dayton et al. 1999). It is becoming increasingly clear that overexploitation not only diminishes populations of species and reduces economic return, but also causes genetic changes in the exploited populations and alters ecological relationships with the species' predators, symbiants, competitors, and prey (Dayton et al. 1999). Fishing affects not only the target species, but also exerts massive pressure on other species. According to Dayton et al. (1999:4) "the destructive impacts of fishing are widespread and so complete that we have few if any habitats worth fishing that have not already been heavily fished." The most serious environmental consequences of fishing are from bycatch, trawling, and dredging. Bycatch results in the almost complete removal or functional extinction of many air breathing marine species such as mammals, reptiles, and birds, as well as many species of elasmobranchs— cartilaginous fishes such as sharks, rays and skates—and other long-lived organisms (Dayton et al., 1999).

Trawls are funnel-shaped nets that are towed behind vessels. Animals are swept into the net and collect at the end of the funnel. As a result, the catch of nontarget species can be very high. Direct trawling effects include damage and often death of target and nontarget species due to contact with the trawl and physical alteration of the seabed. Frequent trawling of the seabed prevents recovery of the marine habitat, altering and impoverishing the physical structure of the ecosystem (Norse 1993).

Dredging is a widespread physical alteration to marine ecosystems, resulting in the alteration of the bottom topography, the destruction of biota and their habitat, and massive sediment resuspension (Norse 1993). Dredging also destroys benthic communities by killing juveniles of target species and epibenthic species. It also alters the substratum such that the community is colonized by opportunistic species capable of living in heavily disturbed habitats.

Other Human Influences

The impacts of salmon fish farming have received much public attention recently. The risks of salmon farming include: pollution and antibiotics entering the marine environment from rearing cages; infectious diseases being carried over to wild stocks; and colonization of rivers by escaped farm fish, including nonnative Atlantic species. These are real threats not only to the native salmon population, but also to other fish, shellfish, and marine mammals (B.C. Environmental Assessment Office, n.d.).

The marine environment is still being used as a dumpsite for much of our refuse. Many cities only have primary sewage treatment. Victoria, the capital of British Columbia, is a case in point. Ships of all sizes also dump refuse into the ocean, including sewage, solid wastes, and ballast. The dumping of ballast has been blamed for the introduction of alien species, which compete with native species and alter ecosystem structure. Abandoned fishnets and plastics floating in the ocean have caused many deaths to fish, marine mammals, and seabirds.

With increasing ship traffic, and the use of acoustic deterrent devices, noise pollution is becoming a potentially serious problem. Not much is known about the effects of noise pollution on the communication of marine mammals. The noise level may interfere with animals' sonar, making it more difficult to find and capture food. The low frequency background noise caused by boat traffic may also interfere with baleen whales using similar frequencies for communication. Acoustic deterrent devices use high frequency sounds to keep marine mammals away from places such as fish farms. These devices disrupt marine mammals' use of their natural habitats. Oil and gas exploration and development has the potential to cause massive habitat destruction. Oil spills, such as the infamous Exxon Valdez spill in 1989, threaten marine life. Seabirds, fish, shellfish, and eggs and larvae of all marine species are extremely vulnerable to oil spills.

Humans have had a profound impact on the oceans. In late 1990, eleven eminent marine biologists met at the Smithsonian Institute in Washington, D.C., to examine the basic dimensions of the marine biodiversity issue. Their conclusion was that "the entire marine realm—from estuaries to coastal waters to the open ocean and the deep sea—is at risk" (Norse 1993). Marine biodiversity is declining, and as a result ecosystem structure and function are less diverse and more vulnerable to additional

Photograph 11.2. Burnaby Strait in the proposed National Marine Conservation Area in Gwaii Haanas, British Columbia is an example of the spectacular west coast scenery that could support tourism development. Photo credit: Sabine Jessen

pressures. In addition, many of our marine habitats may not be able to adapt to climate change in years to come.

Conservation Initiatives

Definition and Role of MPAs

Marine protected areas (MPAs) have long-term legal protection. These areas include the seabed, water column, plants and animals, and their habitats. They can range in size from small to large, and can provide for different levels of protection; from harvest refugia areas completely closed to consumptive and, possibly, other human uses, to multiple-use areas which allow for human uses compatible with the conservation objectives of the area.

In order to ensure that the marine environment receives substantial protection, it is important that human activities that can cause long term, large-scale habitat disruption are prohibited in all MPAs. The following activities should be precluded in all MPAs: oil, gas, and mineral exploration and development; dredging; dumping; bottom trawling; and salmon and other aquaculture. Additional restrictions on human use in MPAs should be determined on a case-by-case basis.

Role of MPAs

Marine protected areas cannot solve all of the problems facing the ocean environment, but they are an important foundation. Evidence that MPAs are effective is surfacing worldwide, and increasingly marine scientists are calling for their use (Murray et al. 1999, Salomon et al. n.d., Sanchirico 2000).

MPAs provide many benefits. MPAs can protect productive ecosystems such as upwelling areas, kelp forests, and estuarine-areas essential to the life stages of marine flora and fauna. They can help serve as "seed bank" areas for the recruitment of groundfish and shellfish, and provide critical sanctuaries to endangered marine species, including the sea otter and killer whale. MPAs can protect commercial and recreational marine resources, and by providing for an array of outdoor recreation and tourism opportunities, they can also contribute social and economic benefits to coastal communities. Such benefits are critical to ensuring the long-term health and future of coastal communities. MPAs can provide for baseline scientific research and help to generate increased public awareness about marine ecosystems and threats to them. They serve as an important insurance policy against unforeseen impacts of future management errors or environmental changes, such as global climate change.

Moreover, MPAs represent a different way to look at how society interacts with the marine environment. The traditional focus has been species-by-species management approaches. MPAs force us to look at marine ecosystems, the role of individual species in these ecosystems, their supporting habitats, and how the different processes and parts are interrelated. In sum, MPAs require a more holistic or systems point of view.

Local community support for marine protected areas is critical. This support is necessary for the attitude shift to occur that will enable us to avoid further damaging the ocean. Education and raising awareness are essential components of MPA planning and management. So too is scientific and management information exchange between areas. MPAs can give local people a sense of stewardship and control over their own futures; this, in turn, fosters responsible attitudes towards the seas and coasts (Agardy 1997).

Table 11.1. Protected Areas in British Columbia with a Marine Component[a]

Classification	Ownership	Size (ha)	Fish Closures
1 national park	federal	21,390[b]	Some
5 migratory bird sanctuaries	federal	2,310[c]	Some
1 national wildlife area	federal	76	?
79 provincial parks and recreation areas	provincial	124,323[d]	Some
15 ecological reserves	provincial	46,651[e]	Some
TOTAL		194,750	

[a]A Canada-British Columbia-Haida agreement is under discussion to create a national marine conservation area, at Gwaii Haanas and Queen Charlottes. This would add 340,000 hectares (839,800 acres) to the MPA system (Jessen and Symington, pers. com. 1999). [b]One national park reserve (Pacific Rim), 21,390 hectares (52,883 acres); [c]Five migratory bird sanctuaries (federal), and 1 national wildlife area totaling 2,310 hectares (5,706 acres); [d]Seventy-nine provincial parks and recreation areas with a marine component, totaling 124,323 hectares (307 078 acres), thirty-four of which are over 200 hectares (494 acres), thirty of these include some fishing closures; and [e]Fifteen provincial ecological reserves with a marine component, totaling 46,651 hectares (115,228 acres), six of these are over 200 hectares (494 acres) and five with some fishing closures.

Existing Marine Protected Areas

The existing system of marine protected areas in the Baja California to Bering Sea Region is inadequate for a number of reasons. The system has many gaps and weaknesses. Most MPAs are small and represent discrete coastal and nearshore biogeographic features. Many have only limited ability to protect threatened resources. Some are not adequately managed or supported by local communities. Preliminary study of MPAs in the study region indicates that they do not function as a network.

Canada, Mexico, and the United States have all engaged in initiatives to protect certain parts of their marine heritage. However, many MPAs are small and established for recreational purposes, such as boat harbors. Such protected areas do little to preserve marine ecosystems. A map of the biogeographic provinces on the west coasts of North America is shown in volume 4 of the 1995 IUCN report *A Global Representative System of Marine Protected Areas.*

Canada : Canada has five federal legislative instruments to establish MPAs, only two of which are controlled by the same agency. These include

- *Canada Oceans Act*, Fisheries and Oceans Canada
- *Canada Wildlife Act*, Canadian Wildlife Service
- Migratory Bird Conservation Act, Canadian Wildlife Service
- *National Parks Act*, Parks Canada, and
- the proposed Marine Conservation Areas Act, Parks Canada

No legally designated marine protected areas have yet been created under the *Oceans Act*. Fisheries and Oceans Canada has five pilot MPAs intended to test aspects of the framework for establishing and managing MPAs (CEC, 1999). Pilot sites have no legal protection, nor are there timelines or action plans set out by the government to protect these sites. The federal government hopes to have a representative network of MPAs in place on the Pacific coast by 2010.

Most MPAs in British Columbia fall under the jurisdiction of British Columbia Parks, in the provincial Ministry of Environment, Lands and Parks. About 1,600 square kilometers (618 square miles), or less than 1 percent, of British Columbia's marine waters have some degree of protection, mostly concentrated in the coastal nearshore region. This 1,600 square kilometer area (618 square miles) is comprised of a national park, migratory bird sanctuaries and a national wildlife area, provincial parks, and ecological reserves (table 11.1).

On the Pacific coast of Canada, the federal and provincial governments are working together to develop a coordinated marine protected areas strategy for establishing a network of MPAs by the year 2010. The strategy also promotes shared decision making with indigenous peoples, the public, and other stakeholders. To date, however, detailed management plans and comprehensive fishery closures are lacking for the marine component of existing MPAs. In addition, neither the federal nor provincial government have adopted even minimum protection standards for all marine protected areas. The contribution of these sites to marine biodiversity conservation is limited (Symington, pers. com. 1999).

Mexico : According to the Mexican Commission for the Knowledge and Use of Biodiversity (México, CONABIO, 1998), Mexico has forty-three natural protected areas with marine and/or coastal components. Of these forty-three, only twelve have areas larger than 100,000 hectares (247,000 acres), and fourteen have areas smaller than 100 hectares (247 acres). The total protected area with marine components in the Baja California region—the Mexican north Pacific, the Baja California coast the Gulf of California, and the Sea of Cortez—is slightly above 2 million hectares (4,940,000 acres) (table 11.2). According to the Mexican National Institute of Ecology (Instituto Nacional de Ecología), however, there are only thirty-one MPAs in the Mexican territory, totaling 7,863,591 hectares (19,423,070 acres) (including both land and water) (CEC 1999 draft).

Table 11.2. Protected Areas with a Marine Component in the Sea of Cortez and the Pacific Coast of Baja California, Mexico[b]

Classification	Designation	Number	Fish Closures
Biosphere reserves	Federal	4	Some
National parks	Federal	1	Yes
Flora and Fauna Protection Area	Federal	1	No

[b] México, CONABIO 1998.

CONABIO states that there is a discrepancy between both terrestrial and marine protected areas on paper and in practice. Most areas do not have a management plan and, even those that do, are generally not managed properly (México, CONABIO, 1998). The report further emphasizes that careful marine classification of Mexico's marine protected areas and their conservation status is needed.

The United States (including Alaska) : The key federal government resource agency with a mandate for ocean-related matters in the United States is the National Oceanic and Atmospheric Administration (U.S., NOAA). Marine protected areas in the United States fall under the following categories of managers:
- National Marine Sanctuary Program administered by the Office of Ocean and Coastal Resource Management (OCRM);
- National Estuarine Research Reserve System under OCRM, National Ocean Service (NOS), and NOAA;
- National Estuary Program administered by the US Environmental Protection Agency (EPA);
- National Wildlife Refuge System administered by the US Fish and Wildlife Service;
- National Park, National Recreation Area and National Seashore system by the National Park Service; and
- Essential Fish Habitat Project administered by the National Marine Fisheries Service.

National Marine Sanctuary Program: The National Marine Sanctuary Program provides for the protection of areas within U.S. waters of special national significance. Administered by the NOAA, five sanctuaries are located along the Pacific Coast (table 11.3). These are: Olympic Coast; Cordell Bank; Gulf of the Farallones, Monterey Bay; and Channel Islands National Marine Sanctuaries. Combined, these marine sanctuaries cover an area of 31,180 square kilometers (12,039 square miles).

Table 11.3. Protected Areas in the Pacific Coast of the United States
with a Marine Component

Classification	Designation	Number	Fish Closures
CALIFORNIA[a]			
Ecological preserves	Federal	1	Some
National marine sanctuaries	Federal	4	No
National parks (national park, national seashore, national recreation area, national research natural area, national monument)	Federal	6	Some
Biosphere reserves	Int'l and federal	2	No
Areas of special biological significance	State	34	Some
Coastal sanctuaries	State	1	Some
Ecological reserves	State	10	Some
Marine resources protection act ecological reserves	State	4	Some
Reserves	State	7	Some
Parks (beaches, historic areas, natural preserves, reserves, and underwater parks)	State	14	Some
Refuges (clam, fish, game, and marine life)	State	20	Some
U.C. natural reserves	State	1	Some
CALIFORNIA TOTAL		104	
OREGON[b]			
Marine gardens	State	7	
Shellfish reserves	State	3	
Research reserves	State	8	
Estuarine research reserve	Federal	1	
National estuary sites	Federal	2	
Biosphere reserve	Int'l and federal	1	
OREGON TOTAL		22	
WASHINGTON[c]			
State parks	State	109	Some
Conservation areas	State	3	Some
Natural resource area	Federal	10	Some
Natural area preserve	State	6	Some
National Wildlife Refuge	Federal	5	Some
Natural estuarine research reserve	Federal	1	Some
National estuary program	Federal	2	No
Biosphere reserve	Federal	1	No
WASHINGTON TOTAL		137	
ALASKA[d]			
Refuges	State	7	Some
Critical habitat areas	State	17	Some
National sanctuaries	Federal	3	Some
ALASKA TOTAL		27	

[a] adapted from: McArdle 1997. [b] Didier 1998. [c] Robinson 1999. [d] Kelleher et al. 1995.

Concern has been expressed that national marine sanctuaries provide limited protection of the marine environment. Dayton et al. (1999) suggest that the sanctuary system must begin by including zones that are closed to all fishing. A process to identify such zones has recently begun for the Channel Islands National Park that would result in 10,118 hectares (25,000 acres), or 20 percent of the area, being declared no-take reserves.

Photograph 11.3. Extractive activities, such as this offshore oil and gas rig just outside of the Channel Islands Marine Sanctuary in California, threaten marine resources along North America's west coast. Photo credit: Sabine Jessen

National Estuarine Research Reserves: NOAA also operates a system of national estuarine research reserves, the newest of which is currently in the designation process in Kachemak Bay to the southeastern entrance to Cook Inlet. NOAA also operates an estuarine reserve in the Tijuana Estuary, adjacent to the Mexican border—the Tijuana River National Estuarine Research Reserve (Roper, et al., this volume).

State MPA Programs: California has a total of 104 marine protected areas under twelve different types of designations including four of the national marine sanctuaries noted above, and two biosphere reserves. State designations account for ninety-one sites. These MPAs range in size from 2.4 hectares (six acres) to the 404,700 hectare (one million acre) Central California Coast Biosphere Reserve. Most are located inshore and adjacent to the coastline. Recreational fishing is permitted in ninety-three MPAs and commercial fishing in ninety-four. Nine MPAs do not provide for any fish harvest. They encompass about 2,428 hectares (6,000 acres) and about thirty-two kilometers (twenty miles) of California coastline. In assessing the current system of MPAs in California, McArdle (1997) notes that there is a problem of overlapping boundaries and designations and that many do not have clearly defined management goals or plans. Lack of financial resources is also a severe impediment to ongoing management and research. Finally, the jurisdictional division of responsibilities between federal and state agencies, especially related to fishing, has impeded the management of living marine resources according to management plans.

The California Resources Agency established a Marine Managed Area Task Force to review the current system of MPAs, and to recommend ways to enhance fish stocks and determine a possible role for no-take reserves (Polakovic 1999). In a draft report, the Resources Agency of California concludes that through a mix of legislative and administrative actions, California's array of state marine managed areas can be redesigned as a system to protect ocean and coastal resources more effectively (California, Resources Agency of California 1999).

In Washington, the state institutions with a role in MPAs are the Departments of Natural Resources, Fish and Wildlife and Ecology, the Washington State Parks and Recreation Commission, and the University of Washington's Friday Harbor Laboratories. Washington has 137 MPAs, which have recently been catalogued and described in a series of reports (Murray 1998, Robinson 1999). Of this total, 102 are in Puget Sound. Protection and enforcement of these sites has been limited, and most are multiple-use oriented with little to no regulation of extractive activities. Three are considered to be "no-take" zones, all of which are located in Puget Sound (Robinson 1999).

Oregon has few MPAs along its 241 kilometers (150 miles) shore. Eleven kilometers (seven miles) of coastline are designated as marine gardens, and 17.7 kilometers (eleven miles) as research reserves. These sites fall under the Oregon Territorial Sea Plan, which provides a framework for state agencies to regulate consumptive and nonconsumptive uses. The sites consist of protected shoreline areas with some protection stretching into the nearshore intertidal area. Generally there are no restrictions on fishing within either designation (CEC 1999).

As of 1995, Alaska had seven refuges, seventeen critical habitat areas, and three sanctuaries (Kelleher, Bleakley, and Wells 1995). The Alaska State Legislature has classified these special areas as essential to the protection of fish and wildlife habitat. The areas are managed by the Alaska Department of Fish and Game, and are usually managed for multiple uses but controlled to prevent habitat changes harmful to the flora and fauna or their habitat. The Glacier Bay National Park and Preserve encompasses 1,121,019 hectares (2,770,000 acres) of marine waters along the Alaskan

Panhandle. A cooperative management plan has been implemented for the regulation of commercial fisheries within the park (CEC 1999).

New Approaches to Conservation

Since the early 1990s, the principles of conservation biology have been applied to several conservation initiatives. The most notable of these is the Yellowstone to Yukon Conservation Initiative (Y2Y). Such initiatives are rooted in conservation biology and aim to realize a series of core-protected areas, connected by wildlife corridors, and surrounded by buffer zones.

To date, such initiatives have been wholly terrestrial, but could in principle be applied to marine environments. The experience gained through the Y2Y initiative will be valuable in setting up a similar project for the Baja California to Bering Sea marine region.

The Y2Y Model

The Yellowstone to Yukon Initiative is a joint Canada-US network of over 140 organizations, institutions, and foundations, plus individual scientists, conservationists, economists, and environmental advocates. They have recognized both the necessity and the advantages of coordinating their efforts transnationally, on a scale that mirrors the area they seek to conserve. The Baja California to Bering Sea Initiative will be based on the Y2Y experience.

Y2Y belongs to the new global family of far-sighted, broad-based biodiversity strategies that have arisen in response to the insights, interpretations, and lessons of conservation biology. The mission is to build and maintain a life-sustaining system of core protected reserves and connecting wildlife movement corridors, both of which will be further insulated from the impact of industrial development by transition or buffer zones. Existing national, state, and provincial parks and wilderness areas anchor the system, while the creation of new protected areas and the conservation and restoration of critical segments of ecosystems will provide the cores, corridors, and transition zones needed to complete it.

Y2Y Guiding Principles

- Y2Y is a network whose governance is democratic, consensual, and participatory. Cooperators acknowledge and value the work of all individuals and all organizations seeking to conserve wildlife and wildlands across the Y2Y region, and they encourage any and all of like minds and ambition to help evolve their program and implement their vision (Y2Y Conservation Initiative n.d.).

- Y2Y seeks to enable, inspire, and energize all individuals and organizations engaged in bringing the principles and practices of conservation biology to localities within the Y2Y region.

- In conjunction with its support for wildlands and wildlife, Y2Y supports, promotes, and encourages the development of sustainable communities and all human activities compatible with the principles of conservation biology within the Y2Y area. Of particular note, Y2Y supports the work of aboriginal communities to safeguard their traditional territories and to ensure the survival of their traditional cultures.

- Y2Y encompasses conservation initiatives that transcend traditional boundaries and borders. Regardless of political boundaries, Y2Y seeks to protect the web of life across public lands—national, state, and provincial parks and wilderness areas—and private lands protected through voluntary conservation programs.

- Y2Y will generate innovative products and tools designed to serve the conservation needs of its network cooperators and the needs of the region. Y2Y participants are working with an Environmental and Cultural Resource Atlas to identify environmental threats and conservation opportunities within the Y2Y sphere.

- Y2Y will initiate and promote events and activities that further the principles of doing together what we cannot do alone.

- Y2Y participants organized a U.S. Canada Forum in which eminent scientists, conservationists, and cultural interpreters addressed regional issues. Workshops were designed to offer activists the opportunity to develop the competencies, establish the contacts, and coinvent the strategies needed to realize the Y2Y vision.

- Y2Y will raise funds solely to support those activities and projects individual groups would not or could not do by themselves.

The B2B Initiative

The Baja California to Bering Sea initiative (B2B) is a cooperative, trinational initiative launched by the British Columbia Chapter of the

Canadian Parks and Wilderness Society. The aim is to establish a network of marine protected areas based on the principles of conservation biology. The ultimate goal is to maintain and restore biodiversity along the 10,000-kilometer reach from Baja California, Mexico to the Bering Sea, Alaska, one of the temperate world's most productive and diverse marine environments. Like Y2Y, B2B aims to link activism and science to generate measurable results. It will provide a forum for learning from collective experiences, and the opportunity to establish protected areas that extend across national boundaries.

In all three countries along the Pacific Coast of North America, long-term conservation strategies are urgently needed to ensure the survival of the many species that call this area home. The approach is to link a network of MPAs with other conservation efforts that will ensure the protection of fully functioning marine ecosystems, and provide for the long-term survival of the full range of marine species. For example, we will work with marine scientists to explore the potential of the *connecting corridors concept* in the marine environment. Such corridors would serve to link individual protected areas, helping to ensure the long-term protection of marine biodiversity.

There are common issues and linkages in the marine environment along the Pacific Coast of North America, and the need exists to foster greater cooperation across national borders to better protect this environment. This has led us to initiate the development of a network of individuals and organizations to collaborate on a B2B campaign. Organizations are working in each country on important marine conservation projects. A larger, cooperative network will build on the strength of these existing initiatives and explore new conservation opportunities for the Pacific Coast as a whole.

Conclusion

Humans have significantly altered the highly interconnected north Pacific marine environment in the past 100 years. Marine biological diversity is threatened at the genetic, species, and ecosystem levels as a result of human exploitation. However, precisely because of the interconnectedness provided by the water medium, the marine environment will likely have the capacity to regenerate if given the chance. Some MPAs currently exist, but the system is inadequate if only because many protected areas are of insufficient size and are not managed adequately to achieve conservation objectives.

The emphasis in marine reserve design must be on a representative network of large and connected areas, larger yet than the terrestrial counterparts. In the sea, currents disperse sediments, nutrients, pollutants, and organisms. Because of the ability of wind and tide generated currents to mix water masses, events originating outside the boundaries of a MPA may affect populations within it. However, partly for the same reasons, it is generally true that marine ecosystems have a capacity for restocking and regeneration exceeding that of terrestrial communities (IUCN 1992). As a consequence, marine habitats are rarely precisely or critically restricted for conservation purposes. In addition, our knowledge and understanding of marine environments is far behind that of terrestrial ecosystems. Thus, in creating MPAs, we must use the precautionary approach and protect large areas of the representative marine ecosystems.

The B2B initiative uses the principles of conservation biology to protect the marine environment. This initiative offers a new approach and new hope for the marine biodiversity. The cooperation of nongovernmental organizations, government departments, indigenous peoples, institutions, scientists, communities, and individuals to protect the Baja California to Bering Sea region will likely create public awareness, and the political will necessary for action to ensue. Such a community may succeed in developing and implementing a comprehensive plan of complementary actions to ensure that future generations—of humans and wildlife—will enjoy the biological riches that define the Baja California to Bering region.

References

Agardy, T. S. 1997. *Marine Protected Areas and Ocean Conservation.* San Diego: Academic Press.

Andres, B. A., and G. A. Falxa. 1995. "Black Oystercatcher Haematopus bachmani", pp. 1-20. In *The Birds of North America, No. 155,* ed. A. Poole and F. Gill. Philadelphia: The Academy of Natural Sciences and Washington, D.C.: The American Ornithologists' Union.

Bloeser, J.A. 1999. *Diminishing Returns: The Status of West Coast Rockfish.* Astoria, Oreg.: Pacific Marine Conservation Council.

California. Resources Agency of California. 1999. *California's State Classification System for Marine Managed Areas. Draft Report of the State Interagency Marine Managed Areas Workgroup.* Sacramento, Calif.: Resources Agency of California.

Cannings, R., S. Cannings, and M. de Jong Westman. 1999. *Life in the Pacific Ocean.* Vancouver: Graystone Books.

Commission for Environmental Cooperation (CEC). 1999. *Marine Protected Areas in North America: Background Paper for the Workshop on Marine Protected Areas, Baja California, Mexico, November 1999. Draft.* Montreal: Commission for Environmental Cooperation.

Connor, J., and C. Baxter. 1989. *Kelp Forests.* Monterey, Calif.: Monterey Bay Aquarium.

Croom, M., R. Wolotira, and W. Henwood. 1995. "Marine Region 15: Northeast Pacific," pp. 55-106. In *A Global Representative System of Marine Protected Areas,* ed. G. Kelleher, C. Bleakley, and S. Wells. Vol. IV. Washington, D.C.: The Great Barrier Reef Marine Park Authority, The World Bank, and The World Conservation Union IUCN.

Dayton, P., E. Sala, M. J. Tegner, and S. Thrush. 1999. "Marine Protected Areas: Parks, Baselines, and Fishery Enhancement." *Bulletin of Marine Science* in press.

Earle, S. A. 1995. *Sea Change: A Message of the Oceans.* New York: Fawcell Columbine.

Estes, J. A., and M. Carr. 1999. "Planning for the Conservation and Management of Coastal Marine Resources in British Columbia." Unpublished Paper.

Gordon, D. G., and A. Baldridge. 1991. *Gray Whales.* Monterey, Calif.: Monterey Bay Aquarium.

IUCN. 1992. *Guidelines for Establishing Marine Protected Areas. A Marine Conservation and Development Report.* Gland, Switzerland: International Union for the Conservation of Nature.

_____. 1995. *A Global Representative System of Marine Protected Areas: Volume IV: South Pacific, Northeast Pacific, Northwest Pacific, Southeast Pacific and Australia/New Zealand.* Washington, D.C.: The World Bank.

Kelleher, G., C. Bleakley, and S. Wells. 1995. *A Global Representative System of Marine Protected Areas. Volume IV: South Pacific, Northeast Pacific, Northwest Pacific, Southeast Pacific and Australia/New Zealand.* Washington, D.C.: The Great Barrier Reef Marine Park Authority, The World Bank, The World Conservation Union.

McArdle, D. A. 1997. *Marine Protected Areas of California: A Summary of a Conference Session.* Santa Barbara, Calif.: University of California.

México. CONABIO. 1998. *Regiones Priotarias Marinas de México.* D.F., México: Comisión Nacional para el Conocimiento y Uso de la Biodiversidad.

Miller, B., R. Reading, J. Strittholt, C. Carroll, R. Noss, M. Soule, O. Sanchez, J. Terborgh, D. Brightsmith, T. Cheeseman, and D. Foreman. 1999. "Using Focal Species in the Design of Nature Reserve Networks." *Wild Earth* 8(4): 81-92.

Murray, M. R. 1998. *The Status of Marine Protected Areas in Puget Sound. Volumes I and II.* Environmental Report Series no. 8. N.P.: Puget Sound/Georgia Basin International Task Force, Work Group on Marine Protected Areas.

Murray, S. N., R. F. Ambrose, J. A. Bohnsack, L. W. Botsford, M. H. Carr, G. E. Davis, P. K. Dayton, D. Gotshall, D. R. Gunderson, M. A. Hixon, J. Lubchenco, M. Mangel, A. MacCall, D. A. McArdle, J. C. Ogden, J. Roughgarden, R. M. Starr, M. J. Tegner and M. M. Yoklavich. 1999. "No-Take Reserve Networks: Protection for Fishery Populations and Marine Ecosystems." *Fisheries* Nov.

Norse, E. A. 1993. *Global Marine Biological Diversity: A Strategy for Building Conservation into Decision Making.* Washington, D.C.: Island Press.

North Pacific Universities. Marine Mammal Research Consortium. 1998. *Annual Report 1997-1998.* n.p.: North Pacific Universities Marine Mammal Research Consortium.

Noss, R. F. 1997. "The Principles of Conservation Biology In Action," pp. 22-32. In *Connections: Proceedings from the First Yellowstone to Yukon Conservation Initiative,* ed. H. Locke. Canmore, Alta.: Yellowstone to Yukon Conservation Initiative, 22-32.

_____. 1995. *Maintaining Ecological Integrity in Representative Reserve Networks.* Toronto and Washington, D.C.: World Wildlife Fund-Canada and World Wildlife Fund-United States.

Pauly, D., T. Pitcher, and D. Preikshot. 1998. "Epilogue: Reconstructing the Past and Rebuilding the Future of the Strait of Georgia," pp. 92-93. In *Back to the Future: Reconstructing the Strait of Georgia Ecosystem,* eds. D. Pauly, T. Pitcher, and D. Preikshot. Fisheries Centre Research Report 65. Vancouver: The Fisheries Centre, University of British Columbia.

Pitcher, T. J. 1998. "Pleistocene Pastures: Steller's Sea Cow and Sea Otters in the Strait of Georgia," pp. 48-52. In *Back to the Future: Reconstructing the Strait of Georgia Ecosystem*, ed. D. Pauly, T. Pitcher, and D. Preikshot. Research Report. 65. Vancouver: The Fisheries Centre, University of British Columbia, Fisheries Centre

Pacific Marine Conservation Council (PMCC). 1999. *Diminishing Returns: The Status of West Coast Rockfish*. Astoria, Oreg.: Pacific Marine Conservation Council.

Polakovic, Gary. 27 August 1999. "Saving a Place for Marine Life." *Los Angeles Times.* http://www.pcffa.org/mpacal1.htm

Recchia, C., and J. Broadhead. 1995. "Marine Protected Areas," pp. 9-17. In *Protecting Canada's Endangered Spaces,* ed. M. Hummel. Toronto: Key Porter Books.

Riedman, M. 1997. *Sea Otters*. Monterey, Calif.: Monterey Bay Aquarium.

Robinson, M. K. 1999. *The Status of Washington's Coastal Marine Protected Areas*. Olympia, WA: Washington Department of Fish and Wildlife.

Salomon, Anne K., Nigel Walter, Cariad McIlhagga, Regina Yung, Carl J. Walters. n.d. "Modeling the Trophic Effects of Marine Protected Area Zoning Policies: A Case Study on the Proposed Gwaii Haanas National Marine Conservation Area. Unpublished paper.

Sanchirico, James. 2000. "Marine Protected Areas: Can They Revitalize Our Nation's Fisheries?" *Resources* 140, Summer 2000: 6-9.

Symington, K. 15 June 1999. Personal communication between S. Jessen and marine campaign coordinator, CPAWS, Vancouver, B.C.

Soulé, M. E., and J. Terborgh. 1999. "The Policy and Science of Regional Conservation," pp. 1-17. In *Continental Conservation: Scientific Foundations of Regional Reserve Networks*, ed. M. E. Soulé and J. Terborgh. Washington, D.C.: Island Press.

Spalding, D. A. E. 1998. *Whales of the West Coast*. Madeira Park, B.C.: Harbour Publishing.

Thorne-Miller, B. 1999. *The Living Ocean: Understanding and Protecting Marine Biodiversity. Second Edition.* Washington, D.C.: Island Press and Sea Web.

United States. National Oceanic and Atmospheric Administration (NOAA). 1999. *National Marine Mammal Laboratory.* NOAA website: http://nmml01.afsc.noaa.gov/ AlaskaEcosystems/sslhome/index.htm. Accessed December 21, 1999.

Yellowstone to Yukon Conservation (Y2Y) Initiative. n.d. *The Yellowstone to Yukon Conservation Initiative to Restore and Protect the Wild Heart of North America.* A pamphlet published by the Yellowstone to Yukon Conservation Initiative, Canmore, Alta.

Zacharias, Mark A., John R. Harper, and Peter Wainwright. 1998. "The British Columbia Marine Ecosystem Classification: Rational, Development, and Verification." *Coastal Management* 26: 105-124.

United States of America

THE TIJUANA RIVER NATIONAL ESTUARINE RESEARCH RESERVE

Tessa Roper, J. G. Nelson, and J. C. Day

Abstract

The Tijuana River National Estuarine Research Reserve (TRNERR) is a 2,500-acre nature preserve located at the southwestern-most corner of the United States, next to the U.S.-Mexico border. A twelve-member board—representing state, federal, and local agencies as well as academic and nonprofit sector interests—manages the reserve. The major agencies are the U.S. Fish & Wildlife Service and California State Parks. It is one of twenty-five national estuarine research reserves under NOAA, the National Oceanic and Atmospheric Administration. TRNERR is an island of natural habitat and green spaces surrounded by the vast metropolitan region of San Diego-Tijuana. It is of special interest because of the ecological and social services it offers to this large urban region. TRNERR represents some of the last remaining habitat of its type in California, where 90 percent of historical coastal wetlands have been lost to development and other factors. TRNERR is located at the terminus of a 1,750-square mile watershed, of which 70 percent is located in Mexico and the remainder in the United States. Over 370 different bird species have been sighted at the reserve, of which seven are endangered. A variety of projects and associated challenges take place at TRNERR, including restoration and education, cooperative endeavors with Mexican partners, water quality monitoring, local public outreach and education, and diverse research activities.

Photograph 12.1. Where the Tijuana Estuary meets the Pacific Ocean, looking north toward Imperial Beach, CA. Photo credit: J.C. Day

Establishment, Purposes, Context

The designation of the Tijuana Estuary (Pritchard 1967) as one of NOAA's national estuarine research reserves, reflects recognition that it represents a significant site for research and education on one of the regional types of estuarine systems in the United States. An extensive review process in the 1970s and early 1980s resulted in the selection of the Tijuana Estuary as a national wildlife refuge in 1981, and a national estuarine reserve in 1982. Results of research on the site were seen as valuable, not only in the locality but the entire natural region of which the Tijuana Estuary is part (Zedler, Nordby, and Kus 1992).

The Tijuana Estuary is located entirely within San Diego County, California. However, three quarters of its watershed lies in Mexico (fig. 12.1). The source of the Tijuana River is in the mountains of Baja California. Water flows from Cottonwood Creek on the U.S. side across the border to join the main stem in Baja before it crosses back into the U.S.

The Tijuana Estuary is a highly variable ecosystem, which has been termed an "intermittent estuary" (Zedler, Nordby, and Kus 1992:3). During the relatively rainy winter, stream flow freshens the estuarine waters. During the drier part of the year, the estuary is little more than an extension of the salty Pacific Ocean. The estuary is not a major

Figure 12.1 Tijuana Estuary and watershed

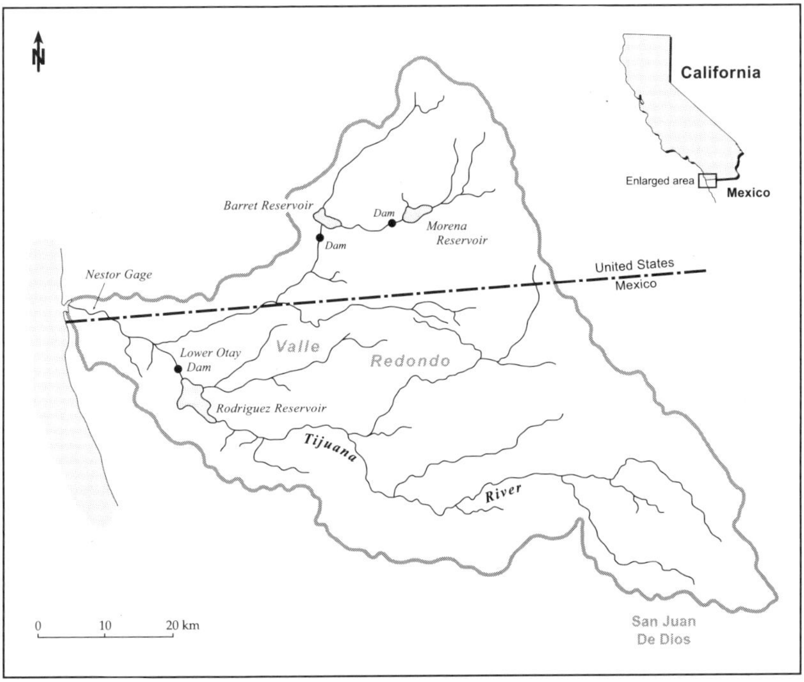

embayment but, rather, a series of channels with a relatively narrow route to the ocean, which has been open to tidal flushing throughout most of the years of record (Photograph 12.1). An intertidal zone supports salt marsh, with mud and sand flats covering only a relatively small part of the area. Figure 12.2 is a map of habitat types of the Tijuana Estuary.

The Tijuana Estuary has been subject to substantial disturbance by both natural processes and human activities (Zedler, Nordby, and Kus 1992; Entrix, PERL, and PWA 1991). Although floods are not frequent events, they can cause major changes in the estuary and its watershed. Flooding in 1980, for example, broadened the riverbed and changed its course. In winter 1983, storms washed sand dunes into the main channel and removed two salt marsh islands. The opening of the estuary to the ocean was blocked in spring 1984, preventing tidal flushing until it was reopened by dredging months later.

The coastal climate and vegetation of southern California are similar to other Mediterranean climates in southern Europe, Africa, Chile, and

Figure 12.2 Habitat Types at Tijuana Estuary

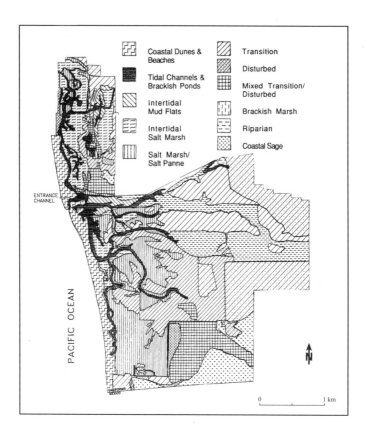

Australia. This is a climate of extremes. Some years can have virtually no rainfall and runoff. Others can have winter storms and severe floods. In general, rainfall and runoff are highly variable. The average annual precipitation is twenty-five centimeters (ten inches). Yet in the 140-year period of record from 1850 through mid-1990, only twenty-one years, or 15 percent of the record, had annual precipitation that fell within 10 percent of the long-term mean (Zedler, Nordby, and Kus 1992).

At all weather stations within the Tijuana watershed, evaporation exceeds precipitation in nearly every month. Hot dry winds can also have a major impact on plants and animals. In fact, all these irregular fluctuations in weather and climate place high stress on the plants, animals, and ecosystems of the Tijuana Estuary and surrounding areas.

Photograph 12.2. The Tijuana Slough research reserve habitats will benefit from the binational sewage treatment facilities under construction by the International Boundary and Water Commission.
Photo credit: J.C. Day.

Ecosystem Disturbance, Valued Species, and Ownership

The reserve is located in an urbanizing area where historic settlement and land use, population growth, and economic development have disturbed and placed much pressure on ecosystems. Sewage disposal practices have presented problems over the years, as have gravel mining, long-term dumping and filling, dike and road construction, and extensive use of off-road vehicles. Military, agricultural, and horse-raising activities have left their marks throughout the southern half of the estuary (Zedler, Nordby, and Kus 1992). Recreational activities are increasing today in parallel with growth in population and income. New disturbances have also arisen with increased illegal immigration into the U.S. through the reserve since the early 1980s. In response, the U.S. Border Patrol roams the reserve area in all-terrain vehicles that cause soil erosion, damage to habitats, nest destruction, and other ecosystem changes. Yet, in comparison to other similar estuaries along the southwest coast of California, the Tijuana Estuary, although battered, is in a condition closer to that of less disturbed estuarine systems in Baja California, Mexico, than more heavily disturbed systems nearer San Diego and Los Angeles in the United States.

Figure 12.3 Historic changes
to the tidal prism of Tijuana Estuary

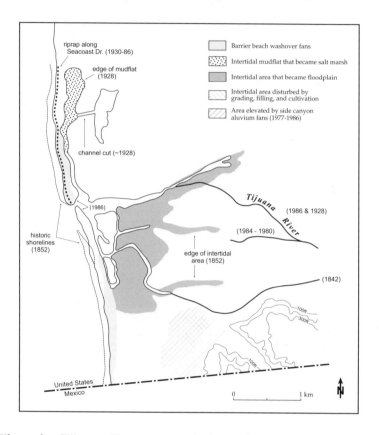

When the Tijuana Estuary was designated as a national estuarine research reserve, one significant consideration was that the site was viewed as relatively undisturbed for a region generally "characterized by degraded wetland and estuarine systems" (Zedler, Nordby, and Kus 1992:5). The site was also recognized as providing habitat for several protected bird species, and as a critical stopover, or staging area, on the Pacific flyway between South and Central America, Mexico, the U.S., and Canada. Only a few water bodies like it had escaped major disruptions by highways, railways, and other developments. A map of changes in the estuary from 1852–1985 is shown in figure 12.3.

Land ownership in and around the research reserve is complex and has required innovative collaborative approaches and stewardship among government agencies, universities, and private organizations in the area. The 2,531 acre (1,024 hectare) NERR site includes: 505 acres (204 hectares) in an endangered species refuge owned by the U.S. Fish and Wildlife Service (FWS); 551 acres (223 hectares) of U.S. Navy land administered by FWS; 418 acres (169 hectares) in Border Field State Park; lands purchased for the NERR to which the city of San Diego has title; San Diego County lands; and some small private inholdings. The County of San Diego is also buying land upstream for a regional park. On the Mexican side of the border the Tijuana River has been converted for long stretches in Tijuana, into a concrete-lined flood-control channel (Zedler, Nordby, and Kus 1992).

Management

Under these circumstances, the reserve has to be managed cooperatively if the process is to be at all effective. In this respect, the mission of the NERR reflects the missions of the three major agencies: NOAA, the U.S. Fish & Wildlife Service's Refuge Program, and California State Parks. The latter is the lead agency in implementing the national research reserve. It created a management authority having broad membership from resource agencies, the county, and two cities. A manager and an education coordinator were employed early on and additional land was secured for the reserve, including the potential site of a power plant. Funding was eventually found for a visitor center, and for ongoing monitoring and research carried out by the Pacific Estuarine Research Laboratory of San Diego State University, which has played a fundamental research role in the area for several decades. The U.S. Fish & Wildlife Service continues to play a pivotal role in the protection of endangered species in the area.

The *Management Plan* is a key element around which the participating agencies build their collaborative efforts. Following the first *Management Plan* released in 1986 (Dobbin and Associates), a series of additional plans, including the latest *Management Plan* (California, Department of Parks and Recreation, U.S. Fish and Wildlife Service, and U.S. National Oceanic and Atmospheric Administration 1999), have focused on an adaptive management approach through long-term monitoring, field studies, manipulative experiments, and restoration.

Tijuana Estuary is a rich laboratory for science. The vegetation-monitoring program that began in 1979 documented several distinct disturbance events. However, many effects were unquantified (e.g., changes to benthic invertebrates and fishes). Monitoring was extended to include channel waters and regular sampling of benthic invertebrates and fishes in 1986. Bird monitoring still needs to be added. Long-term systematic sampling focused to identify cause–effect relationships is an appropriate approach for an estuary that is subject to a highly variable environment. The long-term data track in turn provides an excellent backdrop for specific studies of population, community, and ecosystem dynamics. (Zedler, Nordby, and Kus 1992:123)

Monitoring, research, and education programs at the reserve are carried on interactively with support from a number of agencies and organizations. The State Resource Agency (Environmental License Plate Fund) and the State Coastal Conservancy have sponsored construction of native plant nurseries and large wetland habitats as part of restoration efforts. The wetland habitats provide essential refuges during major ecosystem disturbances, attract animals, and help ascertain how vegetation and salinity influence their use of the area (Zedler et al. 1992).

A vigorous research program at the Tijuana River NERR is essential to the reduction of environmental impacts that plague it and other estuarine habitats along the southern California coast. Many of these impacts have been referred to earlier in this paper. They include sedimentation, beach and dune erosion, stream flow modifications, wastewater discharges, and water quality generally.

Efforts to deal with these and related problems continue to focus on monitoring, research, education, and habitat mitigation and restoration. A number of fairly large-scale habitat restoration projects have been undertaken in the reserve. Restoration is, however, inherently fraught with difficulties for a variety of reasons. According to Zedler and colleagues (1992:139), these include:

- Trying to construct in a short time a system that developed in the absence of man (*sic*) over about five thousand years.
- Determining how the current wetlands developed—there are no blueprints to indicate how the topography developed, what species arrived first, what processes occurred to shape existing communities, what rare and extreme events influence the occurrence and abundance of species.

- Understanding dependencies among the components of the wetland—how species tolerate or depend on specific environmental conditions, how one species uses another as cover or food, or habitat for reproduction.
- Predicting how the dynamics of various populations will change in new surroundings; not enough long-term data are available to know how variable populations can be and still persist in perpetuity. It is unrealistic to expect stability once a habitat is constructed.
- Understanding what factors confer resilience to species and communities. Pickleweed is a good invader after some disturbances, and persists well under a variety of other disturbances. Tolerance to a wide range of salinities and inundation regimes appears to be important to pickleweed's resilience, but we have minimal understanding of why other species are less resilient.
- Lack of experience in constructing wetlands which would provide the basis for predicting the kinds of problems that will arise during construction.

In spite of these challenges and difficulties, or perhaps better to say because of them, Zedler and colleagues conclude that the adaptive management approach is the proper one in light of these uncertainties. Indeed, the Tijuana Estuary offers a standard for all restoration programs in the southern California coastal region. It seems appropriate, however, to move beyond this conclusion and say that the establishment of estuarine and coastal research reserves—through their collaborative monitoring, research, education, and restoration programs—are a necessary part of our attempts to understand and respond to diverse and interactive human impacts, not only in relatively unaltered situations but also in more disturbed urban ecosystems. Research reserves in relatively undisturbed situations can provide knowledge of how ecosystems work in circumstances where there is little human impact. This knowledge can help us understand and deal with changes in more heavily settled and impacted areas. Research reserves in more heavily settled and impacted areas can help us to understand details of the changes and processes involved. This knowledge can be used to protect and restore threatened wildlife, water quality, or other vital functions of natural areas through adaptive management based on monitoring, research, education, conservation, and restoration.

Current Challenges and Needs

Tijuana River NERR faces many challenges today, in great part due to its enveloping urban surroundings with rapidly growing populations in both countries that exert significant pressures on natural habitats and the ecological services that they provide to all life. Sedimentation from eroding upstream settlements as well as U.S. Border Patrol enforcement activities is severe, necessitating a series of sediment retention basins that are planned for key areas. The U.S.-Mexico border, which bisects the watershed, is particularly problematic. Regulation, funding, and other government supported solutions to erosion, pollution, and other watershed problems often stop at the border, while the ecosystems do not. A new, third border fence planned by the U.S. Immigration and Naturalization Service parallel to the current fences could destroy portions of the remaining unique coastal sage scrub habitat, put archaeological sites at risk, add to the sedimentation problem, and severely detract from long-term recreational opportunities on the southern side of the reserve.

A new primary sewage treatment plant and outfall pipe has recently been built to handle Mexican and American sewage flow into the Tijuana River and Estuary, and a secondary plant is under construction. While sewage discharges into the estuary have significantly decreased, wet weather flows that overwhelm the treatment facilities will continue to plague the area, as will industrial pollutants from upstream factories with improper waste disposal systems. Even given the observations of non-governmental organizations that the recently adopted sewage treatment system is not perfect (Ricks 2000), it is a great improvement over the situation that prevailed before international agreement was reached to begin solving the water quality degradation problems in the area (Photograph 12.2).

Endangered species nest near heavily urbanized areas where cats, dogs, horses, surfers, beachgoers, illegal immigrants, and border patrol agents are plentiful. The result is numerous pressures which continue to be a management challenge. While predator control and enforcement of regulations are essential to nesting success, effective public outreach and education will continue to be a long-term goal and one of the few lasting solutions. Finally, scientific and social research are the foundation for additional restoration, and potentially the key to solving many of today's problems. It must therefore continue to be well supported.

While many challenges persist, positive steps are being taken to not only protect the resource but also improve and enhance habitat through restoration. In 1997, a small-scale, two-acre project was completed, linking two large areas of marsh by way of a meandering, planted connector channel in an effort to improve tidal flushing. Fish, birds, and plants have since colonized this constructed marsh and invaluable lessons have been learned about what makes restoration successful. In February 2000, a second phase covering twenty acres was completed. This "model marsh," located in the problematic southern arm of the Tijuana Estuary, has also shown early success and will undoubtedly yield experience and research data to set the stage for future phases. As estuarine habitat loss and degradation continue to occur in heavily populated southern California, efforts to increase the sum total of viable estuarine habitat are an important contribution to overall conservation and management.

In a general sense, there is a need to continue educational and research efforts in the watershed and reserve in an effort to reduce human impacts and enhance local stewardship. Simultaneously this also provides a resource that can be enjoyed by the public. It is also imperative that the mosaic of interested agencies and other stakeholders work together so that this special area is properly managed and cared for. Finally, there is a need for closer cooperation with Mexican partners who share this regional ecosystem and who also stand to gain from its preservation.

Seen in the broader context of the Pacific coast within NAFTA, TRN-ERR is a continuation of a process of estuary preservation that has been underway on the southern California coast over the past quarter century. In spite of the many upland developments that have seen rapid settlement of much of the coastal plain in the region, a surprising amount of estuarine stewardship and habitat conservation has been achieved in this area. This is due, no doubt, to the comparatively strong environment legislation and enforcement related to water quality and coastal management in the United States in comparison to Canada and Mexico. Using a wide variety of institutional mechanisms, a number of bodies are struggling to avoid the destruction of other estuaries in this region. For example, the U.S. Marine Corps is the guardian of one of the best-preserved coastal wetlands associated with the Santa Margarita River on the Camp Pendelton Marine Corps Base. A wide variety of federal and state agencies, and the Cities of Los Angeles and Carlsbad, are cooperating in the Batiquitos Lagoon to enhance the quality of this system. In this context, the Tijuana

River National Estuarine Reserve can be seen as an integral part of an emerging network of estuarine conservation areas along the increasingly urban southwest California coast; a network that sets an example for similar regions elsewhere in North America. As part of this initiative, a civic society is operating a center to educate a large number of school children and adults about the remaining diversity of biophysical resources in the estuary. More than 140 bird species were recorded there since 1993 and an additional thirty species were reported previously that might still visit the area from time-to-time. Similarly, San Diego has invested heavily in the creation of urban wetlands that support a diverse population of coastal birds and other wildlife (City of San Diego 2001).

References

The following references are a basis for understanding the Tijuana River NERR, its character, challenges, and the management responses. These basic references provide more details for the concerned reader. This paper is largely built upon the experience of Tessa Roper, acting reserve manager, Tijuana River NERR, supplemented by field observations of Gordon Nelson and Chad Day in 1996, 1999, 2000. Maps adapted from Zedler et al. 1992

Batiquitos Lagoon, CA. 2000. *Welcome to Batiquitos Lagoon Enhancement Project.* http://www.batiquitos.org/
California. Department of Parks and Recreation, U.S. Fish and Wildlife Service, and U.S. National Oceanic and Atmospheric Administration. 1999. *Comprehensive Management Plan for Tijuana River National Estuarine Research Reserve and Tijuana Slough National Wildlife Refuge.* Berkeley, Calif.: CONCUR, Inc.
City of San Diego. 2001. (http://sannet.gov/park_and_recreation/)
The Conservation Foundation. 1988. *Protecting American's Wetlands: An Action Agenda.* Final Report of the National Wetlands Policy Forum. Washington, D.C.: The Conservation Foundation.
Dobbin Associates, J. 1986. *Tijuana River National Estuarine Sanctuary Management Plan.* San Diego, Calif.: Tijuana River National Estuarine Sanctuary Management Authority.
Entrix Inc., PERL, and PWA, Ltd. 1991. *Tijuana Estuary Tidal Restoration Program.* Draft Environmental Impact Report/Environmental Impact Statement. California Coastal Conservancy (CCC) and U.S. Fish and Wildlife Service, Lead Agencies. Vol. I-III. Oakland, Calif.: California Coastal Conservancy.
Pritchard, D. W. 1967. "What is an Estuary: Physical Viewpoint," pp. 3-5. In *Estuaries,* ed. G. H. Lauff. Washington, D.C.: American Association for the Advancement of Science.
Ricks, Candice. 29 June 2000. "Re: Laws." Waterforum@egroups.com 22:35:37. Reprinted from c.ricks@prodigy.net.
Zedler, J. B., C. S. Nordby, and B. E. Kus. 1992. *The Ecology of Tijuana Estuary, California: A National Estuarine Research Reserve.* Washington, D.C.: National Oceanic and Atmospheric Administration, Office of Coastal Resource Management, Sanctuaries and Reserves Division.

Regional Management Program at Yellowstone National Park [1]

Marvin O. Jensen

Abstract

Yellowstone National Park, the first national park in the United States, was established on 1 March 1872 after a series of reports on Yellowstone's wonders—previously held in disbelief and derision—were finally confirmed by special government expeditions (Establishment of Yellowstone National Park 1872). Yellowstone was "dedicated and set apart as a park or pleasuring ground for the benefit and enjoyment of the people," to be preserved "from injury or spoilation of all timber, mineral deposits, natural curiosities, or wonders, within the park, and their retention in their natural condition." This pattern has been followed in more than 375 units of the national park system in the United States and copied in more than 140 countries around the world. Yellowstone National Park was further designated as a UNESCO international biosphere reserve in 1972 and a world heritage site in 1978, in recognition of its world class values. Yellowstone has been recognized as having set the pattern for the National Park System in the U.S., a pattern that has now been adopted worldwide. The park has long been looked to for leadership in protected area management programs. It has been a leader in addressing critical issue management programs and working

---

1.   An amended version of this paper was presented at the Regional Approaches to Parks and Protected Areas Workshop in Tijuana, B.C., and published in *Environments* 27, no. 3.

Photograph 13.1. Yellowstone National Park is a major source area for water for surrounding regions.

with other entities interested in Yellowstone and its surrounding areas. Science has long played a role in the protection and in the management of Yellowstone Park, its surrounding national forests, and other protected areas. Geographic information systems (GIS) are increasingly being employed to solve management concerns.

Introduction

Yellowstone (fig. 13.1) has been a leader in the National Park System's protection and management programs, which sometimes require cooperative regional approaches. A major concern over preservation of the endangered grizzly bear in the 1960s, 1970s, and 1980s led to an interagency effort and formation of the Greater Yellowstone Coordinating Committee (GYCC) in the 1960s. The interagency effort focused primarily on habitat that encompassed Yellowstone and Grand Teton National Parks, and the six surrounding national forests. This region later became known as the Greater Yellowstone Ecosystem. *A Yellowstone Vision Document*, an interagency coordinated land and resource management plan, was completed in the late 1980s. Strong concerns from national forest constituents resulted in a significantly abbreviated, and less substantive, *Vision Document* and it was essentially shelved. The Greater Yellowstone Coordinating Committee became little more than a periodic social gathering of the forest and park managers. Only recently

Figure 13.1 Greater Yellowstone Region

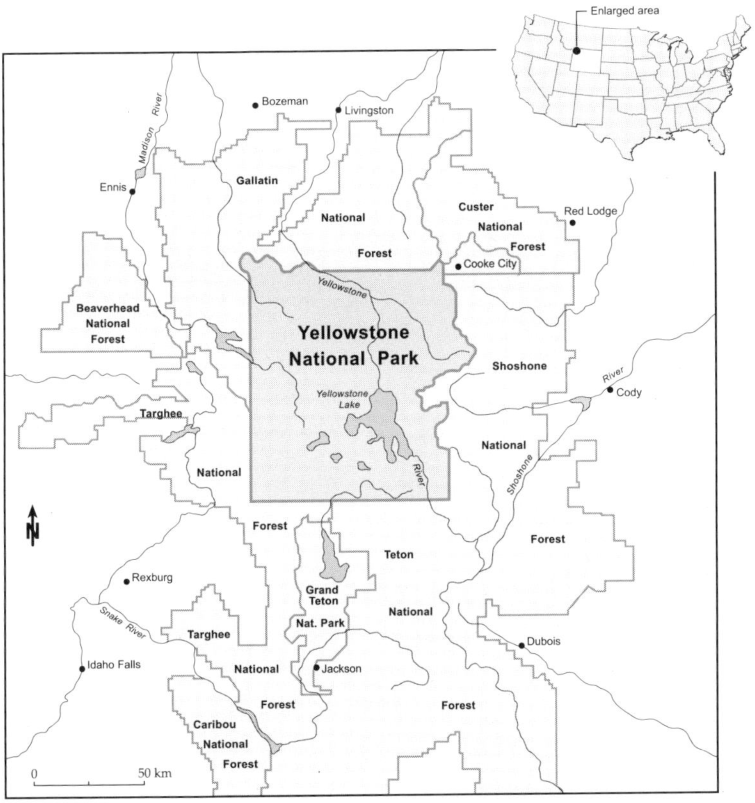

has the group begun to be effective in coordinating management and planning efforts. Many of these projects require collaboration with local, state, and federal government entities. Coordinated regional management efforts are used to address a number of current issues at Yellowstone including: wolf reintroduction; northern range and elk habitat; winter use planning; visitor accommodations and facilities plans; exotic lake trout; external mining proposals; and bioprospecting.

Regional Setting

Yellowstone National Park encompasses 2.2 million acres (890,000 hectares), and ranges in elevation from about 5,000 feet to 11,500 feet

Photograph 13.2 Teton Mountains, Yellowstone National Park area, Wyoming

(1,500 m to 3,500 m) (fig. 13.1). Its primary geographic feature is a major semidormant caldera, which is now a high plateau rimmed by several major mountain ranges. Over ten thousand thermal features are located within the park, along with nine major river systems, and three large lakes including Yellowstone Lake, one of the largest freshwater lakes in North America. Many species of wildlife are also found including: grizzly bear, wolves, bison, elk, bighorn sheep, moose, and deer, and numerous species of birds and fish. Yellowstone is visited by about three million people a year and has two distinct visitor seasons: summer with a wide variety of wheeled vehicular travelers; and the winter snowmobiles, snow coach travelers, and cross country skiers.

To the south of Yellowstone, Grand Teton National Park, and John D. Rockefeller National Parkway are managed together as a single national park system unit. Seven national forests surround Yellowstone: Gallatin, Custer, Shoshone, Bridger, Teton, Targhee, and Beaverhead. Together these federal land units, totaling some 11.7 million acres (4.7 million hectares), comprise what has become known as the Greater Yellowstone Ecosystem (GYE). Thirty-two percent of the GYE is federally designated wilderness. Additional proposed wilderness, if implemented, would result in over half of the Greater Yellowstone Ecosystem being managed as wilderness.

Photograph 13.3 Jackson Hole in Yellowstone National Park area, Wyoming.

Regional Coordination and Cooperation

In large part, probably due to the distinct missions given by Congress to the National Park Service (NPS) and Forest Service, communication and coordination was neither frequent nor substantive until the early 1960s, with some notable exceptions. Concurrently, and in fact until only recently, a general philosophy existed among most NPS and Forest Service managers to view the units under their care as islands. The Greater Yellowstone Coordinating Committee (GYCC) was established in the early 1960s because of recognition of the need to increase the amount and substance of communication between park and forest managers. GYCC began a series of meetings that addressed themselves to more mundane matters (Barbee, Schullery, and Varley 1990). The committee consisted of the superintendents of Yellowstone and Grand Teton National Parks, the forest supervisors of the seven surrounding national forests, the regional director of the National Park Service, and the three regional foresters of the National Forest Service. At the same time, a number of critical issues were facing the GYE managers. Chief among them was a declining grizzly bear population—increasingly alarming to park and forest managers—and other growing management concerns such as seasonally migrating elk, trumpeter swans, and natural fire policies. All of these led to a more focused and aggressive coordination program (Barbee, Schullery, and Varley 1990). The increased interest in ecosystem management expressed by Congress and environmental groups in the mid-1980s, resulted in more frequent and substantive GYCC meetings (Barbee, Schullery, and Varley 1990). The committee established working groups to focus on coordinating management programs across jurisdictional boundaries. One subgroup addressed the grizzly bear issue, which in retrospect was a primary focus of, and vehicle for, the increasing investment of time and effort by the park superintendents, forest supervisors, and their respective staffs.

Leadership Role

Throughout its history, Yellowstone National Park has been considered by managers within the ever-expanding National Park System—and now by park managers throughout the world—as a leader in park protection and management. There is much evidence of this fact. For example, the language found in the *Act* that established the National Park Service (NPS) in 1916 (U.S., *National Park Service Organic Act*) is very similar to the language that established Yellowstone in 1872. That language reads, in part, that the purpose of the NPS is, "to conserve the scenery and the natural and historic objects, and wildlife therein, and to provide for the enjoyment of the same, in such manner and by such means as will leave them unimpaired for the enjoyment of future generations." Similar language is found in enabling legislation, proclamations, or similar instruments establishing essentially all of the other units of the National Park System, with some variation to address the uniqueness of each unit. A postscript worthy of note is that Congress and individual presidents have progressively over the years become more willing, as a result of political compromise, to allow extractive uses in establishing new units of the National Park System.

Yellowstone has continued to be a leader in the management of critical issues since its establishment in 1872. As the early superintendents observed the alarming loss of wildlife due to heavy poaching, they sought, and were given assistance, from the military. The U.S. Cavalry was assigned to Yellowstone and essentially acted to protect the park's wildlife and other resources and values from 1886 through 1916. At that time, Congress established the National Park Service and provided funding for sufficient staff to manage and protect the park. The NPS, very concerned about the dramatic decline in bison numbers, and working through the cavalry, set an aggressive course to "ranch" them back from the brink of extinction beginning in the late 1890s. The program was successful and the bison population is approximately 2,500 today. However, new precedent setting challenges beset these animals. After being part of the program to eliminate wolves from the park by the mid-1920s, and to preserve higher numbers of "more desirable species," the NPS engaged in a recent, highly successful program to reintroduce wolves to the Greater Yellowstone Ecosystem. Yellowstone also has been increasingly known for policies that recognize naturally occurring fires as an essential element of ecosystem processes.

Yellowstone is also currently setting new directions in the area of bioprospecting. Scientific investigation has always been an important part of Yellowstone Park and, indeed, the entire National Park System. Collection of biological specimens has always been a routine part of such research. In recent years, biological specimens from Yellowstone's hot springs have opened the door to major scientific breakthroughs. A major industry has developed as a result of these developments and Yellowstone is setting a precedent for other NPS units in this regard. A percentage of the revenues private companies are deriving from the knowledge gained from Yellowstone's resources must be returned to the park. This could have significant implications for Yellowstone and other national parks in the future.

A few other examples of leadership include:

- taking a position on a proposed mine that would have posed a serious threat to Yellowstone
- establishing the Yellowstone Foundation to raise funding from corporate and private sources to assist in funding programs and projects critical to the protection and enjoyment of the park, and
- developing a business plan that will identify appropriate levels of protection and management in all park operations

Vision Document

In the mid-1980s, a majority in Congress signaled that they would like to see an ecosystem-based method to management of the Greater Yellowstone Ecosystem. This approach was supported by a number of environmental groups interested in Yellowstone (Barbee, Schullery, and Varley 1990), which created a new momentum for managers of the GYE and increased recognition that there was a need for more than an issue-by-issue approach to management. In 1987, GYCC published a list of existing resources and use levels. This led to the understanding that there needed to be a broader set of guidance principles, developed on an ecosystem basis, to direct management efforts (Barbee, Schullery, and Varley 1990). In 1989 the GYCC managers put their respective staffs to work on the creation of such an overarching document of guiding principles. This draft document, the *Vision for the Future: A Framework for Coordination in the Greater Yellowstone Area*, was completed by a team of specialists from the Forest Service and Park Service and released for public comment in August 1990. The draft contained three goals to 1) conserve the sense of naturalness and maintain ecosystem integrity, 2) encourage opportunities that are biologically and economically sustainable, and 3) improve coordination (Barbee, Schullery, and Varley 1990). It included, within these goals, fourteen primary principles that identified guiding management philosophies on how the goals could be achieved while maintaining the overall Greater Yellowstone Ecosystem for future generations (Barbee, Schullery, and Varley 1990). There was no involvement of any state or local governments, or special interest groups who had been active in writing the draft *Vision* document.

A series of public meetings was held in the region to obtain public comment on the draft *Vision* document. A 1990 critique of the draft *Vision* document process was written by then superintendent Bob Barbee, his chief scientist John Varley, and environmental specialist Paul Schullery. They noted that extractive use interest groups dominated the public meetings with firm opposition to the draft *Vision* document. While posing no opposition to specifics within the draft document, the extractive use interests vehemently opposed the whole document as a "giant land grab" or "another federal lockup." At the same time, conservation groups did not engage in the process in any significant way, and the broader national constituency was not engaged in the process at all—perhaps a failing on the part of the GYCC managers. The draft document lacked the force of an environmental impact statement since, by design, care had been taken to avoid specifics that would have required review under the *National Environmental Policy Act*. As a result, many people had little faith in the document being of value.

This sequence of events was a consequence of a series of strategic planning errors. The draft document had not been sufficiently clear in stating that it only applied to federal lands managed by the Forest Service and the National Park Service. There was insufficient understanding on the part of agency staff, both at the field and higher levels, about the draft document and its purpose. Therefore, at critical times when support was needed, such support was lacking.

Significantly, Barbee, Schullery, and Varley noted that, in the world of professional resource managers, everyone was carefully watching; again pointing to the fact that Yellowstone—as the world's first National Park—was being looked upon as a leader in protection and management of natural and cultural resources (Barbee, Schullery, and Varley 1990).

The overwhelming opposition to the draft *Vision* document by regional extractive use interest groups and their constituencies in essence killed this initiative, as drafted and presented for public review and comment. Only the National Park Service and the National Forest Service were clearly in favor of the draft *Vision* document. Eight conservation organizations and state and federal agencies were slightly approving, neutral, or undecided. Forty-four primarily extractive use organizations, also including the U.S. Congressional delegations from the states of Montana and Wyoming, came out emphatically against the draft *Vision* document (Barbee, Schullery, and Varley 1990).

The draft document was subsequently revised and put into a final and approved form. Barbee, Schullery, and Varley noted that the agencies, stunned by the attack orchestrated by extractive use organizations, preserved only a few major points in the final, more limited, version. Curiously, and perhaps indicative of the value of "*The Vision*" itself, the original draft *Vision* document, with no official standing, remains on the shelves of all of the GYCC managers. Its contents are known, understood, and remain in the background of the continuing coordination efforts among the park superintendents and forest supervisors.

After the final version of the *Vision* document was completed, the park superintendents and forest supervisors continued to meet as a Greater Yellowstone Coordinating Committee. However, stung by what was considered a resounding defeat of the *Vision* document—a "rout" as described by Barbee—the continuing coordination efforts were considerably dampened for the next few years.

Current GYCC Activities

By the mid-1990s, most GYCC members who had been part of the team during the draft *Vision* document efforts had moved on to other positions, or retired. During the ensuing years the core issues—driven by biological circumstances and sociopolitical activities—pushed the GYCC members to return to work together on issues, such as those shown in box 13.1.

Box 13.1. Issues of interest to the Greater Yellowstone Coordinating Committee

• Grizzly bear recovery	• Oil and gas land leasing
• Winter use planning	• Water quality
• Wolf recovery	• User fees
• Elk winter migration	• Travel and visitor management programs
• Interaction between bison winter migration and livestock grazing	• Acquisition of critical habitat
	• Air quality
• Exotic weed control	• GIS and data management

Under the basic interagency cooperative agreement and charter, the GYCC, with largely a new cast of players and continuing pressures to address issues, reverted to operating more on an issue-by-issue basis. The ongoing coordination efforts include over thirty separate projects and programs, and cover all of those noted above, plus others. Each of the projects or programs has a number of staff members from parks and forests assigned to it. The makeup of each project or program team varies according to the issue, how it affects each management unit, and the available expertise from the agency units. There is a rapidly developing momentum within GYCC, as evidenced by the expansion of projects and programs and frequency of meetings, to address and coordinate issues. Clear evidence of the increasing commitment to the GYCC effort is found in the fact that the Departments of Agriculture and the Interior have committed over $0.5 million to the coordinating efforts. This funding will be used to fund-facilitate coordination of the GYCC group, and for projects and programs to move forward without affecting ongoing operational needs of the individual units.

Science in Regional Coordination Efforts

Scientific investigation has long been a part of the activities at Yellowstone National Park. Of the more recent issues facing the park, scientific investigation into the questions of grizzly bear ecology probably has the longest history. Science done by the Craighead brothers in the 1950s and 1960s on grizzly bears was of great value in beginning to understand more about these great animals. Though solutions to saving this species from extinction were controversial, and disputed by the Craigheads themselves, the grizzly bear population has begun to show signs of recovery. Another example is the many and varied studies surrounding issues related to elk numbers, and the question of their possible overgrazing of the habitat of which they are a part. Studies on the northern Yellowstone range have shown that while that part of the park has been "fully utilized," by definition it is not overgrazed. Yet this remains a controversial issue with many differences of opinion and continuing pressure to reduce the numbers of elk and bison in the area. In fact, a new study on the overgrazing of Yellowstone's northern range was recently commissioned by direction from Congress, and is to be conducted by the National Academy of Science.

Many other studies have been commissioned into a wide range of subjects within Yellowstone National Park. A few of the more well-known studies include questions regarding bison migration and general ecology over the last several decades, bighorn sheep ecology, coyote biology, soil surveys, geological surveys, seismology, thermal geology, fire ecology, cutthroat trout and grayling ecology, exotic lake trout studies, water quality, air quality, visitor perception studies, visitor impact studies, and many others too numerous to mention. In fact, approximately 250 active research projects are underway each year at Yellowstone. Many of these are not related directly to the management of critical issues. However, a number do pertain to management, and data and information from these studies are essential to approaching critical issues within the park. Yellowstone National Park has cooperative relations with over seventy-five universities and other scientific institutions.

Important for consideration here is that many scientific investigations are undertaken to address critical issues within the park. The Park Service, Forest Service, and other organizations that are interested in management and protection of the Greater Yellowstone Ecosystem jointly fund many such studies. Data and information from these studies are rarely conclusive, nor can they be directly converted into management decisions. Nor, in most cases, should they be. As such, each agency or entity is left to review and analyze the data and information. In the context of agency mandates and sociopolitical circumstances, the agencies make decisions on courses of action that will best achieve the stated goals for each park or forest. The continuation of coordination efforts of the GYCC is essential in evaluating the information from research, and formulating decisions with an understanding of their effects on other units within the Greater Yellowstone Ecosystem.

Geographic Information Systems (GIS) in Management

Only in recent years have geographic information systems been used in Yellowstone or the GYE. It was not until 1997 that the first GIS data became available to Yellowstone National Park managers in the form of a soil survey. Bits and pieces of GIS data were being generated from earlier versions of GIS programs, but nothing comprehensive was available until the last few years. However, as new technology is acquired, and data from current and previous studies are integrated into updated programs, useful information is emerging that is already beginning to bring new understanding to critical resource and visitor issues within Yellowstone and the surrounding parks and forests. Continuing the efforts of GYCC to coordinate GIS across agency boundaries will incrementally create a more complete picture of the Greater Yellowstone Ecosystem and help resolve issues on an ecosystem basis.

Summary and Conclusions

As the world's first National Park, Yellowstone has been looked to as a model for many of the other units within the National Park System. Likewise, the United States' National Park System has been looked to by more than 140 countries around the world as a role model in establishing their own national park systems. Yellowstone has been studied closely for leadership in addressing critical resource issues, such as wildlife and fisheries conservation and restoration, and many other management programs, such as bioprospecting, fund raising, and business management planning. In recent decades, in the process of addressing critical issues and management programs, Yellowstone began working with its neighboring Grand Teton-John D. Rockefeller National Park, and the seven surrounding national forests to come together as the Greater Yellowstone Coordinating Committee. This committee acts to

Photograph 13.4 Yellowstone geysers and lake.

coordinate management projects and programs. The result of its collective efforts in recent years has been the creation of a draft *Vision* document to provide overarching policy guidance to specific decisions on management issues. That particular document was doomed to sit on the shelves without official standing. A more limited version was completed in its place, and the regional coordination efforts of the GYCC were temporarily dampened. However, the coordinating efforts of GYCC have now been revitalized through the need to address grizzly bear, bison, wolf, and other critical issues, as well as sociopolitical controversies such as winter use. Setting aside the debate on whether or not the draft *Vision* document was a failure, it is important to reflect on the process in a broader time frame. In this context it becomes clear that, beginning in the early 1960s, the park and forest managers of the Greater Yellowstone Ecosystem began to place greater emphasis on working across agency boundaries toward solving problems and issues on an ecosystem basis. That commitment grew into an effort to create the draft *Vision* document. Since it was aborted, the GYCC commitment has grown again and with greater emphasis. This new emphasis takes place under the auspices of a basic interagency agreement, rather than the *Vision* document. It works on an issue-by-issue basis, recognizing that many issues are interrelated. With this renewed vigor, it can be anticipated that this form of regional cooperation will continue to grow in the future.

References

Barbee, R. D., P. Schullery, and J. D. Varley. 1991. "The Yellowstone Vision: An Experiment that Failed or a Vote for Posterity?" pp. 80-85. In *Proceedings of Partnerships in Parks & Conservation Conference*. Co-sponsored by the National Park Service, New York State Office of Parks, Recreation, and Historic Preservation, National Parks, and Conservation Association, 9-12 Nov. 1991. Albany, New York.

Clark, T. W., and S. C. Minta. 1994. Greater Yellowstone's Future: Prospects for Ecosystem Science, Management, and Policy. Moose, Wyo.: Homestead Publishers.

Craighead, F. C. 1994. For Everything There Is a Season: The Sequence of Natural Events in the Grand-Teton-Yellowstone Area. Helena, Mont.: Falcon Press.

Craighead, J. J., J. S. Sumner, and J. A. Mitchell. 1995. *The Grizzly Bears of Yellowstone: Their Ecology in the Yellowstone Ecosystem, 1959-1992*. Washington D.C.: Island Press.

Debinski, D. 1997. "Assessing Biodiversity in the Greater Yellowstone Ecosystem." *Geo Info. Systems* 7(7): 42.

Establishment of Yellowstone National Park. 3 March 1872. U.S. Code 16, subchpt. V, para. 21-40.

Freemuth, J., and R. McGregor. 1998. "Science, Expertise and the Public: The Politics of Ecosystem Management in the Greater Yellowstone." *Landscape and Urban Planning* 40(1/3): 211.

Keiter, R. B., and M. S. Boyce. 1991. *The Greater Yellowstone Ecosystem: Redefining America's Wilderness Heritage*. New Haven, Conn.: Yale University Press N.

McNamee, T. 1997. *Return of the Wolf to Yellowstone*. New York: Henry Holt.

Meyer, J. L. 1996. *The Spirit of Yellowstone: The Cultural Evolution of a National Park*. Lanham, Md.: Rowman & Littlefield.

U.S. *National Park Service Organic Act*. 25 August 1916. U.S. Code 16, subchpt. I, para. 1-18.

Cascades International Park:
A Case Study [1]

John C. Miles

Abstract

An alliance of Canadian and American environmental groups proposed a Cascades International Park in 1994. The goal was better coordination of management in the transboundary area, guided by emerging conservation biology, which would lead to better resource protection, especially for biodiversity. Region-wide management of federal and Crown land would, it was hoped, result in greater likelihood of conservation of ecological systems than the current management approaches. No new parks were proposed, but rather greater coordination of management of existing protected areas. Three principal ideas were behind the proposal: landscape management, ecosystem management, and integrated management.

The plan failed. It was perceived by some as a threat to private property and even to national security. There was strong opposition to the proposal from people in communities surrounding the proposed park and stewardship areas. Other reasons for failure included poor timing, specifically in the face of shifting political situations and the provocative presentation of the rationale for the proposed park. The key lesson here is that proponents of ideas, such as those presented in this paper, must be aware of the concerns of those directly or indirectly affected by such proposals,

---

1.   This paper was presented at the Regional Approaches to Parks and Protected Areas Workshop in Tijuana, B.C., and published in *Environments* vol. 27, no. 3.

and they must make every effort to explain the ideas and proposals and respond to their concerns.

Introduction

A three-day conference, entitled *Nature Has No Borders,* was convened in Seattle, Washington on 25-27 March 1994. The meeting aimed to explore the idea for an international park and special management area in the North Cascades of Washington and British Columbia. It was organized by a consortium of fourteen organizations from Canada and the United States seeking a way to provide increased protection for the North Cascades ecosystem. While 200 participants from both nations, including scientists and politicians, discussed the idea, a noisy group of protesters gathered outside the meeting. The proposed *Cascades International Park* as some proponents called the as yet incomplete idea was, said the protesters, a threat to private property and even to national sovereignty. Led by an American antienvironmentalist leader, Chuck Cushman, residents from rural communities around the proposed "park" expressed their fear and anger, attracting considerable media attention. Cushman had written in an "action alert" distributed on 15 March that "The plan is to try to take over this area without legislation by using the Clinton administration to make a treaty with Canada giving up United States sovereignty, control, and traditional uses in the North Cascades Ecosystem" (American Land Rights Association, 15 March 1994).

After the March conference and its protest, the consortium pressed on, releasing its formal proposal in mid-June. They called for linkage of all existing parks and recreation areas as a jointly managed Cascades International Park. Existing agency jurisdictions would continue with increasingly cooperative management. In addition, all U.S. federal and Canadian Crown lands within the ecosystem, but outside the international park, would be designated a *stewardship area* where increased effort to achieve ecological conservation and restoration goals would be pursued. The emphasis would be on greater cooperation between management agencies—both within and between the two countries—in an effort to manage the North Cascades as an *ecosystem.* The consortium was careful to point out that no new parks would be created anywhere; no private lands would be acquired. The aim was to develop a more region-wide management approach to federal and Crown lands, based on a growing scientific understanding of what would be necessary to conserve natural systems in the area. This regional approach would result in greater likelihood of conservation of ecological systems than current management approaches.

The National Park Service (NPS) in the United States issued a news release to coincide with the announcement of the proposal. "Reacting to a proposal to establish an international park in the North Cascades, the National Park Service today took steps to ensure that the public understands the proposal originated with private citizens and not the National Park Service" (USNPS, 13 June 1995). The release noted that the NPS had "co-sponsored an academic conference … at which the subject of international cooperation including a possible international park to protect the North Cascades was discussed." But, readers were assured, no "general agreement or direction emerged from the conference, and the National Park Service has not subsequently pursued the matter."

Reading this NPS release, proponents of the international park knew the idea was in trouble. A poll taken in December of 1994 (Elway Research, Inc.) indicated the public supported the idea by a three to one margin, but the political context had changed drastically since the spring of 1994. Strident antipark voices had been raised, such as that of activist Don Kehoe who was quoted as saying in a meeting in Mount Vernon, Washington—a community in the region—that "This park calls for the first physical breakup of the United States. It will eliminate borders. It will destroy the free and constitutional Republic of the United States of America" (Nemeth, 30 October 1994). Less strident editorials from newspapers in the region, like the *Bellingham Herald*, took the position that "There's no need for an international park. U.S. and Canadian officials can try to agree on common principles that will preserve their respective parks and wildernesses without creating a formal international park" (*Bellingham Herald,* 26 June 1995). At the national level in the U.S., a conservative Congress had been elected in the 1994-midterm elections. Support from federal officials, present in the early stages of proposal development, evaporated. The NPS news release indicated it was keeping to safe political ground. If, as the principal U.S. agency managing the core of the area involved, it were not supportive, the proposal stood little chance of being achieved. Proponents continued to recruit support and encouraged guest editorials in regional newspapers, but by the end of 1995, the likelihood of success seemed so slight that they gave up on the idea and turned their energies in more promising directions.

Photograph 14.1. Lake Ann, North Cascades National Park near the Pacific Crest National Scenic Trail that runs from Canada to Mexico. Photo credit: J.C. Day

Historical Background

The region involved in this proposal has a long history of resource protection and exploitation, and one of the ironies of this case is that

Photograph 14.2. Rugged scenery on the trail to Blue Lake, North Cascades National Park. Photo credit: J.C. Day

because so much land had been protected, more seemed necessary. The British Columbia portion of the area contains two provincial parks and two recreation areas, while in the United States there are a national park, three recreation areas, and seven wilderness areas. The consequence of this level of protection is that "in today's GNCE (Greater North Cascade Ecosystem) still reside every (known) species that was here before white settlement" (Friedman and Lindholdt 1993:2). Some species, like the grizzly, have been extirpated from some parts of the ecosystem, but habitat for them remains there, and management could restore what Friedman calls the "dance of all partners" to these areas. Such restoration was one of the goals of the international park proposal.

In the U.S. part of the region, resource conservation can be traced back to the 1890s when the first federal forest reserves were proclaimed. These reserves became national forests in 1907, and portions of the national forests became primitive and wilderness areas beginning with the North Cascades Primitive Area in the 1930s. The North Cascades National Park, one of a series of proposals for national parks in the area, was established by Congress in 1968, an act that designated most of the primitive area outside the park as the Pasayten Wilderness. Additional legislation in 1984 and 1988 added other parts of the region to the National Wilderness Preservation System, bringing the total to 2,554,047 acres (1,029,979 hectares) of officially designated wilderness.

In British Columbia, the history of conservation reaches back to 1931 and the Three Brothers Mountain Reserve. This became Manning Provincial Park in 1941, and was followed in 1968 by Cathedral Provincial Park. The Skagit Recreation Area was formed in 1973 adjacent to the western boundary of Manning Park, and a Cascade Recreation Area north of the park was designated in 1987. The British Columbia government has also established several small ecological reserves in the Cascade region. Total area conserved in the British Columbia portion of the North Cascades was 153,180 hectares (328,355 acres).

The idea that management of nature in the region should be international began to be explored in the 1970s, when the North Cascades Conservation Council (NCCC) discussed "international wilderness." In 1984, NCCC called again for cooperative park and wilderness planning across the border. At that time, a proposed raising of Ross Dam on the Skagit River, that would flood land valued by environmental groups on both sides of the border, led to international opposition to the dam proposal. The Boundary Waters, Ross Dam Treaty was signed that year by the United States and Canada, which involved agreement that the dam would not be raised, and, among other provisions, established a Skagit Environmental Endowment Commission and Fund which was directed to give "high priority...to the establishment of a firm connection between North Cascades National Park in the United

States and Manning Provincial Park in the Province of British Columbia, forming an International Park..." (NPCA 1994:4).

The 1988 *North Cascades National Park General Management Plan* prepared by the National Park Service (U.S. NPS 1987: 23) did not mention of an international park, but it did address international cooperation. According to this plan, management of the NPS complex was to be coordinated with the management of lands under the jurisdiction of the U.S. Forest Service, Seattle City Light, British Columbia Parks, and others, to provide visitors with a comprehensive overview of the region. The complex was also intended to offer a variety of interrelated visitor experiences, and to maximize the ability to sustain a representative and ecologically healthy sample of this unique ecosystem for the future.

Also in 1988, Congress approved the *Washington Park Wilderness Act* (Public Law 100-688) that made most of the North Cascades National Park Complex part of the National Wilderness Preservation System. Congressional discussion of this *Act* indicated that a higher level of wilderness resource protection was desired than was provided by the national park and national recreational area designations then in place. Development plans for the National Park Complex had, over the years, included proposals that might change the wild character of some areas. The intent of this legislation was to assure that the natural status of the North Cascades and Olympic and Mount Rainier Natural Parks, all of which were included in the bill, would be ensured.

In April 1990, the Skagit Environmental Endowment Commission discussed the idea of an international park or biosphere reserve for the area, and recognized that the idea would be difficult to sell to the local community. It concluded that considerable education would be necessary, and formed a working group to explore the idea. The commission renewed its exploration in 1992 and, at that time, the National Parks and Conservation Association (NPCA) and the North Cascades Conservation Council began considering what sort of process might lead to an international park proposal. The Cascades International Alliance formed and began meeting, and the NPCA received a grant to organize a conference of environmental groups from the United States and Canada. This was the conference, convened in 1994, at which the protesters appeared. The difficulty of "selling" an international park to the local communities, recognized by the endowment commission four years earlier, was more serious and complex than even they had anticipated.

The Proposal and Its Rationale

As noted earlier, what was proposed in 1995 involved no new parks but, rather, greater coordination of management of existing conservation areas. The goal would be greater *integration* of the management of conservation lands in the region. The proposal never reached a stage of detailed specifications as to what management schemes would be involved in this integrated approach. A map was released indicating that the area involved reached from the Coquihalla, Tulameen, and Similkameen Rivers in British Columbia on the north end, to the Snoqualmie and Yakima Rivers in the south (Northwest Ecosystem Alliance 1994). The actual international park included the North Cascades National Park Complex in the U. S., and the Skagit and Cascades Provincial Recreation Areas, along with the Manning and Cathedral Provincial Parks, in British Columbia. Various *restoration areas* were identified in the surrounding British Columbia protected areas and U.S. conservation areas, all of which would be integrated into a *Cascades Stewardship Area*. Management objectives were identified for the stewardship area and included management "...to achieve high quality habitat and security for wide-ranging mammals, including lynx, wolverine, grizzly bear, and gray wolf"; and "reduce fragmentation as needed to restore habitat integrity for wildlife, and control stream sedimentation." These were two of seventeen objectives described on the back of the map depicting the area of the proposal.

The rationale for all of this was well summarized in a talk at the 1994 conference by Karr (NPCA 1994: 58-59):

> In short, setting aside reserves is not adequate to protect landscapes from human actions. A more integrative approach is needed to protect regional resources and human communities that depend on those resources....In regional landscapes such as the North Cascades, four major classes of land use are essential to protect the interests of human society: *commodity* (agriculture or tree plantations); *protective* (natural areas preserving biological integrity and water quality); *compromise* (combination of protective and commodity, such as harvest of fruit or wildlife from natural forest); and *urban-industrial* (the built environment). All these land management options must be included because human society depends on the benefits that each yields to the regional landscape and to human society. The

difficulty will be defining how lands are allocated to these four use classes and how much of each kind is necessary in a regional landscape. Perhaps more difficult will be deciding how each tract of land is used.

The Cascades International Park initiative is a case of trying to build on nearly a century of conservation effort that provided a significant component of the *protective* element that is absent in so many areas. While none of the areas were protected with the conservation of biological diversity in mind, the circumstances, in the minds of international park proponents, provided a critically important and unusual opportunity to build a system that would allow a high level of *stewardship*.

Several principal ideas were behind the proposal. One was *landscape management*; the idea that coordinated planning and management in large areas that have similar and repeatable patterns of physical features, habitats, and human communities could lead to achievement of significant conservation objectives (Salwasser, MacCleery, and Snellgrove 1993). A second was *ecosystem management*; a science-based approach that conserves species and genetic diversity while maintaining the structural and functional integrity of ecological systems and providing economic benefits that can be sustained indefinitely (Karr 1994). A third was *integrated management*; the idea that multiple management objectives could be pursued across conventional boundaries, that multiple objectives could be integrated on landscapes that had, in the past, been managed for a limited set of objectives. Thus, a "working forest" could contribute to restoration of native plant communities even as commodity production was carried out upon it. A fourth principle was *sustainability*; an approach to providing for the needs of the present generation without compromising the potential to meet the needs of future generations.

International park proponents did not hide the fact that their proposal was a response to perceived limitations of traditional approaches to management in the region. Road building associated with extensive logging had caused soil erosion, slope failure, and damage to streams. Logging had degraded and fragmented wildlife habitat. Overgrazing of livestock had impacted streams and fisheries, and damaged plant communities throughout the region. If the protection and stewardship objectives of the proposal were to be achieved, changes in behavior of those who used the land would be necessary. The proposal never reached the point of detailing just what these changes would need to be, but the material released by the Cascade International Alliance left no doubt that change would be necessary.

Lessons Learned From Failure

Why did the Cascades International Park initiative fail, and what lessons can be learned from the episode? The most obvious reason for failure might seem to be bad timing. The proposal happened at a critical stage, just when national politics in the United States took a conservative turn. The extent of the shift of power in Congress took many by surprise, so it may be argued that nothing could have been done about this. No strategy could have avoided the political difficulties that emerged. The Seattle conference in the spring of 1994 heard talks by prominent U.S. and Canadian politicians and resource managers, so proponents were not deluded into thinking they had the political base from which to work. The political winds shifted for reasons beyond their control and blew their plan off course.

This is not, of course, the whole story. Even if national and state politics had not taken the turn they did, opposition in the communities around the proposed park and stewardship areas would have been significant. More than a decade earlier, a proposal had been floated for an innovative international park in the San Juan and Gulf Islands to the west and adjacent to the Greater North Cascades Ecosystem. This idea had met not only powerful opposition but also ridicule. It died quickly. No one wanted to even explore such an idea at that time. The proposals were not comparable because, in the former case, the land involved was mostly private and the "management" would have been focused on the marine interstices of the archipelago and on controlling development. Yet the vehemence in that earlier case—of the response to the idea of big government constraining people's freedoms, even for such good causes as scenic preservation and recreation—should have tipped off Cascades International Park proponents that much groundwork would be necessary to achieve success in their initiative. After their proposal had died, or at least become dormant, the leaders of the effort admitted this and changed their approach to new projects.

The antipark activists did not appear on the scene unprovoked. The proposal may have been based on solid ideas that were emerging out of conservation biology and environmentalism, but the presentation of the rationale for the proposed park was provocative. In a book published in 1993 by the Greater Ecosystem Alliance (now called the Northwest Ecosystem Alliance), Friedman, the leader of the alliance, presented a vision of an international park in the closing essay. He was very specific, writing of drainages currently outside protected areas that should be included in the park. He also suggested that a habitat corridor should link the North Cascades with the British Columbia Coast Range. Friedman (1993: 166) wrote that:

> Lands in the international park would of course be off limits to logging, ranching, and mining. Domestic grazing should also be eliminated from adjacent U.S. wilderness areas, including the Pasayten where it presently continues. Watershed protections should be put in place on all ownerships, to protect salmon runs.

While all of this might be reasonable and necessary to achieve the goals of "protecting an international ecosystem," as the book was subtitled, such ideas were guaranteed to inflame opposition from rural communities.

Also included in this book, and later published in a glossy, poster-sized edition, was a map of the *Greater North Cascades Ecosystem*. A bold black line reached from Everett to Wenatchee to Omak in the United States, and then crossed the international boundary to Princeton, Hope, and ultimately Vancouver in British Columbia. Within the lines fell Bellingham, Skykomish, Leavenworth, Winthrop, and other communities (fig. 14.1). The map was, of course, an attempt to depict the extent of the *ecosystem*, but a casual perusal of it by someone worrying that their freedoms were under siege by big government might, and did, lead to the conclusion that this was the boundary of the *park*. Here was undeniable evidence of the extent of the conspiracy to "take over" their land. Antipark activists, looking for ammunition in their campaign, had all they needed with this map, and Cushman and others made good use of it. A conservative politician from Bellingham, for instance, brandished the map at the Seattle antipark rally as clear evidence that her community was in trouble.

Figure 14.1 The Greater North Cascades Ecosystem

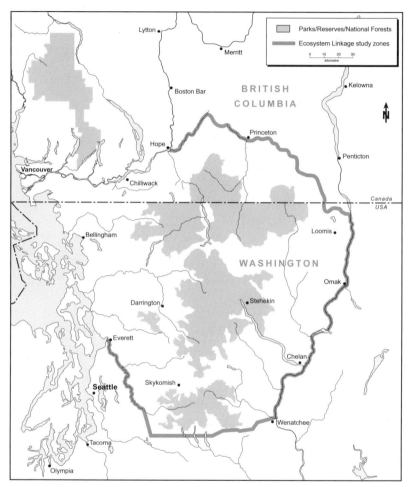

This same map, with the ecosystem boundary this time marked in red, was boldly presented in a publication of the Western Canada Wilderness Committee, copublished with the provocatively titled "World Wilderness Committee," in the spring of 1994, before the Cascades International Alliance had firmed up the details of the proposal. Eighty thousand copies were printed and the world, or at least the potentially affected part of it, knew that "new protected areas" were the goal. Also, new "special management areas" were being proposed, though no details were offered. Readers also learned that the wilderness committee was demanding that "selection logging systems replace clear-cut logging" and "a ban on the export of unprocessed raw logs and cants in order to increase local manufacturing jobs and enable more wilderness preservation". All of these were reasonable goals, but readers might wonder what such demands had to do with an international park.

All of these maps and publications were fodder for an intentional effort to rally opposition. The rhetoric was, in places, inflammatory. Diverse objectives were lumped together, suggesting at least to some that international park proponents had an agenda well beyond that stated up front. Opponents to initiatives of environmentalists in the Pacific Northwest region had long suspected that those bent on preserving the environment had a master plan. They believed that environmentalists "locked up" as much land as they could under wilderness legislation, in a series of efforts culminating in the *Washington State Wilderness Act of 1984* (Public Law 98-406), that designated 1,014,980 additional acres statewide, with 607,204 in the Greater North Cascades Ecosystem added to previously established wilderness. Next, in the view of these critics, the environmentalists conjured up the northern spotted owl to overcome the "release language" in the 1984 legislation which stated "National Forest areas not designated wilderness or for special management by this *Act* are released for multiple-use management and need not be managed to protect their suitability for wilderness designation." The listing of the owl in 1990 under the *Endangered Species Act* (U.S. Public Law 93-205) set in motion a process that resulted in significant reductions in timber harvest in the range of the owl. Then, building on the biodiversity protection approach involved in protecting the owl, came the proposal for an international park, integrated and "ecosystem" management, and a whole new set of reasons to reduce the uses of public lands. While no such master plan existed, proponents of the international park poured fuel on the fire of such thinking with their rhetoric. All of this led to opposition sufficient to kill the idea in 1995.

The lesson here is that proponents of ideas like these must be aware of the concerns of those directly or indirectly affected by them, and make every effort to explain the ideas and proposals and to answer their questions. They must refrain from "loading" a proposal with secondary objectives; from using the opportunity provided by a good idea to pursue other ideas. A clear, straightforward, and related set of objectives must be stated and pursued. While all opposition cannot be eliminated, the opportunity for opponents to whip up hysteria can be minimized. Careful avoidance of provocative rhetoric and extensive work with communities in the region can reduce the opportunity for outside agitators to come into a community and magnify what may be limited opposition. Face-to-face meetings with genuinely concerned citizens that demonstrate respect for their concerns will reduce the likelihood of opponents successfully demonizing proponents of ideas like the international park.

The effort to increase protection in the Cascades transboundary area is not over. The proposal for an international park may rise again. Work continues on other fronts. As this is written, Friedman and colleagues are raising funds to protect critical lynx habitat just south of the boundary by buying the timber rights to 25,000 acres of state timberland. Their approach to this effort has demonstrated that they have learned all of the lessons mentioned above, and more. Opposition has been present, but the Loomis Forest Campaign has avoided inflammatory rhetoric, focused on a clear and limited goal, worked with the communities, and faced head-on concerns of citizens in the region involved. Ultimate success depends on raising $14 million in a short time and is uncertain as of this writing, but the campaign clearly indicates that the work for protection of biodiversity in the Greater North Cascades is ongoing.

References

Cushman, C. 15March 1994. *Action Alert.* Washington, D.C.: American Land Rights Association.
Editorial. 26 June 1995. "Joint Park Isn't Needed." *Bellingham Herald.*
Elway Research, Inc. 1994. *Special Report.* Prepared for the Greater Ecosystem Alliance. Bellingham, Wash.: Greater Ecosystem Alliance.
Friedman, M., and P. Lindholdt. 1993. *Cascadia Wild: Protecting An International Ecosystem.* Bellingham, Wash.: Greater Ecosystem Alliance.
Karr, J. R. 1994. "Beyond Parks: Protecting the North Cascades Landscape," pp. 58-59. In *Nature Has No Borders.* Washington, D.C.: National Parks and Conservation Association.
Nemeth, M. A. 30 October 1994. "Conspiracy in Some Eyes." *Skagit Valley Herald,* Mount Vernon, Wash.
National Parks and Conservation Association. 1994. *Nature Has No Borders: A Conference on the Protection and Management of the Northern Cascades Ecosystem.* Washington, D.C.: National Parks and Conservation Association.
Northwest Ecosystem Alliance. 1994. *Nature Has No Borders.* Bellingham, Wash. (map)
Salwasser, H., D., W. MacCleery, and T. A. Snellgrove. 1993. "An Ecosystem Perspective on Sustainable Forestry and New Directions for the U.S. National Forest System," pp. 44-89. In *Defining Sustainable Forestry,* ed. G. H. Aplet, N. Johnson, J. T. Olson, and V. Alaric Sample. Washington, D.C.: Island Press.
United States. 93rd Congress, 1st sess., 28 December 1973. *Statutes at Large 93-205. Endangered Species Act of 1973.*
———. 100th Congress, 2d sess., 16 November 1988. *Statutes at Large 100-688 Washington Park Wilderness Act of 1988.*

————. Department of Interior. National Park Service. 1987. *General Management Plan and Environmental Assessment: North Cascades National Park, Ross Lake National Recreation Area, Lake Chelan National Recreation Area*. Denver, Colo.: Denver Service Center.

————. 14 June 1995. News Release: *North Cascades International Park a Private Proposal*. Seattle, Wash.

Washington. *Washington State Wilderness Act of 1984* (Public Law 98-406).

Western Canada Wilderness Committee. 1994. "Cascade International Park." *Education Report* 14(4) Spring: 4 pp. (pamphlet, Vancouver, B.C)

THE WILDLANDS PROJECT: The Yellowstone to Yukon Conservation Initiative and Sky Islands Wildlands Network[1]

Steve Gatewood

Abstract

The limitations of existing designated wilderness areas, national parks, wildlife refuges, and other protected areas to safeguard biodiversity in North America have been increasingly recognized in recent years. These protected areas are simply too small, too isolated, and represent too few ecosystem types to perpetuate the biodiversity of North America. Most national parks and other protected areas were selected based not on ecological criteria, but on aesthetic and recreational criteria, or simply because they contained few resources deemed of economic value. The consequence is that the environment of North America is at risk. Parks do not represent complete ecosystems and cannot on their own ensure the survival and recovery of native species biodiversity. The Wildlands Project is based on the belief that bold new vision is needed if native biodiversity is to survive and recover.

The mission of The Wildlands Project (TWP) is to protect and restore the ecological integrity and native biodiversity of North America through the establishment of a connected system of wildlands. The Wildlands Project coordinates the efforts of regional organizations and individuals in the development of conservation reserve design proposals that

---

1.   This paper was presented at the Regional Approaches to Parks and Protected Areas Workshop in Tijuana, B.C., and published in *Environments* 27, no. 3.

are used to construct a continental vision. Several regional efforts have been identified as primary cooperative projects to serve as models. The methods and approaches used by these primary cooperative projects can be adapted for use by other regions. The *Yellowstone to Yukon Conservation Initiative* and the *Sky Islands Wildlands Network* are two such projects. This paper will provide some background on The Wildlands Project and its scientific basis and then introduce two model projects.

The Scientific Foundation

Conservation biology developed in recent decades in response to the biodiversity crisis. It is an effort to link traditional academic disciplines in the interest of biodiversity conservation. Conservation biology has done much to help illustrate and develop the types of approaches and strategies that are required to protect biodiversity and design reserve networks. Studies in conservation biology point to the need for not individual parks and protected areas, but rather systems of protected areas, linked, and buffered—in other words a reserve network system—if biodiversity is to be truly protected. Furthermore, studies are suggesting that between 25 and 75 percent of any region might require some degree of protection in order to meet conservation goals, such as conservation of native biodiversity and ecological and evolutionary processes.

Conservation planning has four basic objectives in an effort to maintain native biodiversity and design reserve network systems (Noss 1992).

1. Represent, in a system of protected areas, all native ecosystem types across their natural range of variation.
2. Maintain viable populations of all native species in natural patterns of abundance and distribution.
3. Maintain ecological and evolutionary processes.
4. Design and manage the system to be responsive to short-term and long-term environmental change.

The three basic components of a wilderness recovery network are: core reserves, buffers, and connectivity. *Core reserves* are protected natural areas managed primarily to maintain or restore their natural values. These areas form the backbone of a reserve network system. Reserves should be selected based on criteria and objectives such as representing all ecosystem types, maintaining viable populations of native species, and maintaining ecological and evolutionary processes.

Buffer or *multiple-use zones* should envelop core reserves and should be managed in a way that is sensitive to natural ecosystems and processes. Well-managed buffer zones will increase the ability of core reserves to maintain biodiversity. Buffer zones can provide supplementary habitat to native species, and allow species to shift their distributions in response to changes such as fire or other natural disturbances. These zones can also provide for many human uses, such as low intensity residential use.

The idea of *connectivity,* or corridors or linkages, is a fundamental principle for designing regional reserve systems. Connectivity helps to reverse the threat of habitat fragmentation, which is the process whereby large blocks of natural habitat are broken up into smaller and isolated pieces. High connectivity in a reserve network system means that individual reserves are functionally united into a whole that is greater than the sum of its parts.

The Wildlands Project

The vision of The Wildlands Project is to foster the recovery of whole ecosystems and landscapes in every region of North America. This requires a long-term conservation plan. This plan is based upon the three key elements of a reserve network system as outlined above: core reserves, buffers, and connectivity. The Wildlands Project is long-range, with individual regional plans expected to be implemented over decades, if not centuries. The proposal is to develop conservation strategies that are based upon the needs of all life, not just human. It is optimistic.

The Wildlands Project is a nonprofit, publicly supported organization. It is made up of a group of conservation biologists and biodiversity activists from across North America. Work is done in cooperation with independent, grassroots organizations throughout the continent to develop proposals for individual bioregions. Over the long term, these individual proposals would be linked together, eventually covering the whole continent. Draft proposals are developed through discussions and conferences that bring together regional activists, conservation biologists and other scientists, and a wide spectrum of conservation groups. The Wildlands Project supports this process through funding, networking, and technical expertise. Education is a key component of the project. The public, the environmental movement, government agencies, and the academic community must all be educated about the importance of species biodiversity and the steps necessary to protect it. Finally, The Wildlands Project rests on a spirit of social responsibility.

Several regional efforts have been identified as model projects. The methods and approaches developed in these models can be adapted and refined for use by other regions. Two such model transboundary projects are introduced below.

Yellowstone to Yukon Conservation Initiative

The *Yellowstone to Yukon Conservation Initiative* (Y2Y) involves most of the northern Rocky Mountain cordillera, from the Greater Yellowstone Ecosystem in the United States to the Mackenzie Mountains in Canada (fig. 15.1). Portions of the states of Montana, Idaho, and Wyoming, and the Canadian provinces of Alberta, British Columbia as well as the Northwest Territories, and Yukon Territory are included in the project area.

Overview

Y2Y was initiated to address conservation of the relatively undeveloped northern Rocky Mountain ecosystem. Large tracts of natural land area in this region continue to support significant populations of many of the large predators, wide-ranging ungulates, and native fish characteristic of the past. Conditions range from a functionally isolated population of grizzly bears in Yellowstone National Park to isolated islands of human development in a matrix of natural lands within the Bonnet, Plume, and Snake River watersheds of the Yukon. The natural character of the region is rapidly changing as a result of impacts from timber harvesting, oil and gas exploration and production, mining, tourism, and general development for human use.

The principal goal of the Y2Y Conservation Initiative is to develop a transnational structure and process capable of identifying and protecting a system of wildlands and linkages that will ensure the survival of key species and maintain the integrity of ecosystems. Key species include important predators like grizzly bear, wolf, mountain lion, and wolverine; wide-ranging ungulates such as elk and woodland caribou; and native fish like bull trout. Old growth forests, pristine watersheds, and large tracts of undeveloped land are also addressed. The transnational structure of the effort involves indigenous peoples as well as Canadian and U.S. groups.

Approach

The Y2Y Conservation Initiative covers the largest geographic area of any cooperator project, and involves the largest number of grassroots groups. Representatives from over one hundred environmental organizations meet as a Governing Council, at least annually, to provide overall direction and set policy. A Coordinating Committee and several subcommittees manage activities between council meetings, and a project coordinator conducts day-to-day operations. The focus of the Y2Y structure is to do together what individual groups cannot do individually.

The Y2Y region supports significant ecological and cultural diversity, and this is reflected in the strategies used to address critical conservation issues. An initial assessment has been completed that summarizes available data, identifies information gaps, and defines methods to integrate various types of information. The environmental and cultural resource atlas, *A Sense of Place—Issues, Attitudes and Resources in the Yellowstone to Yukon Ecoregion* (Wilcox, Robinson, and Haropey 1998), was produced to present and analyze ecological and socioeconomic information. Since the Northern Rockies is under accelerated assault from development, planning is being integrated with immediate efforts to identify threatened biodiversity "hot spots," and to prevent them from being lost while work on a reserve network design is underway. The ultimate goal is to connect existing and proposed wildlands of the region together into a 1,800-mile contiguous system of protected core reserves, transition or buffer zones, and connecting corridors.

A wide range of biological and environmental data is used for the project. These include species distribution maps and metapopulation status; agency databases on land ownership, management, and designation status; vegetation maps and GAP analysis data; distribution of old growth forests; watershed quality and condition; and other geographic information on roads, forest cover, and land use. Cultural and socioeconomic data are also being identified or generated. Most data are processed and analyzed using GIS technology.

Timeline

The first organizational meeting for the Yellowstone to Yukon Conservation Initiative was held in December 1993. A coordinating committee structure was set up in 1995, and by January of 1998 four major tasks had been completed. These included the establishment of a communications network; the appointment of a project coordinator; production of the atlas; and the sponsorship of a grassroots forum of collaborators and interested parties in October 1997 at Waterton Park in Alberta. An outreach coordinator was hired the following year. Current project objectives are to hire a science coordinator, initiate reserve design in the seven designated subregions through the "Conservation Plans 2000" process, host an aquatics workshop, and develop and refine information on economics.

Status

This large project is still in its formative stages. It is an entirely new conceptual approach, and no models exist for guidance. Great progress has been made, and the project is well on the way to meeting objectives. The network structure established in 1995 is operating well and a cadre of over fifty activists and scientists are contributing substantial time and effort. A "circuit rider" has met with dozens of groups on the role of Y2Y in the region. Publicity produced by or about the initiative has been significant, through for example: *Yukon Wild: Natural Regions of the Yukon* (Yukon Conservation Society and Canadian Parks and Wilderness Society, n.d.); a Canadian Broadcasting Corporation program, *The Nature of Things*, featured Y2Y in a one-hour TV program, *Yellowstone to Yukon— The Wild Heart of North America*, that aired in Canada and the US; and publication of several brochures and documents on Y2Y. The Y2Y organization has also played an important role in supporting the efforts of participant organizations to secure protected status for critical areas or to neutralize threats to those areas.

Funding

Cooperating groups cover their costs and the Canadian Parks and Wilderness Society (CPAWS) provides administrative support. CPAWS and TWP provide fiscal sponsorship for grants from Canada and the U.S., respectively. The North American Fund for Environmental Cooperation (NAFEC) of the North American Free Trade Agreement's (NAFTA) Council for Environmental Cooperation (CEC), granted $66,600 Canadian to conduct the grassroots forum. Several foundations; the Brainerd, Bullitt, Kendall, LaSalle-Adams, Lazar, NewLand, and Foundation for Ecology and Development, as well as organizations and individuals have supported the organization with over U.S.$300,000.

Figure 15.1 Location of the Y2Y Conservation Initiative and Sky Islands Wildlands Network

Sky Islands Wildlands Network

The Sky Islands Wildlands Network (SIWN) includes southern Arizona and New Mexico in the U.S., and northern Chihuahua and Sonora in Mexico (fig. 15.1). The network involves a landscape where the Chihuahua and Sonoran Deserts, and the Rockies and Sierra Madre Mountains, all come together and influence the ecology of high-elevation mountain ranges and riparian areas scattered through a vast desert-steppe environment. The project seeks to protect habitat and landscape connectivity for the distinctive and wide-ranging species of the region. Target species include Mexican wolf, black bear, jaguar,

Photograph 15.1. The U.S.National Bison Range, Bitter Root Valley, Montana with Glacier National Park in the background.

mountain lion, desert bighorn sheep, Mexican spotted owl, northern goshawk, tropical and Sierra Madrean birds, Gila trout, and loach minnow.

Approach

Representation of all ecosystems and maintaining viable populations of all native species are not design objectives at this point; rather the focus is on *rewilding* protection of umbrella or flagship species, and maintenance of ecological processes. SIWN seeks to complete a draft reserve design based on initial principles, and then specifically evaluate through the scientific review process how well the draft design does, or does not, address other fundamental wildlands objectives.

Current efforts are primarily the work of grassroots activists and a few key scientists. Several ranchers are involved, but there has been little government participation to date. All available data are processed through GIS services provided by Forest Guardians as part of its Southwest Wildlands Initiative.

Photograph 15.2 Looking West from the San Simon Playa at the entrance to "Sky Islands" of Chiricahua Mountains, Portal, Arizona.

Timeline

Tony Povilitis conceptualized this project in 1993 with an article in *Wild Earth*. The Sky Island Alliance, formed in 1991, adopted the project in 1993, and the Southwest Wildlands Initiative was created in 1996. The SIWN coordinator was hired in late 1996 and a position in Mexico was created in early 1997. A draft reserve design for the U.S. portion was completed in mid-1998 and it was peer reviewed in early 1999.

Status

Numerous regional meetings and workshops have been held over the last few years, including one in Chihuahua, Mexico. The draft reserve design for the U.S. part was used as a model during a Wildlands Project implementation workshop in early 1999. Fieldwork and GIS mapping continue in the northern Sierra Madre.

Funding

Support received to date totals about $150,000 U.S., including grants and membership dues for the Sky Island Alliance. Foundation grants have come from Patagonia, Fund for Wild Nature, The Foundation for Deep Ecology, Mennen Environmental Foundation, Max and Anna Levinson Foundation, Weeden Foundation, and the Town Creek Foundation.

Photograph 15.3 Overlooking the desert with the Peloncillo Mountain "Sky Island", New Mexico, in the background

Conclusion

The Wildlands Project offers a bold new approach to nature conservation and the *rewilding* of North America; one supported by tremendous developments in ecological science since the 1970s. Because the vision offered by The Wildlands Project is new, and unlike any before it, the approaches and techniques used to design reserve networks and to move towards the next stage—implementation—will continue to be refined. Model projects, such as Y2Y and the Sky Islands will help in this process. Support at both the grassroots and other levels continues to grow and evolve.

For More Information Contact

The Wildlands Project 1955 W. Grant Rd., Suite 145
Tucson, AZ 85745
Tel: 520 884 0875
E-mail: wildlands@twp.org
Internet: www.twp.org
Steve Gatewood, Executive Director
Society for Ecological Restoration
1955 W. Grant Rd., Suite 150
Tucson, AZ 85745
Tel: 520 622 5485
E-mail: steveg@ser.org

Further Reading

Forman, D., J. Davis, D. Johns, R. Noss, and M. Soule. 1992. "The Wildlands Project Mission Statement." *Wild Earth* Special Issue: 3-4.

The Nature of Things. 1997. *Yellowstone to Yukon—The Wild Heart of North America.* Toronto, Ont.: Canadian Broadcasting Corporation.

Noss, R. F. 1992. "The Wildlands Project: Land Conservation Strategy." *Wild Earth,* Special Issue: 10-25.

Noss, R. F., and A.Y. Cooperrider. 1994. *Saving Nature's Legacy: Protecting and Restoring Biodiversity.* Washington, D.C. and Covelo, Calif.: Island Press.

Sky Island Alliance online: www.lobo.net/~skyisland

Wilcox, L., B. Robinson, and A. Haropey. 1998. *A Sense of Place: Issues, Attitudes and Resources in the Yellowstone to Yukon Ecoregion.* Canmore, Alta.: Yellowstone to Yukon Conservation Initiative.

Yellowstone to Yukon online: www.rockies.ca/y2y

Yukon Conservation Society and Canadian Parks and Wilderness Society. 1997. *Yukon Wild: Natural Regions of the Yukon.* Np, Np.

Ecoregion-Based Conservation in the Chihuahuan Desert: Summary of Biological Assessment and Biodiversity Vision

Christopher E. Williams and J. G. Nelson

Abstract

The Chihuahuan Desert is one of the foci of World Wildlife Fund's ecoregion-based planning activities globally. This paper reports on the status of the inventory and collaborative work among U.S. and Mexican organizations, scientists, and planners up to approximately 1998, and includes a brief update written in 2001. It also lays out a binational vision for conservation planning of the Chihuahua and indicates the nature of future socioeconomic and other planning.

Introduction to the Chihuahuan Desert

Deserts, by their very nature, are seldom regarded as important reservoirs of biological diversity. But some deserts are extraordinarily rich in species, rare plants and animals, specialized habitats, and unique biological communities. One such desert is the Chihuahuan, which spans almost a quarter-million square miles, stretching from southeast Arizona across New Mexico, west Texas, and southward deep into Mexico (fig. 16.1; Photograph 16.1). It is one of the most biologically rich and diverse desert ecoregions in the world, rivaled only by the Namib-Karoo of southern Africa and the Great Sandy Desert of Australia (Dinerstein et al. n.d.). On a continental scale, the biodiversity of the Chihuahuan Desert far outstrips many of its better-known North

Figure 16.1 Chichuahuan Desert Ecoregion

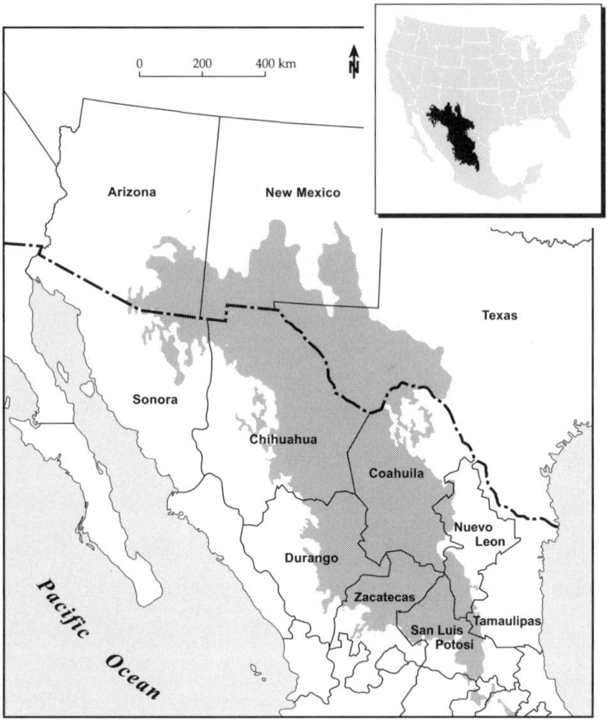

American neighbors. It has more mammal species than Greater Yellowstone, more bird species than the Florida Everglades, more plant species than the forests of the Pacific Northwest, and more reptile species than the Sonoran Desert. In terms of another major measure of biodiversity, *species endemism*, the Chihuahuan Desert is among the top ten ecoregions in the U.S. and Canada.

The Chihuahuan Desert supports a great diversity of cacti species, many endemic to single valleys or hillsides. It is the northernmost range of tropical birds like the elegant trogon and the seven members of the *Momotidae* genus, as well as species more common to temperate climates such as the greater roadrunner, scaled quail, and the rare zone-tailed hawk. Over 250 butterfly species occur in the Chihuahuan, including the giant swallowtail, the largest in North America. The desert is home to wide-ranging mammals such as the pronghorn, the javelina, and the endangered jaguar. The Mexican wolf, believed until recently to be

Photograph 16.1. A sky island and drylands in Northern, Mexico.
Photo credit: J.C. Day.

extinct in the wild, was rediscovered only months ago in the vast expanse of the Chihuahuan.

The Chihuahuan Desert has a great diversity of habitats. Forested mountain ranges rise abruptly like *sky islands* in a desert sea, home to unique assemblages of plant and animal species. In the northern Chihuahuan, Spanish explorers once marveled at the vast grasslands of black grama, tobosa, and giant sacaton. In New Mexico and the Mexican Coahuila State, the wind-blown gypsum soils form a dune scape of white sands; a habitat-type that has given rise to plant species found nowhere else. In the isolated Cuatro Ciénegas basin, spring-fed pools of warm water nurture natural communities of endemic plants and fish like coral reefs in the heart of the desert.

Yet the Chihuahuan Desert is the overlooked desert of North America. The low stature of its rich desert scrub is visually overshadowed by the dramatic architecture of the saguaro, the flagship species of the neighboring Sonoran Desert, or the charismatic Joshua tree of the Mojave Desert. The unimposing creosote bush, the Chihuahuan's dominant plant species, stirs little emotional response. But the images of the Sonoran, Mojave, and Baja deserts belie the fact that the Chihuahuan overshadows these other arid ecoregions in species richness and endemism. Many species of cacti are miniatures. The story of cichlid evolution in the lakes and springs of Cuatro Ciénegas follows a similar pattern to that of the Rift Lakes of Africa, albeit on a smaller scale. Pollination of yucca and some cacti by moths and nectar-feeding bats is a powerful example of coadaptation in nature, seen only rarely by observers.

Table 16.1. Overarching Threats to Biodiversity in the Chihuahuan Desert[a]

Threat	Votes received	Threat	Votes received
Water mismanagement	Unanimous	Unsustainable harvest of native species	9
Growing human population	Unanimous	Altered fire regime	7
Overgrazing and overbrowsing	41	Pesticides	5
Agricultural expansion	29	Loss of indigenous knowledge	5
Lack of law enforcement	24	Road construction, road density	4
Introduced and exotic species	22	Pathogens/disease/parasites	3
Lack of perspective in land use planning	18	Fuel wood harvest	2
Lack of environmental education	16	El Niño	1
Overcollection of biota	14	Mining	0
Air and water pollution	11	Uncontrolled recreation	0
Urbanization	10	Toxic waste disposal	0
Logging	10	Inadequate laws	0
Illegal poaching	9		

[a]Dinerstein et al. n.d.

Land Use Pressures

The Chihuahuan Desert is under tremendous pressure from human population growth and accompanying urban and agricultural development (table 16.1). Many aquatic and riparian habitats in the ecoregion have already been destroyed, notably in the last century, as people compete with wildlife and plants for water and riparian space. As human population centers grow and spread, the limited water resources of the desert are put under ever-greater strain. In Cuatro Ciénegas, for example, a vast lake and wetlands complex has already been reduced to a string of pools. Much of the Chihuahuan has been extensively grazed, and over-grazing remains a serious threat to native flora and fauna. Introduced and exotic species are pushing out native plants in many parts of the desert. Collectors are driving some rare Chihuahuan species towards extinction.

The sweep of the Chihuahuan across two countries and a number of states within the U.S. and Mexico has led to conservation efforts in this, as well as in many other, large, transboundary ecoregions, that are frequently opportunistic and ad-hoc in approach. To conserve biological diversity successfully over the long-term, a more comprehensive approach is needed. Guided by the latest concepts in the emerging science of conservation biology, public agencies, and conservation organizations are embracing ecoregion-based conservation (ERBC) as the most effective spatial scale to achieve conservation objectives.

Ecoregion-Based Conservation (ERBC)

To preserve Chihuahuan biodiversity over the long-term, an ecoregion-based conservation approach (ERBC) has been designed. The goal of this approach is to conserve the full range of species, natural communities, habitats, and ecological processes characteristic of an ecoregion. The Chihuahuan ERBC process began with a series of meetings to promote greater collaboration among many U.S. and Mexican scientists, conservationists, and representatives from government agencies and nongovernmental organizations. An extensive literature review and preliminary mapping study was then conducted of the Chihuahuan Desert. Together with collaborators, including Comisión Nacional para el Conocimiento y Uso de la Biodiversidad (CONABIO), PRONATURA Noreste, The Nature Conservancy, and the Instituto Tecnologico y de Estudios de Superiores Monterrey (ITESM), the World Wildlife Fund U.S. invited over 100 experts to participate in a Chihuahuan priority and assessment workshop. Sixty of the 100 invitees attended, representing a wide array of experts on the ecoregion. Some of those unable to attend the workshop provided peer review for the Chihuahuan work.

The first activity at the workshop was to map important sites and habitats for conservation of six indicator taxa: birds, mammals, herpetofauna, invertebrates, obligate freshwater species, and plants. These 299 locations became known as nominated sites for an ecoregion-based conservation (ERBC) strategy. The second activity was to synthesize the data layers of the overlapping nominated sites to create a smaller subset of sixty-one terrestrial candidate priority sites. However, it is impossible to act immediately on all sixty-one sites. The terrestrial experts therefore adopted a matrix and ranking system to prioritize terrestrial sites based upon the integration of two powerful variables: biological distinctiveness and landscape integrity. The freshwater experts designed a similar matrix, based on biological distinctiveness and habitat intactness (box 16.1).

Box 16.1. Some Relevant Definitions[b]

> *Biological distinctiveness* estimates the relative rarity of biological features at global, continental and ecoregional scales. Classification of this variable ranged from sites that supported high levels of endemism, rare communities, or important ecological and evolutionary processes—the highest ranked features—to multiple sites that support similar species and communities in the lowest ranked category.
>
> *Landscape integrity* estimates the probability of long-term persistence of ecological processes, species assemblages, and other important elements of biodiversity. It is divided into categories based on the size of habitat blocks and their condition: intact or relatively intact, degraded, or highly degraded but still restorable.
>
> *Habitat intactness*, the variable used in the freshwater matrix, is similar to landscape integrity but does not take into account the size of habitat blocks, as this measure is not as relevant or easily measured for freshwater systems.

[b]Dinerstein et al n.d.

Sixteen of the sixty-one candidate priority sites (26%) were selected as highest priority (level one), and eighteen (30%) as high priority, or level two. These sites form the core of the Chihuahuan ERBC strategy. Eighteen more sites were ranked as level three (30%), and six as level four (10%). Freshwater specialists identified thirty-seven priority sites. Twenty-four of these freshwater sites overlap in area by at least 50 percent with a terrestrial priority site (fig. 16.2).

Threats to priority sites were evaluated and scored on the basis of susceptibility to conversion, degradation, and wildlife exploitation over a period of twenty years, and assigned a level of threat of high, medium, low, or unknown. An unacceptably high percentage of level one and two priority sites have a high or medium level of threat. Overall, 24 percent of priority sites have a high threat level, 43 percent a medium threat level, and 25 percent a low threat level.

Protected Areas

Protected areas are the cornerstone of biodiversity conservation. Often, protected areas support the only remaining source populations of endangered species, that is sites where reproduction exceeds mortality. Habitats outside protected areas may be no more than sinks, where populations disperse but do not recruit young in adequate numbers to replace themselves. Analysis of the gaps between protected areas, and the occurrence of significant species and habitats, became a fundamental step

Figure 16.2 Overlap of terrestrial and freshwater priority sites with protected areas

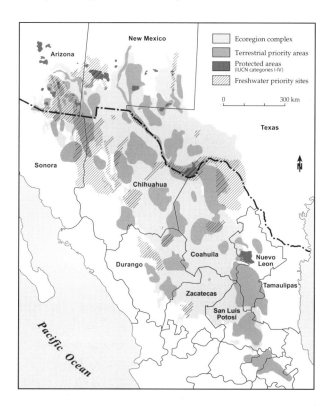

in the ERBC because it illustrates the degree to which protected areas are effectively conserving both species and habitats.

Protected areas are a vital part of the conservation program for the Chihuahuan Desert, although meeting all main targets for the protection of biodiversity will also require other supporting measures such as increasing the commitment to private stewardship. The Chihuahuan Desert ecoregion contains few protected areas established primarily for conservation of biodiversity such as those classified as IUCN categories I-IV (see table 1.1, overview of this book). Only 1.1 percent (6, 900 square kilometers) of the ecoregion is under formal protection; a remarkably low level for such a large, sparsely populated ecoregion. Analysis of overlap between the ninety-eight highest priority terrestrial and freshwater sites and the twenty-eight protected areas shows minimal coverage. Within the sixteen highest priority terrestrial sites (level one), the amount of total protection does not exceed three percent.

The U.S. portion holds eight of the ten protected areas that fall within the highest priority sites, even though (1) 75 percent of the ecoregion is in Mexico, and (2) the American subregion contains only one highest priority site. The U.S. side also contains a number of wilderness study areas, military installations, and NASA facilities. These sites offer wildlife and habitat protection for some species, but do not meet IUCN standards for categories I-IV. This is largely because cattle grazing is permitted in wilderness areas. The analysis does not include the large Mapimi Biosphere Reserve in the Central Chihuahuan subregion, because biosphere reserves do not fall under IUCN categories I-IV.

A biological skew is also evident. None of the protected areas has been designed to conserve freshwater priority sites. This reflects a lack of effort to protect freshwater rivers, streams, and basins, even though the Chihuahuan may be the most globally distinct arid ecoregion in terms of freshwater biodiversity (Dinerstein et al. n.d.).

In sum, the current configuration of protected areas does little to address some fundamental goals of ERBC: giving greater attention to patterns of beta-diversity and conserving large landscapes. The extraordinary beta-diversity of the Chihuahuan is distributed along basins, isolated springs, gypsum habitats, and mountain ranges, and requires a network of reserves distributed widely to capture the complex distributional patterns of many narrow-range endemic species. The overlay analyses of priority sites and protected areas—as determined by CONABIO and this assessment—paint a picture of an extraordinarily diverse desert ecoregion, with a clear sense of where biological priorities are, but vastly inadequate efforts in place to conserve these resources.

A Biodiversity Vision

The core of a biodiversity vision for the Chihuahuan Desert's terrestrial landscape, rivers, and springs, must be idealistic, focusing on what this ecoregion should look like fifty years from now rather than accepting what remains on the map today. Success for the Chihuahuan Desert begins with the conservation in perpetuity of its most distinctive biological features: areas of high endemism for cacti and other endemic plants; globally rare assemblages of freshwater fish species; and representation of all major plant communities in the four biogeographic subregions of the desert. The restoration of landscapes and communities builds on these core features. This includes restoration of flora and fauna associated with prairie dog colonies, desert springs, and desert plant communities affected by overgrazing and overbrowsing, as well as gypsum soil habitats that have been degraded (box 16.2).

Box 16.2. Conservation Targets for the Chihuahuan Desert[c]

To conserve biodiversity at an ecoregion scale, greatest attention should be given to four biological targets:

Distinctive communities, habitats, and assemblages

Representative examples of all habitat types, species assemblages, and ecological or evolutionary phenomena— ideally over their full natural ranges of variation – are important conservation targets. Distinctive units include areas of extraordinary richness, endemism, higher taxonomic uniqueness, or unusual ecological or evolutionary phenomena. These can be evaluated at different biogeographic scales (i.e., globally, regionally, bioregionally, or locally). Some examples found in the Chihuahuan Desert are gypsum dune communities containing many local endemics, assemblages of endemic fish and invertebrates in desert springs, and distinct habitat types such as semi-desert grasslands or montane chaparral.

Large expanses of intact habitats and intact biotas

Intact natural ecosystems and biotas are becoming increasingly rare because of unsustainable human activities. Large units of natural habitat where species populations and ecological processes still fluctuate within their natural range of variation are rapidly disappearing around the world. Larger units are emphasized because principles of landscape ecology and conservation biology suggest that biodiversity will best persist under these conditions. Chihuahuan examples of this target include areas of semi-desert grasslands that still harbor prairie dog communities, pronghorn, and intact floral communities. Other examples are intact pine-oak and chaparral habitats of some desert ranges and spring systems with their full complement of native species still extant.

Keystone ecosystems, habitats, species, or phenomena

At regional and local scales, certain habitats may exert a powerful influence on biodiversity in surrounding habitats and ecosystems. Their persistence and intact ecological processes may be critical for many species and ecological processes in neighboring areas. For example, riparian habitats or springs in the Chihuahuan Desert are vitally important for maintaining vertebrate populations in surrounding habitats. Riparian forests are also essential as feeding, shelter, and resting habitat for migratory songbirds. Other linkage habitats, migration corridors, or drought or fire refugia may also be critical habitats for maintaining ecological processes. Keystone species, such as large mammalian predators and black-tailed prairie dogs, also have a strong influence on the structure and integrity of natural communities.

Distinctive large-scale ecological phenomena

The conservation of distinctive large-scale ecological phenomena – long-distance migration of songbirds or the seasonal, trans-ecoregion migrations of bats – require a combination of site-specific, regional, and policy-level efforts applied over vast continental areas or widely disjunct regions. For example, conservation of flowering cacti across whole landscapes may be important for migratory bats. Habitats or sites that may not be particularly distinctive (e.g., high richness or endemism) or intact may still act as critical habitat for migratory species.

[c]Dinerstein et al. n.d.

Another element of the vision is to manage large "conservation landscapes" of sufficient size and connectivity to maintain important ecological processes and wide-ranging species. This includes restoration, where appropriate, of populations of Mexican wolves, mountain lions, jaguar, black bear, pronghorn antelope, and aplomado falcons. Through the protection of these large conservation landscapes, managed in collaboration with a variety of stakeholders, important gaps in the protected area network will be addressed. Finally, the vision will address the conservation of sites important to hemispherical and regional migrants that spend part of their lives in the Chihuahuan Desert and part in adjacent or distant ecoregions; for example, migratory birds, bats, and monarch butterflies.

For the Chihuahuan ecoregion conservation effort to succeed, the overarching threats identified in this assessment, including mismanagement and diversion of water resources, overpopulation in sensitive areas, overgrazing and overbrowsing of native plant communities, and lack of enforcement of existing laws, must be addressed in a timely and effective manner. Educators, officials, local leaders, and NGOs must sensitize and win support from a cross-section of communities which understand and value biodiversity in their backyard, because of the ecological services it provides as well as its intrinsic value.

A set of restoration targets for terrestrial and freshwater biodiversity, with a clear timetable, must be formulated within the next few years. For the long-term persistence of biodiversity, degraded lands outside of the core areas must be able to sustain seasonal movements of larger vertebrates and other key ecological processes. A long-term vision for the conservation of the Chihuahuan Desert will promote the application of "biodiversity-friendly" land use and wildlife practices. It will also stress the conservation of keystone habitats, such as riparian habitats and springs, in highly managed areas. This effort will help sustain ecological integrity across human-dominated landscapes and within core areas. As partners in the conservation of one of the world's most biologically rich, warm deserts, citizens of the U.S. and Mexico have a joint global responsibility before them. Success in the Chihuahuan initiative will set an example for other nations to follow for the long-term conservation of arid ecosystems.

A firm scientific foundation is only the first step to building a conservation action plan for the Chihuahuan Desert. Although the Monterrey workshop identified major threats to Chihuahuan biodiversity, and a number of measures to address them, success requires a detailed understanding of the social, economic, and political factors that shape human behaviors that lead to biodiversity loss. Thus, in November of 1998, WWF and PRONATURA *Noreste* sponsored a second workshop in El

Paso, Texas. Chihuahuan regional experts in economics, agriculture, history, geography, anthropology, water management, land tenure and use, population and demographics, grazing policy, law enforcement, and other fields, met to help us understand the root causes of biodiversity loss and identify opportunities for conservation.

The El Paso workshop, like the previous biologically-oriented biologists' meeting the year before, examined the Chihuahuan Desert at multiple scales, considering socioeconomic forces at work across the ecoregion and their impacts at specific priority sites. Continuing the process begun in El Paso, WWF, PRONATURA, and other local partners will consult with local officials, conservationists, and stakeholders to create strategies for conservation at priority sites that connect well with efforts to address ecoregion-wide threats to biodiversity. This multiscale approach is necessary if we are to achieve lasting conservation of the desert's wildlife and plants.

Armed with the vision of success created as a result of the first workshop, and the strategies to achieve it identified in the second, the World Wildlife Fund can facilitate the creation of a conservation action plan for the Chihuahuan Desert ecoregion. This plan is not the work of WWF alone, but involves the efforts of partners and collaborators on both sides of the border. The goal is that conservation organizations, academic institutions, federal, state, and local governments, landowners, and other stakeholders will partner with WWF-U.S. to produce and promote the conservation plan.

The biodiversity vision is the foundation on which people with a stake in the future of the Chihuahuan Desert can build a conservation strategy for the ecoregion. It focuses the conservation planning process on species, ecological processes, and geographic areas most important for sustaining and restoring Chihuahuan biodiversity, and suggests priorities for action. The biological vision will shape, and in turn will be shaped by, an analogous analysis of the socioeconomic forces at work in the ecoregion that influence human communities and their interactions with nature. No matter how firmly grounded in the principles of conservation biology and socioeconomic analysis a conservation strategy may be, it can accomplish little, however, without strong commitment from stakeholders within the ecoregion. Thus, WWF and partners are investing significant resources in activities to raise awareness, build constituencies, enlist the aid of governments, academic institutions, and NGOs, and involve local communities in all aspects of Chihuahuan ecoregion conservation.

Postscript

Since 1999, WWF and its many partners in the Chihuahuan Desert have moved forward with the conservation initiatives, while continuing to refine the biological vision and develop the conservation plan. The Nature Conservancy, Pronatura *Norste*, and WWF are combining the biological data of their respective projects in the Chihuahuan Desert to create an integrated multiscale conservation plan. The plan will be completed in draft by late 2001.

The El Paso workshop provided an important overview of socioeconomic forces affecting biodiversity in the Chihuahuan Desert, but general socioeconomic information at the scale of the ecoregion has not proven to be as useful as anticipated. Greater success is being achieved by studying the socioeconomic factors at the scale of priority sites, such as the Rio Grande basin, and by issues such as the economics of irrigated agriculture or the cultural differences that influence cooperation across transboundary protected areas. It is through a combination of overarching policy and understanding of local factors and their effects, on the biodiversity of priority sites, that effective ecoregion conservation strategies will be developed.

References

Much of the information in this paper is derived from Dinerstein et al. n.d. and the inventories, assessment, and cooperation upon which it is based. Chris Williams has also had considerable experience with the WWF work on the Chihuahua, and Gordon Nelson has worked in the Arizona-western New Mexico section of the desert periodically for about five years.

Barbault, R., and G. Halffter, eds. 1981. *Ecology of the Chihuahuan Desert*. México D.F., México: Instituto de Ecología.

Brown, D. E., ed. 1994. *Biotic communities: Southwestern United States and northwestern Mexico*. Salt Lake City, Utah: University of Utah Press.

Dinerstein, E., D. Olson, J. Atchley, C. Loucks, S. Contreras-Balderas, R. Abell, E. Inigo, E. Enkerlin, C. E. Williams, and G. Castilleja. n.d. Ecoregion-Based Conservation in the Chihuahuan Desert: Biological Assessment and Biodiversity Vision. Draft Report. World Wildlife Fund, Comisíon National para el Conocimiento y Uso de la Biodiversidad (CONABIO), The Nature Conservancy, PRONATURA Noreste, and the Instituto Tecnologico y de Estudios Superiores de Monterrey (ITESM).

Noss, R. 1993. "The Wildlands Project: Land conservation strategy." *Wild Earth* Special Issue:10-25.

Soulé, M., and R. Noss. 1998. "Rewilding and biodiversity: Complementary goals for continental conservation." *Wild Earth* 8:18-28.

Tweit, S. J. 1995. *Barren, wild, and worthless: Living in the Chihuahuan Desert.* Albuquerque, N. Mex.: University of New Mexico Press.

PARKS, PROTECTED AREAS, AND ENVIRONMENTAL EDUCATION IN NORTH AMERICA

John C. Miles and James Loucky

Introduction

The goal of this paper is to explore the role that environmental education might play in protection of lands designated for preservation by Canada, the United States, and Mexico. It presents an overview of differing challenges in protection of such areas in the three North American nations, reviews the factors affecting education as a protection tool in each of the three, and suggests avenues that might make education a significant management and protection tool. The intent is to suggest a framework for discussing the role of education in parks and protected area management in North America.

Environmental education in its broadest definition aims to encourage environmentally responsible behavior, most notably behavior that contributes to environmental sustainability; that is, use of the world's resources today without reduction of opportunity for use of those resources by future generations. In the context of parks and protected areas, education entails providing information and a structured experience that engenders understanding of the value of a place to be protected. Park and protected area management may contribute to global goals, but our focus here is specifically on educational measures that may assist in the process of protecting designated areas.

A Complex Challenge for Three Nations

Differences in conservation approaches and challenges in the three nations of North America derive from different histories and cultures, and complicate efforts to prescribe a single management approach that is suitable for all three situations. The same holds true for prescription of educational approaches. The first task, then, is to compare the park and protected area systems of the three nations and their respective approaches to management.

Mexico

The mounting environmental crises in Mexico are a consequence of a development model that places more weight on production than on nature and human justice (Simon 1997, Barkin 1998). In the drive for economic recovery, social and environmental costs of growth have been of secondary concern, which has resulted in several serious problems as outlined below.

- Deforestation related to subsistence cultivation, cattle ranching, and the timber industry has resulted in the loss of over one million acres per year. Only a fraction of tropical rainforest remains; the Lacondon Rainforest in southern Mexico, for example, has been reduced to half its original size, in large part through colonization programs designed to diffuse peasant unrest in the highlands.
- Erosion is another consequence of intensive agriculture and extensive cattle grazing. An estimated 560 million tons of topsoil are lost each year.
- Desertification is accelerated as a result of the overdrawing of aquifers, deforestation, and erosion. This is nowhere more evident than the lunar landscape of much of the Mixteca region of Oaxaca.
- Mexico, one of the world''s most biodiverse nations, is also experiencing one of the highest rates of loss of biological diversity.
- Toxins are ubiquitous with pesticides banned in the U.S. widely used in agriculture, resulting in contamination of fields and of field workers.

Mexico is a developing nation, unlike its two larger neighbors to the north. Its economic situation is precarious, its environmental problems massive, yet it is attempting to conserve natural areas of exceptional value.

Mexico's political economic history helps explain contemporary differences in environmental policy compared to Canada and the United

States. All "national" space is already owned by local people, and often has multiple claims on it. The 7,232 square kilometer Calakmul Biosphere Reserve on the Yucatan Peninsula borders 114 communities whose 25,000 residents have practiced agriculture, forestry, and cattle ranching long before the tropical reserve was established in 1989 (Ayers 1998). Similarly, the twenty square kilometers that constitute the Monte Alban archaeological park in Oaxaca, involve land used by fifteen local communities (Garcia and Corbett 1995). Parks and protected areas tend to be perceived as usable spaces by people who often have limited resources to support themselves. Even seemingly clear processes, such as deforestation, are perceived very differently by colonists than by scientists and policy makers (Arizpe, Paz, and Velaquez 1996).

Parks and protected areas in Mexico are thus considered by the people living around, and in, them as part of the landscape upon which they depend for their livelihoods, or even as their homeland. Biologists, historians, archaeologists, and environmental activists identify values in landscapes, which are viewed by policy makers as of national or even global value, and lawmakers impose a protected status upon such areas. But, people still live there and may not understand the values imposed by others, seen as outsiders, upon these places. Too often, rural peoples have been displaced from other lands, have been unable to continue traditional resource management practices, and even faced little choice but to use and sometimes degrade physically attractive yet productively precarious areas in their efforts to survive. In other words, the root causes of pressure to exploit resources in existing parks and potential protected areas, and to minimize attention to impacts of that use, are embedded in official economic policies.

Canada

The situation in Canada is quite different. While Canada is geographically large and has an extensive rural and indigenous population, it is considered a developed nation with an advanced economy. The county has pursued a policy for protecting places of national significance since the 1880s, when the first national and provincial reservations were established. Initial motivation for establishment of parks was the desire to protect from the excesses of private development, areas judged of provincial and national value. In the wake of damage to resources, as occurred for example at Niagara

Falls, the Canadian government assumed a role as protector of places that had great potential for public recreation, inspiration, and education (Shultis 1995). An extensive system of national parks was established over the ensuing century, with considerable progress in recent decades. The goal is a system that includes a national park in each of Canada's thirty-nine natural regions, with all parks managed to maintain their ecological integrity. Provinces have also moved to increase their park systems, with Ontario establishing 155 new provincial parks in 1983 alone, and British Columbia doubling its provincial park system in the 1990s to 12 percent of the land base (see McNamee, this volume).

The Canadian story regarding protection of lands as parks and other protected area designations, is one of slow progress for decades with occasional spurts of activity. In a country of geographic immensity, with a relatively small population and low overall density of settlement—except along the border with the United States—recognition of the need to set aside large tracts of land as parks and protected areas has been slow to build. Successive federal governments have been reluctant to preserve wilderness as such, since there was pressure to develop a country that seemed so empty. Until recently, public support for preservation has been modest. In addition, controversies over cultural and sovereignty issues, and outstanding aboriginal land claims, have further complicated efforts to decide which areas to protect and how to protect them.

Park and protected area management in Canada encounters some of the same challenges in certain areas as those faced by Mexico, while in others the challenges are very different. Some large national parks in the far north, for instance, such as Wapusk in Manitoba and Northern Yukon in the Yukon, involve aboriginal people who live upon land that is protected. In the Northern Yukon case, a park was established as part of the Western Arctic Inuvialuit Land Claims Agreement, covering critical habitat for the Porcupine caribou herd, and thus protecting wildlife used by aboriginal people for subsistence. In Wapusk, the management structure of the park involves an advisory board whose members include both Aboriginal and non-Aboriginal peoples who live in and around the park. In these instances, the management of the park involves the people who live there, aboriginal cultural values, and strong integration of local communities into the challenges of achieving park goals such as protection of ecological integrity.

In other parts of Canada, the parks and protected areas do not physically include human communities. These range from wild and unsettled forests, to coastlines, and mountain regions. In such places, protection of wildness does not directly affect the daily lives of people, but does so indirectly by placing areas off-limits to development and regulating ways in which people can use such areas for any activity, including recreation. Thus, while there are not communities *in* these areas, there are communities *around* them that are affected by park and protected area designation. In virtually every case, designation of an area for protection is contentious, and achievement of management goals after designation involves the community and general public.

United States

Finally, in the United States, with its large and diverse system of national parks and wilderness areas, the challenges of managing parks and protected areas differ in certain respects from both of the other nations. The United States has the most extensive system of protected areas in North America, with over 100 million acres designated as part of the National Wilderness Preservation System; the consequence of a preservation movement historically much stronger than those in either Canada or Mexico. In the United States, no communities are located within national parks and wilderness areas in the sense found in the other countries, with the exception of Stehekin in the North Cascades, and developed resorts within the parks. No communities depend upon protected lands for traditional subsistence, although in Alaska subsistence has been incorporated into management of several of the national park system units.

Protected reserves in the United States are increasingly surrounded by development. Gateway communities grow on park boundaries along major access routes. Mining, timber harvest, tourist and even residential development, pose external threats to the scenic and ecological integrity of protected areas. Parks and other protected areas become increasingly part of regional communities as the human population grows in the American West. Visitation to national parks grows all the while, and Americans unknowingly impact parks and protected areas by "loving them" too often and with too much enthusiasm.

The U.S. park and protected area system is extensive, but many argue it is far from complete. Most protected areas were not established with ecological goals in mind, but rather for maintaining scenic and recreational values. The work of conservation biologists has revealed that the protected area system is more incomplete than once thought, as essential functions involving biological diversity have been identified (Noss and Cooperrider 1994). Drive is currently underway in the United States to protect remaining roadless areas, and other parts of the public land system, for a variety of reasons; conservation of biological diversity prominent among them (Kerr 1999).

The situation in the United States, while different in many respects from that in the other two nations, involves similar educational challenges. The goals of protection of resource values like ecological integrity, biological diversity, and other natural and cultural values, involve human communities and depend upon support of those communities for success. Great differences are found in the situations of the three nations. In all cases, the future of parks and protected areas will require involvement in management decisions of people, who live near, and use, these areas. Such involvement will require education of these residents by managers, and conversely, education of managers by the local people. This interactive process is a form of environmental education.

A Role for Education

What role might there be for education in meeting the parks and protected area challenges in these three different situations? What generalizations can be offered about education as a management tool for parks and protected areas in Mexico, Canada, and the United States?

The term "education" here is used in the sense of the process of informing people about parks and protected areas. Its goals are to motivate them to be curious about and interested in these areas, to understand the values of these areas and their protection to themselves and the larger community, and to be willing to act to assure protection. Education, in this context, is a companion process to regulation and provision of incentive for proper action. If the goal of protected area management is to protect the resources of that area, whatever they may be, then the process of management entails preventing people from taking actions that would harm those resources, while motivating them to take actions that will help protect them. Achieving management goals in parks and protected areas often involves management of people more than of physical resources (Cole, Petersen, and Lucas 1987). Education can and must be part of any program aimed at management of visitors and residents.

Education has been an integral part of park and protected area management in the United States and Canada nearly since the beginning of the movement that established such areas (Mackintosh 1986). At least since the 1920s, the emphasis has been upon helping people understand and appreciate what they have experienced in these areas. Interpreters, as these educators are called, used the drama of creation and stories, which explain the values that the parks were often established to protect. Gradually this process of interpretation broadened to explain general processes of the landscape, ecological relationships, and management issues. Interpretation remains the most common form of education in parks and protected areas today. Using firsthand experience of an object, artifact, landscape, or site, it seeks to reveal the meaning and relationship of the subject to the visitor.

Other educational approaches have complemented interpretation in parks and protected areas. College and university classes have used them as outdoor classrooms and natural laboratories, bringing students for varying periods during which they receive instruction, or conduct research. Where park areas are close to communities, field trips have exposed younger students to interpretation and other approaches to learning. Nonprofit, cooperating associations have sold publications about parks and protected areas to visitors, and supported other public relations and educational efforts with the funds raised by their activities. Park management agencies have reached out to communities, sending interpreters and educators into schools and other youth group settings, though poor funding has seriously limited the outreach that could have been achieved. In recent years, partnerships with nonprofit educational institutes, such as the North Cascades Institute and the Yosemite Institute, have evolved for offering a variety of educational programs to people of all ages. In short, education in and for national parks and protected areas is not a new idea.

What is new, however, is a growing recognition that brief visitor focused interpretation challenges—the dominant form of education currently being practiced—misses much of the potential of education to assist in meeting resource protection. The interpretive educational experience, while better than no educational experience, is too brief and consequently too superficial to teach very much. Most participants in interpretive programs are "passing through." This is not to criticize interpretation or suggest that less of it should be offered, but simply to recognize its limitations.

The U.S. National Park Service (NPS) recently recognized this challenge. A report from its *Education Initiative Symposium* stated (NPS 1997):

> Changing demographics, emerging technologies, and national priorities are necessitating additional approaches. Few fields have changed more rapidly in the last few years than education and communications.... There are exciting possibilities for educating broad sectors of society—people of all ages and ethnicities, even if they never visit an NPS area. Understanding different perspectives and making programs and materials relevant to diverse groups increases the potential to engage millions throughout the country in learning about the parks, the resources, and the importance of stewardship.

The report suggests that the educational process leading to an ethic of stewardship of parks and protected areas must reach well beyond park boundaries. If protection is to be national policy, then the broad community must understand what is being valued and why and how it can be protected.

Inclusion of people in the management of and education about parks is clearly also important in Mexico. Given the struggles for resources and consequent sets of conflicts where parks and people overlap, perhaps the most critical challenge for Mexico is to include local involvement and benefits as an integral part of park management. It may be unrealistic, even undesirable, to envision some parks without people in Mexico (Keck 1995). The environmental education discourse is, in fact, shifting from viewing these people as perpetrators of environmental damage to consideration of them as holders of valuable environmental knowledge and integral participants in potential solutions.

The current state of environmental education in Mexico is somewhat distinct from that outlined above for the United States and Canada. While increasingly in vogue (Simonian 1995), it is bedeviled by lack of agreement as to what the term really means. Some treat it as equivalent to field biology, others as practical housekeeping; for example, do not pour oil down the drain. Still others see it as a potentially separate field. Nonetheless, growing recognition of the depth of ecological deterioration has heightened realization of the need to strengthen environmental awareness in the family as well as schools. Mexican teachers share with their northern neighbors the challenge of fitting new material into existing programs of study, which inevitably also needs to be authorized at a high level and sanctioned by unions. Yet there are many more children's books with environmental themes and teachers are far more informed than even a few years ago. Direct experiences by schoolchildren are also becoming more common, whether it be through releasing baby sea turtles in Chacagua National Park on the Pacific Coast, adopting a tree in a cloud forest in Chiapas managed by the nongovernmental agency Pronatura, or field trips to the monarch butterfly reserve several hours west of the Mexico City metropolis.

The educational challenge relating to parks and protected areas in Mexico thus involves people who can learn about, and who may visit, these areas as well as those who live in or near them. Since three-quarters of the population in Mexico today lives in cities, the urban orientation of environmental education is crucial. Environmental education has also been an increasing focus of nongovernmental efforts, perhaps most notably by the "Grupo de Cien," a coalition of one hundred of Mexico's most noted artists, authors, and statespersons who have become active defenders of the environment and proponents of educating in, and about, parks and protected areas.

What, in view of all of this, can be said about how education can and should become part of the management of parks and protected areas? An obvious first point is that once the decision has been made to include education in the management toolkit, the goals and objectives of programs must be clear. These will vary from country to country, park to park, even from place to place within large parks and protected areas. In Mexico and Canada, for instance, the overriding goal in some parks where people live on the landscape must be to include local people in discussions regarding the benefits to, and perceived difficulties in, protecting the resources of the area under consideration. If people understand the value of the place and its resources for them, and if in the long-term their welfare can truly be enhanced by protection, they will likely help design and promote measures necessary for maintenance of resource values. A necessary part of this effort must be to develop, or add to, the understanding of resource values sufficiently for local people to participate in setting of management policy and regulation. As the Canadian Environmental Advisory Council stated in *A Protected Areas Vision for Canada* (1991:49); "[a]chieving this goal will result in a better informed public that will appreciate the area's natural and cultural heritage and transfer acquired values and experiences into the broader context of increased personal responsibility and improved lifestyles."

The goal of this effort is not to impose resource values on local people, but to collaborate in finding ways to mediate local resource values with those perceived by the national community beyond the immediate area. The problem may not be a lack of understanding of the larger resource values by local people, but a lack of options. Local people often recognize the values of local resources to the larger community, but they must make a living, even if doing so affects the resource in question. On the other side of the ledger, for managers and staff of protected areas, the challenge is to work with the local people to identify and establish sustainable resource use patterns acceptable to all parties. Where necessary and possible, alternate ways should be provided for local people to generate necessary income.

Another problem to be addressed by a management program may be threats to the resources of parks and protected areas posed by development outside area boundaries. In this case, the target group of an educational program may be different than the resident or proximate local populations, and the approach and delivery systems must also be different. Local entrepreneurs generally attempt to gain as much benefit as they can from visitors attracted to a park, and in doing so may threaten the very resources that attract these visitors. In such cases, the challenge is to support a local community in taking a long-term view of the opportunity it has, particularly by providing comparative perspectives on threats to resources, as well as analyses of potential long-term consequences if shortsighted actions jeopardize the resource that is the attraction itself. The goal in these situations is to inform so as to stimulate enlightened self-interest of thoughtful people in the community, which in turn will encourage voluntary restraint of problematical activities.

While traditional interpretive and educational approaches should continue to address the worthy goals to which they have always been directed, careful analysis of emerging management problems and identification of new educational goals is essential. Traditional interpretation directed at visitors will simply not reach local populations. Programs reaching beyond the boundaries of parks and protected areas, geographically and conceptually, are required. Educational outreach poses many problems. These include: funding as there is seldom enough even now to meet visitor education needs; local resistance to what is perceived as outside agency interference in local prerogatives and autonomy; and paucity of existing venues for educational programs. Still, it is essential that ways be found to undertake outreach simultaneously with in-park interpretation, if educational approaches with local populations are to be of any significance.

Education for Parks and Protected Areas

In making the case that education has a significant role to play in management of parks and protected areas, we here suggest some pragmatic considerations, offering these in no particular order of priority.

1. Build the educational approach on the extensive foundation of work that has been done in interpretation and environmental education. As noted earlier, interpretation has been practiced for nearly a century, and much has been learned. Environmental education has been explored for three decades and provides an extensive foundation of insights into how to go about identifying and addressing environmental education goals and objectives in many settings. Programs specifically designed to assist in the protection of parks and protected areas should build on this work.

2. Set educational goals and objectives systematically and with full involvement of the communities that will be targets of educational activities. Common sense, as well as much educational literature, dictates that goals and objectives must be carefully developed. As the old proverb observes, "If you don't know where you are going, any road will get you there." Crucial to success of any educational enterprise is a clear endpoint toward which effort can be directed and by which that effort can be effectively evaluated. Additionally, target communities must be involved in the definition of the end points. Goal and objective setting is ideally done by teams comprised of educators (for process), resource specialists (for content), managers (to check feasibility), and community members (to assure social and cultural appropriateness and acceptance). One task for these partners is to decide what key concepts should be taught. The Biodiversity Project, a nonprofit organization based in Madison, Wisconsin focusing on conservation and restoration of biological resources, provides an example of key concepts identified around "community biodiversity" (1998:42).

• Everyone lives in an ecosystem

- Native species add ecological richness and value to the local landscape and to the services that nature provides the local community
- Native plant species are adapted to the local climate and soils, require less maintenance, are less susceptible to disease, and provide important habitat for native wildlife
- Nonnative (alien or exotic) species harm native ecosystems and native species by usurping niches and disrupting food webs

Since the process of designing an educational program of any kind begins with identification of what is to be taught, clear articulation of concepts within learning objectives sets any educational effort off on the right foot.

3. The learning process aimed at achieving goals and a team involving local resource people should similarly design objectives. After the goals and objectives are set, the next major task is deciding the best path to reach the "end points." This effort is also best achieved by teams and with "local" perspective.

4. Identify the "stories" central to parks and protected areas that are relevant to various groups, and find ways to "tell" these stories. Each area is special for a reason, and its special qualities can and must be presented not in dry technical language but in ways that allow people to relate an area's values to their lives. This is storytelling, which is faithful to fact but compelling to the imagination. It is also storytelling which relates to the ethos and experiences of local people.

5. Adapt the message and approach to the cultural heritage(s) of the learners. In the context of the previous point, an approach appropriate for a resident of a city in the United States may not be effective for a rural Mexican learner, or for Inuit in the Canadian north. This dimension of educational program development has been elusive because, since most park and protected area visitors have been relatively affluent travelers from urban centers, the limited funds available for education have been directed toward this dominant visitor group. In their struggle for budget and bureaucratic power, management agencies cater to those believed to be the most effective constituency group (Clarke and McCool 1985). They have perceived this constituency to be mostly the affluent traveler, and thus have not expanded their scope to other groups.

6. Work with partners, such as locally based organizations, to reach out to nearby communities, adjacent landowners, and commercial

operators to develop understanding of common interest in protection (CEAC 1991). Where community-based educational organizations already exist, they should be enlisted in leading, or at least participating in, the parks and protected area educational effort. Since they are already embedded in the local community, they can assist with goal setting, assessment of appropriate educational approaches, and development of the critical shared commitment to long-term success of the educational effort.

7. Link programs and services to state and local curricula. This applies only to the aspects of educational programs for parks and protected areas that involve formal learning, as in elementary and secondary schools. Given the substantial responsibilities faced by most teachers, units that contribute to achieving existing student learning objectives will be most readily embraced. Furthermore, the more easily a learning unit or resource can be incorporated into a teacher's curriculum, the more likely it will be used.

8. Educate the educators. Incorporating learning involving parks and protected areas into curricula is also most likely when teachers recognize the tangible benefits of doing so. Thus, an essential step toward inserting concepts and stories that address park and protected area educational objectives, is teacher development. This may include: conferences for teachers with appropriate credit or other reward-based incentives attached; training programs offered through professional organizations; programs that bring teachers to the parks and protected areas and involve them directly in programs and efforts there; use of internet and distance education learning programs, in partnerships with agencies and universities; and incorporation of essential learning about parks and protected areas into preservice teacher education programs.

9. Encourage involvement of community-based environmental education organizations in furthering the educational goals established for parks and protected areas. Such organizations enjoy a freedom to experiment and a base of community support that may be denied government agencies. An excellent example of this approach is the North Cascades Institute in Washington State, which was encouraged by the U.S. National Park Service and the Forest Service. The institute has assisted with educational programming in the North Cascades National Park Complex and three national forests. Two park rangers conceived of a nonprofit field school focusing on the North Cascades mountain region. They shared their idea with superintendents of North Cascades

National Park, one of whom supported initial development of the organization and promoted cooperation of the park. Both the Park Service and the Forest Service, traditionally rivals, were housed together in one administrative setting, and the superintendent assisted the institute in its educational goals as a way of complementing existing educational efforts of the two agencies in the region. This relationship has grown and matured for fifteen years and achieved a high level of effective educational activity in cooperation with both agencies.

10. Promote the use of protected areas as extensions of conventional classrooms. Direct experience of resource values is the most powerful learning experience that can be enjoyed by people. Whenever learners are in reasonable proximity to parks and protected areas, managers should encourage use of these areas for educational activities.

11. Incorporate teaching about the full range of resource values into educational programs. Learners can come to appreciate that humans attach a range of values to resources that are given measures of protection in parks and protected areas. While resources have market value, they usually also have vital life-support value for the human community as providers of essential ecological services, genetic diversity value, historical and cultural symbolization value, esthetic, and religious value (Rolston 1986).

12. Periodically assess the effectiveness of educational programs and adapt approaches based on knowledge gained from these assessments. After an educational program properly based on clear objectives has been implemented, it should be examined to evaluate whether it is achieving the ends for which it was designed. It can be continued and enhanced, modified, or replaced. While common sense dictates this, modification of educational programming based on assessment is not as common as might be expected.

While not exhaustive, these points are offered as topics for stimulating exploration of how education might be used to support effective management of parks and protected areas.

Conclusion

The future of parks and protected areas in North America presents many challenges, some of which have been touched upon in this discussion.

The greatest challenge comes from a growing human population with a growing appetite for natural resources. A big question is: can the needs and wants of North Americans be satisfied without degradation of the places that have been, or may yet be, designated as having special natural or cultural value? Even though the rate of population growth in North America is declining, absolute growth will continue for decades. Along with this pressure, growth of consumption to unprecedented and unsustainable levels requires an ever-growing input of natural resources. In the face of these pressures, the three nations of North America struggle to protect remnants of their natural and cultural heritage from human-induced change that is destroying the heritage values of these places.

The argument presented here is that education is critical to any effective and long-term management of parks and protected areas and the human pressures on them. While hardly a new idea, the urgency of considering it is perhaps greater than ever before. The goal of education in these areas, pursued for nearly a century in the United States and Canada, has been to help the visitor appreciate and understand the values of the area they are experiencing. The aim has been to use these precious places as educational resources for the enhancement of the lives of people who visit them. This noble aim should continue to be a goal of education in parks and protected areas. But, in the twenty-first century this must be complemented by educational strategies, which directly help to achieve the goals of resource protection. In essence, education must become a management "tool" as well as a process of enrichment and growth for visitors.

Environmental education is usually considered a process directed primarily at children. The aim is to develop understanding, appreciation, and motivation in the young so that when they grow up they will support environmental protection. The young must continue to be the target of such education, but not only the young. Development in North America is progressing at such a rapid rate that scarce resources such as wilderness and threatened and endangered species cannot wait for future generations to come to their defense. This requires a re-examination of the very meaning and implications of terms such as "development" and "protection." The need is for shifting focus towards accountability, for defense in the present as well as the future. Education must therefore be integrated into management processes that work with current visitors

and leaders to assure that the natural and cultural heritage currently protected in parks and other protected areas is present for future generations
to benefit from and enjoy.

The focus of most environmental educators has not been on many of
the goals discussed here. Educating for parks and protected areas should
be added to the goals of organizations like the North American Association for Environmental Education. More of the accumulated knowledge
of how to do effective environmental education needs to be applied to
park and protected area management than has been the case to date.

References

Arizpe, L., F. Paz, and M. Velazquez. 1996. *Culture and Global Change: Social Perceptions of
Deforestation in the Lacandona Rain Forest in Mexico.* Ann Arbor: University of
Michigan Press.

Ayers, T. 1998. "Scientists Engage Mexican Residents in Conservation Efforts." *Science*
281: 1372-1373.

Barkin, D. 1998. *Wealth, Poverty, and Sustainable Development.* Mexico: Centro de Ecología
y Desarrollo.

The Biodiversity Project. 1998. *Engaging the Public on Biodiversity: A Road Map for
Education and Communication Strategies.* Madison, WI: The Biodiversity Project.

Canadian Environmental Advisory Council. 1991. *A Protected Areas Vision for Canada.*
Ottawa: Ministry of Supply and Services Canada.

Clarke, J. and D. McCool. 1985. *Staking Out the Terrain: Power Differentials among Natural
Resource Management Agencies.* Albany: SUNY Press.

Cole, D. N., M. E. Petersen, and R. C. Lucas. 1987. *Managing Wilderness Recreation Use:
Common Problems and Potential Solutions.* General Technical Report INT-230. Ogden,
UT: U.S. Forest Service, Intermountain Research Station.

Garcia, N. R., and J. Corbett. 1995. "Land Tenure Systems, Economic Development, and
Protected Areas in Mexico," pp 55-61. In *Sustainable Society and Protected Areas*, ed.
Robert M. Linn. Hancock, MI: The George Wright Society.

Keck, M. E. 1995. "Parks, People and Power: The Shifting Terrain of Environmentalism."
NACLA Report on the Americas 28 (5): 36-41.

Kerr, A. 1999. "Big Wild: A Legislative Vehicle for Conserving and Restoring Wildlands
in the United States." *Wild Earth* 9:4, 77-86.

Mackintosh, B. 1986. *Interpretation in the National Park Service: A Historical Perspective.*
Washington, D.C.: History Division, National Park Service.

National Park Service. 1998. *Findings and Recommendations: Education Initiative Symposium.*
Washington, D.C.: U.S. Government Printing Office.

Noss, R. F., and A. Y. Cooperrider. 1994. *Saving Nature's Legacy: Protecting and Restoring
Biodiversity.* Washington, D.C.: Island Press.

Rolston III, H. 1986. *Philosophy Gone Wild: Essays in Environmental Ethics.* Buffalo, NY:
Prometheus.

Shultis, J. 1995. "Improving the Wilderness: Common Factors in Creating National Parks
and Equivalent Reserves During the 19th Century." *Forest and Conservation History*
39: 125-127.

Simon, J. 1997. *Endangered Mexico: An Environment on the Edge.* San Francisco: Sierra Club
Books.

Simonian, Lane. 1995. *Defending the Land of the Jaguar: A History of Conservation in Mexico.*
Austin: University of Texas Press.

United States of Mexico

CONSERVATION AND SUSTAINABLE USE OF NATURAL RESOURCES IN BAJA CALIFORNIA [1]

Exequiel M. Ezcurra

Abstract

The region of Baja California and the Sea of Cortes is one of extraordinary environmental heterogeneity, and is one of Mexico's richest areas in terms of natural resources. The region has an inordinately high biological richness and an extremely high level of endemism. In addition to the abundance of its natural resources, Baja California holds one of Mexico's fastest growing regional economies. The maquiladora industries in northern Baja California, the high-input crops in the agricultural valleys, and the booming tourist industry, are all powerful driving forces of economic and demographic growth.

   Driven by the attendant rapid increase in demand for resources, the region is confronting a series of environmental threats. Chief among these threats are: uncontrolled urban sprawl along the Mexico-U.S. border; exhaustion of the underground aquifers; replacement of native vegetation by weedy exotic grasses; off-road vehicles; tourism in the fragile environments of the islands; degradation of estuaries and coastal lagoons; and unsustainable commercial fishing in the Sea of Cortes.

---

1.   This paper was originally prepared as a briefing report for San Diego Dialogue's Forum
        Fronterizo policy luncheon series and was used in amended form as an overview briefing
        paper for the 1999 Workshop on Regional Approaches to Parks and Protected Areas in
        North America in Tijuana, Mexico.

Photograph 18.1. The ecologically diverse coast between Tijuana and Ensenada, Baja California, has been subject to rapid urbanization between the highway and the sea in recent decades without effective development and pollution controls. Photo credit: J.C. Day

In recent years, both the Mexican government and nongovernmental organizations have worked to protect the incredibly rich and increasingly endangered ecosystems of Baja California. The region now has eleven natural protected areas, including six that have been created during the last five years. Efforts have been developed to promote the sustainable use of fisheries and natural resources.

It is difficult to say at this time if the increasing pace of conservation efforts in Mexico will be able to stall the rapid environmental degradation that the region is experiencing. There seems to be a growing awareness of the importance of environmental protection. Conservation groups, research institutions, federal and state governments, NGOs, conscientious business people and ecotourism operatorshave all been contributing to the growing appreciation of the environment, and to the attendant conservation actions. The new Secretary of the Environment also deserves a great deal of credit for recent advances. The time seems to be perfect to promote true cooperative work, not only within Mexico but also across the border, between Mexican and U.S. conservation groups.

Figure 18.1 Baja California

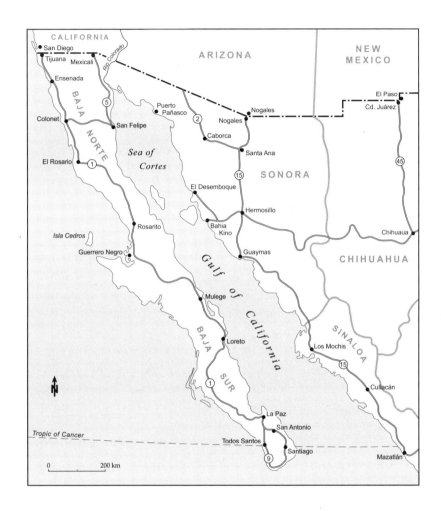

Introduction

The history of Baja California (fig. 18.1) is one of evolution in isolation. It is a natural account of the deep causes of the diversity of life on Earth. All along Baja the driving theme is *insularity*. During the last six million years, the Gulf of California (also known as the Sea of Cortes) has kept the long and dry Baja California peninsula separate from the Mexican mainland, and the peninsula has kept the Sea of Cortes literally engulfed in its own depths, sequestering it from the Pacific Ocean. On this landscape of sea and land that mutually embrace each other, keeping in solitude the genetic secrets of their founding life forms, smaller patches of insularity are superimposed at even smaller scales. Marine islands surround the peninsula on all sides, and high mountains, true sky islands in a desert sea, imprint the landscape all the way from the U.S. border down to Los Cabos, the southern end of the peninsula. Palm oases in deep, disjunct canyons form thousands of wetland islands within the rocky matrix of the peninsular ranges. The seacoast is fringed by coastal lagoons that repeat in a fractal manner the isolation theme in smaller and smaller bodies of water.

These patches of segregation are the driving force of biological speciation, of adaptation to local conditions, of specializing to particular isolated environments. After millions of years, fragmentation yields unique life forms. It also yields unique cultures. Quite separated from the rest of Mesoamerica, the Cochimí Indians developed one of the most incredible assemblages of cave paintings in the world. Later, during the Spanish colony, the Jesuit fathers founded their own Utopia in a system of missions that evolved in complete independence from the hard and cruel rules of the mainland *conquistadores.*

True to the etymology of the word, the peninsula has been indeed almost an island. Even in recent decades, some journalists in Mexico City have referred to Baja California as "the other Mexico" (*el otro México*). It has always been a land of fantasy and adventure, of surprising, often bizarre growth-forms, and of immense natural beauty. At present, however, modern transportation, population growth, urban sprawl, agricultural technology, and modern fishing techniques, among other causes, seem to be putting stress on the fragile peninsular environment. This paper is an attempt to discuss some of the issues related to environmental degradation and natural resource conservation in the region within a regional perspective.

The Shaping of a Singular Landscape

While most of the continental mainlands of Mexico and the United States are attached to the North American Plate, the southwestern part of California, along with all of Baja California, is a sliver of continental

Photograph 18.2. Severe aridity characterizes the eastern side of the Baja coastal mountains. Looking east to the Sea of Cortez. Photo credit: J.C. Day

crust that has become affixed to another slab of the Earth's crust–the Pacific Plate–and rides on it. The peninsula of Baja California is being very slowly torn away from the Mexican mainland by a series of rifts that are gradually opening up the Gulf of California, moving the whole plate towards the northwest. In Southern California the drifting movement of the peninsula generates a long line of friction, where the two plates are neither pulling apart nor squeezing together, but rather they are sliding against one another. This line is known as the San Andreas Fault. The ridges and crumples that are formed by this very active tectonic interface are the main causes of the regional topography, which in turn drives local climates and, ultimately, is a major causal force of the region's unique biological diversity. South of San Diego, at the Mexican border, the main ecosystems of Southern California, the coastal plains, inland deserts, and mountain backbone, spill naturally into Baja California. Ecological corridors link the region from north to south. The long continuum of the peninsular ecosystems defines a homogenous natural region: Greater Baja California.

Cycles of Abundance and Scarcity

In the same way as the geological processes are the force that shaped the abrupt geology of the peninsula of Baja California, the circulation of winds and oceanic currents is the underlying mechanism that generated the region's incredible ecosystems, and is the motor that maintains their existence.

On the Pacific coast of Baja, the cold California current, which runs from north to south, is deflected westward by the rotational movement of the Earth; an effect known as the "Coriolis force". The deflected surface layers of the California current are replaced by an upwelling of deeper cool water that is transported upwards from the nutrient-rich layers of the ocean floor, bringing fertility to the surface. Local currents produce similar upwelling phenomena in the Sea of Cortes, making it one of the most productive seas on Earth.

Cold seas are also the major cause of the aridity of the land, as the moisture-laden northwesterly winds that run from the cold Pacific into the warm peninsula become hotter and hence drier. Only in the mountain ranges does ascending air cool sufficiently to generate significant rainfall and sustain temperate forests. In the northern part of Baja California the land cools sufficiently in winter to cause atmospheric condensation and induce winter rains.

During El Niño years, random variation in the earth's flow of air weakens the trade winds, and the westward deflection of oceanic currents decreases. Warm oceanic waters accumulate in the coasts of the American continent, the upwelling of nutrient-rich waters decreases, and the sea becomes less productive while the abundant rainfall that originates from the now warm ocean waters soaks the land.

Biological Uniqueness

Few places show the extraordinary environmental heterogeneity of the peninsula of Baja California and of the Sea of Cortes. Regional climates vary from Mediterranean-type winter rains in the north, to monsoonal-type summer rains in the south. The steep slopes of the mountain ranges generate some of the most dramatic environmental gradients on Earth. The northern part of the peninsula extends from a coastal sclerophyllous scrub in the east to a dry subtropical desert in the west, with a sequence of Mediterranean scrubs (chaparral) and temperate pine-oak forests covering, respectively, the intermediate and the highest altitudes of the central mountain ranges. A rare form of tropical deciduous forest occupies the lowlands of the Cape region, in the southern part of the peninsula. Also in the Cape region, but at higher elevations, temperate pine-oak forests are found in the mountains of the Sierra de la Laguna. This unique temperate ecosystem—a relictual memory of past glaciations—has evolved in extreme isolation, and is composed mostly of rare, highly endemic species. Similar areas of geographic isolation and biological rarity are found in the central mountain ranges—San Francisco, Guadalupe, and La Giganta—and in the oceanic islands of the Sea of Cortes and of the Pacific coast.

Wiggins' (1980) *Flora of Baja California* describes 2,958 species and 686 endemic plants. Adding recent discoveries and a more complete review of the literature, the flora possibly consists of more than 3,500 plants with a very high proportion, almost 30 percent, of these being endemic species. Endemism, or the property of being uniquely restricted to a small area, is particularly high in the island ecosystems of the region, both in the Pacific and the Sea of Cortes, and in the isolated *sierras* such as San Pedro Martir, Jurez, San Francisco, Guadalupe, and La Laguna. Similar levels of endemism are found in reptiles and land mammals. For example, the terrestrial mammals of Greater Baja California comprise 109 species, twenty five (22%) of which are endemic.

Even in the case of birds, which by their volant nature are more cosmopolitan, the region of Southern California and Baja California harbors eleven strictly endemic species and 114 endemic subspecies out of some

550 species and around 700 taxa (species + subspecies). In short, 2 percent of the avian species' richness is endemic, and a remarkable 22 percent of the diversity at the subspecies level is unique to the Baja/ Southern California Region. Additionally, extinction is already a major threat for many avian species. The Guadalupe storm petrel (*Oceanodroma macrodactyla* Bryant), a rare and highly endemic marine bird, is extinct, as are other local, very restricted subspecies. Some of these subspecies, like the Guadalupe crested caracara (*Caracara plancus lutosa* Ridgway) were sufficiently distinct that they were considered separate species by some taxonomists. Many other endemic species and subspecies, such as the least storm petrel (*Oceanodroma microsoma*), the yellow-footed gull (*Larus livens*), or the Yuma clapper rail (*Rallus longirostris yumanensis*) are rapidly disappearing or becoming increasingly threatened by habitat destruction.

In the same way as the peninsula is isolated from the Mexican mainland by the Sea of Cortes, the Sea itself is also a sort of "marine peninsula," isolated from the rest of the Pacific by the 1,500 kilometers of land of Baja California. Biologically, the Sea of Cortes is one of the most productive and diverse seas in the world, harboring some 4,500 known invertebrate species (excluding the single-celled protozoans), with a very high level of endemism. Some authors estimate that a similar amount of invertebrate species remains undescribed in this extraordinarily rich environment. A similar situation of exceptionally high diversity is found in marine fish. Around 872 species have been recorded in the gulf, eighty-six (10%) of which are endemic to the region. Of these, teleostean fish comprise some 750 species. Reef fish, in general, have more restricted distributions than deep-sea, pelagic, or sandy shore species. Of 271 known reef fish in the Sea of Cortes, some fifty-two species (19%) are endemic to the region. The gulf is also extremely rich in marine mammals, harboring thirty-three species. Of these, twenty-eight are cetaceans, including the highly endemic *vaquita* porpoise (*Phocoena sinus*) that is only found in the Upper Gulf.

The high diversity of the Gulf of California is largely due to two phenomena. First, the great variety of general habitats that are found in the gulf, including mangrove swamps, coastal lagoons, coral reefs, shallow and deep-sea basins, hydrothermal vents, and a diverse array of shore and subtidal substrates. The second phenomena are the complex geological and oceanographic histories of the gulf. These include: past invasions of animal immigrants from tropical South America; the Caribbean Sea before Earth's tectonic forces sealed the Panama seaway; the cold shores of California during past glacial periods; and the vast stretches of the Pacific Ocean from the tropical West Pacific.

The gulf is important both biologically and economically. It houses an inordinately high proportion of the marine species richness of Mexico, and yields some 30 to 50% of the catch of national fisheries. The sustainable use and the conservation of the Sea of Cortes are critical issues.

Table 18.1 Selected Indicators of Economic Development in the Peninsula of Baja California[a]

	Illiteracy	Houses with Electricity	Mean No. of Live Offspring
Baja California	3.16	86.95	2.3
Ensenada	4.09	83.97	2.4
Mexicali	3.14	93.58	2.4
Tecate	3.72	77.32	2.4
Tijuana and Playas de Rosarito	2.80	83.29	2.2
Baja California Sur	3.60	86.93	2.4
Mulegé	4.25	86.44	2.6
Comondú and Loreto	5.15	87.36	2.6
La Paz	2.74	91.72	2.3
Los Cabos	3.55	70.13	2.4

[a](a) percentage of the population that is illiterate, (b) percentage of houses that have electricity, and (c) mean number of live children per woman older than twelve years (source: INEGI: Instituto Nacional de Estadística, Geografía e Informática).

The Socioeconomic Background

The Baja California Region is not only one of Mexico's richest areas in terms of natural resources, it also holds one of Mexico's fastest growing regional economies. The *maquiladora* industries in northern Baja California, the high-input crops and associated agro industries in the agricultural valleys (Mexicali, Tecate, San Quintín), and the booming tourism industry, are all powerful driving forces of economic and demographic growth. Selected indicators of economic development show values that suggest relatively high economic development compared to the rest of Mexico (table 18.1). Globally, the peninsula of Baja California has levels of illiteracy of less than 4 percent (illiteracy was calculated as the proportion of illiterate adults in the whole population).

The number of houses with electricity approaches 90 percent. This calculation includes rural dwellings; in urban areas this percentage is even higher. The mean number of live children per woman over twelve years is around 2.4. By comparison, the state of Oaxaca in southern Mexico has 17 percent illiteracy, only 73 percent of its houses have access to electricity, and the mean number of live children per woman above twelve years of age is 3.1.

With some 2.5 percent of the population of Mexico, the peninsula of Baja California produces almost 3 percent of the country's gross domestic product. That is, the *per capita* contribution of the peninsular inhabitants to the GDP is more than 20 percent above the national average. The *per capita* income in the peninsula in 1996 was $3,774 ($3,722 in Baja California, and $4,068 in Baja California Sur). Although this may seem low by the standards of a developed country, it is substantially higher than the national average of Mexico, which was $2,880 for the same period.

The success of the peninsular economy has brought a large population increase to the region, mostly derived from immigration (table 18.2). While national demographic growth rates in Mexico have descended considerably in recent decades, from a national average of more than 3 percent to less than 2 percent, the growth rates in the peninsula of Baja California still remain very high. Between 1990 and 1995, the state of Baja California grew at an annual rate of 4.77 percent, while neighboring Baja California Sur grew at a rate of 3.34 percent. The cities with the most dynamic and active economies grew even more rapidly. Tijuana, fueled by the immigration magnet of the *maquiladora* industry, grew at a rate of 6.52 percent, while the population of Los Cabos, under the impulse of a rapidly increasing tourism boom, grew at the extraordinary rate of 9.67 percent. If these rates were maintained, the Tijuana population would double every eleven years, while Los Cabos would double every seven years. When these remarkably rapid growth rates are analyzed against the demographic data on female fertility (table 18.1) it becomes obvious that the fast population growth of the region cannot be ascribed to reproductive habits, as Baja families have a relatively low number of children compared to the rest of the country. The population increase is chiefly the result of migration within Mexico, from the impoverished southern states into the more dynamic economy of Baja's border region.

These economic indicators highlight some of the most pressing environmental problems of the peninsula. On the one hand, it is extremely difficult to adequately supply services such as running water and sewage to cities that double in size every ten years. Rapid demographic growth means, almost by definition, an increasing lag in water and electricity supply, and an overloading of sanitary infrastructure, including poor drainage and lack of water-treatment facilities. The consequence is pollution and environmental degradation. On the other hand, rapid growth means an ever-increasing demand for water and other natural resources, which are scarce in the peninsula, chiefly due to aridity of the region. Thus, rapid expansion of the peninsular population is mostly at the expense of depleting underground aquifers and of destroying the natural ecosystems and the watersheds that surround the large urban areas.

Table 18.2. Population in the Municipalities of the States of Baja California and Baja California South for 1990 and 1995, and Calculated Exponential Yearly Percentage Growth Rates[a]

	1990	1995	Rate (%)
Baja California	1,660,855	2,108,118	4.77
Ensenada	259,979	314,281	3.79
Mexicali	601,938	695,805	2.90
Tecate	51,557	62,617	3.89
Tijuana (Playas de Rosarito)	747,381	989,287 (46,128)	6.52
Baja California Sur	317,764	375,450	3.34
Mulegé	38,528	45,887	3.50
Comondú (Loreto)	74,346	65,969 (10,003)	0.43
La Paz	160,970	182,348	2.49
Los Cabos	43,920	71,243	9.67

[a]INEGI. The Municipalities of Playas de Rosarito and Loreto were created after 1990. Their 1995 values, indicated in parentheses, were added to those of Tijuana and Comondú, respectively, to calculate growth rates.

Environmental Threats Confronting the Region

Driven by the rapid increase in resource demand, the biologically unique region of Baja California is confronting a series of growing environmental threats. Among them, the following are of pre-eminent relevance.

   1. Along the Mexico-U.S. border, growing industrialization is generating uncontrolled urban sprawl that puts long-term conservation of the chaparral scrub under grave danger. At the other extreme of the peninsula, in the Cape Region, the rapid growth of tourism is also creating a similar phenomenon of explosive urban expansion. In both areas, the growing demand for drinking water is depleting aquifers.

2. Some agricultural areas that were developed in the mid-twentieth century are now facing the exhaustion of underground aquifers, which were used in an unsustainable manner with no consideration for recharge. For example, some specialists estimate Ciudad Constitución, some fifty kilometers north of La Paz, is facing the closure of most of its wells within a time horizon of ten years. Whatever the true time horizon turns out to be, the final result once the aquifer is exhausted will be a barren wasteland of salinized agricultural soils that present a challenge for ecological restoration. In some parts, the descent of the regional aquifers has also meant the drying-up of surface water springs with the consequent degradation of freshwater wetlands. In many parts of the Baja deserts, water is indeed a nonrenewable resource, or a resource with a very slow rate of natural replenishment. Regional agricultural techniques, however, frequently use water wastefully, with a very low efficiency of conversion of water input to crop yields. The consumptive use of the aquifers for wasteful agricultural activities is a major determinant of long-term ecological deterioration.

3. In some areas, vegetation cover is being rapidly destroyed for agricultural development and the planting of weedy exotic grasses—such as African buffel (*Pennisetum ciliare*)—to improve forage productivity for cattle in desert environments. In southern Baja, the weedy buffel grass does not seem to need previous land clearing to become established. Highly adapted to the hot and dry tropical environment, buffel is rapidly invading some overgrazed desert lands. Once invaded by the rapidly growing and leafy buffel, the accumulated biomass burns easily during the dry season, turning the Baja desert into a fire ecosystem that burns seasonally and prevents the re-establishment of the original biologically-rich scrub.

4. Adventure-tourism has had a large impact on some of the peninsular ecosystems. Perhaps the most destructive form of wildland recreation is the use of off-road vehicles in the open desert and the coastal sand ridges. Vegetation in these environments has an extremely slow growth rate. For example, a barrel cactus, which can be destroyed in seconds by a rash driver, may have taken centuries to grow to its adult size. The destruction wrought by a vehicle on a single weekend may take centuries to recover.

5. Additionally, nature tourism has had an increasing impact in the island ecosystems of the Gulf of California, which are extremely fragile. Biological evolution in isolation has made the islands of the Gulf of California highly vulnerable to ecological impacts associated with the introduction of exotic species, habitat deterioration, hunting, and fishing. In particular, the introduction of exotic species such as rats, cats, or goats may cause true ecological catastrophes to the population numbers of plants, marine birds, or island reptiles. Finally, the growing demand of nature tourism has, in turn, generated increasing pressures to develop the islands. Although to date no development has been authorized in the Gulf Islands, the number of proposals and of associated environmental impact statements has been increasing steadily over the last decade.

6. The estuaries and coastal lagoons of the region are facing increasing threats from industrial and tourism developments, and from runoff of terrestrial pollutants. The deterioration of coastal lagoons affects a large number of marine organisms that spend part of their life cycle in these ecosystems, from the gray whales in the Pacific lagoons, to shrimp, mollusks, and fish in the Sea of Cortes. It also affects a large number of migratory birds that use these wetlands along their travel routes. Thus, coastal lagoons provide unique ecological services that are crucial for the maintenance and survival of species that migrate later into other, often distant, ecosystems. These services, however, are not easily perceptible by developers, who have tended to consider such environments as "wastelands" that should be used for more direct economic profit. The cutting of mangroves for aquaculture or for coastal resorts is a typical example of this problem. While the seminal importance of mangroves for open-sea fisheries and marine life in general is not easy to perceive, the immediate utility of their clearing for other less productive purposes seems to be more comprehensible.

7. Finally, the use of shrimp dragnets in the Gulf of California, gill nets with inadequate mesh sizes, and longlines in both the Gulf and the Pacific, are creating serious concerns for the long-term sustainability of the marine ecosystems around the Baja California peninsula. For example, incidental by-catch in the shrimp fisheries is often more than 90 percent of the total harvest, creating an immense waste of resources that are consumed neither by humans nor by other marine species that depend on these organisms.

Table 18.3. Protected Areas in the Peninsula of Baja California, the Sea of Cortes, the Mexican Pacific Ocean, and the Gulf Coasts of the Sonoran Desert[a]

Name	Area (ha.)	Category[b]	Date of decree	Ecosystems
STATE OF BAJA CALIFORNIA				
Alto Golfo de California y Delta del Río Colorado	934,756	BR	15 June 1993	Sand dunes, halophilic scrub, intertidal mudflats, estuary
Constitución de 1857	5,009	NP	27 March 1962	Pine-oak forest and chaparral
Sierra de San Pedro Mártir	63,000	NP	26 April 1947	Fir, pine-oak forest, and chaparral
STATE OF BAJA CALIFORNIA SUR				
Bahía de Loreto	206,581	MP	19 July, 1996	Mangroves, coastal dunes, rocky reefs, desert scrub
Cabo Pulmo	7,111	MP	6 June, 1995	Coral reef
El Vizcaíno	2,546, 790	BR	30 Nov., 1988	Desert scrub, coastal dunes, halophilic scrub, mangroves, coastal lagoons
Sierra de la Laguna	112,437	BR	6 June, 1994	Pine-oak forest, tropical dry forest, palm oases, columnar cacti, and desert scrub
ISLAND RESERVES IN THE PACIFIC & SEA OF CORTES				
Archipiélago de Revillagigedo	636,685	BR	1 Jan., 1994	Tropical dry forest, coastal scrub, coastal shrub lands
Isla de Guadalupe	25,000	AR	27 Oct., 1928	Pacific coastal scrub
Isla Rasa	61	AR	30 May, 1964	Coastal scrub
Isla Tiburón	120,800	AR	15 March, 1963	Sonoran Desert scrub
Islas del Golfo de California	150,000	AR	2 August, 1978	Sonoran and Gulf Island scrub
OTHER COASTAL RESERVES IN THE SEA OF CORTES				
Cajón del Diablo	147,000	AR	14 Sept., 1937	Desert Canyon oasis
El Pinacate y Gran Desierto de Altar	714,556	BR	10 June, 1963	Sonoran Desert scrub

[a]SEMARNAP

[b]Categories: BR: Biosphere Reserve (Reservas de la Biosfera); NP: National Park (Parque Nacional); MP: Marine Park (Parque Marino); AR: Areas currently under recategorization (Areas en Recategorización).

Of Whales and Cacti: Conservation Efforts in Baja California

Both the Mexican government and conservation nongovernmental organizations (NGOs) have developed actions to protect the incredibly rich and increasingly endangered ecosystems of Baja California. The region now harbors eleven natural protected areas, including five biosphere reserves (El Vizcaíno, Alto Golfo de California y Delta del Río Colorado, El Pinacate y Gran Desierto de Altar, Sierra de la Laguna, and Archipiélago de Revillagigedo), two national parks (Constituciõn de 1857, and Sierra de San Pedro Martir), and two marine parks (Bahía de Loreto and Cabo Pulmo) (table 18.3). Formally protected by older and outdated decrees, the islands of the Gulf of California, the island of Guadalupe in the Mexican Pacific, and a canyon in the midriff coast of

Sonora, are being recategorized to conform to new Mexican legislation on protected areas. It is clear from the data in table 18.3 that since 1993 there has been an immense effort to decree and protect new areas. Indeed, between 1993 and 1998 six new protected areas, totaling 2,612,126 hectares were placed under some category of protection.

In 1993, the Mexican government issued two decrees protecting the strip of desert land and coastal ecosystems that join the Sonoran Desert with the Baja California Peninsula, under the category of biosphere reserves. The creation of these wilderness-protected areas was achieved largely thanks to the initiative and the support of local conservation groups and academic institutions. Both the Pinacate-Gran Desierto Biosphere Reserve and the Upper Gulf of California Biosphere Reserve gained immediate national and international support. The Gran Desierto Biosphere Reserve protected the remarkable endemisms of the largest continental sanddune system and volcanic shield in North America, while the Upper Gulf Biosphere Reserve protects two highly endangered marine species: the vaquita porpoise (*Phocoena sinus*) and the totoaba (*Totoaba macdonaldi or Cynoscion macdonaldi*). In conjunction with Organ Pipe Cactus National Monument and Cabeza Prieta Game Reserve in the United States, these two Mexican reserves form the largest ecological corridor of protected areas in the Lower Colorado Valley desert lands.

The most remarkable aspect of the project has been the wide cooperation and the partnerships that it involved. The creation of these desert and coastal reserves involved the participation of many groups, including indigenous peoples like the Tohono O'odham, conservation groups like Pronatura, Conservation International, The Nature Conservancy, and the Audubon Society, together with a myriad of academic and research organizations. Some of these organizations eventually coalesced into a conservation bloc called the Sonoran Desert Alliance.

During 1993 the Mexican government prepared a series of documents that were presented to UNESCO to dedicate the Vizcaíno Biosphere Reserve as a World Heritage Site within UNESCO's World Heritage Committee. Shortly afterwards, new decrees followed. With the cooperation of researchers from the Instituto de Ecología, A.C., the California Academy of Sciences, and the University of California, Los Angeles, the Mexican government issued a decree for the protection of the Revillagigedo Archipelago in the Mexican Pacific. Six months later, in June

1994, a decree was issued to protect the Sierra de la Laguna, in Baja's Cape Region. In 1995, following an initiative from Pronatura Peninsula de Baja California (a Mexican NGO), the greatest and most diverse reef of the Sea of Cortes became officially protected under the name of *Parque Marino de Cabo Pulmo*. Finally, in July 1996, a decree was issued to protect the Bay of Loreto, also as a marine park. It is remarkable that the creation of this last park was totally the result of a grassroots initiative from the local fishermen, who were concerned about the continuing decline of their catches and the degradation of hatching grounds.

Efforts have also developed to promote the sustainable use of fisheries and natural resources, in general. In July 1998, the governors of the four states surrounding the Sea of Cortes (Baja California, Baja California Sur, Sonora, and Sinaloa) and the Secretary of the Environment, Julia Carabias, signed an agreement to pursue a joint program for the sustainable use of the Sea of Cortes.

Concluding Remarks

It is difficult to say at this time if the increasing pace of conservation efforts in Mexico will be able to stall the rapid environmental degradation that the region is experiencing. The optimistic note is that there seems to be, at least in the peninsula of Baja California and in the Sea of Cortes, a growing awareness, as never was observed before, of the importance of taking urgent action to protect the environment. The swelling number of conservation actions that have been taking place is not the sole merit of any sector. Conservation groups, research institutions, federal and state governments, NGOs, conscientious businesspersons, and ecotourism operators have all contributed to the growing appreciation of the environment, and to the attendant conservation actions. But the new Secretary of the Environment deserves great credit in having listened to these rising voices, and in having acted accordingly.

It was not by chance that the first Mexican protected areas along the U.S. border were created in the state of Sonora. A number of institutions and organizations on both sides of the border have been working together for years promoting the conservation of these areas. For years, research institutions from both Mexico and the United States, conservation groups and organizations, the traditional government of the Tohono

O'odham people, and governmental officers both from state and the federal levels have been working together to prepare plans and proposals for a joint binational project to preserve the *Gran Desierto*. Eventually, all the nongovernmental and academic institutions coalesced into the Sonoran Desert Alliance, a truly participative organization with a great capacity to influence decision-making and to draw the attention of public opinion towards environmental affairs. A time came in which the proposal to protect the Gran Desierto and the coasts of the Colorado River Estuary was ready and had the consensus and support of hundreds of environmental leaders from both sides of the border. The Gran Desierto is now protected all the way from the Tohono O'odham (Papago) Reservation to the waters of the Upper Gulf of California.

To preserve their shared ecosystems, Southern California and the peninsula of Baja California require a similar effort. It seems to be a perfect time to promote true cooperative work, not only within Mexico but also across the border, between Mexican and U.S. conservation groups from Baja California and Southern California. Recently, a number of Mexican institutions with an interest in the conservation of Baja California and the Sea of Cortes formed the Coalition of the Gulf of California (*Coalición del Golfo de California*), with the participation of several conservation NGOs and academic and research groups. It is the right moment to bring U.S. institutions into this alliance, or into a similar one with a regional scope of interest. The region is one large continuum, with shared watersheds, species, and natural resources that do not recognize a boundary line. The protection of these unique environments is of the uttermost importance for the survival and well-being of all of us, for generations to come.

References

Alvarez, Juan, and V. M. Castillo. 1986. "Ecología y Frontera/Ecology and the Borderlands." Papers presented at a meeting held 10 April 1986 at the Universidad Autónoma de Baja California, Tijuana, Mexico. Tijuana, Mexico: Universidad Autónoma de Baja California, Escuela de Economía,

Arriaga, L., and R. Rodríguez Estrella. 1997. *Los oasis de la peninsula de Baja California*. La Paz, Baja California Sur: Centro de Investigaciones Biológicas del Noroeste.

Camarillo R., J. L., and F. Rivera A. 1990. *Areas Naturales Protegidas en México y Especies en Extinción / Proyecto Conservación y Mejoramiento del Ambiente*. Iztacala, México: Universidad Nacional Autónoma de México.

Ordóñez Díaz, María de Jésus, and Oscar Flores Villela. 1995. *Proyecto Conservación y Mejoramiento del Ambiente (Mexico)*. Pronatura, México, D.F.

Wiggins, I. L. 1980. *Flora of Baja California*. Stanford, Calif.: Stanford University Press.

Conservation and Management of Ecosystems Within and Without Protected Natural Areas, Baja California, Mexico [1]

Roberto Martínez and Ileana Espejel

Abstract

Mexico has several ways of preserving flora and fauna, depending on geographical scale and land ownership. Until recently, fifty percent of the land was common property called *ejidos*,[2] which denotes communal land and protected areas. Wildlife management and natural resources conservation practices occur in these types of land tenure. There is a gradient of land use intensities, from cities and agricultural lands to almost pristine sites. Eighty percent of Baja California is under a conservation or management policy. There is a regional plan for the whole state, and three plans for the coastal zone. Several public policies have been created for nature protection and management as well as for creating social interest in environmental issues. Fifteen terrestrial and marine areas are considered a priority for national conservation. Nature protection occurs in one biosphere reserve, three special biosphere reserves on the islands, two national parks in the mountains, and three areas for protection of forests and desert vegetation. Wildlife management

---

1.   This paper was presented at the Regional Approaches to Parks and Protected Areas Workshop and published in *Environments,* 27, no. 3.

2.   For *ejidos* see footnote 1, Chapter 4.

is conducted in thirty units (called UMAS) and around the buffer zones of the biosphere reserves. Nevertheless, this system does not work well. Challenges include: highly modified and fragmented areas; endangered species and vegetation types; land tenure conflicts; several exotic cultural land use practices; and the absence of natural areas in cities and agricultural fields. We present an updated plan for the conservation and management of Baja California landscapes, ecosystems, communities, and natural resources. We also present our own landscape-scale design for the conservation and management of wildlife. Two main strategies must be followed to reach the conservation goals, within and without protected areas, regardless of the legal status of land ownership.

Introduction

Protected areas have long been the most effective and widespread measure for conserving nature and natural processes. But, according to Lewis (1996), protected areas are based on a myth. A charming myth, but still a myth; that nature is separate from people, and that nature is diminished whenever people try to live within it. At the most recent academic meetings, the issue of whether protected natural areas are enough to protect nature was widely discussed (Simonetti 1995; Wright 1996; Soulé and Terborgh 1999). Conflictive demands on land and particular monitoring processes, show failures but also successes. The literature is rich in developing new tools to solve social-nature problems. Old ideas are incorporated into new ones to formulate approaches and policies, which are being adopted to solve conflicting resource use demands while still preserving important species populations or keystone ecosystem processes.

The conservation of natural areas as well as the management of natural resources have been major tasks of recent federal and state policies in Mexico. The percentage of land and sea dedicated to preservation and management in Baja California has increased considerably in the past ten years. Two huge biosphere reserves have been created and many hectares have been designated for wildlife management. Because Baja California is mostly an unpopulated, arid land, setting aside land for conservation in unproductive areas has been relatively easy. Conservation and management areas cover almost all undeveloped land, far from urban nuclei and productive lands. Therefore, the real challenge is to preserve species and manage ecosystems in urbanized and agricultural areas, where more frag-mented natural ecosystems are dominant and smaller and lower quality remnants are common.

In this paper we explain the legal instruments available at the federal and state scale to enforce conservation and management practices in Baja California. We also discuss the possibilities of reaching the goal of pre-serving species and ecosystem processes. We present a map with our pro-posal to preserve and manage natural resources, both within and outside of protected areas.

Mexican Public Policy for Nature Protection and Management

Several public policies in Mexico deal with conservation issues (México, Secretaría de Medio Ambiente y Recursos Naturales (SEMARNAP) 1999). At a large scale, regional plans, or ecological ordinances, must be created legally. These are analogous to urban development plans but were created for rural areas. Plans can be regional, state, municipal, or for specific areas with intensive and conflicting use. Depending upon scale, environmental impact assessments can also assist with nature protection and management practices. Watershed councils are a new social and institutional arrangement seeking to improve and maintain high water quality and management of natural resources within drainage basins.

Mexican protected areas belong to a national system (El Sistema Nacional de Áreas Naturales Protegidas, or SINAP) that consists of eight categories. These areas are managed by the National Ecology Institute (Instituto Nacional de Ecología or INE). Under this system, ninety-four protected areas cover a total of 11,288,503 hectares (approximately 5.5% of the country). Twelve protected areas are included in UNESCO's Man and the Biosphere (MAB) world network; four are World Heritage sites, and four, soon to be six, are designated as important international wet-lands under the RAMSAR convention. Other areas where conservation approaches have been developed are older in administrative terms: lakes, rivers, wells, watersheds and basins, wood and nonwood forestry lands, and large areas where soil must be protected. These involve 218 govern-ment decrees and cover 61,658,432 hectares. In addition, there are scien-tific reserves and other heritage areas or protected areas as outlined in the

World Conservation Union's categories of protected areas (México, CONABIO 1999).

Another new administrative program is related to wildlife conservation and productive rural diversification. Two political instruments have been developed in recent years. The first involves individual projects for the conservation and rehabilitation of priority species, including populations of plants and animals at risk or with economic or cultural values. Sanctuaries and repopulating practices are also promoted. One other instrument is a large system of Wildlife Management and Sustainable Use Units (UMAS, by its Spanish acronym Unidades de Manejo y Aprovechamiento Sustentable). These areas can be private, communal, or owned by local communities or businesses. This system is complementary to the protected areas system. To date, many *ejidos*) have been declared as UMAS.

Mexican Fund for Research on Nature Conservation and Natural Resources Management

Besides the national public policies for nature conservation, mention should be made of the National Commission for the Conservation of Biodiversity (Comisión Nacional para el Conocimiento y Uso de la Biodiversidad, CONABIO). It is an important financing agency, setting priorities for conservation in the whole country, inside as well as outside protected areas. Fifteen areas of Baja California have been considered priorities for conservation research purposes and are currently being updated: eight terrestrial areas (CONABIO 1999), four marine areas (Arriaga 1998a), and four watershed areas (Arriaga 1998b). Nine projects have been funded for botany, zoology, and aquatic resources, especially for collection and database support, and four other projects deal with ecology and management studies. In addition, this agency has also supported several projects in the Gulf of California.

This information is also useful for other national financing agencies like the Mexican Fund for Nature Conservation (Fondo Mexicano para la Conservación de la Naturaleza, A.C., FMCN). Such programs fund basic or applied projects such as: floristic databases and geographic information systems; endangered species projects for the marine mammal vaquita and some fish species; landscape conservation planning of coastal sage scrub; and environmental education activities in Punta Banda and San Quintín (FMCN 1999).

Figure 19.1 Ecological regional planning model for Baja California

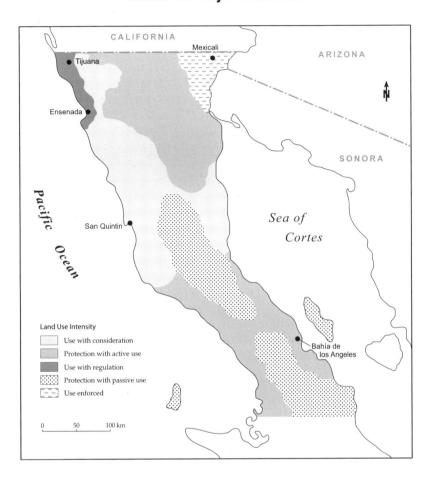

Regional Planning

Baja California is one of the few states in Mexico where a state regional plan for development, based on ecological data, has been decreed. This regional planning program distributes policies on land use intensity gradients (fig. 19.1). Large areas are classified and land use capacity is evaluated. Together with environmental impact assessments, maps are produced to show homogenous land units selected for specific recommended uses. We understand that protection is a category of use since it competes with using the land for other "values," such as economic development activities (Escofet et al. 1993). Most of the maps assign public policies such as protection with passive use through intermediate use policies such as consolidated use, regulated use, and protection with active use. The Baja California State regional planning process was completed in 1995. There are ten "regions" with five land use intensities; each region, as well, has adopted its own use intensities.

Watershed Management

In Mexico, a new public system has been organized for water management. Most regional plans are based on watersheds and managed at the state or county level. Few watershed councils have been created to date. This is a starting point to join diverse interests around the same natural resource, water, as well as shared biotic communities. Baja California still has not established this system, but it is a promising instrument for some of the most important watersheds in the state (Meza 1998).

Protected Areas and Wildlife Conservation, Management and Sustainable Use Units

Baja California contains half of the categories of the national protected areas system. The large marine ecosystem and island biosphere reserves are mainly in the Gulf of California and are shared with neighboring states, Sonora and Baja California Sur. The national parks are small and located inside two pine forests created for protection of natural resources. The largest protected area in the state is a natural resources protection area called Valle de Los Cirios, created to preserve desert ecosystems. There are currently no protected areas along the Pacific Coast, although Punta Banda and San Quintín are locally protected for research, environmental education, and landscape management. Only the core zones of all of the biosphere reserves have preservation policies. Sustainable use practices are permitted and enforced in the buffer zones of the biosphere reserves as well as the other protected areas that have no core zones for strict nature preservation. All natural protected areas need management plans. Research staff in both of the biosphere reserves worked on developing management plans, but this kind of work has not been done in the other protected areas.

The idea of the UMAS was to create units for one or diversified species management; for instance, private people owning a nursery or an association producing quail on a farm. In Baja California, however, the concept of a UMAS has been applied differently; almost all *ejidos* of the state have been declared UMAS. Therefore, there are thirty UMAS covering almost half the state, even if an area had a previous declaration as protected land. For example, the Valle de los Cirios and seven UMAS, or ejidos, share almost the same area. The main aim of the UMAS is intensive use, with control, and hunting or fishing depending on the availability of useful species. In Baja California, large UMAS, or *ejidos*, were necessary because the bighorn sheep was the focal species and its home range is large. Also, operation of the UMAS has to consider seasonal movements of the animal group, as well as the individual movement, which differs according to sex as males have larger home ranges.

All UMAS need operating management plans, which consider the needs of the species to be managed. Nevertheless, the implementation of the UMAS has proceeded slowly and few UMAS have operating management plans in place. As protected areas, most of these conservation and management areas are virtual, or on paper only; they have a decree but do not have management plans and do not really function as protected lands.

Present and Future Needs

Numerous but confusing policies exist for protecting and managing nature in Mexico. There are almost too many, especially since the existing ones are not fulfilling their goals. We believe that one way to guarantee consideration of conservation issues will be when local people find a better way of living in protected areas, UMAS, or elsewhere, according to their regional environment and local natural resources. Conservation of natural resources and ecosystems urgently needs both administrative changes at the municipal level and the design and implementation of local management plans.

Municipal administrative units are not ecological entities. This makes the decision-making process difficult for ecologists as well as for social and political agencies. For instance, the *UMAS Ejidos Asociados* belongs to two municipalities, with different political parties governing them and two different development plans. A new design for municipalities based on watershed areas has been proposed by some (Dourjeanni et al. 1994, Espejel et al. 1998). This could be a way of ameliorating social and ecological conflicts. Such an ecological administrative unit should have an information center with a wide variety of biological and socioeconomic information available. Both would help to design municipal planning and specific management plans, relating for example, to priority species and to areas for protection and/or sustainable use (Arendt 1999; Tillman 1999).

As priority sites for conservation research, protected areas and UMAS focus attention on particular places and ignore the rest of the land where, in general, local communities are found. So, for example, we have inventories for special areas, but not for *ejidos*, which urgently need plans for sustainable use of ecosystems and species. That is why we need integrated conservation planning—ecological and social systems together—within and beyond protected areas. As some of the centers of endemism in Baja California are not in nature reserves, these sites have to be preserved despite the presence or absence of protected areas.

Our proposal is shown in figure 19.2, where we suggest two strategies for implementing broader regional conservation and management plans, beyond those for more limited areas. There is a need to support the conservation of highly biodiverse areas by intensifying use in proper sites. One strategy has to consider the desert and mountains, because they are almost unpopulated. Conservation in very large areas is still possible. These huge lands still belong to *ejidatarios* whom, if organized can manage on a more integrated basis, for example for species such as bighorn sheep, or for natural processes such as patterns of fire.

A second strategy, small nature reserves and wildlife corridors, has to be designed for the urbanized and agricultural matrix. This patchy design must have a new legal framework to be implemented, since neither the urban nor the regional plans consider these kinds of smaller protected areas. Perhaps the best opportunity to acquire land in Baja California for conservation purposes is presented by The Nature Conservancy, as is done in the U. S. A. Efforts are directed towards that policy, although we think that local people have to keep their land while working it, using wildlife for their own benefit, and preserving their culture and natural inheritance (Goldman 1998). A wise man from the Paipai Indian group

Figure 19.2 Proposed land use designations for Baja California North

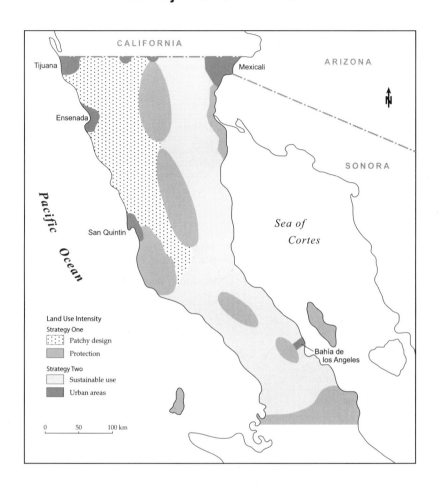

who recently died, Don Benito Peralta, said: "this land is big, is ours, is dry but rich, we know how to use it, how to enjoy it and nobody is going to damage it or take it away from us."

In the memory of Benito Peralta, it is our commitment to implement landscape conservation plans only if they bring wealth to their owners.

References

Arendt, R. 1999. *Growing Greener: Putting Conservation into Local Plans and Ordinances.* Washington, D.C.: Island Press.

Arriaga, L., E. Vázquez-Domínguez, J. González-Cano, R. Jímenez-Rosenberg, E. Muñoz López, and V. Aguilar Sierra. 1998a. *Regiones Prioritarias Marinas de México.* D.F., México: CONABIO.
Arriaga, L., V. Aguilar S., J. Alcocer D., R. Jímenez R., E. Muñoz L., and E. Vázquez Domínguez. 1998b. *Regiones Hidrológicas Prioritarias: Fichas Técnicas y mapa escala 1:4 000 000.* D.F., México: CONABIO.
Dourjanni, A. November 1994. "Políticas públicas para el desarrollo sustentable: la gestión integrada de cuencas." *Proceedings, Second Latin American Congress on Watershed Management.* Universidad de Los Andes, Centro Interamericano de Desarrollo e Investigación Ambiental y Territorial (CIDIAT) and Comisión Económica para América Latina y El Caribe (CEPAL). Mérida, Venezuela.
Escofet, A., I. Espejel, J. L. Fermán, L. Gómez Morín, and G. Torres-Moye. 1993. "Manejo de fragmentos en al zona costera," pp. 182-193. In *Biodiversidad Marina y Costera de México,* ed. S. Salazar-Vallejo and N.E. González. D.F., México: CONABIO y CIQRO.
Espejel, I. November 1998. *El municipio ecológico: una idea descabellada?.* El Colegio de México (COLMEX). Proceedings of "Foro del Ajusco". D.F., México.
Fondo Mexicano para la Conservación del al Naturaleza, A.C. (FMCN). 1999. Information accessed online: http://www.fmcn.org.
Gobierno del Estado de Baja California. 1995. *Plan de Ordenamiento Ecológico del Estado de Baja California.* Tomo CII. No. 42. Mexicali, B.C.: Periódico Oficial del Estado de Baja California: 2-153.
Gobierno del Estado de Baja California. Comité Técnico. 1994. *COCOTEN Programa Regional de Desarrollo Urbano Turístico y Ecológico del Corredor Costero Tijuana-Ensenada.* Mexicali, B.C.: Secretaría de Asentamientos Humanos y Obras Públicas, Dirección de Estudios y Proyectos.
Goldman, M. 1998. *Privatizing Nature.* New Brunswick, N.J.: Rutgers University Press.
Lewis, C. 1996. *Managing Conflicts in Protected Areas.* Gland, Switzerland: International Union for the Conservation of Nature-The World Conservation Union.
México. Comisión Nacional para el Conocimiento y Uso de la Biodiversidad (CONABIO). 1999. *Regiones Prioritarias Terrestres.* D.F., México.
México. Secretaría de Medio Ambiente y Recursos Naturales (SEMARNAP). 1996. *Programa de Áreas Naturales Protegidas:1995-2000.* D.F., México.
———. 1997. *Programa de Conservación de la Vida Silvestre y Diversificación Productiva en el Sector Rural: 1997-2000.* D.F., México.
———. 1999. Information accessed online, http://www.semarnap.gob.mx
Meza, M. 1998. *Los Consejos de Cuenca. Tesis de Maestría. Administración Integral del Ambiente.* Tijuana, Baja California: Colegio de la Frontera Norte.
Peck, S. 1998. *Planning for Biodiversity: Issues and Examples.* Washington, D.C.: Island Press.
Simonetti, J.A. 1995. "Wildlife Conservation Outside Parks is a Disease-mediated Task." *Conservation Biology* 9(2): 454-456.
Soulé, M. E., and J. Terborgh. 1999. "The Policy and Science of Regional Conservation," pp. 1-17. In *Continental Conservation: Scientific Foundations of Regional Reserve Networks,* ed. M. E. Soulé and J. Terborgh. Washington, D.C.: Island Press.
Tillman, L. J. 1999. *Design for Human Ecosystems.* Washington, D.C.: Island Press.
Wright, R. G. 1996. *National Parks and Protected Areas: Their Role in Ecosystem Protection.* Cambridge, Mass.: Blackwell Science.

Feasibility of Sustainable Investment Projects in the Northern California Gulf and Colorado River Delta Biosphere Reserve, Mexico [1]

Noél Arón Fuentes and Carlos Israel Vázquez

Abstract

This paper presents the objectives, methodologies, and preliminary results of a feasibility study on potential sustainable investment projects in the Northern California Gulf and Colorado River Delta Biosphere Reserve, Mexico. The main objective of the study is to identify, select, and evaluate investment projects that will provide employment and income alternatives for the population in the area influenced by the core zone of the Northern California Gulf and Colorado River Delta Biosphere Reserve. The first two sections of this paper examine environmental and socioeconomic issues affecting the communities in the area of influence of the reserve core zone. The next section explains the methodology used to evaluate the projects. A fourth section presents some preliminary analyses. The study concludes with policy recommendations.

1.　　Translated from Spanish by Christina Novo Perez and J. C. Day.

Introduction: Environmental Issues

Environmental Deterioration

The northern waters of the California Gulf form a calm sea between the coasts of Puerto Peñasco and Santa Clara in the Mexican State of Sonora, and the coasts of San Felipe in the State of Baja California (B.C.). The predominant climate is continental, influenced by the Sonoran Desert. Terrestrial and marine conditions result in high concentrations of plankton, making this coastal ecosystem one of worldwide importance in terms of primary productivity. A large number of species breed and seek shelter in the region, particularly in the area influenced by the Colorado River Delta.

The status of two species at risk that are endemic to the region illustrates the severe deterioration of ecosystems in the Northern California Gulf. The marine vaquita (*Phocoena sinus*), a sea mammal, is considered endangered in the U.S., in Mexico, and by the World Conservation Union (IUCN). It is also listed under the *International Convention on International Trade in Endangered Species* (CITES). The population of marine vaquita, about one hundred individuals, grows less than ten percent annually. Its main threat is accidental mortality as a result of fishing activities, which alone reduces the population by five to ten percent annually. This species will become extinct if current trends are not reversed (Godinez 1995). The giant totoaba (*Totoaba macdonaldi* or *Cynoscion macdonaldi*), a fish species, is considered endangered in the U.S. and is listed under CITES. Its situation is similar to that of the marine vaquita (Chávez and Arizú 1972, Román 1994). Population decline is mainly due to overexploitation, poaching of adult fish, juvenile mortality as bycatch, and habitat deterioration.

Environmental Protection

The region of the Northern California Gulf and the delta of the Colorado River are high in marine species diversity, and have long been recognized as valuable habitat for the breeding, feeding, and protection of marine species. Protection measures such as seasonal closures have been in place since 1940. The creation of a protected area at the mouth of the Colorado River in 1974 forbade the exploitation of certain resources. Finally, in 1993, the Northern California Gulf and Colorado River Delta Biosphere Reserve, covering over 900,000 hectares, was

Figure 20.1 Northern California Gulf and Colorado River Delta Biosphere Reserve

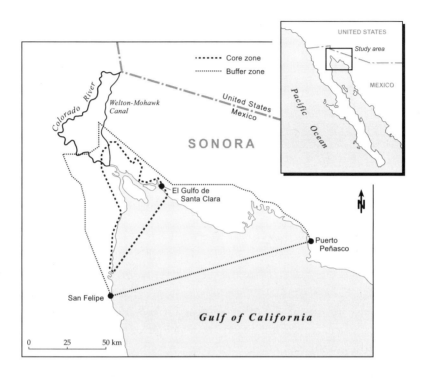

established (DOF 1993) (fig. 20.1). The reserve consists of a core zone and a surrounding buffer zone. In the buffer zone, which constitutes about 82 percent of the reserve area, resource use is not as restricted as in the core zone, thus allowing investment in projects to provide economic alternatives for the communities affected: San Felipe, B.C. and Puerto Peñasco, Sonora. The core zone comprises the remaining 18 percent of the reserve area, protecting ecosystems of particular interest. Activities in this area are restricted to research, technical education, and preservation. Resource use restrictions in the core zone have had a negative impact on the community of El Golfo de Santa Clara and the "*ejidos*" or communal lands of Luis Encinas Johnson, El Doctor, Mesa Rica; and Flor del Desierto (Sonora), and Salinas de Ometepec, Playa Blanca, and Playa Paraiso (B.C.).

Socioeconomic Issues in the Core Zone of the Reserve

Economic Structure

The reserve is a necessary long-term solution to environmental problems, but in the short-term, it will detrimentally affect the well-being of the communities that depend on the fishing resource. In the community of El Golfo de Santa Clara, fishing is the main activity in the primary sector, occupying 74 percent of a total working population of 434 people (INEGI 1990).

Twenty-four percent of fishers had an income below the poverty line by Mexican standards in 1990. Monetary earnings from fishing accounted on average for 46 percent of a fisher's total income, nonmonetary returns accounted for 53 percent, and only 1 percent of total income came from monetary earnings from other sources (El COLEF and SIMAC 1994-1997).

The average fisher is thirty-seven years old, has lived in Santa Clara for 29.2 years, has been a fisher for twenty years, and has only six years of school. The average fisher's home has a family of five, 3.6 of them dependants. Fishers work 9.1 months in fishing activities, 13 percent of them receive income from other sources for 6.5 months, and only 13 percent of fishers are qualified to do other kinds of jobs. With regards to housing, the average number of people per household is almost six. Twelve percent of houses have walls made of cardboard, corrugated metal, and adobe, nine percent have dirt floors, and none of them have running water. Most people (85%) own the houses they live in (COLEF and SIMAC 1994-1997).

This socioeconomic profile of the community of Santa Clara reveals high inflexibility towards any change in type of employment, income, and location of residence, and therefore indicates a strong pressure on the marine resources of the reserve. Under these conditions, the participation of the community in management of the reserve is essential. Establishing a reserve is an adequate measure to protect resources and the environment, but it is not sufficient. It is important to integrate fishing objectives and policies with resource protection, always involving local communities.

Fishing Crisis

In the last twenty years, fishing activities in the community of Santa Clara have concentrated on shrimp. Fishing for shrimp and "chano" (low value fish species) has been the basis of industry and exports in El Golfo de Santa Clara and other communities located in the area of influence of the reserve's core zone. These two fisheries contribute 90 percent of the production and monetary value of the total fishing production. In the past few years, there have been drastic declines in catch, and there are no signs of recovery in the short-term. Recognized causes of decline include overexploitation, declining fresh water inflows, low nutrients in the Colorado River, and lack of enforcement of seasonal closures (Godinez 1995). The shrimp catch increased from 135 tons in 1991 to 500 tons in 1994, then decreased to 132 tons in 1996. Economic indicators of fishing activity indicate a crisis. The number of cooperatives, partnerships, and boats has decreased. In 1996, all fourteen existing large boats dedicated to shrimp fishing were mortgaged. The number of smaller boats decreased from 240 to 180.

These results demonstrate the importance of considering economic and social impacts in order to achieve the environmental goals of the reserve. As long as there are no feasible economic alternatives to generate employment and income levels comparable to those existing prior to the biosphere reserve, the population directly affected by reserve restrictions will have incentives to violate resource-use regulations before attempting emigration or adopting new kinds of employment.

Project Sensitivity Analysis and Community Participation in the Area of Influence of the Reserve's Core Zone

Identification of Projects

Under the existing legislative structure, affected communities must be involved in the design and approval of a reserve's management plan. In the Northern California Gulf, stakeholders include commercial and sport fishers, tourism developers and business owners, farmers, non-governmental organizations (NGOs), and the general public. Stakeholders may participate through three channels:

- written proposals to federal authorities
- direct consultation by the Technical Committee for the Design and Approval of the Biosphere Reserve Management Plan; the committee holds public meetings and there is a representative from each community on the committee, and
- indirectly through recommendations drawn from the results of socioeconomic studies in the fishing communities

A questionnaire answered by the regional stakeholders resulted in twenty-one proposals for different investment projects. These represent market opportunities that may contribute to economic growth through employment and income generation. However, projects may have detrimental social and environmental impacts on communities and biodiversity in the area. Investment projects were selected according to criteria of conservation and sustainable use of resources, as well as preservation of cultural values and lifestyles.

Box 20.1. Criteria applied to project selection

• preserve biological diversity; project viability depends on the sustainable use of resources • avoid abrupt changes in residents' customs and lifestyles • adhere to the principles of sustainability	• independence: the costs or benefits of one project must not affect implementation of another project • mutually exclusive: the same project may be implemented in different locations or at different scales • not contingent on implementation of another project

Project Selection

In order to select those projects that are sustainable, this study used the Man and the Biosphere Program (MAB) established by UNESCO in 1972 as the conceptual basis to operationalize a set of criteria to define a sustainable investment. The premise is that it is possible to achieve an equilibrium between biological and cultural diversity, and economic development. Development must meet the needs of present generations without compromising the needs of future generations, and must not undermine existing resources and ecological systems (box 20.1).

Based on the criteria, eight investment projects were selected for further evaluation: shrimp farming, fresh water fish farming, mollusk farming, a shrimp freezing plant, a fishing products distribution center, sport fishing and ecological tourism, sport hunting, and a textile factory. These projects represent market opportunities that adhere to the sustainability requirements. Further project assessment includes market research and analyses of their financial, economic, and social feasibility.

Market Analysis

An analysis of market conditions is necessary to ensure a high probability of success. The analysis should include both a private and a social perspective, since the ultimate decision about project feasibility will depend upon the perspective taken. There is no rigid methodology to guide project approval decisions, due to project diversity and their different implications. However, decisions should be based on an integrated evaluation comprising financial, economic, and social analyses. Cost/benefit analysis (CBA) may be used to examine financial, economic, and social implications of projects in an integrated evaluation approach. The analysis needs information on six project aspects: lifetime of the project; initial capital investment; sales returns (benefits) from year zero and throughout the project lifetime; operating and input costs; product price; and discount rate. Data for evaluating specific projects were obtained from similar projects evaluated and approved by FIRA-FOPESCA (Banco de México, Fideicomiso para fondos de la Agricultura - Fomento de Pesca). A survey of expectations, perspectives, and participation in projects of local stakeholders was used to check the relevance of the data. Results should be interpreted as "subject to confirmation of the relevance of data to the area under study. "

Project Evaluation Perspectives

The cost-benefit analysis includes the following evaluative perspectives.

1. *Financial analysis* uses market prices, which may not reflect actual resource scarcity and values. They may include taxes and subsidies, which in a macroeconomic context are simply money transfers. This analysis determines net project benefits from the point of view of a private investor.

2. *Economic analysis* uses shadow prices, which are adjusted as needed to reflect actual values for society of inputs and outputs. Shadow prices reflect the opportunity cost for society of embarking on the use and production of goods and services. The economic analysis should concentrate on those adjustments to financial accounting that will probably influence the final decision of investing in a project.

3. *Social analysis* incorporates impacts on employment and income distribution among stakeholder groups involved in each project. This method adjusts monetary benefits against social objectives, such as employment and income, which are ignored by financial and economic analyses.

Shadow prices were calculated using the commercial goods method (Squire and Van der Tak 1975; Little and Mirreless 1974), since most projects need a high proportion of imported inputs and equipment, and involve exporting products.

Three decision criteria were used to determine which projects should be implemented. They allow comparison of projects and hence their priorization. The criteria used are:

1. *Net Present Value (NPV)*. This is the present value of benefits minus the present value of costs. If the NPV is negative, the project under study is not profitable for the chosen discount rate (this study used 13%), and vice versa if the NPV is positive.

2. *Internal Rate of Return (IRR)*. The IRR is the discount rate that would be required for the NPV to equal zero. If the IRR exceeds the discount rate, the decision rule is to go ahead with an investment.

3. *Benefit-Cost Ratio (B/C)*. The B/C compares the present value of benefits to the present value of costs. The decision rule is to adopt independent projects having a B/C equal to, or greater than, one.

The benefit-cost ratio (B/C) and net present value (NPV) are criteria that consider the value of money over the lifetime of a project and its capital costs. The internal rate of return (IRR) has an advantage over the other two criteria; not needing to consider explicitly the capital costs of the project. However, it assumes that all net returns generated during a project's life are reinvested at that rate.

Project evaluation

The following results correspond to the financial, economic, and social evaluation of the projects selected previously. The objective of this evaluation is to obtain quantitative indicators of the degree to which investment projects contribute to private benefits (financial), net social benefits (economic), and the generation of employment and income (social). This triple bottom-line evaluation allows the detection of difficulties that overall project implementation may encounter, as well as particular problems facing each project. The evaluation results are presented first project-by project for each analysis, in order to detect differences and make recommendations. Next, evaluation results are presented across projects to be able to compare and prioritize them. The financial analysis included a calculation of internal rate of return (IRR), net present value (NPV), and benefit–cost ratio (B/C), using market prices (not adjusted) (table 20.1).

Table 20.1. Financial Analysis of Projects[a]

Project	Internal rate of return (IRR)	Benefit-cost ratio (B/C)	Net present value (NPV)	Total Investment. (Pesos)
Shrimp farming	22%	1.56	144,406	555,448
Fresh water fish farming	29%	1.69	23,845	199,750
Mollusk farming	31%	1.53	120,000	375,000
Freezing plant	18%	1.18	17,150	781,000
Distribution center	18%	1.23	53,152	583,158
Ecotourism: sport fishing	37%	1.83	2,750	175,000
Ecotourism: sport hunting	21%	1.49	1,793	150,000
Textile factory	16%	0.94	5,782	359,746

[a] Direct information and projects FIRA-FOPESCA 1997
Note: Minimum rate of return of 8%, minimum reference rate of return of 16%. The rates of return are based on benefit and costs flows for similar projects in 1997.

All projects should be approved according to the NPV criterion. The NPV permits the assessment of a project in absolute terms, but not the ability of a project to generate returns per unit of input. The B/C ratio provides that information, showing which project provides higher returns given a level of input. The textile factory performs poorly under this criterion (B/C = 0.94). Sport fishing has the highest B/C at 1.83, followed by fish and seafood farming (fish at 1.69, shrimp at 1.56. mollusks at 1.53), sport hunting (1.49), the distribution center (1.23), and the freezing plant (1.18). Following the B/C decision rule, all projects except the textile plant should be implemented. Finally, projects with an IRR greater than 13 percent (the discount rate used in this study) are viable. The results for the IRR criterion confirm those of the NPV and B/C.

The economic analysis compares the values obtained for the financial internal rate of return to an economic internal rate of return (table 20.2). Values for the economic rate of return are adjusted using shadow prices. Project costs are adjusted according to a conversion factor, which accounts for the increase or decrease in price of a good or service in the international market to compare it to national prices.

Table 20.2 Economic Analysis of Projects[b]

Project	Financial Internal rate of return (IRR)	Economic Internal rate of return (IRR)
Shrimp farming	22%	14%
Fresh water fish farming	29%	35%
Mollusk farming	31%	32%
Freezing plant	18%	9%
Distribution center	18%	15%
Ecotourism: sport fishing	37%	40%
Ecotourism: sport hunting	21%	24%
Textile factory	16%	13%

[b]Direct information and projects FIRA-FOPESCA 1997
Note: Minimum rate of return of 6%, minimum reference rate of return of 14%. The rates of return are based on benefit and costs flows for similar projects in 1997. However, calculations have been adjusted for the specific region of the Northern California Gulf and Colorado River Delta.

The economic analysis shows mixed results with regards to the net social benefits of projects. The economic internal rate of return decreases with respect to the financial IRR for the freezing plant (economic IRR of 9%), the textile plant (13%), shrimp farming (14%), and the distribution center (15%). For these projects, the economic internal rate of return is not statistically higher than the price of money (the discount rate used in this study, 13%). Therefore, they are not really acceptable. The rest of the projects have an economic internal rate of return statistically higher than the price of money, hence they should be implemented according to this analysis. The order of preference would be: sport fishing (economic IRR of 40%), fish farming (35%), mollusk farming (32%), and sport hunting (24%).

The social analysis also uses the internal rate of return as an indicator of project viability. In this analysis, values are adjusted, using shadow prices that have also been corrected with the purpose of indicating how projects affect the generation of employment and income for stakeholder groups (table 20.3). The viability of each project depends on how they affect employment and income, saving, and consumption. Generally, large investments have a measurable impact on employment, income, and saving.

Table 20.3. Social Analysis of Projects[c]

Project	Financial internal rate of return (IRR)	Economic internal rate of return (IRR)	Social internal rate of return (IRR)
Shrimp farming	22%	14%	19%
Fresh water fish farming	29%	35%	18%
Mollusk farming	31%	32%	25%
Freezing plant	18%	9%	28%
Distribution center	18%	15%	26%
Ecotourism: sport fishing	37%	40%	10%
Ecotourism: sport hunting	21%	24%	8%
Textile factory	16%	13%	34%

[c]Direct information and projects FIRA-FOPESCA 1997

Table 20.4. Sensitivity Analysis

Sensitivity scenarios	Evaluation perspective	Internal Rate of Return (IRR)							
		Shrimp farm	Fish farm	Mollusk farm	Freezing plant	Distribution center	Sport fishing	Sport hunting	Textile plant
Normal operation	Financial	20%	29%	31%	18%	18%	37%	21%	16%
	Economic	18%	35%	15%	10%	25%	60%	24%	13%
	Social	19%	10%	25%	8%	21%	27%	8%	34%
10% + input costs	Financial	4%	20%	10%	7%	13%	19%	4%	20%
	Economic	6%	33%	15%	4%	20%	40%	6%	33%
	Social	10%	5%	14%	1%	15%	18%	10%	5%
10%+ operating costs	Financial	8%	24%	19%	4%	4%	5%	8%	24%
	Economic	10%	13%	9%	2%	14%	20%	10%	13%
	Social	6%	4%	18%	5%	12%	15%	6%	4%
10%- returns	Financial	0%	10%	18%	7%	8%	9%	0%	10%
	Economic	9%	31%	14%	5%	5%	2%	9%	31%
	Social	10%	9%	19%	4%	5%	2%	10%	9%

Note: these values do not necessarily match those in previous tables, because this table's results are based on scenarios.

The textile plant would require a high capital investment and would cause a large social impact, while ecotourism activities (sport fishing and hunting) have the least social impact. Sport fishing and hunting generate mostly direct employment, with a substantial part of investment going to individual consumption, saving only a small portion for reinvestment. In the long-term this could negatively impact project viability. On the other hand, the textile plant, freezing plant, distribution center, and mollusk farming have important impacts on employment and income, based on medium to high investment levels. These four projects have a social IRR well over the cost of money, making them viable according to the social analysis. Shrimp farming (social IRR of 19%) and fish farming (18%) are within the range of viability. Finally, according to the social analysis, sport fishing (10%) and hunting (8%) are not viable.

There are elements of uncertainty in the estimations used in the project evaluation, in particular with regards to assumptions around the decision criteria and estimates based on secondary information. A sensitivity analysis shows how the calculated internal rates of return vary with changes in estimates. Project variables that have been estimated include: the lifetime of the project; initial capital investment; sales returns (benefits) from year zero and through the lifetime of a project; operating and input costs; product price; and discount rate. The sensitivity analysis involves three scenarios: ten percent increase in input costs, ten percent increase in operating costs, and ten percent decrease in returns (table 20.4).

In general, the internal rates of return are not sensitive to changes in the different scenarios. The higher the decrease in returns, the higher the probability of rejecting the projects. At the project level, the freezing plant and shrimp farming are very sensitive to increases in the cost of inputs. Sport fishing and hunting, and fish and mollusk farming are more sensitive to changes in returns. These results underline the importance of increasing the certainty of the project variables estimated. However, the stability of the estimated internal rates of return suggests that the evaluation results are reliable.

Identification of Projects that Are Sustainable and Feasible

Environmental and socioeconomic issues in the region under study point to a need to find a model of regional development that is sustainable. The concept of sustainable development is understood here as a process of interaction between human activity and nature, where the socioeconomic well-being of local communities is maximized, while resources are used and at the same time are conserved. Studying the feasibility of sustainable investment projects allows an exploration of the possibilities for economic growth based on an economy more diversified and stable, which makes efficient use of marine resources, increases well-being, and conserves the environment of the region.

A short-term strategy involves new fishing activities in the region, which will guarantee the socioeconomic well-being of fishers. Benefit-cost ratios and internal rates of return are useful project evaluation criteria. They provide information on the most suitable order for the implementation of projects, given that constraints on the amount of capital available would not allow all projects to start simultaneously. The results indicate the following projects should be implemented:

- promote fishing and commercialization through a distribution center of new commercial species
- farming of traditional commercial species such as shrimp and mollusks
- farming of different species of herbivorous fresh water fish
- develop sport hunting and fishing activities, and
- establish a textile factory and a freezing plant

From the perspective of private investment (financial analysis), the most viable options are sport fishing, fish, mollusk, shrimp farming, and sport hunting. The distribution center and freezing plant are less feasible, and the textile plant is not profitable.

From the perspective of the economic analysis (net social benefits), the most preferable projects are sport fishing and fish and mollusk farming. Sport hunting is less viable and the distribution center, freezing plant, and textile factory are not viable. In the economic analysis, the internal rate of return depends on the mechanical equipment required as an investment. Those projects that need the equipment generate a lower IRR than is indicated in the financial analysis, due to price distortions.

From a social perspective, the most feasible options are the freezing plant, the distribution center, mollusk farming, and the textile plant. Fish and shrimp farming are less viable and sport hunting and fishing are not viable. This analysis considers project impacts on employment and income generation among stakeholder groups.

Finally, it is essential to redefine credit policies for fishing activities in order to provide resources for project implementation. It is also convenient to improve physical infrastructure and social services in the area. Physical infrastructure is needed to support the productivity of local fishing activities and to attract nonfishing activities. The improvement of social services will increase the level of well-being in the communities, providing fishers with access to education, health, and recreation.

Recommendations

The purpose of this paper was to propose an approach to resolve environmental and social issues in the Northern California Gulf. The approach integrates several methodologies to evaluate the feasibility of sustainable investment projects in the area influenced by the core zone of the Northern California Gulf and Colorado River Delta Biosphere Reserve. The implementation and operation of projects is the responsibility of fishers, business people, government authorities, research institutions, NGO's, and generally of the local, national, and international public.

Acknowledgements

This study was financed by International Conservation Mexico (Conservación Internacional México, A.C), based in Guaymas, Sonora. The authors acknowledge J. Alberto Godínez Placencia for his suggestions and valuable literature, Jacaranda Acuña for her assistance, and Teresa Contreras for editorial support.

References

COLEF (Colegio de la Frontera Norte) and SIMAC. *(Sistema de Investigadores del Mar de Cortés (Research Systems for the Sea of Cortez)) 1994-1997.* El Colegio de la Frontera Norte: Tijuana, México: Estudio Socioeconómico del Sector Pesquero del Alto Golfo de California.

Chavéz F., and T. Arizú. September 1972. *Informe sobre los Trabajos del Proyecto: Evaluación y Mortalidad de Totoaba* (mimeo). Ensenada, B.C.: Instituto Nacional de Pesca, Secretaría de la Pesca, Centro Regional de Investigaciones Pesqueras.

Diario Oficial de la Federación (DOF). 1993. *Propuesta para la Declaración de la Reserva de la Biósfera del Alto Golfo de California y Delta del Río Colorado.* Hermosillo, Sonora, México: Comité Técnico para la Preservacion de la Vaquita y la Totoaba (Technical Committee for the Preservation of the Marine Vaquita and the Totoaba).

Godínez, P. A. 1995. *Economìa Pesquera y Especies en Peligro de ExtinsiÚn en el Alto Golfo de California* Tijuana, Mexico: El Colegio de la Frontera Norte, Department of Economic Studies (Departamento de Estudios Economicos)..

——— 1994. *Pobreza y Especies en Peligro de Extinsión en el Alto Golfo de California.* Tijuana, Mexico: El Colegio de la Frontera Norte, COLEF IV.

México. Instituto Nacional de Estadistica y Geografia (INEGI) (National Institute for Statistics and Geography). 1990. *Censo General de Población y Vivienda.* D.F., México.

Little, I., and J. A. Mirreless. 1974. *Project Appraisal and Planning for Development Countries.* New York: Basic Book Inc.

Roman, B. March 1994. *Plan de Recuperación de la Vaquita (Phoceana sinus).* D.F., México: Depto. de Zoología, Instituto de Biología, UNAM.

Squire, L., and H. Van der Tak. 1975. *Economic Analysis of Projects.* Baltimore: Johns Hopkins University Press.

PARKS AND PROTECTED AREAS IN LOCAL AND REGIONAL CONTEXT IN NORTH AMERICA: A Multisectoral, Transdisciplinary Approach

Gustavo D. Danemann

Abstract

The objective of this paper is to highlight the need for a wider focus to analyze and address problems related to natural protected areas (NPAs) in North America. In order to achieve this, I describe the limitations of current decision-making processes related to NPAs by comparing the general characteristics of the problems to be addressed, to the approaches commonly used for diagnosis, and analysis of such problems.

Introduction

In the first issue of the *Journal of Environmental Management*, Sewell (1973) pointed out that in the decision-making process regarding natural resource management, it is imperative to consider broadly the environmental, social, institutional, economic, and financial consequences of each decision. Sewell also indicated that the procedures used to generate the information necessary for decision-making excluded social sciences, reflecting "institutional biases towards some strategies rather than others." According to Sewell, many of the weaknesses of the procedures—as well as many of their consequences—could be overcome through the incorporation of social research into the natural resources management field. Social sciences could contribute particularly in "the identification of the nature and magnitude of resources problems and the demands for resources-related goods and services; the delineation of alternative strategies for dealing with resources problems; hindsight reviews of projects and policies; examination of alternative ways of identifying public views; and development of more sophisticated techniques for taking account of multiple objectives, multiple strategies, and a wide range of values" (Sewell 1973: 34).

More than one quarter of a century after Sewell's observations, comparisons carried out during the *Workshop on Regional Approaches to Parks and Protected Areas in North America* suggest that in Canada, the United States, and Mexico, the decision-making processes related to parks and other natural protected areas (NPAs) are still using the classic analytical reductionist approach to deal with wicked problems. This approach considers social aspects at best partially, and also does not generally define the system, or holistic, context that determines problems related to NPAs and the use of their natural resources.

Problems Related to Protected Areas

Generally, management of an NPA in any country should address problems that are not strictly problems of the areas or individual resources within them. Rather, they are "human problems that we have created at many times and in many places, under a variety of political, social, and economic systems" (Ludwig, Hilborn, and Walters 1993:36). These are considered to be "composed problems" (Clayton and Radcliffe 1990:160), defined with the following characteristics (after Söderbaum 1987):

> *They are multidimensional, multisectoral, and multidisciplinary.* The problems present diverse dimensions, which will be given an importance related to the interests of whoever is judging a situation. Thus, a problem related to the use of a natural resource is evidenced in the legal, political, cultural, social, economic, biological, and environmental dimensions, among others. The study of such a variety of dimensions requires a similar variety of specialists and disciplines. Some of these dimensions will have a monetary representation, or market value, while others will not. The system involved in this situation will always be com-

posed of actors from diverse sectors, according to the diversity of interests converging in natural areas and resources.

They have spatial and temporal ramifications. NPA problems are not limited to geographical regions, or to the moment at which they are described. Supporting this statement is the definition of sustainability, when it refers to effects that the utilization of natural resources at a certain time and place may have in other areas or on future generations.

They extend beyond the immediate actors. Besides some agents directly involved in the use of NPAs and their resources, numerous actors exist, both nearby and distant, who are interested in such areas and their resources, or are suffering in some way from the consequences of problems within NPAs.

They involve conflicts among interests and ideologies. The interests around NPAs and their resources, and the ideologies that support them, can be as diverse as the actors involved in each case.

They involve uncertainty and risk, which also tends to be expressed multisectorally. Any problem related to the use of NPAs represents a risk to the interests of the actors involved. There is also uncertainty about the future evolution of the situation and induced future risks. As the actors involved in a given situation belong to diverse sectors, both the risk and the uncertainty have transverse effects that may involve several sectors simultaneously.

The problems related to NPAs are rarely expressed in an isolated way. Such problems are perceived through networks of symptoms that could show interdependence, multicausality, concatenation, variable coefficients of interrelation, positive or negative feedback, cumulative effects, circular causality, vicious circles, unstable equilibriums, dynamism, constant change, and adaptation (Clayton and Radcliffe 1996).

Limitations of Traditional Approaches to Problems in NPAs

The complexity and characteristics of problem situations regarding NPAs indicate that protecting natural areas and conserving their resources is not only a bioecological process, but a sociocultural one as well (Fiske 1992). However, most resource management issues are expressed solely in ecological imperatives to protect threatened resources. A review of NPA declarations and their management programs and regulations, shows that these processes usually follow a bioecologically-driven pattern, not addressing the complexity of the problems they intend to solve nor the situations they seek to improve (Feick 1996; Enríquez-Andrade and Danemann 1998). Instead, the diagnoses and analysis of wicked problems in which NPA design and administration have been based, commonly present the characteristics and limitations outlined below.

Unisectoral Approach

In public administration, academic, and conservationist sectors, the analysis of wicked NPA problems has been usually carried out considering only the sectoral perspective of the agency, institution, or group in charge of the analysis. Even in those cases in which the research included transectoral elements, the analysis started from an *a priori* definition of the problem, which caused other stakeholders to respond to interests and objectives from the sector in charge of the study. Consequently, diagnoses have generally been directed to only one part of the challenge, and the proposed solutions have been fragmentary and overwhelmed by the complexity of the problem situation.

Guha (1997) provided a strong argument regarding bioecologically-driven programs promoted by conservation organizations and government: "Wildlife conservation programs in the Third World have all too often been premised on an antipathy to human beings. In many countries, farmers, herders, swiddeners, and hunters have been evicted from lands and forests which they have long occupied to make way for parks, sanctuaries and wildlife reserves." This was the case for the "Montes Azules" Biosphere Reserve, in Chiapas, southeastern Mexico, where in May 2000, the Mexican government offered some of the local communities economic compensation to leave the reserve and settle in other areas, in order to prevent impacts on the natural ecosystem (Alvarez-Icaza 2000; Reveles 2000a). Little consideration was given to the fact that biosphere reserves are intended to provide a framework to search for "rational and sustainable use of ecosystem resources and, hence, for close cooperation with the human populations concerned" (Batisse 1986); the governmental perspective in this case was that the local population *was* the problem. Not surprisingly, the initiative generated a strong reaction from the affected sectors (Barreda 2000; Hernández 2000; Reveles 2000b).

Reductionist Approach

Scientists from the natural sciences, such as biologists, ecologists, and geographers, have carried out the majority of the analyses of problems in NPAs. The classic reductionist method, although useful in natural sciences, is generally inappropriate to solve problems related to the use of NPAs and their resources, that include not only natural but social elements as well, organized in a system of great complexity.

An example of this is provided by land-use planning techniques to define NPA zoning. The model is based in the definition of "environmental units," which are portions of territory sharing similar physical and bioecological characteristics (Cendrero 1982). Environmental units defined in this way are meant to respond homogeneously to environmental impacts, therefore being susceptible to a common set of management regulations. However, when NPAs involve people and their economic activities, as is the case in biosphere reserves, this reductionist scheme fails. Human users are neither homogeneous in their characteristics or interests, nor do they respond in the same way to a given set of rules or regulations. For instance, the intention of managing fishing activities in the "Upper Gulf of California and Colorado River Delta" Reserve of the Biosphere (Gobierno de los Estados Unidos Mexicanos 1993) through this kind of zoning method failed. Social, economical, and operational determinants in the use of fishing areas, as well as the implementation costs for the proposed regulations, were never considered (Instituto Nacional de Ecología 1995). Lately, comanagement efforts have been implemented to improve the former map-based fisheries management initiatives (Cudney and Turk 1998).

Partial, Inadequate, or Nonexistent Analysis of Social Components

As noted above, most analyses of NPAs problems have been carried out by researchers from the natural sciences. The lack of emphasis on social science research explains the vague or nonexistent evaluation and attention that has been given to interested actors, and such factors as roles, norms, values, concepts, and applications of power. These relationships define the structures as well as the operations of the social systems involved in the complex situations under study (Checkland and Scholes 1990; Clayton and Radcliffe 1996). Feick (1996) assigned to this "narrowness in perspective resulting from bureaucratic and disciplinary constraints," the failure of many biodiversity conservation programs in North America. According to this author, biologists in charge of endangered species recovery programs "devise solutions rooted in biological assessments and conclusions," and "frequently overlook the chief cause of species endangerment: the insidious and intricate economic, social and cultural attitudes and values."

The reintroduction of wolves into the Yellowstone National Park provides an example on this point (Kluger 1998). After a successful transplant of wolves from Canada into the park by the U.S. Fish and Wildlife Service in 1994, the program encountered opposition from ranchers and representatives of tourism businesses, who were concerned about wolf attacks on cattle and tourists, respectively. In 1995, those opposed filed suits against the program, and in 1997, a federal judge ruled that while the program's goals might be noble, its methods were illegal, declaring that the only solution was to remove the reintroduced animals. The unplanned reaction from opposing human actors in this case was, by far, more problematic to wolves than their readaptation to bioecological conditions in the park.

Inadequate Assignment of Causal Relations to Observed Symptoms

Human beings are inherently predisposed to attribute a cause and effect relationship to events that occur consecutively (Clayton and Radcliffe 1996). However, symptoms of problems form networks in which the original causes are frequently neither immediate nor apparent (White 1983). The actions designed as a result of direct cause and effect analysis address only the symptoms of a problem, not its evolution and interactive causes. In other words, such solutions often fail to address the true nature and cause of the problems.

That is the case when "the problem" for a NPA is defined as, for instance, fragmentation of habitat via logging and road building (Primm and Clark 1995 in: Feick 1996), or overfishing (Instituto Nacional de Ecología 1995). Backstep analysis (Fischer 1999) shows that those are not problems, but consequences of the present definition of economic incentives that promote logging and road building, and the open access condition of the overexploited fishery (McGoodwin 1990). In both cases, local symptoms are generated beyond the NPA frontiers. Therefore, management initiatives designed in the form of prohibitions of activities or actions that locally conflict with the "ecological integrity" of an NPA, are not likely to be effective if they are not supported by a more general work focused on the root causes of the unwanted behaviors.

Lack of definition of the system in which symptoms of a problem are located

It follows from the foregoing that the definition of NPA problems has generally been limited to a superficial description of symptoms, without considering the systems that generate, define, and maintain those symptoms. This is aggravated in cases where diagnoses are prepared without adequate and sufficient information, which typically happens when agencies or institutions that undertake diagnoses are unfamiliar with the area, or lack the expertise in fields of study necessary to fully understand the problem in all of its complexity. Fischer (1981) pointed out that the complex nature of environmental problems is such that no researchers from outside the local or regional context could ever fully capture all the subtleties, actors, and interests involved. This is applicable to the analysis of problem situations in NPAs, in which the local components of the system involved have a prominent role.

Fiske (1992) provided an example of the consequences of lacking a definition of the system to be affected in establishing an NPA. This author described the case of "La Parguera," a proposed marine sanctuary in Puerto Rico. It was designed in the late 1970s by the Puerto Rico Department of Natural Resources to protect tropical coral reefs, seagrass beds, and bioluminescence phenomena, from dumping of raw sewage from boats and shoreline homes. When presenting the project to the public, promoters faced the total and radical opposition of almost all local actors, who feared the sanctuary might limit their business or affect other private interests. This opposition caused the initiative to be abandoned by 1985. In this case, the government's approach to the problem focused on the threats to the biological elements in the system, and the managers designed their strategy considering that single aspect. A systemic perspective would have exposed the complex network of sectoral interests and relationships converging in the area, providing managers with better information for policy analysis and strategic design of their project.

Conclusions

The complex characteristics of problems related to NPAs and the use of their natural resources clearly surpass the methods commonly used to describe and address them. The reductionist, unisectoral, and bioecologically-driven approach used to describe problems and design solutions only give partial pictures of the situations being addressed. As every decision-making process depends primarily on the definition of the problem to be solved, it is not surprising that partially described problems receive only partial solutions. This has caused the inefficacy, and even complete failure, of many managerial initiatives in NPAs of North America. In the process, inter- and intrasectoral conflicts arise, threatening natural areas and resources, and causing NPA administrations to lose public credibility.

A better decision-making process for NPAs requires two changes in the current analytical methods:

1. Problem situations should be described following a multisectoral, radically transdisciplinary, and systemic approach; and
2. Policy analysis should evolve from the current technical approach—in which problem definition and management objectives are set *a priori* by the analyst—to a flexible approach, more suitable to the uncertainty and risk usually involved in the development of situations involving human activity systems.

Upgrading the traditional methods to consider the complexity of environmental problems would allow the management of NPAs in North America to be better adapted—in both their strategic and tactical aspects—to objectives and expectations determined at local, regional, and national levels.

Acknowledgments

This paper was developed as part of my Ph.D. research on system analysis and natural resources administration at the Faculty of Marine Sciences of the Universidad Autónoma de Baja California. It focused on natural protected areas of North America through the fruitful discussions we shared at Working Group 3—(S. Brennan, C. Castillo, M. Castillo, G.

Forbes, M. Jensen, P. Morales, G. Nelson, S. Santiago, E. Vázquez, and Gustavo Danemann)—which was dedicated to the analysis of planning, management, and deciding upon parks and protected areas in a local regional context in North America. I thank Gordon Nelson, Lucy Sportza, and Chad Day for their editorial assistance.

References

Alvarez-Icaza, P. 2 May 2000. "Montes Azules." *La Jornada.*

Barreda, A. 10 May 2000. "Los Incendios, Coartada para la Guerra." *La Jornada.*

Batisse, M. 1986. "Developing and Focusing the Biosphere Reserve Concept." *Nature and Resources* 22(3): 2-11.

Cendrero, A. 1982. *Técnicas e Instrumentos de Análisis para la Evaluación, Planificación y Gestión del Medio Ambiente.* CIFCA, Serie Opciones, Política y Planificación Ambiental, N°6. Madrid, Spain. 67 pp.

Checkland, P., and J. Scholes. 1990. *Soft Systems Methodology in Action.* New York: John Wiley & Sons.

Clayton, A. M., and N. J. Radcliffe. 1996. *Sustainability: A Systems Approach.* Boulder, Colo: Westview Press. 258 pp.

Cudney B. R., and P. J. Turk B. 1998. *Pescando Entre Mareas del Alto Golfo de California: Una Guía Sobre la Pesca Artesanal, su Gente y sus Propuestas de Manejo.* Puerto Peñasco, Sonora, Mexico: Centro Intercultural de Estudios de Desiertos y Océanos (CEDO), A.C. 166 pp.

Enríquez-Andrade, R., and G. Danemann. 1998. *Identificación y Establecimiento de Prioridades para las Acciones de Conservación y Oportunidades de Uso Sustentable de los Recursos Marinos de la Península de Baja California.* Technical report presented to the Mexican Fund for Conservation of Nature. Damas N°49, Col. San José Insurgentes, 03900 Mexico D.F. 77 pp.

Feick, J. 1996. *Evaluation of Ecosystem Management in the Columbia Mountains of British Columbia.* Ph.D. Dissertation Research Proposal. Calgary, Alta: University of Calgary, Department of Geography. 81 pp.

Fischer, D. W., ed. 1981. *North Sea Oil: An Environmental Interface.* Bergen, Norway: Univeritetsforlaget. 330 pp.

Fischer, D. W. 1999. *Técnicas para la Formulación de Políticas en Zonas Costeras.* Mexicali, Baja California, México: Universidad Autónoma de Baja California. 243 pp.

Fiske, S. 1992. "Sociocultural Aspects of Establishing Marine Protected Areas." *Ocean & Coastal Management* 18: 25-46.

México. 10 June 1993. Decreto por el que se Declara Area Natural Protegida con el Carácter de Reserva de la Biósfera, la Región Conocida como Alto Golfo de California y Delta del Río Colorado, Ubicada en Aguas del Golfo de California y los Municipios de Mexicali, B.C., de Puerto Peñasco y San Luis Río Colorado, Son. *Diario Oficial*: 24-28.

Guha, R. 1997. "The Authoritarian Biologist and the Arrogance of Anti-humanism: Wildlife Conservation in the Third World." *The Ecologist* 27(1): 14-19.

Hernández N., L. 9 May 2000. "Militarización y Ecología en la Lacandona." *La Jornada.*

Kluger, J. 1998. "The Big (not so Bad) Wolves of Yellowstone." *Time* 151(2): 22-25.

Ludwig, D., R. Hilborn, and C. Walters. 1993. "Uncertainty, Resource Exploitation, and Conservation: Lessons from History." *Science* 260:17, 36.

McGoodwin, J. R. 1990. *Crisis in the World's Fisheries. People, Problems, and Policies.* Palo Alto, Calif: Stanford University Press. 235 pp.

México. Instituto Nacional de Ecología. 1995. *Programa de Manejo de la Reserva de la Biósfera "Alto Golfo de California y Delta del Río Colorado."* México, D.F.: Secretaría del Medio Ambiente, Recursos Naturales y Pesca. 97 pp.

Reveles, J. 25 May 2000a. "Descartan Usar a la PFP para Desalojar la Reserva de Montes Azules". *El Financiero*: 46.

_____. 24 May 2000b. Reclaman Tzeltales y Tzotziles el Derecho de Vivir en Predios de Montes Azules." *El Financiero* :48.

Sewell, W. 1973. "Broadening the Approach to Evaluation in Resources Management Decision-Making." *Journal of Environmental Management* 1:33-60.

Söderbaum, P. 1987. "Environmental Management: A Non-Traditional Approach." *Journal of Economic Issues* 21(1):139-165.

White, C. 1983. "Problem Solving: The Neglected First Step." *Management Review* (January): 52-56.

TOURISM, PROTECTED AREAS, NATURE CONSERVATION, AND SUSTAINABLE DEVELOPMENT IN MEXICO

Nora L. Bringas Rabago and Lina Ojeda Revah

Abstract

This study explores the differences among some existing forms of alternative tourism. Ecotourism stands out as an alternative source of income for the maintenance of protected natural areas and thus the conservation of biodiversity. Although its benefits are generally highlighted, poorly managed ecotourism can cause the same harmful effects as mass tourism. Unfortunately, in developing countries such as Mexico, the prefix "*eco*" in front of tourism is not a guarantee of sustainability or respect for nature, though it can be an easy lure for external financing. This paper makes use of off-road races, such as the Baja 1000 and Baja 500, which take place in Baja California, Mexico, as illustrations of the potential threats of nature-based adventure tourism to protected areas and environment generally.

Introduction

Every time a new economic development model is implemented, it brings with it profound sociocultural, environmental, and territorial changes. In tourism development, these changes are associated with the introduction of an outside element to the local culture—the tourist—who causes modifications in the economic structure, in the behaviour of the local population, and, most importantly, in their values. As Marie-

Françoise Lafant said, "With tourism, what you are importing to a country is not only the tourists with their luggage, but a new model of society" (Cazes 1992). This contact between visitors and hosts gives rise to complex relationships that differ depending on how dissimilar the two groups are, and on the intensity of the relations. The larger the volume of visitors, the larger will be the effect of tourism.

Since World War II, mass tourism has been profiled as the most important kind of tourism worldwide. All predictions from the World Tourism Organisation (OMT 1998) indicate that mass tourism will continue to grow in importance and size. However, with an increase in environmental awareness, this kind of tourism has been widely criticized for its environmental destructiveness. Consequently, in recent decades there has been increasing interest in finding and developing alternative forms of tourism, which take place mostly in natural areas. Different forms of alternative tourism have appeared in the market, creating confusion about its definition and its effects on the environment.

Tourism: General Context

In the period following World War II, better socio-economic conditions and the emergence of the middle class facilitated an increase in the demand for tourism services, which previously were only available to a small, privileged group. The "baby boom" generation started worldwide mass travel. These travellers, most of them young couples, were looking for a relaxing holiday, passively enjoying the sea, sun, and sand.

During this period, the prevailing development model consisted of building large beach hotels including a variety of amenities. Each hotel would operate as a self-contained unit, hindering contact between tourists and the local community. Managing the coastal zone for such tourism resulted in rapid development, without adequate planning or measures to mitigate the negative environmental impacts of construction and visitor pressure.

The widespread use of air transportation, as well as the pressure exercised by the international tourism industry to reduce hotel and air fares, played a fundamental role in the massive growth of tourism. Operations which could not compete were forced to leave the market. A swarm of tourists seeking cheap packages and trips developed quickly (Ungefug 1992)—lured more by low prices than by destination—and resulted in an increased flow of visitors toward low-cost destinations, intensifying environmental deterioration.

In 1997, 613 million international tourists generated approximately $444 billion[1] in economic benefits. By 2000, an estimated 692 million tourists will generate profits of about $560 billion—a figure expected to increase in the following decades (OMT 1998). Based on an annual growth rate of 4.3 percent, projections for 2020 indicate that there will be 1,600 million international tourists. The growth rates for both the number of travelers and the profits they generate will grow faster than world wealth, projected to grow 3 percent annually (OMT 1998). The magnitude of tourism activity since the mid-1980s has caused increasing concern for the environment. Alternative tourism, based in nature travel, has emerged as a form of tourism that can help lessen the negative effects of mass tourism.

The Current Models: Traditional and Alternative Tourism

In the light of the previous remarks, two types of tourism will likely prevail in the next years: mass or traditional tourism and alternative tourism (table 22.1).

Table 22.1. Differences Between Traditional and Alternative Tourism Models

Traditional Tourism	Alternative Tourism
Standard product	Unique product
High initial investment on tourism infrastructure	High initial investment in knowledge, organization, and information
High impact initially	Gradual growth
Advertised through mass media	Specialized advertising
Market selection criteria: • Income level	Market selection criteria: • Interest groups
Subject of advertising: • Tourism facilities	Subject of advertising: • Activities and experiences
Standard life style	Personal life style
Tourist behavior: • Observing without interacting	Tourist behavior: • Experiencing the region
Travel program: • Pre-established	Travel program: • Open
Risk: • Loss of control	Risk: • Organizational complexity

1.   See http://www.cec.org/files/pdf/BIODIVERSITY/eco-eng_EN.pdf

Mass or traditional tourism

Mass or traditional tourism continues to be very important and is growing as people have more free time. This kind of tourism generally consists of bargain packages including air transportation and lodging, with destinations not being as important as price. Low to medium income tourists normally expect fun and entertainment on beaches. Generally, the destination is a self-contained resort and visitor mobility is reduced to airport–hotel–beach. Its motto could be summarized as "many tourists and few profits." In countries like Mexico, tourism is promoted as the economic development solution for impoverished regions with diverse cultural and natural resources. During the first quarter of 1998, tourism profits exceeded those from oil exports in Mexico making it the second largest source of foreign income for the country (SECTUR 1998a). Tourism advances regional development generating profits, employment, and other sociocultural impacts, as well as increasing awareness of environmental health, which is essential for sustainable success.

Of the 92.9 million visitors to Mexico in 1997, 73.5 percent came for only one day, and only 19.4 percent were tourists. Total income from international visitors was $7,593.7 million, 75.7 percent being from the tourism sector and the remaining 24.3 percent from excursionists. Thus, one fifth of the total tourism generated 75 percent of the income. Even though Mexico occupied eighth place as a tourist destination globally, it is sixteenth in terms of currency generated (SECTUR 1998b). The average tourism expense in Mexico is $297, compared to an average of $730 in the rest of the world. In Mexico, the presence of unique attractions is undervalued; it seems that the country is competing for low prices, which is unfortunate given the great competitive advantage of its natural and cultural resources.

Alternative tourism

Alternative tourism is a new segment of global tourism that is increasingly gaining importance. This type of tourism attempts to organize trips to unknown places away from mass tourism, normally in natural environments, and according to clients' needs and schedules. As opposed to mass tourism, alternative tourists are willing to pay high prices for unique natural or cultural attractions. This sector relies on attracting interest in exceptional resources, such as the Egyptian pyramids or the ceremonial centers of Mexico, giving these destinations an international competitive advantage.

This kind of tourism attracts those who travel to experience the existence of cultural resources, natural resources, or some combination of both. This kind of tourism involves rural or agrotourism, adventure tourism, and ecotourism. Both ecotourism and agrotourism generally help to improve an area, through monetary, time, or work contributions. On the other hand, the natural environment contributes to the enjoyment of adventure tourism, but the activity does not necessarily contribute to improvement of the area affected (Burton 1998).

All these types of alternative tourism, and their vague definitions, have created confusion around them. The term "ecotourism" has been used as an advertising catchword, creating the illusion of the commercial product always being beneficial for the environment. This, unfortunately, is not necessarily true. Ceballos-Lascurain (1988), considered one of the pioneers of ecotourism, defined it as travel to relatively pristine areas to study, admire, and enjoy landscapes, flora, fauna, or cultural manifestations. Ecological tourism implies a scientific, aesthetic, or philosophical appreciation, even though the tourist is not necessarily a scientist, artist, or professional philosopher.

What is ecotourism and how does it arise? What does the ecotourist desire? Does ecotourism generate economic benefits? This document will try to answer these questions. Because different types of alternative tourism are not clearly defined, all of them are encompassed here under the generic term *ecotourism*.

The search for enriching experiences which characterized the 1960s, the popularity of outdoor activities of the 1970s, and the concern for health and physical condition of the 1980s were the basis for the development of ecotourism (Budowski 1989). With tourism being criticized as an activity detrimental to the environment, ecotourism emerged as a possible way to reconcile ecology with economy and change the negative reputation of tourism. In fact, some consider ecotourism as the development model closest to sustainable development, implying respect and care of natural resources, without compromising their enjoyment by future generations (Marajh and Meadows 1992). This is achieved by allowing local communities to live off the rational use of those resources. Under this perspective, ecotourism is conceived as an alternative source of income for rural communities, permitting them to subsist without having to destroy their resources. Ecotourism can offer an economic justification to protect areas which otherwise would not receive any protection (Boo 1990). However, some critics caution that ecotourism may open the door to the destruction of the same areas it is trying to protect (Ziffer 1989).

The tourism industry is booming as a consequence of the growth of ecotourism (Boo 1990). Although no statistical data exist on the numbers of ecotourists visiting different zones of the world, or the revenues generated as a result, interviews with tourism industry operators by Ziffer suggest ecotourism is in constant expansion, growing by approximate 20 percent annually (Ziffer 1989).

The United States National Parks System received 270 million visitors in 1989, while state parks received about five hundren million. In Canada, provincial and national parks received twenty and forty-seven million visitors respectively (OMT-PNUMA 1992). Birdwatchers in Point Pelee National Park of Ontario spent $3.8 million in twenty-four days, of which $2.1 million were spent locally (Mendelsohn 1994).

The data suggest the economic potential of ecotourism. In 1986 approximately 5,000 travel agents specialized in nature-based travel in the United States (Budowski 1989). Indeed, adventure and ecological tourism is the fastest growing tourism sector in the U.S. Around four to six million Americans travel abroad each year to natural areas. The average cost of a trip, excluding airfare, was approximately $3,000 dollars. Revenues remaining in receiving countries amount to around $12 billion (Budowski 1989).

The total expense of visitors from Europe and the United States to natural areas in less developed countries has been estimated at $ 1.7 billion (Ziffer 1989). For countries such as Costa Rica, Ecuador, Belize, Rwanda, and Kenya among others, this kind of tourism is of major economic importance (Boo 1990, Ziffer 1989, Budowski 1989, OMT-PNUMA 1992, OMT 1992, Marajh and Meadows 1992). In 1988, approximately fifteen million tourists visited Latin America, many of them drawn by the flora and fauna of protected natural areas (Mendelsohn 1994). In Parc National des Volcans de Rwanda, tourists who watch gorillas generated one million dollars in revenues from park admissions, in addition to all other expenditures (OMT-PNUMA 1992).

One of the most effective ways of protecting certain animal species is their economic profitability. Economic models applied in Amboseli

National Park, Kenya, suggested that observing a lion generated an annual revenue of approximately $27,000. The value of a herd of elephants was estimated at $610,000 annually, also due to ecological tourism (OMT-PNUMA 1992). This suggests the importance of ecological tourism for wildlife conservation as well as for revenue generation in local communities. However, in order for ecotourism to be an effective conservation strategy, those who plan land use should ensure that ecotourism is more profitable than competing land uses. For example, Amboseli National Park is estimated to gain forty dollars annually for each hectare dedicated to ecological tourism, in comparison to eighty cents per hectare if the same land was dedicated to agriculture (OMT-PNUMA 1992).

Are these models incompatible?

Ecotourism, as opposed to traditional tourism, requires low investment in infrastructure and high investment in training, organization, and information. Ecotourism demands a greater level of preparation and an ability to withstand competition, which is based on the existence of unique resources. The alternative tourist looks for a novel product and participates in trip planning, demanding an experience that allows personal growth and interaction with the local community (Pearce 1988). Conventional tourism advertises through the media and is marketed largely towards the income level of travelers. Alternative tourism, on the other hand, aims for a niche market. Therefore, the former focuses on growth, whereas the latter rewards organizational capacity, which makes it more complex.

Although ecotourism is gaining importance every day, this new form of tourism will not displace mass tourism. On the contrary, the latter continues to grow. In this context, given the fragility of ecosystems and their exposure to mass tourism, those responsible for tourist planning face an important environmental challenge. Innovative strategies must be developed to persuade large hotel chains to participate in a more rational and sustainable use of natural resources (Wall 1997).

While ecotourism has contributed to revenue generation, profits generally remain in the countries of origin of the tourism industry operators. Most tourists come from developed countries in the Northern Hemisphere, where large tourism operators are located. Most travelers' expenses are paid in the country of origin and there are few shopping opportunities at destinations, which often are wilderness areas. Consequently, both tourism industry operators and receiving regions have the potential to increase revenues by attracting more tourists. However, this raises the danger of ecotourism becoming mass tourism. Could ecotourism simply be a precursor of large-scale tourism development (Wall 1997)?

Why Limit Conservation to Protected Areas?

Conservation of biodiversity and natural ecosystems has focused primarily on the creation of protected areas, whereby portions of land are set aside and sheltered from human development. Although it is necessary to continue this approach, it will not be sufficient in the long-term, given the current rate of loss of species and ecosystems. Ecological, social, and economic issues inside and outside protected areas are closely related, but are often addressed as though they were independent of each other. However, conservation problems will only be solved through the integrated planning of conservation and development initiatives regionally and locally. The success or failure of sustainable development will depend upon the creation of regions that are ecologically sustainable (Lineham and Gross 1998). This precondition is used as a point of departure to analyze some of the problems of protected areas in the next section.

Ecological issues

One of the most important problems of protected areas is their isolation and small size. Many protected areas are too small to protect biodiversity, including both species and habitats. The small size and isolation of many protected areas also means that the processes necessary for the long term adaptation and survival of species and habitats are not protected.

Disturbances are environmental changes or destructive events that alter the structure and function of a system, such as fires, floods, or human intervention (Pickett and White 1981). Disturbances produce heterogeneity by deviating communities from their paths of succession. Protected areas were often established before the role of natural disturbance in preserving biodiversity was understood, and they are often too small to maintain the natural disturbance regime.

Protected areas are also often too small and isolated to protect species that have large home ranges over the long-term. This isolation also decreases opportunities for exchanging genetic material between different populations, reducing the ability of species to adapt to disturbances and, hence, threatening their survival. Roads also contribute to the isolation of habitat patches, by impeding the movement of small mammals. As well, roads are often the main cause of mortality of large mammals (Peck 1998).

Habitat fragmentation refers to the subdivision of a continuous habitat into small units, mainly due to natural and human disturbances. Human population growth, economic development, agriculture, and resource extraction inevitably result in habitat fragmentation (Reed and Noss in Szaro and Johnston (n. d.), 574–589). Fragmentation of anthropogenic origin has resulted in a decline of biodiversity due to loss of original habitat, isolation of the remaining habitat, edge effects, and an increase of unsuitable habitat in the landscape (Andren 1994). Changes in area, shape, and connectivity of habitat patches affect species richness and distribution, as well as the disturbance regime (Franklin and Forman 1987).

Several studies have shown that problems affecting protected areas often originate beyond their borders, indicating the importance of analyzing what occurs outside protected areas. Fragmentation of natural habitats increases with human development. Protected areas become small islands in a hostile matrix that could destroy them in the medium term. In this context, it is obvious that seminatural and managed landscapes will play a vital role in conserving populations, species, ecological processes, and even the survival of protected areas.

When ecotourism is proposed as an alternative for financing protected areas, it is often assumed to be an environmentally benign activity. However, like any type of tourism, ecotourism may have negative environmental impacts. It focuses on particular areas that are protected precisely because of their fragility. It does not plan itineraries to avoid critical times such as mating periods; on the contrary, it often chooses such times. Finally, ecotourism assumes that there is a lineal relationship between volume of use and associated impacts. In fact, this is probably not true as even a small number of visitors may cause negative impacts (Wall 1997).

Socioeconomic issues

In Mexico, human communities often form an integral part of the ecosystem, depending on resources for subsistence. This is why protected areas have been based on the model of the biosphere reserve, with a core area preserved from human disturbance, and a buffer area where activities based on sustainable resource uses are allowed. However, biosphere reserves are not without problems, partly due to inadequate management plans. The main constraint, though, is that protected areas and their populations are isolated from the surrounding economic environment. They are expected to adhere to sustainable development principles that are in conflict with the driving external economic forces that demand high economic gains in a short time. Keeping protected areas isolated from their surroundings is a luxury in any country, but is particularly difficult in poor countries with meagre resources for environmental protection.

Another problem originates in efforts to assign an economic value to nature. The complexity of the natural environment will always be under-valued. It is important to repudiate the notion that the environment can be compartmentalized into those resources and services which are of value to humans. Indeed, it cannot be if the biodiversity that is so treas-ured is to be maintained sustainably.

If protected areas are insufficient to maintain biodiversity, and if ecot-ourism is an initial form of mass tourism, then alternative tourism should be considered both inside and outside protected areas. The next section makes use of off-road races, such as Baja 1000 and Baja 500, which take place in Baja California, Mexico, as examples to illustrate the potential threat of nature-based adventure tourism.

Environmental Effects of Off-road Vehicles

Ecosystems in the Baja California peninsula are mainly arid, containing a diversity of natural resources. About three thousand flora species are present, of which 23 percent are endemic to the peninsula (Wiggins 1980). Endemic species can be extremely vulnerable to the pressures of activities like tourism, because their distribution is restricted to small populations. Under such conditions, the effects of tourism are generally negative, especially when legislation regulating environmental protection and tourism is lacking. Off-road vehicle use illustrates this situation.

Mexico, and Baja California in particular, have become a paradise for off-road vehicle users and organisers of races after off-road vehicle use was restricted in the U.S. because of the widespread ecological damage associated with this use (Kockleman 1983a). Although there has been little research that examined the effects of off-road vehicles on Baja California ecosystems, such effects can be inferred from numerous studies undertaken in California, where the ecosystems are similar.

Off-road vehicles impact the desert ecosystem in many ways, particularly damaging soil, fauna, and flora. Constant vehicle transit erodes and compacts the soil and destroys vegetation, accelerating erosion. Organic decomposition is faster, leaving an inorganic surface crust that increases water run-off. Less oxygen and water penetrates the soil, impacting species that inhabit it. The general result is environmental degradation. The environment becomes more hostile to both flora and fauna, and sediment in streams increases with erosion (Dregne 1983, Kockelman 1983b).

Vehicles detrimentally affect coastal dunes in Baja California, destroying the vegetation that stabilize them. This has an adverse impact on neighbouring urban and tourist areas that are negatively affected by increased quantities of wind-blown sand (Escofet and Carvacho 1988). In areas frequented by off-road vehicles, vegetation patterns and species composition are often dramatically changed (Lathrop and Rowlands 1983). Noise caused by off-road vehicles has a negative impact on neighbouring communities as well as on animal species (Brattstrom and Bondello 1983, 167-206).

Currently, the area most used by off-road vehicles extends from the U.S. border to 100 kilometers south of Ensenada on the west side of the peninsula, south to San Felipe on the Gulf side, and over the hills to the vicinity of San Pedro Martin National Park (fig. 22.1) (Parkhurst 1988). This activity has negatively affected an extensive area that includes most vegetation types. The routes of the Baja 500 and Baja 1000 races cut across the range of bighorn sheep (*Ovis canadensis*) in the region. Bighorns are endangered in Mexico. In 1997, the Mexican Secretariat of the

Figure 22.1 Natural protected areas and off-road vehicle races

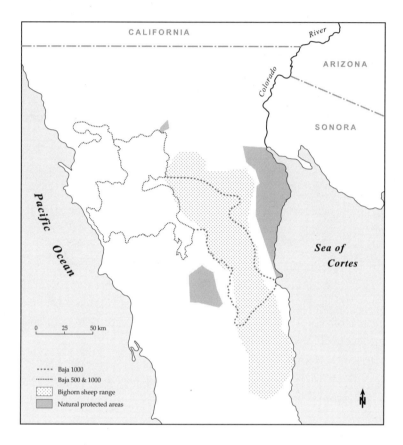

Environment, Natural Resources, and Fisheries (Secretaría de Medio Ambiente, Recursos Naturales y Pesca, SEMARNAP), and the Secretariat of Tourism (Mexico, Secretaría de Turismo, SECTUR) issued a joint ecotourism program for protected areas (Programa de Ecoturismo en Areas Naturales Protegidas de Mexico). While measures to restrict hunting of bighorn sheep are in place, the indiscriminate use of off-road vehicles remains unregulated, based on claims that off-road races, disguised as a form of ecotourism, generate high economic gains. This claim is contradicted by the research, as noted above, on the detrimental effect of off-road vehicles on geomorphology and vegetation in desert environments.

Establishing a connected system of protected areas that include representative ecosystems is one of the tools available to preserve species and habitat diversity. Although 27 percent of the State of Baja California is protected, these sheltered areas are isolated and not representative of all ecosystems. For example, ecosystems along the Pacific coast are missing. Protected areas in Baja California include low numbers of endemic species, and conditions make them vulnerable to extinction (Villaseñor and Elias 1989; Riemann, personal communication). Moreover, protected areas in Mexico not only present problems of isolation and inadequate ecosystem representation, but also of insufficient budgets, which result in virtually no enforcement of environmental protection regulations. Hence, it is possible for off-road vehicles to enter such areas and seriously damage the environment.

Final Comments

In modern society, tourism offers an opportunity for cultural interaction. Often people travel to experience a different culture, which stimulates their creativity and is important in realising individual potential. Awareness of the economic importance of tourism in the 1960s led the government to plan and finance tourist destinations. Whereas tourism has sometimes contributed to regional development, it has had negative impacts as well. Local populations are often excluded from the benefits of development. Social and environmental costs have frequently been irreversible, and higher than economic benefits.

Acapulco is a good example of negative social and environmental impacts caused by tourism development. In Acapulco Bay, the local population was displaced from the coastal zone to the base of the local mountains. This resulted in the loss of basic water, sewage, and electrical services for the displaced population because of the high costs of their construction in steep topography. In addition, the water in the bay was polluted by waste water and garbage discharged to it during the rainy seasons (Bringas 1999; Ramírez Sáez 1986).

All around the world, tourism perspectives predict growth in nature-based travel, particularly from developed to developing countries. In this context, ecotourism offers an opportunity to redirect the focus of tourism into novel ways of spending free time which achieve benefits for the individual, generate economic profits for the entrepreneur and the host region, and help conserve natural resources and environments. In summary ecotourism presents three planning challenges if it is to contribute to sustainable development. Mexico must ensure that eco-logical tourism is:

- economically viable, both locally and nationally
- culturally supportive of, and acceptable to, local communities, and
- ecologically sustainable over the long-term (Mendelsohn 1994).

Ecotourism is not a panacea, and when badly planned it may have the same negative impacts as mass tourism. In Mexico there are many unfortunate examples of the risks of mass tourism disguised as "green" tourism. Numerous visitors watching marine turtles lay their eggs in South Pacific beaches, together with high light intensities from nearby hotels, often cause turtles to return to sea without laying their eggs. On the Baja California coasts, the high numbers of whale watchers are alarming and viewed as threatening to the animals (Paget and Begley 1996).

Clearly a greater effort is needed to involve local communities in con-servation if the potential of ecotourism to diversify economic activity while preserving ecological, social, and cultural values is to be realised. In 1994, less than 1 percent of economic benefits generated in Bahía Magdalena, Baja California, stayed in the receiving communities. Most of the profits went to tourism industry operators in California, U.S.A. If receiving communities retained a greater share of economic revenues, they would have a powerful incentive to conserve their resources. To do so would require ecotourism targets to be managed by experienced nationals, following management plans that provide for enforcement of protected area regulations.

The concepts of ecosystem health and integrity are useful to promote ecologically sustainable landscapes. Ecosystem health is determined by the continuance of ecological processes, independent of species composi-tion. Ecosystem integrity refers to ecological processes as well, with an emphasis on preserving native biodiversity and community structures (Callicot and Munford 1997). These concepts include ecosystems in areas of human occupancy in such a way that land uses are linked to natural ecosystems where they take place.

A more integrated vision of biodiversity conservation, would consider protected areas as part of a landscape mosaic of different types and inten-sities of land use, oriented to maintain ecosystem health and integrity, managed by local communities. Ecotourism areas, designated for differ-ent land uses according to ecosystem fragility, would support different levels and forms of alternative tourism. Undertaken at a landscape level, the objective should be to produce enough economic revenue to maintain areas of restricted access. Experimentation is warranted to determine the sustainability of such a management approach.

Not all types of nature-based tourism are ecologically and socially sustainable. Nor do local communities always receive the economic revenues from environmentally based tourism. Generally, commercial groups have a strong interest in increasing the number of tourists. Clearly, such a policy would create serious risks for local people without promoting increased sustainable local economic benefits. Ideally, the income distribution from these kinds of tourism should be the inverse of the current policy. That is, a much greater proportion of the associated profits should remain in the local communities.

Ecotourism has an enormous potential in Mexico. It could be a viable alternative to diversify the activities offered by current approaches to mass tourism, and to increase local economic benefits at the same time. In order to achieve such a policy change, however, local communities must be involved in the conservation of future ecotourism sites in an attempt to ensure that ecological, and sociocultural—not just economic—factors, are considered.

References

Andren, H. 1994. "Effect of Habitat Fragmentation on Birds and Mammals in Landscape with Different Proportions of Suitable Habitat: A Review." *Oikos* 71: 355-366.

Boo, Elizabeth. 1990. *Ecotourism: The Potentials and Pitfalls.* Washington, D.C.: World Wild Fund for Nature.

Brattstrom, B. H., and M. C. Bondello. 1983. "Effects of Off-road Vehicle Noise on Desert Vertebrates," pp. 167-206. In *Environmental Effects of Off-road Vehicles,* ed. H. R. Webb and H. G. Vilshire. New York: Springer-Verlag.

Bringas Rábago, Nora. 1999. "Políticas de Desarrollo Turístico en Dos Zonas Costeras del Pacífico Mexicano." *Región y Sociedad, Revista de El Colegio de Sonora* 17: 3-52.

Budowski, Támara. 1989. "Ecoturismo a la Tica." *Tecnitur International Magazine.* Costa Rica.

Burton, Fiona. 1998. "Can Ecotourism Objectives be Achieved?" *Annals of Tourism Research* 25(3): 756

Callicot, J. B., and K. Munford. 1997. "Ecological Sustainability as a Conservation Concept." *Conservation Biology* 11(1): 32-40.

Cazes, Georges. 1992. *Tourisme et Tiers Monde. Un Bilan Controversé. Les Nouvelles Colonies de Vacances?* Tome 2, Collection Tourismes et Sociétés. Paris: Editions L'Harmattan.

Ceballos Lascurain, Hector. 1988. "The Future of Ecotourism." *Mexico Journal* 17: 13-14.

Dregne, H. E. 1983. "Soil and Soil Formation in Arid Regions," pp. 15-30. In *Environmental Effects of Off-road Vehicles,* ed. H. R. Webb, and H. G. Vilshire. New York: Springler-Verlag.

Escofet, A., and A. Carvacho. 1988. "The Effect of Tourist Activity on Coastal Ecosystems of Baja California," pp. 194-198. In *Proceedings of the International Conference on Natural and Man Made Coastal Hazards,* ed. S.F. Ferraras y G. Pararas-Carayannis. Ensenada, Baja California.

Franklin, J. F., and R. T. T. Forman. 1987. "Creating Landscape Patterns by Forest Cutting: Ecological Consequences and Principles." *Landscape Ecology* 1(1): 5-181.

Kockleman, W. J. 1983a. "Introduction," pp. 447-493. In *Environmental Effects of Off-road Vehicles,* ed. H. R. Webb, and H. G. Vilshire. New York: Springler-Verlag.

_____. 1983b. "Management Practices," pp. 1-14. In *Environmental Effects of Off-road Vehicles,* ed. Webb, H. R. and H. G. Vilshire. New York: Springler-Verlag.

Lathrop, E. W., and P. G. Rowlands. 1983. "Plant Ecology in Deserts: An Overview," pp. 113-152. In *Environmental Effects of Off-road Vehicles,* ed. H. R. Webb, and H. G. Vilshire. New York: Springler-Verlag.

Lineham J. R., and M. Gross. 1998. "Back to the Future, Back to Basics: The Social Ecology of Landscapes and the Future of Landscape Planning." *Landscape and Urban Planning* 42: 207-223.

Marajh, Oumatie, and Deborah R. Meadows. 1992. "Ecotourism in Latin America and the Caribbean: Strategies and Implications for Development." Presented in *Envitour-Vienna '92,* 10-12 November 1992, Vienna, Austria.

Mendelsohn, Robert. 1994. "The Role of Ecotourism in Sustainable Development," pp. 511-515. In *Principles of Conservation Biology,* eds. Gary K. Meffe and C. Ronald Carroll. Sunderland, Mass.: Sinauer Associates, Inc.

México. Subsecretaría de Desarrollo Turístico (SECTUR). 1998a. *Movimiento y Gasto de Turistas Internacionales en el Primer Semestre de 1998 y Pronóstico de Cierre del Mismo Año.* D.F., México.

_____. 1998b. *Estadísticas Básicas de la Actividad Turística 1997.* D.F., México.

Padget, Tim, and Sharon Begley, 1996. " Les Baleines Victimes de la Vague Verte." *Corrier International* 283: 28[Paris, France].

Parkhurst, J. 1988. "Baja and Motorcycles: The Worlds Most Exciting Dirt Biking." *Baja Traveler* 1(1): 50-53.

Pearce, Douglas. 1988. *Desarrollo Tturístico, su Planificación y Ubicación.* México: Trillas.

Peck, S. 1998. *Planning for Biodiversity: Issues and Examples.* Covelo, Calif. and Washington, D.C.: Island Press.

Pickett, S. T. A., and P. S. White. 1981. *The Ecology of Natural Disturbance and Patch Dynamics.* Orlando, Fla.: Academic Press.

Ramírez Sáez, Juan Manuel. 1986. *Turismo y Medio Ambiente: El Caso de Acapulco.* D.F., México: Universidad Autónoma Metropolitana, Cuaderno Divisional 4.

Szaro, R. C., and D. W. Johnston. n.d. *Biodiversity and Managed Landscape: Theory and Practice.* New York: Oxford University Press.

Ungefug, Hans-Georg. 1992. "Tour Operators and Suppliers See Tourism to Mediterranean as being in Grip of Transition: More Round Trips and Quality Gaining Ground." *FVW* 27: 92.

Villaseñor, J. L., and T. Elias. 1989. Endemism and Conservation in Baja California, Mexico. 1er Simposio sobre Recursos Vegetales (1st *Symposium on Vegetation Resources)* ESC. UABC, 17-18 November (manuscript).

Wall, Geoffrey. 1997. "Is Ecotourism Sustainable?" *Environmental Management* 21(4): 29.

Wiggins, I. 1980. *Flora of Baja California.* Palo Alto, Calif: Stanford University Press.

Organización Mundial del Turismo (OMT). 1998. *Turismo Panorama 2020: Nuevas Previsiones de la Organización Mundial del Turismo, Avance Actualizado.* Madrid.

_____. 1992. *Directrices: Ordenación de los Parques Nacionales y de Otras Zonas Protegidas para el Turismo.* Madrid.

——— (OMT-PNUMA). 1992. *Aliar el Medio Ambiente, la Economía y el Turismo.* Informe de la 24a. reunión de la Comisión de la OMT para Africa. (Report of the 24th meeting of the OMT Commission for Africa.) Madrid.

Ziffer, Karen A. 1989. *Ecotourism: The Uneasy Alliance.* Washington, D.C.: Conservation International & Ernst & Young. 36 pp.

PUBLIC PARTICIPATION IN MEXICAN PROTECTED AREAS: Terminos Lagoon, Campeche

Bruce A. B. Currie-Alder and J. C. Day

Abstract

Recent legislation opens new opportunities for greater public participation in managing Mexican protected areas. This case study of one protected area presents an example where public participation was used to resolve civil protests over oil-related development. Through the development of a management plan and a joint management body, local people and other stakeholders participated in planning and decision-making for the protected area. The national oil company inadvertently prompted greater public participation by creating a crisis over the management of the protected area that led to public demands for a joint management body, and later by providing funds that made this body possible. The joint management body enjoyed moderate success between 1997 and 2000. Yet it failed due to issues that extended beyond the protected area's boundaries, uncertainty regarding the joint management body's purpose, and confusion among stakeholders related to each other's roles and responsibilities.

Protected Areas in Mexico

Despite Mexico's wealth of biodiversity, it is difficult to justify setting areas aside for conservation and deny rural people access to natural resources given the high levels of poverty and inequity in Mexico. Few traces of unaltered wilderness remain in Mexico, and newer protected areas are often established in populated regions already experiencing environmental degradation and conflict over natural resource use.

While, in the United States and Canada, land enclosed in protected areas is often government owned, Mexican protected areas seldom change existing land tenure when they are created. Mexican conservation policies depend upon voluntary action of landowners. As a consequence, protected area management in Mexico must not only encompass conservation science, but also manage conflicting interests and coordinate the activities of a wide range of stakeholders. A key means of achieving these goals is through public participation. Articles 157 through 159 of the *Federal Environment Law* provide the main description of public participation and declare society "coresponsible for the planning, execution, evaluation, and monitoring of environmental policy and natural resources." Public participation in protected areas management is specifically mentioned in article 47:

> In the establishment, administration, and management of protected areas ... the (federal) Secretariat of the Environment shall promote the participation of (the protected areas') inhabitants, property owners and overseers, local governments, indigenous groups, and other social organizations, whether public or private, with the goal of creating integrated development of the community and assuring the protection and preservation of ecosystems and their biodiversity. (México, Diario Oficial 1988, 1996)

While the *Federal Environmental Law* assigns responsibility for federal protected areas with the National Institute of Ecology (INE—*Instituto Nacional de Ecología*), there is an understanding that this agency is to coordinate its activities with state and local governments. This coordination occurs through an informal relationship between these governments through a local office (*Dirección*) that INE establishes within each protected area. Additionally, the *Federal Protected Areas Program of 1995-2000* established the opportunity for a form of contract-based collaboration under which certain management responsibilities may be transferred from the federal government to other stakeholders.

> The *Federal Environment Law* ... opens the possibility for a decentralized management of protected areas with the participation of local residents and society in general. The law creates

the option of transferring the administration, total or in part, of protected areas to state governments, the Federal District, individuals, or organizations so that they may assume the responsibility for the conservation, development, and monitoring, for the time established, for the purposes of research, tourism, recreation, or as otherwise described. (México, SEMARNAP 1996, 103).

While such references are vague and distributed among multiple pieces of legislation, they create an unprecedented opportunity for improving the efficiency of protected area management though increased public participation.

Methods

This case study is based upon fieldwork conducted in early 2001, including direct observation, archival research, and focused interviews. Archival research included consulting past issues of local newspapers, local publications, project reports, and video tape recordings of key meetings concerning the protected area. A total of fourteen interviews were conducted with government representatives, oil workers, local environmental groups, fishing cooperatives, and academics. Focused interviews are short sessions where the questions asked are often open-ended and assume a conversational manner, but are derived from a previously developed protocol (Yin 1994, 84). The case study used representative sampling where more evidence and more respondents were sought out until additional evidence gathered no longer yielded any new variation (Strauss 1987). Once a full variety of information had been uncovered, findings were drawn when information from one source of evidence corroborated information from another source, or when there was agreement across multiple interviews. This process is sometimes referred to as triangulation (Yin 1994, 13).

Figure 23.1 Terminos Lagoon

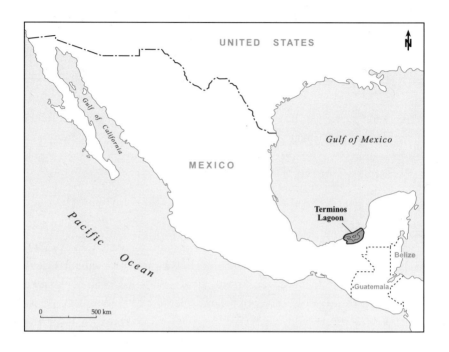

Figure 23.2 Terminos Lagoon Protected Area

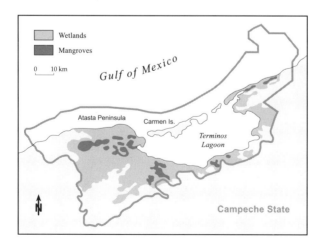

Historical Background: 1670s to 1980s

The Terminos Lagoon Protected Area is located in Campeche State, at the base of the Yucatan Peninsula (fig. 23.1). Terminos Lagoon is a shallow water body that is semi-isolated from the Gulf of Mexico by Carmen Island (fig. 23.2). The lagoon acts as an interface between nutrient-rich fresh water from the south and marine waters from the Gulf of Mexico to the north (David and Kjerfve 1998). The mixing of these waters results in a flow of nutrients into the gulf that supports one of the most productive fishing areas in Mexico (Yañez-Arancibia and Day 1988).

Terminos Lagoon has long been a net exporter of natural resources and subject to boom and bust cycles in resource use. After the conquest of present-day Mexico by Spanish forces, the Gulf coast was left relatively defenseless and became a refuge for pirates. By 1671, some pirates had settled on the shores of Terminos Lagoon to become foresters, harvesting trees for sale in Europe for furniture making and textile dyes. Although Spanish forces attacked the pirates' settlements within the lagoon several times, pirate activity continued until 1824 (Rodríguez 1984, 57). In the first decades of the twentieth century, Terminos Lagoon experienced resource booms in chicle extraction and copra. Development of commercial shrimp fisheries in the 1950s converted the region into one of the country's most important commercial fishing centers. Today many people living around Terminos Lagoon are either fishers, or consider themselves children of fishers. The Terminos Lagoon Region has been living in an oil and gas boom since the 1970s. The country's most important hydrocarbon reserves are located offshore in the Gulf of Mexico, producing three quarters of Mexico's oil and half of its national gas output (Bustillos 2000, 33).

During each of these cycles, resources were harvested to feed consumer demands outside the region. These markets were primarily controlled by outside entrepreneurs. As only a small portion of this wealth was reinvested in the area, local living standards remained poor compared to the national average. Locals have come to resent outsiders for appropriating local wealth and corrupting local culture; and perceive oil workers as the modern day equivalent of seventeenth century pirates.

Since the 1970s, the loss of wetland habitat coincided with a silent crisis in local fisheries of declining production. The federal government declared Terminos Lagoon a fishing reserve on 13 March 1974, but this effort was largely unsuccessful, due to a lack of enforcement, and illegal fishing continued (Rodríguez 1984). The 1980s witnessed the emergence of environmental awareness as budding environmentalists formed a number of small, local environmental groups to promote the region's ecology as a part of local identity and to lobby for greater conservation (interviews).

Protected Area Decree: 1990 to 1994

In the early 1990s, local environmental groups were concerned that exploration studies being conducted by the national oil company, Petróleos Mexicanos (PEMEX), meant the company was to increase its presence in the region. These groups approached the state government and proposed that Terminos Lagoon be made a protected area. The state government worked with INE to fund a preliminary study, and on 6 June 1994 the federal government published a decree (decreto) establishing the region as a part of the federal system of protected areas. The decree applies to a 7,061 square kilometer area, including Terminos Lagoon and its shoreline, Carmen Island, Atasta Peninsula, and the coastal zone up to ten meters of water deep (fig. 23.2; México, Diario Oficial 1994).

Unlike national parks or biosphere reserves, Mexican legislation places few restrictions upon land or resource use within the category of Protected Area for Flora and Fauna. Instead, the four-page decree is a mission statement by the federal government committing to coordinate its activities in the region. Consequently, the decree does not specifically forbid anything and continues to permit the multiple use of the protected area for a wide range of activities (México, Diario Oficial 1994).

In Mexico's federal protected area system, a management plan (*programa de manejo*) is developed for each protected area. A management plan is intended to be a general framework that describes the goals of a protected area, any restrictions on the human use of an area's resources, and the responsibilities of each government agency involved in its management. Under pressure from local groups, the Terminos Lagoon plan was developed through a public consultation process. A first round of consultations was held in 1994 to identify problems to be addressed by the management plan. A draft plan was prepared and a second round of consultation was held in early 1995 to seek feedback on the draft. Over 110 open meetings were held throughout the protected area, attracting over forty-five different organizations representing a cross section of civil society (México, SEMARNAP 1997).

This process had two legacies: the variety of issues to be considered in management, and a role for public participation. Although the decree states the area exists to protect endangered species, the process addressed a variety of environmental and social problems in the region. The consultation process also created a sense of ownership over the process and many participants began to speak of "our protected area." Through their involvement, many stakeholders felt they were exercising a right to participate in developing and managing what they now came to consider their protected area (interviews).

Protest and Crisis: 1995 to 1997

For decades PEMEX has exploited oil and gas deposits offshore beyond the protected area. Within the protected area, the oil company had previously constructed pipelines and an industrial plant to receive oil and gas from offshore platforms and ship these products to Tabasco State. This infrastructure is a source of tension between PEMEX and local people. Local farmers and fishers repeatedly accuse PEMEX of damaging local crops and fisheries through oil pollution. Locals occasionally seek legal action against the company, and have even resorted to civil protests such as blockading roads or occupying oil wells.

In the 1990s, changing social values and an interest in exploring the Terminos Lagoon Region inspired PEMEX to adopt a practice of giving monetary compensation to individuals claiming to be adversely affected by its activities. Rather than basing compensation on evidence of damages, payments were often allocated in proportion to the inconvenience protests caused either through media attention or interference with PEMEX's operations (interviews). The policy successfully reduced the number of protests disrupting PEMEX's operations, yet it also created a cycle of dependency. With the precedent that PEMEX pays those who protest, protesting became a form of income generation as well as a means of gaining attention for local problems (interviews). In an effort to reduce social tension, the federal and state governments negotiated an agreement in 1995 between PEMEX and one of the more important protest groups, the Campesino and Fishers Movement of Atasta Peninsula (*Movimiento de Campesinos y Pescadores de la Península de Atasta*). In return

Figure 23.3 Zoning map of Terminos Lagoon protected area

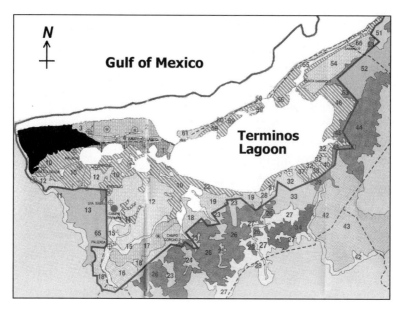

for ending the protests, PEMEX committed funding for agricultural projects to offset losses local people claimed to have suffered.

In March 1996, while the management plan was still under review, INE approved a PEMEX proposal to drill two exploration wells within the protected area. The region again erupted in protest. Feeling the new oil wells betrayed the purpose of the protected area and sensing a threat of expanded oil activity, environmental groups quickly formed an alliance with the campesino movement under the name of Citizen's Council for the Defense of the Terminos Lagoon Protected Area (*Consejo Ciudadano para la Defensa del Área Natural Protegida Laguna de Términos*). The citizen's council gained national media attention through a petition calling on PEMEX to cancel the drilling project and by distributing white flags that local people hung in front of their homes as a symbol of their protest (interviews).

PEMEX argued that oil exploration was a matter of national interest and noted that the draft management plan accepted the presence of all pre-existing oil infrastructure. The company asserted the new wells would simply count as part of that infrastructure once the plan was published. Meanwhile the citizen's council retorted that any new drilling went against the spirit of the management plan, and the new wells were part of an effort that would see expanded oil exploration within the protected area. The citizen's council pointed out an inconsistency in the actions of the federal government: On the one hand, INE was conserving the protected area, and on the other hand it approved PEMEX's drilling project. Two activities working at cross-purposes had been approved by the same government agency.

The federal Secretariat for the Environment (SEMARNAP—*Secretaría de Medio Ambiente, Recursos Naturales y Pesca*) sought a solution by returning to the draft management plan. A subtle shift occurred. Whereas the plan was previously a matter of consultation with local interests, the plan now became the focus of negotiation to avoid further protests in the region. Over the next months, the citizen's council consented to the drilling project in return for a commitment from PEMEX to fund the protected area. The draft management plan expanded to include a zoning map and a new chapter on organizational structure (fig. 23.3).

The zoning map (*ordenamiento ecológico*) was a key advance in making the management plan less ambiguous. Instead of listing objectives, the plan now restricted certain activities spatially within the protected area. An ordenamiento ecológico is a form of suitability assessment introduced in the 1988 *Federal Environmental Law* (México, Diario Oficial 1988, 1996). An ordenamiento ecológico examines the geography and ecology of a particular landscape and assigns categories of land and resource use based on physical hazards, ecological sensitivity, and soil fertility. The product of an ordenamiento ecológico is a zoning map that restricts certain activities that are inappropriate for sensitive parts of the landscape.

Creating such a zoning map for the Terminos Lagoon Region moved the management plan away from polarized positions and created an opportunity to negotiate the multiple use of the protected area. Rather than a simple mapping exercise, the zoning map created the terms on which participants worked out how they could achieve their distinct goals for the protected area. Stakeholders involved in creating the map stated that part of the protected area was sacrificed to oil development in order to obtain commitments from PEMEX and government to safeguard the rest (interviews).

The second major advance in the management plan was a new organizational structure for managing the protected area. In addition to a local government office (*Dirección*) common to all Mexican protected areas, a joint management body was proposed to include other stakeholders in management.

Joint Management: 1997 to 2000

A resolution was presented to the public on 21 February 1997 at a press conference held in the Carmen City Hall. The purpose of the press conference marked both the official release of the management plan and the announcement of a joint management body known as the Consultative Council (*Consejo Consultivo*). Government, oil, and local representatives were unanimous both in their enthusiasm for what they had accomplished and their high expectations for the council (Bustillos 2000, 56).

The council began operating late in 1997 with at least thirty members, although some respondents recall more than seventy members. Members included representatives from the three levels of government, PEMEX, environmental groups, fisher organizations, and other local groups. The council operated as a roundtable where everyone had a voice and vote (interviews). A protected area director, appointed by INE, was responsible for calling meetings and setting the agenda. Council members debated proposals for the protected area's programs and allocated project funding, making decisions either by consensus or, occasionally, through an open vote.

The council (fig. 23.4 and table 23.1) operated with moderate success from 1997 to 1999. This success can be partially explained by the availability or lack of funding for the protected area. PEMEX provided a substantial amount of the council's funding and gave the council the means to manage the protected area through research, monitoring, and other actions. The opportunity to have a say in these decisions was a powerful incentive for local people to participate. Lack of funding also explains the willingness of the federal government to allow the council such powers. While the *Federal Environment Law* assigns authority for managing the protected area with INE and other government agencies, these agencies are underfunded in comparison to their mandates. Yet through the council, INE worked with local governments and environmental groups to establish an informal network to monitor poaching.

Figure 23.4 Organizational structure for Terminos Lagoon Protected Area management

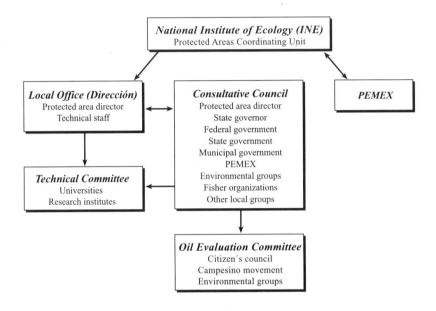

Table 23.1 Management Bodies within the Terminos Lagoon Protected Area

Authority	Name	Description	Part of Mgt. Plan	Legal Recognition
Official	Local Office	Small INE office dedicated to managing the protected area	Yes	Yes
	Consultative Council	Participatory management body composed of representatives from government and interested stakeholders	Yes	No
Quasi-Official	Technical Committee	Panel of researchers responsible for providing technical information to the Direction Office and Consultative Council	No	No
	Oil Evaluation Committee	Committee created by the Consultative Council to monitor the oil industry within the protected area	No	No

Collapse: 2000 to 2001

By late 1999, the Consultative Council was in trouble. Social capital created while developing the management plan had been undermined, funding had been redirected, and government was no longer as supportive of the council. Government representatives began to perceive the council as a threat to their authority. Fearing local stakeholders had captured the council, government representatives believed that only they could ultimately act in the public interest and began to ignore the council (interviews). When government made decisions without the council's input, local people felt the federal government had betrayed earlier promises and responded by withdrawing their support for the council (interviews). Despite a promising start, the enthusiasm expressed in the 1997 press conference was replaced by frustration, misunderstanding, and debate over the council's purpose.

The council lacked transparency in its financial records and allegations of corruption became common. The council was accused of funding unnecessary projects and INE was accused of misdirecting funds intended for the council. Local groups became antagonistic with the protected area director, and wished to replace the INE appointment process by making the director an elected position voted by the council members (interviews). PEMEX reacted to the accusations of financial mismanagement by stopping its direct funding of council. PEMEX distanced itself from financial questions by recruiting organizations from outside the region to allocate funds the company donated for the purpose of funding conservation. Consequently, both the Consultative Council and local INE office were subsequently required to submit proposals to these outside organizations in order to receive PEMEX funding. INE and PEMEX's actions isolated the council and diminished its powers. INE was both unable and unwilling to make up for this shortfall as the council had allowed them to question the legitimacy of federal actions and policy.

While the council continued to meet throughout 1999, its last meeting was held in January 2000 when INE appointed a new protected-area director (interviews). This new director never again convened the council, and three years after it was created the Consultative Council simply ceased to exist.

Today, Terminos Lagoon is, at first glance, a paper park that exists only in government documents (Gómez-Pompa and Kaus 1999). The City of Carmen continues to dump raw sewage into the lagoon, cattle feed on the shores, fishers bring marginal catches to port, and life continues much as it was before the decree. The casual visitor to the region is unaware that he or she is standing within a protected area. The current state of affairs is a stalemate between two factions, with the government agency on one side and local stakeholders on the other. With the failure of the Consultative Council, formal management of the protected area became centralized within INE. While salaries for its staff and director come from the INE budget, the local office must apply to the PEMEX-chosen organization to fund its activities. Some groups that participated in the Consultative Council have disintegrated, due to lack of funding or burnout among their members. Those that remain run a variety of projects ranging from aquaculture to crocodile breeding. Feelings of frustration and deception are widespread among those who participated in the council, and many comment with sadness that the management plan is now dead (interviews). Both sides continue with their own initiatives, but with a focus on individual projects rather than the more integrated programs outlined in the management plan. Without the benefit of coordination the Consultative Council and management plan provided, projects are duplicated and programs such as enforcement and habitat restoration have been abandoned altogether.

Why the Council Failed

During its brief three-year history, the Consultative Council was a unique solution for managing what is arguably Mexico's most complex protected area. The council was expected to continue the remarkable degree of public participation that had been achieved while developing the management plan, yet there were signs that the council was in trouble from the beginning. The management plan was overly ambitious given the financial and human resources available to the council. The council was not legally recognized despite the agreement expressed during the February 1997 press conference. The council's purpose was open to interpretation by its members and it created a confusing array of other management bodies (fig. 23.4 and table 23.1). These were symptoms, however, of root causes that led to the council's failure. The root causes for the failure of the Consultative Council were management issues that extended beyond the protected area's boundaries, uncertainty regarding the council's purpose, and confusion among stakeholders regarding their roles and responsibilities.

Boundary Problems

Oil-Related Development

Local people have suffered three decades of detrimental impacts, both environmental and social, related to the presence of the oil industry, and they feared even greater hardship should PEMEX expand its activities within the region. Many local people were motivated to participate in the management plan and the Consultative Council, by a desire to protect their communities and the regional environment against the threat of new oil drilling (interviews). Although the management plan restricts new drilling, the protected area management bodies have no authority to manage environmental risks beyond its boundaries, such as offshore oil platforms in Campeche Sound. Despite the potential for dialogue the Consultative Council offered, the oil industry's relationship with local people cannot be adequately addressed solely within the protected area framework.

Fisheries Decline

Another issue that extends beyond the protected area's boundaries is a slow decline in local fisheries over the past two decades. While the reasons for this decline are not clear, the most likely causes are overfishing combined with the detrimental impacts on habitat and water quality of industry, agriculture, and urban development. For example, fishing effort is concentrated closer to shore as fishers are excluded from old fishing grounds adjacent to offshore oil infrastructure in the Gulf of Mexico (Barbier and Strand 1998). Without the benefit of impact assessments or baseline studies, it is impossible to distinguish the relative impacts of overfishing versus oil-related impacts (Simon 1997, 175). The protected area could contribute to a solution by providing habitat protection and no-take sanctuaries to support economically important fish species, yet an alternate solution must be found beyond the framework of the protected area.

Roles and Responsibilities

The other root cause of the council's failure was the confusion related to which stakeholders have the right to decide the fate of the protected area. Roles and responsibilities refer to how stakeholders participate in managing a natural resource. Responsibilities describe the activities a stakeholder performs in support of management, and are derived from the property rights held by a stakeholder (Schlager and Ostrom 1993). When a stakeholder is involved in management, each activity in which he or she participates corresponds to a right and responsibility being exercised either formally or informally by that stakeholder. While stakeholders can include local people, nongovernmental organizations, private interests, and government agencies, any of these groups may play a range of roles such as decision-maker, planner, data collector, enforcer, advisor, critic, and so on. Roles imply both the degree to which a stakeholder participates in management and the relative power he or she possess to influence decision-making.

Jurisdiction

Confusion exists over jurisdiction and the role for each level of government in managing the protected area. The *Coastal Zone Regulation, National Waters Law,* and *Federal Oceans Law* grant the federal government jurisdiction over about half of the protected area including a twenty-meter strip of land adjacent to the coast, coastal lagoons, and the seaward section of the coastal zone (México, Diario Oficial 1992, 1991, 1985). The remaining landmass of the protected area is under the jurisdiction of the Campeche State government and includes sections of three municipalities (fig. 23.2). Although the protected area was not initially a source of conflict, the protected area challenged the authority of local governments when its management plan began to cover issues beyond biodiversity and habitat protection. These governments began to see the protected area as an imposition of federal authority on lands under their jurisdiction. The creation of the Consultative Council temporarily resolved this conflict by coordinating governmental efforts. Yet with the council's failure, there is renewed tension between the environmental agencies of each level of government as to who has the authority to make decisions within the protected area.

Council's Purpose

Through protests, local groups won a position of power that allowed them to negotiate the management plan with INE and PEMEX as equals. Local groups saw the council as a vehicle for citizen control and believed it represented a transfer of authority from INE to local people. Local governments saw the council as a form of shared authority, where control of the protected area was to be shared among government representatives, with some input from others. For INE, the council was a forum for actively consulting with local people to bring concerns to the agency's attention. INE acknowledged the role local stakeholders had played in the management plan and welcomed community input, yet intended that decision-making for the protected area would remain within the government agency (interviews).

Members' Roles

Through their participation, groups representing local people came to continuously expect more of a role in managing the protected area and began to perceive themselves as joint managers, equal to the government agency (interviews). Stakeholders were allowed to define their own roles because the Consultative Council never formally defined the rights or responsibilities of its members. INE had little experience in collaborating with local groups, and believed that the positive experience of developing the management plan could be continued without defining rights, roles, or responsibilities. Without understanding the rights of others, each stakeholder interpreted the council as representing the form of public participation that best justified his or her role in management (interviews). When stakeholders felt others did not respect their particular roles, they were apt to argue over details, abandon their responsibilities, or ignore the council.

Governments' Roles

Government representatives comprised a large proportion of the Consultative Council's membership and there was little effort to filter the membership of other groups. At one time or another, over twenty of the council's members represented different government agencies, or levels of government. While a number of government agencies held responsibilities related to the management plan, including all of them in the council made for a large, unmanageable membership and diluted the local and regional voices that were the reason for the council's creation. In effect, the layers of governments had a variety of management obligations, which often conflicted.

Moving Beyond the Council

Currently, the management system within Terminos Lagoon is divided between formal, government stakeholders and informal, local stakeholders. On the one hand, government representatives manage the protected area through their offices, while on the other hand, a number of groups claiming to represent local people continue with a diversity of projects related to the protected area. The lesson of Terminos Lagoon is that a successful joint management body must balance the official government apparatus with local desires for a say in decision-making. Assessing the Consultative Council demonstrates that future efforts in joint protected area management approaches could allay government fears regarding local control by building trust among council members and establishing limits to what the council can perform, or decide, without government approval.

The federal *Protected Area Regulation*, passed in November 2000, describes the creation of technical advisory committees (CTA—*Comités Técnicos Asesores*). The *Regulation* limits CTA membership to a maximum of twenty-one members. Each CTA must create a formal, written agreement that both legally recognizes the management body and describes its organizational structure and rules. While their name implies that CTAs are simply advisory bodies without formal decision-making powers, CTAs have the power to review and advise on annual management plans, to propose projects, and may exercise significant influence over a protected area's director (México, Diario Oficial 2000).

Unfortunately, the framework proposed by the *Regulation* perpetuates some defects that contributed to the Consultative Council's failure in Terminos Lagoon, including a large number of government representatives and few restrictions on membership. The *Regulation* states that CTA membership must include the state governor, the protected area director, and the president of all municipalities located within the protected area. Yet the *Regulation* also provides that members may appoint a substitute to represent them in meetings (México, Diario Oficial 2000), and some logistical nightmares could be avoided by carefully selecting substitutes for the state governor and municipal presidents. For the remaining CTA members, the *Regulation* simply states that they must be people with ties to the use or conservation of natural resources within the protected area. This includes representatives of local organizations, nongovernmental organizations, landowners, or the academic community (México, Diario

Oficial 2000). Without a more critical process for selecting members, there are no safeguards against a CTA becoming dominated by individual interests rather than the common good.

Yet with careful implementation the CTA model may replace the Consultative Council and solve the current stalemate in the Terminos Lagoon Protected Area. A CTA in Terminos Lagoon could benefit by implementing a more rigorous selection process for its members, creating mechanisms for community accountability, and offloading some responsibilities to a coastal management committee.

Clear Membership and Purpose

Not all local people are necessarily interested in all aspects of protected area management. Instead they wish to be involved in decisions concerning the resources that most affect them. Care should be taken in selecting members for a protected area CTA to ensure that they represent legitimate interests connected to the protected area, provide the management body with needed skills or knowledge, and demonstrate a willingness to understand the needs of others. With the upper limit on membership in the CTA, a process will be needed to select members for the new management body. Each potential member could be interviewed by a selection committee to determine how well he or she represents some interest within the protected area, his or her understanding of other interest groups, and ability to work with others (Abrams 2000, Pinkerton 1991). With such a selection process, the members would be chosen based on their commitment to the common good. Dialogue within a CTA would be elevated towards finding more workable solutions and away from purely interest-based conflicts that plagued the Consultative Council. Once a CTA membership is decided, members will have to negotiate a common vision for the CTA, including each other's roles and responsibilities. This common vision would ideally emerge during a guided process of creating the formal document describing each CTA's organizational structure and rules as required by the *Regulation*.

Community Accountability

Local representatives could always hold government representatives accountable by citing legislation, complaining to politicians, or by embarrassing government representatives in the media. There were, however, no such controls on local representatives. The federal government's distrust of the Consultative Council was caused, in part, by this absence of accountability on behalf of the council's members. The fears of government representatives, that local interests had captured the council, could have been allayed if there had been mechanisms for community accountability within the council. Such mechanisms have already been identified as critical for the success of joint management bodies (Abrams 2000, Pinkerton, and Weinstein 1995), and could restore the government's faith in public participation.

Coastal Management

The CTA´s tasks could be simplified by transferring some of the management plan's responsibilities to a new statewide forum for coastal management. Some authors have already called for the creation of a coastal management committee and legislation in Campeche State (Zárate-Lomelí et al. 1999, Yañez-Arancibia et al. 1999). A coastal management committee would include all levels of government with jurisdiction along the coast and coordinate government actions across a range of programs, reducing the need for government representation within the protected area. A coastal management committee would also be in a better position to address conflicts that extend beyond the protected area's boundaries, such as detrimental impacts of the oil industry and declining fisheries production.

Conclusion

Public participation in protected area management was attempted in the Terminos Lagoon Protected Area to resolve civil protests over the presence of the oil industry. Through the development of a management plan and a joint management body, local people and other stakeholders participated in defining objectives and decision-making for the protected area. Joint protected area management would not have occurred without the presence of the national oil company, which both prompted a crisis that led to the joint management body, and provided funding that made the work of this body possible. The joint management body enjoyed moderate success between 1997 and 2000, but failed due to issues that extended beyond the protected area's boundaries, uncertainty regarding the joint management body's purpose, and confusion among stakeholders related to each others' roles and responsibilities.

Mexican legislation opens opportunities for public participation, yet the federal government does not clearly define stakeholders' roles and responsibilities critical to the success of the joint management body. Public participation in the Terminos Lagoon Protected Area occurred when there was a fortunate coincidence of conflict, policy, laws, and people; unfortunately the institutions created were insufficiently developed and stakeholders' commitments were short-term. While Terminos Lagoon served as a role model for the country, the Consultative Council promised more than government or PEMEX was willing to support in the long run. The government agency, INE, was open to involving local people in specific management responsibilities, but the agency was poorly prepared for working with local people.

The potential remains to use public participation to improve the efficiency of protected areas management in Mexico. One strategy for Terminos Lagoon is to create a new management body for the protected area and transfer other responsibilities to a new forum for coastal management. A technical advisory committee (CTA), as outlined in the new *Protected Area Regulation*, could replace the now defunct Consultative Council. It would have the added benefit of providing a formal set of rules for the management body and limiting the number of potential members. By subjecting potential members to a more critical selection process, the management body could avoid incorporating conflicts between private interests into its structure and better foster a vision of the common good among its members. Such a management body would have significant de facto powers over activities within the protected area and would continue to provide a local forum for public participation. The tasks of the CTA could be simplified by transferring some responsibilities currently included in the protected area's management plan to a coastal management committee for Campeche State. This new committee would be in a better position to address conflicts that extend beyond the protected area's boundaries and could coordinate government actions across a range of programs, reducing the amount of government representation required within the protected area's management body.

The Final Word

In considering the current state of affairs in the Terminos Lagoon Protected Area, and the challenge of public participation in Mexican protected areas, a facilitator's comment during one of management plan workshops remains relevant today:

> There exists the proposal for a Consultative Council, but what else are we going to do? At the heart of the issue is the question: How can I ensure that my voice is heard when it is time to make decisions?... All this work is to ensure that the management plan considers the opinions of everyone because, in the end, we will all be the beneficiaries or the losers. Ultimately, it is important to ensure that you have a voice and vote in the decisions. (Anonymous facilitator, México, Universidad Autónoma del Carmen 1995)

The Terminos Lagoon Protected Area was established to conserve habitat for endangered species, but over the course of seven years the area came to represent much more. Through protest and negotiation, stakeholders in Terminos Lagoon attempted to improve the quality of the local environment through greater public participation in protected area management. This effort was not entirely successful, but the potential remains for Terminos Lagoon to recover and improve upon its experiences. Regardless of the protected area's future, Terminos Lagoon Protected Area serves as an inspirational example for Mexican society and the international community as to what sustainability could be.

References

Abrams, Peter. 2000. "Overcoming Obstacles to Implementing Community-based Collaborative Governance of Natural Resources: the Case of the Clayoquot Sound Central Regional Board." Master's thesis. Burnaby, B.C.: School of Resource and Environmental Management, Simon Fraser University.

Barbier, E. B., and I. Strand. 1998. Valuing Mangrove-Fishery Linkages: a Case Study of Campeche, Mexico. *Environmental and Resource Economics* 12: 151-66.

Bustillos, J. 2000. *Petróleo, área naturales y gestión ambiental.* Mexico City: SEMARNAP and United Nations Development Program.

David, L. T., and B. Kjerfve. 1998. Tides and Currents in a Two-inlet Coastal lagoon: Laguna de Terminos, Mexico. *Continental Shelf Research* 18(10): 1057.

Gómez-Pompa, A., and A. Kaus. 1999. From pre-Hispanic to Future Conservation. Alternatives: Lessons from Mexico. *Proceeding of the National Academy of Sciences* 96: 5982-86.

México. Diario Oficial de la Federación. 30 Nov. 2000. *Reglamento de la ley general del equilibrio ecológico y la protección al ambiente en materia de áreas naturales protegidas.*

————. 6 June 1994. *Decreto por el que se declara como área natural protegida, con carácter de área de protección de flora y fauna, la región conocida como Laguna de Términos, ubicada en los municipios de Carmen, Palizada y Champotón, Estado de Campeche.*

————. 24 Nov. 1992. *Ley de aguas nacionales.*

————. 21 Aug. 1991. *Reglamento para el uso y aprovechamiento de mares territoriales, aguas navegables, playas, la zone federal de tierras costeras y bienes que se encuentran en las zonas portuarias.*

————. 28 Jan. 1988. *Ley general del equilibrio ecológico y la protección al ambiente.* (Law revised 13 Dec. 1996).

————. 18 Dec. 1985. *Ley federal del mar.*

————. Secretaría de Medio Ambiente, Recursos Naturales y Pesca. 1997. *Programa de manejo del área de protección de flora y fauna Laguna de Términos. D.F., México*: SEMARNAP.

————. Secretaría de Medio Ambiente, Recursos Naturales y Pesca. 1996. *Programa de áreas naturales protegidas de México 1995-2000. D.F.*, México: SEMARNAP.

————. Universidad Autónoma del Carmen. 1995. "Taller para la elaboración del plan de manejo del APFF de la Laguna de Términos." Video No. 648. Video tape recording of meeting. Carmen, Campeche: Universidad Autónoma del Carmen.

Pinkerton, E., and M. Weinstein. 1995. *Fisheries that Work: Sustainability through Community-based Management.* Vancouver, B.C.: David Suzuki Foundation.

Pinkerton, E. 1991. Locally-based Water Quality Planning: Contributions to Fish Habitat Protection. *Canadian Journal of Fisheries and Aquatic Sciences* 48: 1326-33.

Rodríguez, R. 1984. *Los pescadores de la Laguna de Términos.* D.F., México: Centro de Investigaciones y Estudios Superiores en Antropología Social.

Schlager, E., and E. Ostrom. 1993. Property Rights Regimes and Coastal Fisheries: an Empirical Analysis. In *The Political Economy of Customs and Culture: Informal Solutions to the Commons Problem,* T.L. Anderson and R.T. Simmons, eds. 13-41. Lanham, Md.: Rowman and Littlefield.

Simon, J. 1997. *Endangered Mexico: an Environment on the Edge.* San Francisco: Sierra Club Books.

Strauss, A. L. 1987. *Qualitative Analysis for Social Scientists.* New York: Cambridge University Press.

Yañez-Arancibia, A., A. L. Lara Dominguez, J.L. Rojas Galaviz, D. J. Zarate, G. J. Villalobos Zapata, and P. Sanchez-Gil. 1999. Integrating Science and Management on Coastal Marine Protected Areas in the Southern Gulf of Mexico. *Ocean & Coastal Management* 42: 319-44.

Yañez-Arancibia, A., and J. W. Day. 1988. *Ecology of Coastal Ecosystems in the Southern Gulf of Mexico: The Términos Lagoon Region.* D.F., México: UNAM.

Yin, R. K. 1994. *Case Study Research: Design and Methods.* 2nd Ed. Applied Social Research Methods Series vol. 5. London, England: Sage Publications.

Zárate-Lomelí, D., T. Saavedra-Vásquez, J. L. Rojas-Galavíz, A. Yáñez-Arancibia, and E. Rivera-Arriaga. 1999. Terms of Reference Towards an Integrated Management Policy in the Coastal Zone of the Gulf of Mexico and the Caribbean. *Ocean & Coastal Management* 42: 345-68.

PHYLOGEOGRAPHY, HISTORICAL PATTERNS, AND CONSERVATION OF NATURAL AREAS

Ella Vázquez-Domínguez

Abstract

Genetic diversity, a fundamental component of biodiversity, has been largely ignored up to this point in the creation of parks and protected areas. However, the theory is now available to confront this unexplored dimension of diversity given more advanced theoretical models, molecular technologies, and conceptual frameworks. The comparative analysis of phylogeography allows for evaluation of the geographic patterns of the genetic component of biodiversity, emphasizing the evolutionary differentiation and historical demography within and among populations. These advances make it possible to incorporate genetic diversity and evolutionary processes as goals in the assessment of conservation priorities.

Introduction

From a biological perspective, there is a major deficiency in the ecological research that has been undertaken to date related to parks and protected areas. After identification of important sites or areas because of their high species richness, or high endemic values, it is now evident that more detailed ecological research is needed to maximize representation of different taxa, and to incorporate evolutionary processes as primary goals within natural protected areas. Accordingly, genetic diversity is now recognized as a fundamental component of biodiversity and the need for its protection has been incorporated into conservation programs and policies (Humphries, Williams, and Vane-Wright 1995). However, little priority has been given to the direct estimation of genetic diversity, partly because of the absence of suitable data and an appropriate conceptual framework (Avise 1992), but also because it has been erroneously assumed that by protecting diversity at or above the species level, the underlying genetic and evolutionary diversity will also be protected (Avise 1989, Moritz et al. 1996).

Table 24.1. Comparison of the Terrestrial Ecosystem Diversity in Some Latin-American Countries (Dinerstein et al. 1995)

	Mexico	Brazil	Colombia	Chile	Argentina	Costa Rica
Kind of ecosystems	5	5	4	3	3	3
Kind of habitat	9	8	6	4	6	4
Ecoregions	51	34	29	12	19	8

Mexico as a Megadiverse Country

Although Mexico is ranged fourteenth for its size among the countries of the world, it is fourth for its biological diversity and is defined as "megadiverse" (Mittermeier 1988). Such remarkably high diversity is a consequence of its dominant vegetation types, which can be subdivided in thirty to fifty subtypes, or ecoregions, depending on the classification used (Ramamoorthy et al. 1993). Among Latin-American countries, Mexico has the highest number of ecoregions (Dinerstein et al. 1995; table 24.1). At the species level, and only considering angiosperms, insects (butterflies), and vertebrates, Mexico has approximately 10 percent of the species described in the world, 1 percent of which are endemic (table 24.2). Marine biodiversity, however, is less well known as is the case worldwide, and many new species are described regularly (Vázquez-Domínguez et al. 1998). The nation's genetic diversity, only recently being directly evaluated, ranges from the genetic variability of many endemic or threatened species to, for example, genes of *Zea diploperennis*, the only wild relative of maize. Topography, together with climatic variability, have produced heterogeneous landscapes within every ecosystem, in which speciation and evolution have yielded an immense genetic and evolutionary variability.

Table 24.2. Number of Species and Endemic Species in Mexico, and Ranking of Mexico Among the 17 Most Megadiverse Countries

Group	# species in Mexico	# endemic species	# species globally	Megadiversity Rank by group	by endemics
Mammals	450	140	4,629	5	3
Birds	1,050	125	9,040	12	6
Reptiles	717	368	6,458	2	2
Amphibians	284	169	4,222	4	6
Freshwater fishes	347		8,411		
Vertebrates[a]	2,501	802	10,680	6	3
Butterflies	2,237	200		6	7
Plants[b]	18-30,000	10-15,000	250,000	4	8

[a]without fish; [b]angiosperms, gymnosperms, ferns, and bryophytes (Data from Mittermeier et al. 1998)

Toward Improved Understanding of Genetic Diversity

Species should not be visualized as monotypic entities, but rather as a series of populations that differ geographically, with a distinguishable genetic and historical structure. A great number of species studied in different environments, such as tropical forests, show a marked genetic divergence as well as structured populations (Moritz, J. Cunningham, and Schneider 1997, Patton et al. 1997, Moritz and Faith 1998, Schneider, M. Cunningham, and Moritz 1998), which are not evident from phenotypic comparisons (Vázquez-Domínguez et al. 2001). This suggests that the descriptions of biodiversity based on the distribution of vegetation types, number of species or number of endemic species, do not adequately represent the evolutionary diversity of the biota. Accordingly, we have started to better understand the temporal, spatial, and evolutionary processes that have shaped the present distribution of biodiversity; information that is essential to guarantee the long-term viability of natural systems.

The fragmentation of habitats, one of the main challenges for the conservation of natural resources, has two components: current anthropogenic alterations, and long-term natural processes. Habitats and ecosystems have experienced contractions and expansions in their distribution during geologic history such as glacial and interglacial periods (Flenley 1979). These changes can be appreciated through geographic patterns of genetic variation, which would be congruent among different species that have been affected by similar means. Accordingly, since historical changes in the distribution of ecosystems are strong determinants of the current distribution of genetic diversity and of species, it is essential to consider the historical perspective in order to have a more complete knowledge about biodiversity (Nix 1991, Joseph, Moritz, and Hugall 1995).

Protection of genetic diversity should consider the amount of genetic diversity within and among populations, as well as the maintenance of historical patterns of independent evolution and of evolutionary potential among populations within species. Thus, the assessment of conservation priorities on a regional basis also depends on an understanding of the genetic uniqueness and genetic diversity of local populations. Common conservation approaches are likely to encompass the adaptive component of genetic diversity, but fail to recognize explicitly the genetic diversity accumulated through geographic isolation per se.

Genetic surveys of regional biotas have become a practical goal only recently with the development of rapid, molecular methods of genetic evaluation. The analysis of mitochondrial DNA (mtDNA) in animals is an effective tool in evolutionary biology (Hillis, Moritz, and Mable 1996), but also has a high potential for practical studies in conservation (Moritz 1994a, Moritz et al. 1996). Because it is homologous across animals, analysis on mtDNA variation permits objective, quantitative comparisons across independently evolving taxa and provides a particularly useful tool for regional biotic surveys; it is especially useful to detect frontiers between genetically different populations (Smith and Wayne 1996). Molecular studies can also reveal the phylogeny of alleles within species, allowing us to discern historical biogeographic and population processes which were inaccessible before (Avise 1994, Joseph, Moritz, and Hugall 1995, Moritz, J. Cunningham, and Schneider 1997). The information from mtDNA variability within species has two applications or advantages: to know (a) the phylogenetic interrelations among the DNA molecules themselves, and (b) the geographic distribution of the phylogenetic groups. Together, these two elements form part of the discipline of phylogeography. Phylogeography has helped prove that many species have a different phylogenetic history and are geographically structured (Avise et al. 1987, Joseph, Morris, and Hugall 1995). It is possible, through the comparative analysis of the phylogeography of codistributed species, to know the geographic patterns of the genetic component of biodiversity; in turn, this can be used as an element to allocate conservation and management priorities (Avise 2000, Newton et al. 1999).

History, Populations, and Conservation

A different conservation approach emphasizes historical and current isolation among populations. The study of the phylogenetic content of the mtDNA sequences is particularly valuable to evaluate the evolutionary differentiation and the historical demography within and among populations. This kind of study is useful to identify groups of populations that have been historically isolated and which together comprise the evolutionary diversity of a taxon; these groups allow us to define or delimit geographic regions in which multiple species have populations that are genetically unique (Evolutionary Significant Units, ESUs *sensu* Ryder 1986). Thus, these historically isolated populations are identified as those with phylogenetically distinct clusters of alleles; where multiple species are surveyed across the same sites, such information can be combined to identify areas where patterns of isolation coincide across multiple species (Crandall et al. 2000, Moritz 1994b).

Geographic areas also can be identified within which the populations of a high proportion of a species present in a region have been evolving independently from conspecific populations from other areas (Avise 1992). This allows different conservation priorities to be assigned to different areas, because each one would comprise an evolutionarily different or divergent community (Moritz, J. Cunningham, and Schneider 1997). Information obtained through these kinds of studies, for the design and conservation of natural areas, is important because combining information on the distribution of genetic variation and of species can be useful in prioritizing areas for protection and management. It is also useful in developing more sensitive criteria in the selection of future parks and protected areas (Crandall et al. 2000, Soberón, Rodríguez, and Vázquez-Domínguez 2000). High priority areas can be identified, although they might not have a collection of endemic species as it is usually acknowledged under conventional methods.

Potential Applications

1. Endangered or vulnerable single species

a) Genetically divergent populations increasingly are being recognized as appropriate units for conservation, regardless of their taxonomic status. The ghost bat (*Macroderma gigas*) of Australia, a vulnerable species, requires warm and humid caves, so it has a naturally, patchy distribution. Genetic studies of four of the contracted populations of this species—as found in suitable caves or abandoned mine shafts—indicate that these represent effectively separate populations. Thus, it is clear that the extirpation of regional breeding populations will not be reversed by natural immigration within a time frame relevant to management. Also, each of the four populations represents a substantial fraction of the species' genetic diversity that should be protected (Moritz et al. 1996).

b) Successful translocations of individuals, the most plausible conservation strategy for some endangered species, depend upon precise knowledge of their genetic structure. The hairy-nosed wombat (Lasiorhinus krefftii) is one of the most endangered species of mammal in Australia, restricted to a single population of fewer than seventy individuals. For its recovery, the immediate actions are to protect and increase the size of this population through habitat management and future translocations to new sites. Genetic studies have provided fine-scale analysis of mating systems, information used as a guide for the managed movement of individuals and for future design of an appropriate translocation strategy (Moritz et al. 1996).

2. Parks and protected areas

a) An exciting application of phylogeography is to define geographic regions within which multiple species have genetically unique populations or ESUs. This leads us from species to community genetics, testing for congruence of phylogeographic patterns among species, in order to define geographic regions within which a substantial proportion of species has had evolutionary histories separate from their respective conspecifics (Avise 1992, Crandall et al. 2000, Moritz 1994b). The significance of this is that regions with a high proportion of ESUs should be accorded high conservation priority. A study on the distribution of montane endemic bird species in Cameroon and Equatorial Guinea, in which morphologic data was combined with information on phylogeographic structure and endemism, permitted the identification of three biogeographical regions for their conservation and management (Smith et al. 2000).

Figure 24.1 Marine priority and natural protected areas

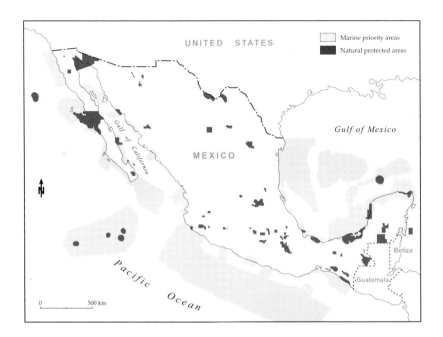

b) Adaptive management of reserves requires information on population size and connectivity, both to assess their current status and to predict outcomes of specific management actions. Molecular phylogenies can provide insights into long-term population trends and patterns of gene flow, to be used as a basis for management of populations (Milligan, Leebens-Mack, and Strand 1994). This information also is valuable for a wide range of applications: such as the design and evaluation of potential or actual biological corridors adjoining natural vegetation fragments; the analysis of complementarity among conservation areas; or the description, on a regional or continental scale, of the geographic distribution of intraspecific biodiversity, which would serve as a basis to direct the conservation of biological diversity (Moritz and Faith 1998, Taberlet 1998).

In Mexico, seventy priority coastal and oceanic areas have been identified, delimited and characterized based either on their high biodiversity, the lack of information regarding biodiversity, or the diversity of their resource uses. This prioritization was done with the

Figure 24.2 Terrestrial priority and natural protected areas in Mexico

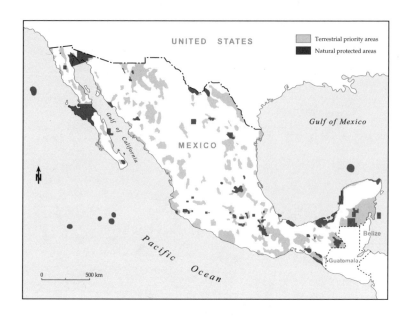

objective of developing a framework that would contribute to the planning, conservation and sustainable use of marine as well as terrestrial environments in the country (Arriaga et al. 1998; figs. 24.1 and 24.2). Together with more biological and ecological research, these areas will benefit from detailed genetic surveys, especially those where biologically important populations and species exist. Use of the different phylogeographic applications described here, in the design and delimitation of parks and protected areas within these priority marine areas, will allow for protection of the evolutionary diversity within them. Establishment of such areas would be valuable in their own right and could assist with the building of the Baja to Bering Sea Marine Conservation Initiative (see Jessen and Ban, this volume).

References

Arriaga Cabrera, L., E.Vázquez–Domínguez, J. González–Cano, R. Jiménez Rosenberg, E. Muñoz López, and V. Aguilar Sierra, coords. 1998. *Regiones Prioritarias Marinas de México*. D.F. México: Comisión Nacional para el Conocimiento y Uso de la Biodiversidad.

Avise, J. C. 1989. "A Role for Molecular Genetics in the Recognition and Conservation of Endangered Species." *Trends in Ecology and Evolution* 4: 79-281.

————. 1992. "Molecular Population Structure and the Biogeographic History of a Regional Fauna: A Case History with Lessons for Conservation Biology." *Oikos* 63: 62-76.

————. 1994. *Molecular Markers, Natural History and Evolution.* New York: Chapman & Hall.

————. 2000. *Phylogeography: The History and Formation of Species.* Cambridge, Mass.: Harvard University Press.

Avise, J. C., J. Arnold, R. M. Ball, E. Bermingham, T. Lamb, J. E. Neigel, C. A. Reeb, and N. Saunders. 1987. "Intraspecific Phylogeography: The Mitochondrial DNA Bridge Between Population Genetics and Systematics." *Annual Review of Ecology and Systematics* 18: 489-522.

Crandall, K. A., O. R. P. Bininda-Emonds, G. M. Mace, and R. K. Wayne. 2000. "Considering Evolutionary Processes in Conservation Biology." *Trends in Ecology and Evolution* 15: 290-295.

Dinerstein, E., D. Olson, D. Graham, A. Webster, S. Primm, M. Bookbinder, and G. Ledec. 1995. *Una Evaluación del Estado de Conservación de las Ecoregiones Terrestres de América Latina y el Caribe.* Washington D.C.: Banco Mundial, Fondo Mundial para la Naturaleza.

Flenley, J. R. 1979. *The Equatorial Rainforest: A Geological History.* London: Butterworth.

Hillis, D. M., C. Moritz, and B. K. Mable. 1996. *Molecular Systematics.* 2d ed. Sunderland, Mass.: Sinauer Associates Inc.

Humphries, C. J., P. H. Williams, and R. I. Vane-Wright. 1995. "Measuring Biodiversity Value for Conservation." *Annual Review of Ecology and Systematics* 26: 93-111.

Joseph, L., C. Moritz, and A. Hugall. 1995. "Molecular Support for Vicariance as a Source of Diversity in Rainforest." *Proceedings of the Royal Society of London B.* 260: 177-182.

Milligan, B. G., J. Leebens-Mack, and A. E. Strand. 1994. "Conservation Genetics: Beyond the Maintenance of Marker Diversity." *Molecular Ecology* 3: 423-435.

Mittermeier, R. A. 1988. "Primate Diversity and the Tropical Forest: Case Studies from Brazil and Madagascar and the Importance of the Megadiversity Countries," pp. 145-154. In *Biodiversity,* ed. E. Wilson. Washington, D.C.: National Academic Press.

Mittermeier, R. A., C. G. Mittermeier, and P. Robles-Gil. 1998. *Megadiversidad: Los Países Biológicamente más Ricos del Mundo.* D.F. México: CEMEX.

Moritz, C. 1994a. "Application of Mitochondrial DNA Analysis on Conservation: A Critical Review." *Molecular Ecology* 3: 401-411.

————. 1994b. "Defining Evolutionary Significant Units for Conservation." *Trends in Ecology and Evolution* 9: 373-375.

Moritz, C., and D. P. Faith. 1998. "Comparative Phylogeography and the Identification of Genetically Divergent Areas for Conservation." *Molecular Ecology* 7: 419-429.

Moritz, C., W. J. Worthington, L. Pope, W. B. Sherwin, A. C. Taylor, and C. J. Lipus. 1996. "Applications of Genetics to the Conservation and Management of Australian Fauna: Four Case Studies from Queensland," pp. 442-456. In *Molecular Genetic Approaches in Conservation,* ed. T. B. Smith and R. K. Wayne. Oxford: Oxford University Press.

Moritz, C., L. Joseph, C. Cunningham, and C. J. Schneider. 1997. "Molecular Perspectives on Historical Fragmentation of Australian Tropical and Subtropical Rainforest: Implications for Conservation," pp. 442-454. In *Tropical Forest Remnants: Ecology, Management and Conservation of Fragmented Communities,* ed. W. Laurence and R. Bierregard. Chicago: University of Chicago Press.

Newton, A. C., T. R. Allnutt, A. C. M. Gillies, A. J. Lowe, and R. A. Ennos. 1999. "Molecular Phylogeography, Intraspecific Variation and the Conservation of Tree Species." *Trends in Ecology and Evolution* 14: 140-145.

Nix, H. A. 1991. "Biogeography: Patterns and Processes," pp. 11-39. In *Rainforest Animals: Atlas of Vertebrates Endemic to Australia's Wet Tropics.* Canberra, Australia: Australian Nature Conservation Agency.

Patton, J. L., M. N. F. da Silva, M. C. Lara, and M. A. Mustrangi. 1997. "Diversity, Differentiation, and the Historical Biogeography of Nonvolant Small Mammals of the Neotropical Forests," pp. 455-465. In *Tropical Forest Remnants: Ecology, Management and Conservation of Fragmented Communities*, ed. W. Laurence and R. Bierregard. Chicago: University of Chicago Press.

Ramamoorthy, T. P., R. Bye, A. Lot, and J. Fá, eds. 1993. *Biological Diversity of Mexico: Origins and Distribution*. Oxford: Oxford University Press.

Ryder, O. A. 1986. "Species Conservation and Systematics: The Dilemma of Subspecies." *Trends in Ecology and Evolution* 1: 9-10.

Schneider, C. J., M. Cunningham, and C. Moritz. 1998. "Comparative Phylogeography and the History of Endemic Vertebrates in the Wet Tropics Rainforests of Australia." *Molecular Ecology* 7: 487-498.

Smith, T. B., and R. K. Wayne, eds. 1996. *Molecular Genetic Approaches in Conservation*. Oxford: Oxford University Press.

Smith, T. B., K. Holder, D. Girman, K. O'Keefe, B. Larison, and Y. Chan. 2000. "Comparative Avian Phylogeography of Cameroon Guinea Mountains: Implications for Conservation." *Molecular Ecology* 9: 1505-1516.

Soberón, J., P. Rodríguez, and E. Vázquez-Domínguez. 2000. "Implications of the Hierarchical Structure of Biodiversity for the Development of Ecological Indicators of Sustainable Use." *Ambio* 29: 136-142.

Taberlet, P. 1998. "Biodiversity at the Intraspecific Level: The Comparative Phylogeographic Approach." *Journal of Biotechnology* 64: 91-100.

Vázquez-Domínguez, E., C. Aguilar, V. Aguilar, and V. Arenas. 1998. Áreas Prioritarias Marinas de Alta Biodiversidad, pp. 109-126. In *Regiones Prioritarias Marinas de México*, coord. L. Arriaga Cabrera, E. Vázquez-Domínguez, J. González-Cano, R. Jiménez Rosenberg, E. Muñoz López, y V. Aguilar Sierra. México, D.F.: Comisión Nacional para el Conocimiento y Uso de la Biodiversidad.

Vázquez-Domínguez, E., D. Paetkau, N. J. Tucker, G. Hinten, and C. Moritz. 2001. "Resolution of Natural Groups Using Iterative Assignment Tests: An Example from two Species of Australian Native Rats (*Rattus*)." *Molecular Ecology* (in press).

Retrospectives

RETROSPECTIVE FROM CANADA

Graham Forbes

Main Observations

In listening to discussions and presentations at the Tijuana workshop, it seems apparent that there are many similarities and some substantial differences in ideas on protected areas in Mexico, the United States, and Canada. The emphasis or trend in Mexico towards biosphere reserves instead of national parks appears to be, at least partially, a function of economic contributions. In Canada there is a feeling that fully protected lands should, and can be, removed in whole or in part from resource extraction activities. Our society can afford it in many regions. This separation of land use also has fostered a perception that humans are part of the problem, and must be "removed" from these areas. By contrast, Mexico appears to favor biosphere reserves, generally a less rigid model of protection where zoning incorporates increasing amounts of human activity. Parks become a means of conserving resources for future human use. In Canada, the emphasis is on using parks as a means of preserving resources from human abuse.

The incorporation of science and ecological criteria in selecting, designing, and managing parks is prevalent in Canada. A major initiative is the use of ecological integrity as the foundation for park management. Of interest at these meetings is the extent that social sciences are mentioned as either lacking or unapplied in all three nations. It is evident that the social sciences are important, particularly in models using greater ecosystem and bioregional planning approaches.

Trends in Canada

Marine protected area programs are likely to become a major initiative in Canada. Legislation and case studies are being established by various government agencies to address this gap in the Canadian protected areas network. Recent, high-profile cases of mismanagement of Atlantic cod stocks on the east coast, and salmon stocks on the west coast, highlight the need for better management and provide impetus for growing public support for parks as part of that management.

Planning for network connectivity is at the earliest stages in Canada, though several sites are being considered in North American networks such as *Yukon to Yellowstone* and *Baja to Bering Sea*. Only a few connected systems exist in Canada because the need has not been plainly evident. Unlike states such as Florida, where the isolated forests highlighted a need for connectivity, much of Canada is still forested and many of the parks are not surrounded by urban development. So, though it may be harder to initiate a network program with the public, it should be easier to accomplish one. If we wait for the areas to become isolated, it will be harder to "claw back" the natural landscape. The limited network initiatives that exist between the U.S. and Canada likely are related to much of Canada's population being located along the international boundary. There is a trend underway to increase cooperation in land management, largely because Canada is seen as a source for large carnivore restoration in the northern United States; an example is the reintroduction of wolves to Yellowstone.

Future Role of a Trinational Working Group or Association

Such a group could facilitate the exchange of information and experience in order to avoid repeating costly mistakes. This information should include web-page access to limit publication costs and increase dissemination. Some questions that this group could focus on include:

1. what ecological services are provided by parks to adjacent people, to the environment, and to the economy, based on IUCN categories?
2. how do we get park managers and planners to incorporate social science dimensions into park design and management?
3. what have been the successes and failures in our approaches to public participation, support, and involvement in park establishment and management? What can we learn from these experiences to guide future planning processes?

RETROSPECTIVE FROM THE UNITED STATES

James Loucky

This forum on parks and protected areas in North America generated as many questions as answers, as a valuable first gathering should, while highlighting significant similarities as well as differences in the establishment, management, and associated values of parks. It became clear that while there is growing awareness that few environmental issues today are confined to political borders, equally essential is basic understanding of the geographies, resource bases, and histories of each country. The international and interdisciplinary mix and sharing of practical experience with scientific knowledge are also vital for demonstrating the opportunities to be gained from transborder and trinational collaboration.

The role of people is undoubtedly the most complicated arena associated with parks and protected areas. Recognizing that human ecology is a crucial dimension of an ecosystemic approach is fundamental to identifying continuities and discontinuities across countries, particularly in regards to how "protection" is defined and implemented. Canadian and U.S. parks were often established in scenic areas prior to scientific considerations and also opportunistically, primarily as preservation from use and for aesthetic, recreational, and limited commercial purposes. Parks in Mexico are generally newer, on the other hand, and have been established in the context of differing levels of resources and human needs. Beauty of landscapes is often secondary to the need for providing natural resources for human use. The question of whether people need parks can be rephrased to ask in what ways parks may need people. This reveals how different needs, levels of resources, and priorities set the context for distinctive action and management strategies in the three countries.

The North American countries are increasingly seeing common challenges as well, such as those associated with incorporating sciences and securing adequate funding for sustainable park management. Whereas U.S. and Canadian parks have long been essentially government-funded, today there is a growing need for partnering and corporate sources. Similarly, each country is seeking means to identify local models of stewardship and benefit from best community practices. This requires commitment to ensure full partnership with stakeholders and active involvement from the onset. This approach is in contrast to an all-too-frequent pattern of community participation in which people are included, at either early or late stages of parks planning in a paternalistic manner, and then ignored as management begins. Fully integrating human populations into ecosystems planning may not be the most efficient way to manage parks. However, all three countries have promising examples of the substantial benefits to be gained from the buy-in and long-term continuity associated with including affected peoples from the start. Similarly, the close relationship between biodiversity and cultural diversity is increasingly recognized as of critical value across the continent.

Another set of commonalities relate to the shared space of border regions. Borderlands are particularly vulnerable to environmental degradation because of accelerated flows of people, products, and pollutants. They are also critical insofar as they can become key settings for forging further positive international relationships. The well-being of shared ecosystems and migratory resources are clearly enhanced by international cooperation. Nonetheless, attention to parks in all three countries has, to date, been focused mainly on domestic issues, with few researchers and managers concerned with binational situations and virtually none with trinational issues. What is needed is a shift in perspective from borders as problems to borders as opportunities. This, in turn, requires commitment to transborder training, investigation, and monitoring from a continental perspective, and involvement of multiple levels of governments and interest groups.

Many benefits can be gained from the directions pursued by this pioneering workshop. Knowledge and experience gained in binational protected areas extend widely to other park situations. They have considerable potential, even for nonpark areas, when protected areas are viewed as part of a larger strategy involving public and private spaces. Comparative attention to North American parks also provides an array of invaluable environmental educational opportunities, ranging from public school students to policy makers. Greater interdisciplinary, and trinational collaboration in research and training are needed in order to produce the working knowledge and policy applications necessary to address effectively the resource management and development issues associated with parks and protected areas in North America.

RETROSPECTIVE FROM MEXICO

Alejandro Robles

I do not want to speak from the point of view of Mexicans, in general, since I am not sure that my Mexican colleagues would agree with what I am about to say. Rather, I speak as someone who participated in the meeting and learned from the experience. I will concentrate on four points that I consider important with respect to developing a regional perspective on protected areas.

First, I think we all agree that there is a need to maintain protected areas in order to conserve biological diversity and ensure the preservation of the ecological services of particular sites. However, if we do not keep a regional perspective on conservation, it will be difficult to preserve biological diversity and the environmental services it provides in the long-term. Therefore, I agree that in order to deal with this issue we need tools that work across spatial and temporal scales, considering carefully the context within which these tools are applied. On the other hand, it is important to acknowledge the great differences between terrestrial and marine environments, observed mainly with respect to the representativeness of natural protected areas. In terrestrial environments, connectivity depends on corridors and it is threatened by changes in land use. In marine and aerial environments this condition does not apply. Rather, sites along migration routes of birds or whales, as well as biodiversity donor and receiving sites, are of greater importance.

My second point relates to the assumed antagonism between local and regional, between scientific and empirical, as well as between top-down and bottom-up planning initiatives. Instead of looking at these as antagonistic, it would be more productive to consider them as complementary.

Local or regional perspectives do not, in themselves, provide an advantage in our ability to make good decisions. I think that good decisions are a function of how clear our values are, what information we have available, as well as of our education and principles. And, since environmental problems depend partly on the point of view of those involved, it may be possible that no one understands the whole picture. Thus, the sharing of perspectives and information becomes essential for good decisions.

Third, the importance of values was not discussed adequately in any of the groups. While I believe that there is a consensus on how to proceed at a scientific, technical level, I think that value differences are at the root of the issue. The fact that culture is intimately linked to values makes me believe that there could be important discrepancies with regards to this point, both between countries and between different cultures within the same country, as with Native Americans.

Finally, I do not think the subject of institutions was considered adequately, hence, I deem it important to reflect upon this subject. It may be that governmental, private, and civic institutions are not yet prepared to work effectively within a broad regional context. For this reason it is necessary to examine the adequacy of existing institutional frameworks and identify those areas where institutional improvement is required.

The Growing Role of the Commission for Environmental Cooperation in Biodiversity and Protected Area Planning in North America

Hans Hermann, Jürgen Hoth, and J. G. Nelson

Introduction

From the tropical, humid forests to the treeless tundra, and from the Gulf of California to the Gulf of Maine, North America is home to a great wealth of natural diversity. Migratory species such as the gray whale and the monarch butterfly, and transboundary ecoregions such as the Great Plains, are linked across the continent and are consequently affected by action—or lack thereof—in each of the three countries. North Americans, in the broad sense, are seeking new means to protect the richness of life on our shared continent. One such means is through collaboration promoted by the *North American Agreement on Environmental Cooperation* (NAAEC)—a side agreement of the *Free Trade Agreement*—which has, as one of its objectives, to "increase cooperation to better conserve, protect, and enhance the environment, including wild flora and fauna." (NAAEC 1993: article 1c). As seen in the Tijuana conference, it is becoming increasingly clear that regional and continental action is not only a potentially effective approach, but also an essential one. And the North American Commission for Environmental Cooperation (CEC) is in a unique position to tackle this challenge.

Major changes were underway in protected area thought and practice at the time of the Tijuana conference in March 1999. Paramount among these was the growing tendency to see the conservation of protected area plants, animals, and natural communities as heavily dependent on connections with other outlying natural sources of genetic diversity. In other words, protected areas were dependent upon the larger natural landscape of which they were part. Conversely, the environmental health and sustainability of the larger region depended on a well functioning network of protected areas. Protected areas and regional planning were inextricably linked.

The Tijuana conference papers demonstrated that this was true at many scales, ranging from individual protected areas, such as Fundy National Park, through larger landscapes such as the *Yukon to Yellowstone* or the *Chihuahua Desert*, to continental-scale initiatives such as *Wings Across the Border* or the *Baja California-Golfo de California to Bering Sea* (B2B). At the time of the Tijuana conference, considerable planning was underway at the first two scales, although less so at the continental scale.

Since the 1999 Tijuana meeting, however, the Commission for Environmental Cooperation (CEC) has emerged as a new player engaged in developing regional approaches to conserve and manage biodiversity. Although CEC is a relatively young institution—operating since 1995—this intergovernmental organization has already carved itself a special niche within the realm of conservation agencies and organizations. It is the only environmental organization which resulted from a trade agreement, and which convenes both governmental and nongovernmental sectors from all three North American countries. Through its four program areas—biodiversity conservation; economy and trade; pollutants and health; and law and policy—environmental challenges tackled by CEC have the possibility to be undertaken in a holistic manner. CEC is strategically positioned to bring together diverse issues and experts needed to address complex conservation problems and challenges effectively and efficiently.

Regional Approach

In the past, CEC concentrated its efforts in developing continent-wide vehicles and tools for conservation: current efforts are, however, gradually concentrating in priority regions. Examples of the former include the CEC *North American Bird Conservation Initiative* (NABCI), launched in 1999 to conserve all birds in all habitats in North America (CEC 1999a). Earlier on, the CEC supported and facilitated developing an atlas of the terrestrial ecological regions of North America (CEC 1997[1]), which in turn became the foundation for developing the bird conservation regions (BCR) map of North America. Another example is the development of the *Directory of North American Important Bird Areas* (IBAs) (CEC 1999b[2]).

Current CEC biodiversity-related programs are focusing more and more on priority regions. In the late 1990s, CEC began developing a strategic plan on biodiversity, in consultation with relevant scientists and key stakeholders. The first part of the process sought to assess the state of, and major threats to, biodiversity in the continent and opportunities and priorities for collaboration (Hanson, Agardy, and Pèrez Gil 1999) ; the second part of the process elicited feedback from stakeholders in various sectors. These two parts led to the development of the third component: a set of priorities on issues and regions of common continental concern. The CEC *Biodiversity Strategy* is currently being reviewed by the three North American governments.

To maximize the impact of the strategy, it was necessary to define working scales that were realistic, pertinent, and effective for given challenges. Some CEC project work is best undertaken at a North American scale. In other instances, collaborative approaches based on ecosystems, or regions, are fundamental to effective and efficient biodiversity conservation.

In order to identify regions of trinational conservation concern, CEC convened leading ecologists from Canada, Mexico, and the United Stares to identify regions that, due to their high level of biological continental significance and threats thereto, are prime candidates for focused North American attention. Fourteen regions were identified: 1. Arctic Tundra/ Archipelago; 2. Arctic Coastal Tundra/North Slope; 3. Bering to Baja; Gulf of California Coastal/Marine Systems; 4. Yukon/Yellowstone/Sierra Madre Corridor; 5. Prairies/Chihuahuan Desert Corridor; 6. Northern Forests/Softwood Shield; 7. Great Lakes/St. Lawrence Lowlands; 8. Greater Gulf of Maine/Coastal/Marine System (Nova Scotia to New England), Gulf of St. Lawrence/Grand Banks; 9. Chesapeake Bay; 10. Southern Appalachians; 11. Rio Bravo/Laguna Madre Corridor; 12. Transverse Neovolcanic Belt; 13. Maya Reef and Southern Florida

---

1.   See http://www.cec.org/files/pdf/BIODIVERSITY/iba-ang_EN.pdf
2.   See http://www.cec.org/files/PDF/BIODIVERSITY/draftstatus-e_EN.pdf

Photograph 28.1. Prairie dog mounds in Grasslands National Park, South Saskatchewan, Canada.

Coastal/Marine Systems; and 14. "Selva Maya," Tropical Dry and Humid Forests.

These priority regions offer unique opportunities to establish projects on issues of common concern, and to build synergies among CEC program areas as well as with other institutional partners. More recently, projects are underway in two of these new priority regions; namely in the North American Central Grasslands and the Baja California-Golfo de California to Bering Sea (B2B).

Grasslands

On a continental scale, the wildlife services of Canada, U.S., and Mexico, have agreed to collaborate to conserve seventeen species of wild mammals and birds, known as "species of common conservation concern" (SCCC). The majority of these species are associated with grasslands, including the tall, mixed, short, and desert grasslands, which are considered to be among the most threatened ecosystems in North America (Samson and Knopf 1996). CEC consequently hosted a workshop and follow-up activities for protection of these species, primarily through conservation of their habitats on a continental scale (Hoth 2001). This program currently involves developing a common framework and tools to promote cooperation in grassland conservation

Photograph 28.2. Drylands in the border area of New Mexico, U.S.A. and Sonora, Mexico

throughout North America. Among the expected results are an assessment of common issues and needs, as well as maps showing existing conservation planning units, such as protected areas and important bird areas (IBA's).

Marine and Estuarine Ecosystems

CEC is focusing its work on marine conservation though the stewardship of a North American marine protected area (NAMPA) network. It is supporting the development of common tools, as well as the identification of trinational conservation priorities related to species and areas. While some of activities of the NAMPA Network are North American-wide, others focus on the Pacific Coast Region of North America, also known as the Baja California-Golfo de California to Bering Sea (B2B) Region. The NAMPA network includes over 250 stakeholders from government and nongovernment organizations, local communities and indigenous organizations, business and academic groups, all working at the different regional scales.

The North American MPA Network seeks to enhance and strengthen the protection of marine biodiversity in North America by:

Figure 28.1   Fall migrations of the monarch butterfly in North America

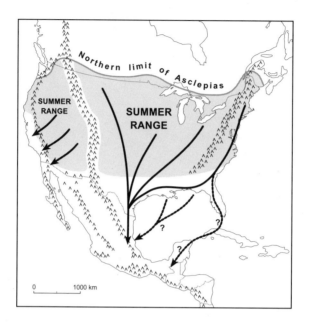

Source. Brower, L. 1995 (see keynote presentation in the preface
section at: http://www.cec.org/programs_projects/conserv_biodiv/
na_bio_cons/monarchs/%20Preface.pdf)

- protecting critical marine and coastal habitats through shared conservation approaches, and by developing cross-cutting conservation initiatives
- enhancing collaboration among the three countries to address common marine biodiversity challenges and to jointly prioritize conservation actions
- building regional, national, and international capacity to conserve critical marine and coastal habitats by sharing lessons learned, new technologies, and management strategies, and by increasing access to relevant information
- facilitating the future design and establishment of a globally representative system of MPAs throughout North America.

CEC has also supported regional collaboration based upon valued shared species. A prime example is the effort carried out with the monarch

Figure 28.2 Spring migrations of the monarch butterfly in North America

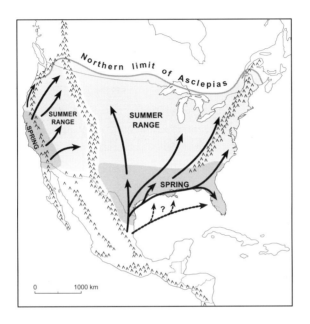

butterfly (*Danaus plexippus*). Since 1996, CEC has had the mandate to foster cooperation among the three North American countries to protect this migratory species (figs. 28.1 and 28.2).

In 1997, CEC organized a trinational and multistakeholder conference. It brought together, for the first time, scientists, farmers, politicians, government officials, NGOs, and concerned citizens to develop a common understanding about the continental issues and opportunities for conservation of the monarch butterfly throughout North America (Hoth et al. 1999). In addition to enhancing communication among diverse groups, this meeting resulted in recommendations and guidance for action. One such recommendation was to review the presidential decree that established North America's first monarch reserve in Mexico in 1986. Follow-up involved the World Wildlife Fund and resulted in the establishment in 2001 of a new decree augmenting the size of the protected area three-fold.

Conclusion

Nature does not recognize borders. Hence, regional multistakeholder planning to conserve spaces and species is an increasingly important field if nations are to more effectively, efficiently, and equitably address common concerns related to biodiversity conservation.

Although the CEC work has gathered momentum since the Tijuana workshop, its role in achieving successful stewardship of North America's biodiversity remains a huge and complex challenge. Nonetheless, through its ongoing efforts in the terrestrial and marine realms, CEC is proving to be an attractive cooperation model for other regions of the world. Cooperation and understanding among groups at all levels is of paramount importance to achieving a common goal: the conservation of biological diversity and human well-being.

References

Brower, L. 1995. Understandings and misunderstanding the migration of the monarch butterfly (Nymphalidae) in North America: 1857-1994. *Journal of the Lepidopterists's Society* 49: 304-385.

Commission for Environmnental Cooperation. 1997. *Ecological Regions of North America: Toward a Common Perspective.* Montreal: Commission for Environmental Cooperation. 71 pp. Also available at: http://www.cec.org/files/pdf/ BIODIVERSITY/eco-eng_EN.pdf

————. 1999a. *North American Bird Conservation Initiative.* Council Resolution 99-03. Montreal: Commission for Environmental Cooperation. Also available at: http:// www.cec.org/files/pdf/COUNCIL/99-03e_EN.pdf

————. 1999b. *North American Important Bird Areas: A Directory of 150 Key Conservation Sites.* Montreal: Commission for Environmental Cooperation. 359 pp. Also available at: http://www.cec.org/files/pdf/BIODIVERSITY/iba-ang_EN.pdf

Hanson, A. J., T. S. Agardy, and R. Pérez Gil S. 1999. *Securing the Continent's Biological Wealth: Towards Effective Biodiversity Conservation in North America.* Montreal: Commission for Environmental Cooperation. 162 pp. (unpublished). Summary available at: http://www.cec.org/files/PDF/BIODIVERSITY/draftstatus-e_EN.pdf

Hoth, J., ed. 2001. *Grassland Species of Common Conservation Concern. [Especies de los pastizales de Interés Común para la Conservación].*Report on the First Trinational Workshop. Nuevo Casas Grandes, Chihuahua, México, 21-23 March 2001. Unpublished report, also available at: http://www.cec.org/files/PDF/BIODIVERSITY/Chihuahua_Meeting_Final_report-Reporte_final.PDF

Hoth, J., L. K. Merino, I. Oberhauser, S. Pisanty-Price, and T. Wilkinson, eds. 1999. *Proceedings of the North American Conference on the Monarch Butterfly.* Montreal: Commission for Environmental Cooperation. 428 pp. Also available at: http:// www.cec.org/programs_projects/conserv_biodiv/na_bio_cons/monarchs/

Hoth, J., and T. Wilkinson. 2001. CEC setting biodiversity priorities. *TRIO* (newsletter of the Commission for Environmental Cooperation) Winter 2000-2001. Also available at www.cec.org/trio/stories/index.cfm?ed=2&id=18&varlan=english

NAAEC. 1993. North American Agreement on Environmental Cooperation between the government of Canada, the government of the United Mexican States, and the government of the United States of America. Also available at http://www.cec.org/ pubs_info_resources/law_treat_agree/naaec/download/Naaec-e.doc

Samson, F. B., and F. L. Knopf. 1996. "Preface." In *Prairie Conservation: Preserving North America's Most Endangered Ecosystem*, ed. F. B. Samson and F. L. Knopf. Washington, D.C.: Island Press.

Conservation of Biodiversity: The North American Conservation Area Database

David Gauthier and Ed Wiken

Abstract

Biodiversity conservation has gained wide acceptance as a term to describe the initiatives and measures to protect nature's assets at levels covering genetics, species, and entire ecosystems. Ecosystem level protection has commonly taken place through protected area systems plans, or through related types of conservation areas and practices. However, why do we need to know what is happening in and among jurisdictions or, indeed, major ecosystem types? What value do such data have in shaping strategies, identifying gaps, and improving operational efficiency? This paper addresses these questions in North America. It traces the evolution and integration of databases in Canada, Mexico, and the United States, their potential uses, and remaining problems related to lack of information and weakly developed coordination among protected area networks. Until baseline information is consolidated and strengthened to contribute to broader, more integrated, objectives with measurable indicators, current approaches to establishing innovative conservation strategies, gap analyses, and priority setting will remain suspicious and ineffective.

Introduction

It is easier to think about conservation areas as isolated and independent places. Last Mountain Lake (National Wildlife Area), Banff (National Park), and Yellowstone (National Park) are examples of seemingly distinctive and disjunctive areas that North Americans seek out to experience as wilderness areas. Many wildlife species need such areas for survival. For species that possess small home ranges, the lands and waters enclosed by a singular conservation area like Banff may suffice. However, for species that have large home ranges like bears, caribou, and whales, singular conservation areas are of limited value unless they are very large. Wide-ranging bird species require a series of conservation areas to act as stepping-stones across large migratory routes. Here too, one isolated conservation area would not suffice in meeting their life cycle and habitat needs.

The success of conservation practices therefore depends on many activities taken across the continent's landscapes or seascapes. Sometimes these activities are more symbolic conservation measures such as Ramsar or world heritage sites. Others, including national and provincial parks, national wildlife areas, and migratory bird sanctuaries are more formal types of protected areas (Wiken, Robinson, and Warren 1998c). Associated legislation and regulations can be used to control land use pressures and enforce conservation more directly. Areas such as biosphere reserves can embrace protected areas, general conservation practices and agreements, and working landscapes into one conservation mosaic.

Establishing the North American
Conservation Area Database

NCAD was designed on the same template as the Canadian Conservation Area Database (CCAD) (Beric 1999). Each list covers formal protected areas as well as other conservation designations. NCAD and CCAD evolved under a number of associated principles:

- conservation areas and protected areas alone are not viable solutions for protecting species, habitats, and ecosystems
- conservation needs to be viewed as a suite of activities practiced across protected areas and nonprotected areas, landscapes, and seascapes

- managing species, habitats, and entire systems requires an underlying ecosystem framework and approach.
- species crossover, fly, and swim across borders; yet conservation agencies, governments, and institutions often do not have the capacity to manage across political lines

The Canadian Council on Ecological Areas (CCEA) (CCEA home page) and the Canadian Plains Research Center (CPRC) combined efforts to develop a standardized, integrated, georeferenced database of major conservation areas for North America (Canada, Mexico, and U.S.A.). This was to be made both accessible through GeoGratis and CEONet (Canada 1999b), and suitable for representation in the national atlas of Canada.

The North American Conservation Area Database (NCAD) is a hybrid that was woven together from many sources. Two major Canadian geospatial datasets were used to create NCAD: the Canadian Conservation Areas Database (CCAD) (Beric 1999), and the Terrestrial Ecosystem Framework for Canada (Wiken et al. 1996). In addition, levels 1 and 2 of the international North American Ecological Regions Framework (CEC 1997) were used, as well as the U.S. Managed Conservation Areas Database and the Mexican Protected Areas Database.

Goals for the project included:

1. developing a standardized database design for integrating conservation area databases for the three countries are available through GeoGratis and CEONet
2. integrating seamlessly, for easily accessible query and analysis, the conservation area databases of the three countries
3. producing thematic analyses of the integrated database as a demonstration of its usefulness for the conservation community and projects such as national atlases
4. building upon similar conservation area initiatives conducted in the past

The project benefits partners in the conservation community in a variety of ways. These include:

- increasing and improving ecosystem-based conservation and management data
- improving the ability of CCEA and other organizations to plan for protected areas nationally and internationally on a cooperative basis
- contributing to communications and education about conservation areas

Photograph 29.1. Lakes and wetlands in the McKenzie Delta Region, West Arctic, Canada

- improving databases for protected area research, especially in regard to opportunities for analysis of macro ecosystems—such as grasslands—both nationally and internationally

Placing NCAD in Context

To facilitate the application of NCAD in a more informed manner, CCEA worked with the Commission for Environmental Cooperation (CEC) to develop terrestrial and marine ecosystem frameworks for North America. These strategic geospatial databases provide an ecological frame of reference within which to apply numerous databases, including NCAD. The collective efforts of the North American Ecosystem Working Group (CEC 1997) in mapping and classifying natural regions, led to the development of a standardized ecosystem map and framework for North America, now sanctioned by the North American environment ministers. This standardized mapping approach is intended to provide a base within which international, national, and regional issues can be addressed.

In meeting these needs, this project followed recommendations from the North American Workshop on Environmental Information, the Tri-Lateral Committee on State of the Environment Reporting, and the

World Commission on Protected Areas (WCPA) (Wiken and Gauthier 1998a). Prior to this project, there was no standardized or comprehensive conservation area database within North America to allow comparison and evaluation of protection within and among the three countries. Without a standardized, accessible, and integrated database of conservation areas, it is not possible to meet a variety of local to international needs. These include a rigorous assessment of biodiversity and ecosystem protection, gaps in protection, and development of appropriate international policy and management alternatives. This project directly supported objectives related to ecosystem education, conservation, information, and public outreach.

- developed an easily accessible electronic database linking various levels of North American ecosystems as well as territorial, provincial-state, and country jurisdictions
- linked the standardized protected area databases to GIS compatible files for North American ecological regions and jurisdictions
- provided mapped and tabular analysis of the status of protected areas by jurisdiction and ecosystem
- developed these data for representation on GeoGratis, CEONet, and in the National Atlas of Canada
- built upon North American Protected Areas initiatives already undertaken through the North American Tri-Lateral Committee (Pisanty-Baruch et al. 1999).

NCAD provides an overview of protected areas throughout North America. These can be used for initiatives in cooperative environmental and resource sector planning as agreed to under the North American Free Trade Agreement. Such information is commonly required by organizations such as the Canadian Council on Ecological Areas (CCEA), the Canadian Wildlife Service (CWS), Wildlife Habitat Canada (WHC), Parks Canada, the World Conservation Monitoring Centre (WCMC), Mexico's Instituto Naciónal de Ecología, the World Wildlife Fund, the Commission on National Parks and Protected Areas (CNPPA), and many others.

Through the provision of an accessible, standardized, and integrated information base on North American conservation areas, many current barriers to assessment, collaboration, and interjurisdictional education will be overcome. NCAD provides an important means by which governments, industry, and environmental and nongovernmental groups can market their success in the field of conservation, provide status reports on international and national commitments, and develop indicators and track progress and trends.

Planning and management efforts for conservation areas were hampered by the lack of consolidation of comprehensive databases (Turner, Wiken, and Lopoukhine 1999; Wiken 1999a). NCAD will serve a pivotal role in the integration of major conservation areas at the continental scale. NCAD will act as a catalyst for the multiparty development of management plans at local, national, and international scales. NCAD is a value-added component to CCAD, in that it uses and promotes Canadian geospatial data as a primary data model and important primary data source. Canada shares many ecosystems that are of continental and world significance.

CCAD has provided the catalyst to further integrate and use other GIS data sets, particularly from the standpoint of an ecosystem database (Rubec, Turner, and Wiken 1993; Turner, Wiken, and Moore 1997). It has also permitted factors to be considered that stress conservation areas, such as pollution levels and surrounding land use patterns and types. The GIS mode, combined with the ecosystem model, has been the most successful way to promote an enhanced awareness of issues, of varying perspectives, of possible monitoring plans, of key conservation priorities, and of means to solve problems (Wiken and Gauthier 1998a and b).

How Continental Conservation Areas Differ

NCAD as well as CCAD have already been used to analyze several aspects of conservation areas across North America (Gauthier and Wiken 1999). This work includes terrestrial as well as marine conservation areas. Some examples can be used to show the difference between an ecosystem and a jurisdictional approach. Figure 29.1 shows national parks according to jurisdictions, such as states, provinces, territories, and countries. When expressed as a percentage of the total area of a jurisdiction, such as Canada, the greatest success is achieved in creating systems of parks and protected areas in the north. While a jurisdictional analysis is interesting, its main function is to show what key authorities have done, and who has the main mandate to further conservation initiatives.

Ecological regions can provide a more informative framework for assessing ecosystem, habitat, and species conservation. (fig. 29.2). The

Figure 29.1 Total area of national parks in North America by jurisdiction

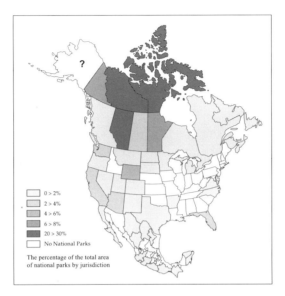

0 > 2%
2 > 4%
4 > 6%
6 > 8%
20 > 30%
No National Parks

The percentage of the total area
of national parks by jurisdiction

Figure 29.2 Total area of national parks in North America by ecological region

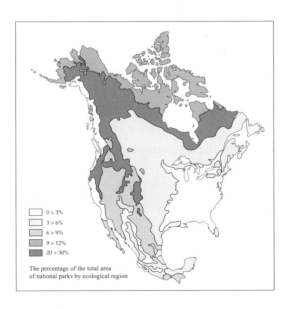

0 > 3%
3 > 6%
6 > 9%
9 > 12%
20 > 30%

The percentage of the total area
of national parks by ecological region

percentage occurrence map of national parks shows a higher proportion

Photograph 29.2. Kluane National Park near the Yukon-Alaska border, Canada and U.S.A.

of parkland in Arctic, northern forest, and mid- to northern-mountain ecosystems. While this might suggest that the authorities in these areas had a better comprehension of conservation needs, it really reflects where human settlement has been sparse or recent. Areas of longstanding settlement are often favored for human occupancy by flat terrain, a warm climate, and productive land. To protect far-ranging species, proper habitat and ecosystem protection require a network of protected areas linked by appropriate corridors as proposed in initiatives, such as the Yukon to Yellowstone (Y to Y) and Baja to Bering Sea (B to B).

The maps prepared to date, reveal trends and conditions pertaining only to national parks. More important and strategic questions need to be confronted next. They should be couched in the context of the set of protected areas that would include national wildlife areas, migratory bird sanctuaries, and ecological reserves. To date, NCAD has only partially incorporated, or coded, these types of conservation areas.

Conclusion

Many organizations promote conservation activities to enhance the establishment and understanding of conservation areas (Canada 1966). These include: the North American Waterfowl Plan, the North American State of the Environment Coordination Committee, the

Photograph 29.3 "Cienaga," a formerly much more extensive type of wetland in the San Pedro Valley, Arizona, U.S.A.

Canadian Council on Ecological Areas, the Commission for Environmental Cooperation, Wildlife Habitat Canada, and the North American Section of the World Commission on Protected Areas (Canada 1999a; Wiken 1999a; Wildlife Habitat Canada 1991). Marine areas continue to be underrepresented in most protected area plans (Wiken 1999b).

Lack of information and weakly developed coordination among protected area networks are fundamental problems in advancing integrated planning. Because of the restricted way most conservation area organizations set their mandates, and the limitations of jurisdictional boundaries, information consolidation and standardization remain weak and ineffective. This situation has created a chronic problem in obtaining up-to-date, relevant, ecosystem-based information on a North American scale that can be used in promoting sustainable resource use and regional ecosystem management (Wiken and Gauthier 1998a). Biodiversity, wildlife habitat conservation, and species protection are universal concerns and not the exclusive domain of any organization. Until baseline information is consolidated and strengthened to contribute to broader, more integrated, objectives with measurable indicators, current approaches to establishing innovative conservation strategies, gap analyses, and priority setting will remain suspicious and ineffective to many stakeholders. The North American Conservation Database

(NCAD) ecosystem framework is a critical tool that could contribute to the solution of these problems at a continental level. This work urgently requires support by the NAFTA nations if all significant North American ecosystems are to be accurately identified and protected.

References

Beric, R. 1999. *Overview of the Canadian Conservation Database* (CCAD). CCEA Newsletter no. 12. Ottawa. http://geogratis.cgdi.gc.ca/frames.html

Canada. 1996. "Understanding Connections," Records, pp. 185-354. In *State of the Environment Report of the Conserving Canada's Natural Legacy.* Ottawa: Minister of Public Works and Government Services Canada. (CD-ROM)

Canada. Environment Canada. 1999a. *Canada's Plan for Protecting Species at Risk: An Update.* Ottawa. http://www.ec.gc.ca

Canada. Natural Resources Canada. GeoAccess Division. 1999b. *NCAD—North American Conservation Areas Database, GeoGratis.* Ottawa. http://geogratis.cgdi.gc.ca/frames.html

(CEC) Commission for Environmental Cooperation. North American Ecosystem Working Group (NAEWG). 1997. *Ecological Regions of North America.* Montreal.

Gauthier, D. A., ed. 1992. *Framework for a Nation-Wide System of Ecological Areas in Canada: Part 1—A Strategy.* Occasional Paper Series no. 12. Ottawa: Canada Council on Ecological Areas.

Gauthier, D. A., K. Kavanagh, T. Beechey, L. Goulet, and E. B. Wiken. 1995. *Ecoregion Gap Analysis: Framework for Developing a Nation-wide System of Protected Ecological Areas.* Occasional Paper Series no. 13. Ottawa: Canadian Council on Ecological Areas.

Gauthier, D. A., and E. B. Wiken. 1999. "Reporting on Macro Ecosystems: The Great Plains of North America." *George Wright Forum* 16: 52-63.

Gauthier, D. A., and E. B. Wiken. 2002. "Conservation of biodiversity in North America: The North American Conservation Area Database (NCAD)," pp. 1480-1489. In *Managing Protected Areas in a Changing World*, Proceedings of the Fourth International Conference on Science and Management of Protected Areas, 14-19 May 2000, ed. S. Bondrup-Nielsen, N. W. P. Munro, G. Nelson, J. H. M. Willison, T. B. Hermann, and P. Eagles, SAMPAA. Wolfville, N.S.

Pisanty-Baruch, I., Jane Barr, E. B. Wiken, and David A. Gauthier. 1999. "Reporting on North America: Continental Connections." *George Wright Forum* 16: 22-36.

Rubec, C.D.A., A. M. Turner, and E. B. Wiken. 1993. "Integrated modeling for protected areas and biodiversity assessment in Canada," pp. 157-176. In *Sustainable Landscapes.* Proceedings of the Third Symposium of the Canadian Society for Landscape Ecology and Management. Morin Heights, Que.: Polyscience.

Turner, T., E. B. Wiken, and H. Moore. 1997. "Modelling Risk to Biodiversity in Canada: an Ecosystem Approach," pp. 657-667. In *Linking Protected Areas with Working Landscapes Conserving Biodiversity*, Proceedings of the Third International Conference on Science and Management of Protected Areas, 12-16 May 1997, ed. N. W. P. Munro and J. H. M Willison. Wolfville, N.S.: Science and Management of Protected Areas Association.

Turner, A. M., E. B. Wiken, and N. Lopoukhine. 1999. "Reporting and Indicators for Protected Areas and Ecosystems: a National Perspective." *George Wright Forum* 16: 37-51.

Wiken, E. B., D. Gauthier, I. Marshall, K. Lawton, and H. Hirvonen. 1996. *A Perspective on Canada's Ecosystems: An Overview of the Terrestrial and Marine Ecozones.* Occasional Paper no. 14. Ottawa: Canadian Council on Ecological Areas.

Wiken, E. B., and D. Gauthier. 1997. "Conservation and Ecology in North America," pp. 5-15. In *Proceedings of Caring for Home Place: Protected Areas and Landscape Ecology,* 29 September - 2 October 1996. Regina, Sask.: University Extension Press and the Canadian Plains Research Center.

————. 1998a. "Reporting on the State of Ecosystems: Experiences with Integrating Monitoring and State on the Environment Reporting Activities in Canada and North America," pp. 233-238. In *Proceedings of the North American Symposium on Towards a Unified Framework for the Inventorying and Monitoring Forest Ecosystem Resource*, ed. C. A. Bravo and C. R. Franco. Held in Guadalajara. Technical Report RMRS-P-12. Fort Collins, Colo.: Rocky Mountain Research Station, U.S. Department of Agriculture. 533 pp.

————. 1998b. "Ecological Regions of North America." pp. 114-129. *Linking Protected Areas with Working Landscapes Conserving Biodiversity.* In Proceedings of the Third International Conference on Science and Management of Protected Areas, 12-16 May 1997, ed. N. W. P. Munro and J. H. M Willison. Wolfville, N.S.: Science and Management of Protected Areas Association.

Wiken, E. B., J. Robinson, and L. Warren. 1998c. "Return to the Sea: Conservation of Canadian Marine and Freshwater Ecosystems for Wildlife," pp. 7-18. In *Proceedings of the Marine Heritage Conservation Areas Workshop*, 3 April 1998. Waterloo, Ont., ed. B. S. Iisaka, K. Van Osch, and J. G. Nelson. Heritage Centre Working Paper 14. Waterloo, Ont.: Heritage Resources Centre, University of Waterloo.

Wiken, E. B. 1999a. "The Importance and Principles of State of Ecosystem Reporting and Indicators." *George Wright Forum*, vol. 16: 14-21.

————. 1999b. "Casting the Bottom Line on the Blue Planet, " pp. 8 -10. In *Proceedings of the Conference on Protected Areas and the Bottom Line*. Canadian Council on Ecological Areas (CCEA), 1997 Annual General Meeting. Fredericton, N.B.: Atlantic Forestry Centre, Canadian Forest Service, Natural Resources Canada.

Wildlife Habitat Canada. 1991. *The Status of Wildlife Habitat in Canada: Realities and Visions*. Ottawa, Ont. www.whc.org

Attendee List

Authors & Workshop Attendees

Canada

Kenneth W. Cox
North American Wetlands Conservation Council
Ottawa, ON

J. Chad Day
Simon Fraser University
Burnaby, B.C.

Graham Forbes
University of New Brunswick
Fredericton, N.B.

David Gauthier
Canadian Plains Research Center
University of Regina,
Regina, Saskatchewan

Sabine Jessen
Canadian Parks and Wilderness Society
Vancouver, B.C.

J. G. Nelson
Heritage Resources Centre
University of Waterloo
Waterloo, ON

Lucy M. Sportza
University of Waterloo
Waterloo, ON

Ed Wicken
Science and Policy
Wildlife Habitat Canada
Ottawa, ON

United States
Scott Brennan
Western Washington University
Bellingham, WA

Steve Gatewood
The Wildlands Project
Tucson, AZ

Marvin Jensen
Yellowstone National Park
Wyoming

James Loucky
Western Washington University
Bellingham, WA

John C. Miles
Western Washington University
Bellingham, WA

Tessa Roper
Tijuana River National Estuarine Research Reserve
San Diego, CA

Chris Williams
World Wildlife Fund
Washington, D.C.

Mexico
Noel Arón Fuentes
Colegio de la Frontera Norte
Tijuana, B.C.

Nora L. Bringas Rábago
Colegio de la Frontera Norte
(Dept. Urban and Environment Studies)
Tijuana, B.C.

Carlos Castillo Sánchez
Director, Reserva de la Biosfera El Pinacate y Gran Desierto de Altar
Instituto Nacional de Ecología
Puerto Peñasco, Sonora, México

Exequiel Ezcurra
Instituto Nacional de Ecología
SEMARNAT
D.F., México

Gustavo Danemann
Pronatura Península
de Baja California
Ensenada, B.C.

Ileana Espejel
Facultad de Ciencias, UABC
Ensenada, B.C.

Rocio Esquivel
Instituto Nacional de Ecología
D.F., México

José Luis Fermán
Facultad de Ciencias Marinas, UABC
Ensenada, B.C.

Cuitláhuac Hernández
Colegio de la Frontera Norte
Student: Master in Environment Administration
Tijuana, B.C.

Juan Galindo
Colegio de la Frontera Norte
Student, Master in Environment Administration
Tijuana, B.C.

Hans Hermann
Head, Biodiversity Conservation Program
Commission for Environmental Cooperation
Montreal, Que.

Jürgen Hoth
Manager, Biodiversity Conservation Program
Commission for Environmental Cooperation
Montreal, Que.

Rubén Lara
Pronatura Península de Baja California
Ensenada, B.C.

Roberto Martínez Gallardo
Facultad de Ciencias, UABC
Ensenada, B.C.

Pablo Morales
Colegio de la Frontera Norte
Student: Master in Environment Administration
Tijuana, B.C.

Lina Ojeda Revah
Colegio de la Frontera Norte
Dept. Urban and Environment Studies
Tijuana, B.C.

Oscar Pedrín
Instituto Nacional de la Pesca
Ensenada, B.C.

David Ortiz Reyna
Upper Gulf of California Biosphere Reserve Agency
Puerto Penasco, Sinaloa

Hugo Riemann
Colegio de la Frontera Norte
Dept. Urban and Environment Studies
Tijuana, B.C.

Alejandro Robles
Conservación Internacional
Washington, D.C., U.S.A.

Ella Vázquez-Domínguez
Conabio/Instituto de Ecología
D.F., México

Carlos Israel Vázquez León
Colegio de la Frontera Norte
Master in Environment Administration Program
Tijuana, B.C.

Index

153, 154, 156, 157, 187, 188, 203, 217, 220, 237, 258, 274, 293, 324, 382, 389, 392, 395, 396
cooperative(s) 7, 21, 110, 118, 127, 128, 144, 185, 186, 187, 193, 206, 214, 215, 220, 224, 236, 280, 295, 311, 349, 401, 403
coordination 61, 64, 66, 68, 77, 147, 156, 209, 212, 213, 214, 216, 217, 219, 226, 348, 359, 399, 407
coral reefs 80, 249, 286, 327
Cordell Bank 181
core reserves 166, 236, 237, 239
core reserves *See also* reserves
Coriolis 163, 164, 284
corridors 6, 78, 97, 100, 127, 128, 144, 167, 185, 187, 237, 239, 284, 304, 375, 387, 406
Costa Rica 336
cost-benefit analysis 313
crisis 49, 236, 311, 347, 351, 365
criteria 17, 76, 82, 83, 85, 94, 97, 99, 116, 118, 235, 236, 312, 314, 318, 319, 373, 381
cross-border 5, 7
cross-disciplinary 21
cross-sectoral 142, 156, 157
cultural 4, 11, 17, 46, 76, 79, 81, 83, 84, 85, 92, 124, 186, 213, 239, 258, 264, 266, 269, 271, 272, 274, 275, 276, 298, 300, 312, 322, 326, 334, 335, 343, 344, 384
cumulative 323
currents 163, 164, 166, 188, 284
cycle of dependency 353
cycle(s) 351, 353

Dakota 45
decision-making 1, 5, 6, 13, 40, 76, 79, 80, 86, 129, 142, 146, 295, 303, 321, 322, 328, 347, 361, 362, 363, 365
decree 63, 70, 293, 303, 352, 353, 358, 395
degradation 1, 64, 65, 70, 100, 202, 203, 252, 275, 279, 280, 282, 289, 290, 294, 341, 348, 384
Department of Interior 233
desert 241, 247, 248, 249, 250, 254, 257,

258, 282, 285, 290, 293, 297, 302, 304, 341, 342, 392
desertification 262
Desierto de los Leones 61
development *See* economic development
Directory of North American Important Bird Areas (IBAs) 391
discipline, disciplinary 84, 91, 326, 372
discipline, disciplinary *See also* cross-disciplinary, multidisciplinary, transdisciplinary
discount rate 313, 314, 315, 316, 318
District of Muskoka 129
disturbance 13, 28, 108, 173, 195, 200, 338, 339, 340
diversity *See* biodiversity, biologcial diversity, genetic diversity, natural diversity, species diversity
Dominion Parks Branch 29
dredging 175, 177, 195
drilling 354, 355, 360
Ducks Unlimited 159, 160
dumping 176, 177, 197, 327

easements 81, 91, 97, 124, 129, 145
Ecological and Environmental Advisory Committee (EEAC) 93
ecological integrity 5, 40, 42, 66, 75, 103, 105, 111, 113, 114, 118, 120, 121, 126, 130, 166, 235, 256, 264, 265, 266, 327, 381
Ecological Land Classification System 101
ecology 5, 21, 51, 57, 75, 78, 79, 82, 91, 114, 215, 241, 300, 335, 352, 355, 383
economic
  benefits 6, 178, 227, 333, 335, 343, 344, 345
  development 18, 79, 197, 287, 302, 312, 331, 334, 339
  growth 17, 312, 318
  needs 79
ecoregion(s) 98, 99, 101, 109, 154, 247, 250, 251, 253, 254, 256, 257, 258
ecosystem
  management 76, 81, 82, 85, 108, 127, 155, 210, 219, 227, 407
  management *See also* ecosystem-based management

harvesting 97, 238, 351
heritage 6, 30, 37, 38, 91, 96, 99, 100,
    129, 145, 179, 205, 269, 272, 275, 276,
    299, 400
Heritage Resources Centre 3, 131, 132,
    409
heterogeneity 279, 285, 338
hierarchy, hierarchical 65, 76, 83, 94, 106,
    164
history, historical 4, 5, 14, 15, 21, 25, 45,
    52, 54, 55, 59, 61, 68, 78, 92, 105, 109,
    113, 118, 154, 158, 171, 172, 174, 193,
    210, 215, 222, 224, 257, 262, 274, 281,
    359, 369, 371, 372, 373
holistic 76, 81, 91, 108, 128, 161, 178,
    322, 390
homogeneous 325
homologous 372
human dimensions 13, 16, 121, 127, 130
human ecology 21
hunters, hunting 28, 31, 39, 140, 171,
    174, 291, 303, 312, 315, 316, 317, 318,
    319, 324, 342
hydroelectric projects 37

Iceland 175
ideologies 323
immigration 197, 288, 374
implementation, implementing 41, 64,
    103, 109, 110, 116, 126, 127, 128, 129,
    147, 149, 150, 158, 188, 199, 243, 244,
    303, 304, 314, 319, 320, 325, 364
incentive 266, 344, 356
inclusive 8, 104, 142
income distribution 314, 345
Indians 282
indicators 8, 127, 287, 288, 311, 314, 399,
    404, 407
indigenous knowledge See knowledge
infrastructure 53, 67, 70, 99, 100, 155,
    156, 158, 289, 319, 337, 353, 354, 360
in-holding 138, 141
Instituto Nacional de Ecología (INE) 62,
    69, 180, 299, 325, 326, 329, 348, 412,
    413
insularity 281
integrate, integration, integrative 12, 20,
    81, 82, 86, 103, 128, 130, 153, 155,

158, 216, 219, 226, 227, 231, 239, 251,
    258, 264, 275, 304, 310, 313, 338, 344,
    348, 359, 399, 401, 403, 404, 407
interactive 7, 114, 120, 124, 142, 144,
    145, 201, 266, 326
intercontinentally 12
interdependence 323
interest groups 212, 213, 364, 384
interjurisdictional 14, 403
Internal Rate of Return 314
international cooperation 147, 221, 225,
    384
International Fur Seal Treaty 174
International Whaling Commission 175
interpretation 54, 130, 267, 270, 271, 359
intraspecific biodiversity 375
Inuvialuit 31, 264
invertebrates 99, 167, 168, 200, 251
irrigation 135
isolation 104, 281, 285, 291, 338, 339,
    343, 372, 373

jaguar 241, 248, 255
Japan 170, 175
Jasper National Park 41
joint management See management
jurisdictional 184, 210, 404, 407
jurisdictional See also interjurisdictional
justice 262

kelp forest(s) 166, 170, 173, 178
Kitlope Valley 39
knowledge 17, 21, 75, 76, 77, 82, 99, 122,
    125, 148, 150, 167, 168, 188, 201, 211,
    268, 274, 276, 364, 372, 374, 383, 385
    indigenous 6, 20
    local ecological 80, 83
    scientific 20, 83
Krakow 7

La Giganta 285
Labrador 35
land claims
    mineral 26
land claims See also aboriginal land claims
land tenure 64, 69, 138, 257, 297, 348

North American Association for Environmental Education 276
North American Bird Conservation Initiative (NABCI) 153, 158, 390, 396
North American Conservation Area Database (NCAD) 399, 401, 408
North American Ecological Regions Framework 401
North American Ecosystem Working Group 402, 408
North American Free Trade Agreement (NAFTA) 8, 16, 154, 240, 403
North American Fund for Environmental Cooperation 240
North American Plate 282
North American Waterfowl Management Plan 147, 148, 149, 158, 159, 160
North American Wetlands Conservation Act 152, 157, 160
North American Wetlands Conservation Council 160, 411
North American Workshop on Environmental Information 402
North Cascades Conservation Council 224, 225
North Cascades National Park 222, 224, 273
Northwest Territories 35, 39, 238
Nova Scotia 38, 391
Nunavut 35
nutrients 164, 188, 311, 351

Oaxaca 262, 263, 288
Office of Ocean and Coastal Resource Management 181
off-road races 331, 340, 342
oil 26, 32, 33, 37, 39, 69, 176, 177, 238, 268, 334, 347, 349, 351, 352, 353, 354, 355, 356, 360, 365
old growth forests See forest(s)
Olmstead, Frederick Law 30
Ontario 16, 28, 29, 38, 39, 43, 87, 91, 92, 93, 96, 97, 98, 99, 101, 113, 115, 124, 129, 131, 132, 145, 264, 336
opportunity cost 313
Oregon 172, 184
Oregon Territorial Sea Plan 184
Organic Act of 1916 29

outreach 68, 118, 128, 130, 193, 202, 240, 267, 270, 403
overfishing 326, 360
overgrazing 215, 255, 256
ozone 18

Pacific 2, 27, 28, 161, 162, 163, 164, 170, 172, 173, 174, 180, 181, 187, 188, 189, 190, 194, 198, 199, 203, 231, 248, 269, 282, 283, 284, 285, 286, 287, 291, 292, 293, 302, 343, 344, 393
Pacific flyway 198
Pacific Northwest 231, 248
Pacific Plate 283
paper park 358
Parks Canada 21, 30, 40, 41, 43, 114, 118, 120, 121, 122, 124, 125, 126, 127, 128, 130, 131, 132, 179, 403
participation, participatory 6, 21, 40, 61, 66, 68, 69, 79, 185, 242, 293, 295, 310, 313, 347, 348, 349, 353, 359, 362, 365, 366, 367, 382, 384
Partners in Flight (PIF) 153, 158
partnerships 68, 71, 100, 147, 149, 152, 153, 156, 267, 273, 293, 311
Pasayten Wilderness 224
pesticides 262
petroleum 167
petroleum See also oil
PetrÛleos Mexicanos (PEMEX) 352, 353, 354, 355, 356, 358, 359, 360, 361, 366
phenotypic 371
philosophy, philosophical 21, 29, 42, 209, 335
phylogenetic 372, 373
phylogeography 15, 369, 372, 374
pipelines 353
planning
    adaptive 114, 129, 142
    bioregional 75, 78, 381
    participative 76, 79, 84, 85
    rational 129
    regional 1, 2, 5, 7, 8, 11, 12, 15, 16, 17, 18, 20, 76, 78, 82, 85, 86, 87, 88, 96, 301, 302, 390
    transactive 7, 124, 142
pleasuring ground 27, 50, 205
poaching 210, 308, 356

Contents

Aerial view of
The J. Paul Getty Museum

Foreword

I thought it worthwhile to create one building in the Roman tradition. The Greco-Roman buildings that remain to us have had hard usage during the last couple of thousand years. I suppose that 99.99% of the buildings of Imperial Rome have disappeared. The few buildings left are all more or less incomplete. They have been worn by time, and, if they were in the Mount Vesuvius region, they suffered severe damage in the volcanic eruption and earthquake. Fortunately some of the villas around Mount Vesuvius have been excavated, and, while none of them are complete, we know after studying them how a typical Roman villa looked even though we can't make an accurate facsimile of any particular one.

The Villa dei Papyri at Herculaneum served as an inspiration for the museum. The Villa has not been excavated but, fortunately for us, many years in the eighteenth century were spent in exploring the Villa by means of galleries, and we have good engineering information about the peristyle garden and much of the building. I believe that the ancient Roman proprietor would find the peristyle garden in the museum very close to the one at Herculaneum. And, even though there are some changes, I believe that he would recognize the floor plan of the main level.

J. Paul Getty

J. Paul Getty
January 1974

Main peristyle garden

Introduction

If a museum is alive and thriving, it is bound to keep changing and improving itself. This is good for our visitors and good for our staff. But it means that guidebooks quickly go out of date.

This is the fifth edition of the Guidebook since the new J. Paul Getty Museum building opened in January 1974.

No guidebook can advise you how best to spend your time during a visit to the museum. Certainly we hope that you will visit all three collections – Antiquities on the Main Floor, Paintings and Decorative Arts on the Upper Floor. But please allow time to walk round the gardens, perhaps slipping from gallery to garden and garden to gallery to rest both feet and eyes. There is a lot to see. Only you can decide whether you would prefer to see everything fleetingly or a few things at leisure.

Please respect the few simple regulations that we impose on your visit. Most especially – please do not touch any of the art objects. We are proud to be the custodians of such superlative collections, and we wish you – and future generations – to enjoy them.

Our founder and benefactor Mr. J. Paul Getty, who died in June 1976, did not live to see the museum that he had created. But he is very much alive in everything that you will find here. During his lifetime, he gave his personal consideration to everything that was acquired and took a highly active interest in all aspects of the museum. Mr. Getty has endowed the musuem in a manner which will enable it to develop over the years ahead so that it will make a worthy contribution to the cultural life in California and become one of the great museums of the world.

Whether you came for light-hearted enjoyment (and we think that there is much to please you) or out of scholarly concern for our collections, we hope that you will be pleased with what you see. But further – we hope that you will discover *more* than you expected. We would like you to be stimulated and surprised at the quality and enchantment of what you find here and that you will enjoy not only this visit to the J. Paul Getty Museum but return frequently in the future.

Stephen Garrett
Director
September, 1980

South porch

History of the Museum

INTRODUCTION

It was in the 1930s that Mr. J. Paul Getty began, as a private individual, to collect works of art. From the outset he was interested in three distinct areas: Greek and Roman antiquities, Renaissance and Baroque paintings and French eighteenth-century decorative arts. In the course of his travels, and with increasing enthusiasm on his part, Mr. Getty's collection expanded. When the present property in Malibu was acquired in the late 1940s, he assembled the collection in the large Spanish-style house to the north of the new museum.

In the early 1950s Mr. Getty decided to form an educational trust, administered by a Board of Trustees, that would take charge of the collection and open it to the public. After it opened in 1954, the original J. Paul Getty Museum attracted an increasing number of visitors drawn by the quality of the three collections and the charming intimacy of the galleries set within the original house.

During the years that followed, the size of the collection increased steadily. Although new galleries were added, the space was rapidly outgrown. Rather than continue to modify the existing facilities, the Trustees decided to construct a new and separate building that would be tailored to the needs of the expanded collection.

The Trustees did not wish to commission a modern building, numerous examples of which – both good and bad – already existed among museums. Neither were they satisfied with the usual design concept whereby the structure would be a mere backdrop for art objects. They felt that a museum building should

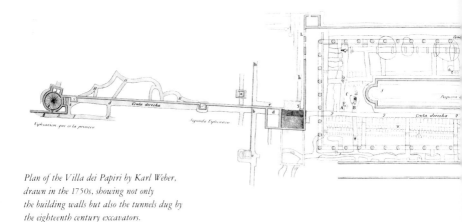

*Plan of the Villa dei Papiri by Karl Weber,
drawn in the 1750s, showing not only
the building walls but also the tunnels dug by
the eighteenth century excavators.*

be a statement in itself – that is, be of interest for its own sake – as well as providing a harmonious setting for the collections.

Mr. Getty's interest in Greek and Roman antiquities was one of long standing. During his frequent and often lengthy stays in Italy, he had been able to visit not only museums but also the classical sites of Pompeii and Herculaneum. He was fascinated with one particular building: the Villa dei Papiri at Herculaneum, which had been destroyed along with the rest of the city by the eruption of Mount Vesuvius. A structure patterned after it would certainly be exciting archaeologically; it would also provide the ideal setting for the antiquities collection, one of the finest in the United States.

The Trustees decided that the new museum would be a reconstruction, as close as possible, of the Villa dei Papiri.

VILLA DEI PAPIRI
The home of wealthy patrician families from the first or second century B.C.

until it was destroyed by volcanic eruption in A.D. 79, the Villa dei Papiri was a large Roman seaside villa. It was located in the ancient town of Herculaneum, which lay on the Bay of Naples a few miles east of Neapolis, the Greek predecessor of Naples. Herculaneum was relatively small in size – the population was approximately 5,000, a quarter that of Pompeii's – and was principally a fishing village which had become a fashionable resort area for wealthy Romans. Little is known of its actual history, though it was traditionally believed to have been founded by the legendary Greek hero Herakles (known to the Romans as Hercules). It was probably established by the Greeks and then passed successively through the hands of the Etruscans, the Samnites, and finally the Romans.

In August of the year A.D. 79, the long dormant volcano Vesuvius erupted and obliterated the city along with a number of others including Pompeii and Stabiae. While these sites were covered with volcanic ash, Herculaneum was buried by a river of volcanic mud which

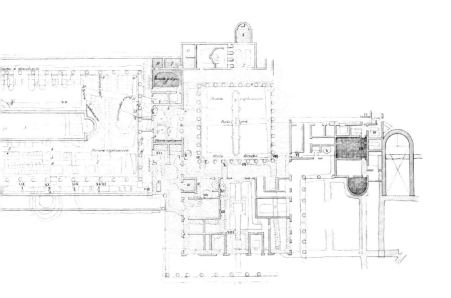

soon solidified into rock. Because the town was situated on the coastline, almost all the inhabitants were able to escape. A few survivors returned and attempted to rescue abandoned valuables but were discouraged by the hardened mud. Eventually even the location of the city was forgotten. Its depth of burial was increased by later eruptions, climaxed by a tremendous lava flow in 1631.

The site of the town was discovered by chance in 1709 when monks, digging a well, came upon a tier of carved seats. The precious cut marbles that were found prompted further digging, and the marbles were sold for decoration of a nearby villa. In 1738 the partially looted structure was identified as a theater, and soon afterwards an inscription was found that named the town as Herculaneum. From that time on the excavations were eagerly supported by Carlos III, the new Bourbon king of Naples. The excavations were accomplished by tunneling, and the goal continued to be treasure rather than archaeological information.

In June 1750, when a well was sunk in another monastery garden just outside the city, an exquisite circular floor (now in the National Museum, Naples) was discovered. Made of vari-colored marbles, this floor belonged to a garden pavilion and led eventually to the discovery of the Villa dei Papiri.

The excavation of the villa – which involved digging down to a depth of over sixty feet and then tunneling horizontally – was done under the supervision of Karl Weber, a Swiss engineer. As the villa was gradually exposed, Weber made a detailed plan of the structure (illus.) with dimensions, and kept a diary of his discoveries – a novel practice for that time.

The method of excavating by means of tunnels was both difficult and dangerous. Interest in the findings waned, and the tunnels became filled with poisonous volcanic gases. After about eighteen years of work, the project was abandoned and the tunnels gradually fell in. Today the surface of the site is covered with a tomato patch, and the Villa dei Papiri remains underground, parts of it still unexplored. Only Weber's plan and notes were readily accessible to provide the basis for the modern reconstruction of the building.

The villa evidently lay on a gentle slope parallel to and not far from the sea. It was surrounded by extensive gardens, possibly reaching down to the shore, while the high road from Naples leading to other coastal towns passed to the north. Two main parts of the villa are recognizable: the residence proper, built around a square peristyle or court, and a large rectangular peristyle to the west. The original house may date back to the second century B.C., but it must have been extended and remodeled several times and apparently changed hands shortly before the eruption of Vesuvius.

The square inner peristyle was surrounded on four sides with deep porticoes. There was a narrow pool in the center set in a garden with small marble fountains at each corner. To the south of the court was the large atrium, the principal room of the house. The floor of the atrium was inlaid with black and white mosaic, and in the center was a shallow pool – the impluvium – placed below an opening in the roof·to catch rainwater. Two alcoves, or alae, were on either side, and the atrium was connected with the tablinum (a sort of sitting room) which opened onto a colonnaded porch facing the sea. Several doors within the room were blocked and the space converted for display cabinets, but they must have once led to the traditional cubicula or bedrooms which were normally adjacent to the atrium. The arrangement of the rooms around the atrium indicates considerable remodeling.

The portion of the house to the east of the peristyle is sketchy on Weber's plan. What is shown includes an extensive private bathing area, a library or room for storing papyrus volumes and indications of stairways to an upper floor.

The section to the north of the peristyle is also incomplete on Weber's plan. Recognizable are a room with a semicircular apse – perhaps the lararium or private chapel – and a curvilinear room with a curious low wall. The northeast corner – blank on Weber's plan – may have been the location of an entrance from the main road.

The west side of the peristyle was dominated by a large hall that connected the smaller inner peristyle with the rectangular one outside. On four sides of this great court stood colonnades, and in the center was a long pool with curving protuberances at each end. This pool was apparently quite deep and probably served as a reservoir. Presumably this area was an addition – possibly from the second half of the first century B.C. – to the original house.

The circular floor that first led to the discovery of the villa was located in one of the decorated structures in the garden some distance from the end of the great outer peristyle. That floor was only the first of many to be found, and periodic reports to the king of Naples emphasized the quantity of marble removed from them.

The villa also yielded a treasure in sculpture. Of the original collection, there are now thirty bronze busts, thirteen large bronze statues, eighteen smaller ones, fifteen marble busts and seven marble statues to be seen in the Naples Museum.

Others have been found in fragments or have since been lost. The excavations yielded the greatest find of antique bronzes ever to be discovered in one building. Reproductions of many grace the museum gardens.

But the discovery that was of special interest to scholars – and one that gave the villa its name – was the unearthing of an extensive library of Greek and Roman texts written on rolls of papyrus. Carbonized by the heat of the eruption, the papyrus rolls have now been partially deciphered. The works were principally philosophical in nature, especially Epicurean, and featured works of a certain Philodemus, who lived in the first century B.C. and was patronized by

South façade

Lucius Calpurnius Piso, the father-in-law of Julius Caesar. On this basis, it has generally been supposed that one owner of the villa was Piso and that the library was that of Philodemus. At one time, there may have been a school at the villa, and one unenthusiastic pupil added a graffito to the marble bust of the author complaining that he was extremely boring. It is known from the records that many statues were removed from the estate shortly before the eruption, probably to be sold, and one of the rooms near the atrium was filled with grain. Apparently, the last owner had neither artistic nor literary tastes.

The decision to recreate the Villa dei Papiri as the basis for the new museum was made in spring 1970.

CONSTRUCTION OF THE NEW MUSEUM

Many difficulties arose in translating Karl Weber's original records into a modern structure. There existed such myriad considerations as the nature of the available site, the practical needs of a museum and its visitors, the necessity of employing modern workmen and equipment, and the requirements of a rigid building code. In addition, it was necessary to supply information for those incomplete or missing portions of Weber's plan: several areas on the ground level and the entire floor above. Fortunately, Dr. Norman Neuerburg agreed to act as consultant for the project. An architectural historian, he combined years of scholarship in antiquities – including research and excavation of Pompeii and Herculaneum – with an acute sense of design and construction problems.

The Building and Gardens

ENTRANCE

Entering from Pacific Coast Highway and passing under an imposing gatehouse, the visitor travels up a landscaped driveway to the south facade of the Main Peristyle. The lower portion, which contains a parking structure, is faced with tufa stone in a pattern popular in Italy at the time of the villa's construction. Above it is a loggia with Corinthian columns.

MAIN PERISTYLE GARDEN

An elevator and staircase provide access from the ground level vestibule to the upper level where the visitor passes through a colonnade into the Main Peristyle Garden. Here the monumental facade of the museum can be seen beyond the great reflecting pool and garden.

Embellished with replicas of some of the bronze statues found in the Villa dei Papiri, the formal garden is landscaped with trees, shrubs and flowers such as might have been planted by the original owners of the villa. The Romans welcomed the beauty of ornamental plants as an extension of their buildings, and their interest in gardens and nature is evidenced by the great variety of flora that they collected and cultivated. The Main Peristyle Garden is planted with jonquils, violets, roses and many flowering shrubs and trees. Pomegranate, oleander, laurel and arbors covered with grape are also present. The garden is planned for seasonal variety, and each visit will provide a new experience as the flowers and foliage change. The borders of formal hedges and the carefully trained ivy mounds reveal the Roman interest in topiary gardening.

Entrance vestibule

The garden has deep porticoes on all sides; on three sides the columns are of the Doric order, while the colonnade in front of the museum proper is of a particularly magnificent Corinthian style. The tile used on the roofs was custommade to Roman specifications, and the eaves are fronted by antefixes (ornaments used in classical times to conceal the ends and to prevent swallows from nesting within). The floor of the Doric porticoes combines mosaic and marble with *opus signinum,* the Roman equivalent of modern terrazzo paving; the floor of the portico by the museum is paved with colored marbles set in geometric patterns.

The walls around the garden are decorated with illusionistic painting of architecture. A practice fashionable in the latter half of the first century B.C., its principal aim was to expand the space by visual rather than physical means. The ceilings are based on a fine wooden one found in a villa at Boscoreale, near Pompeii. After dark, lighting in the garden is provided by lamps adapted from a Pompeian lantern. The semicircular stone seats surrounding the black slate and white limestone floors were modeled after examples found in public locations in Pompeii.

VESTIBULE

The museum proper is entered through bronze doors at the end of the Main Peristyle Garden. Inside, the magnificent Vestibule (Gallery 101) displays a floor and walls inlaid with colored marbles in designs from Herculaneum. The entire floor and parts of the wall were recut from antique marbles that came from quarries closed over a millennium and a half ago. The ceiling, painted as a grape arbor, is adapted from one found in Pompeii.

INNER PERISTYLE GARDEN

At the center of the museum is the square Inner Peristyle Garden. Its thirty-six columns are topped by four-sided Ionic capitals popular in Pompeii during the second and first centuries B.C. The walls reproduce decorations from a peristyle of the House of the Faun in Pompeii while the ceiling uses motifs still visible in a fragment of a stone on the Street of the Tombs in the same city. Colors used here and on other painted surfaces of the museum were matched to ancient samples. At the center of the garden, the long narrow pool and the five bronze maidens repeat a feature of the original villa, as do the four small fountains in the corners. The mood is one of serene formality.

EAST GARDEN

The walled garden to the east of the building is dominated by a colorful mosaic niche fountain which reproduces one found in the House of the Large Fountain in Pompeii. In the center of the garden are a second fountain and a pond. Plantings in this garden include European sycamore, bay, campanula, English boxwood and seasonal flowers for color. Each garden of the museum was designed to evoke a feeling appropriate to the purpose of the space, and the solitary contemplative mood of the East Garden contrasts effectively with the open and social nature of the Main Peristyle.

HERB GARDEN

At either end of the portico to the museum are entrances to smaller gardens. On the west side is the agricultural garden with its geometric plantings

Inner peristyle garden

of apple, fig, pear, and citrus trees. Kitchen gardens were an important part of Roman homes, and the carefully tended beds of thyme, fennel, basil, dill, rosemary, and seasonal vegetables demonstrate the versatility of such gardens as sources of food and decoration. On ramped terraces of the hill stands the traditional olive grove.

MAIN FLOOR

Housing the antiquities collection, some of the galleries which surround the peristyle are based on typical rooms of the period and vary in their decoration. They display a wide spectrum of ceiling types used during the Roman period, including plaster, relief stucco, wood and mosaic. Floors are principally marble, mosaic, or terrazzo and range from simple to elaborate in their patterns. Two of the finest marble floors reproduce ones at the Villa dei Papiri. The walls are of plain and painted plaster, relief stucco, brick, and marble. The woodwork and hard-

ware used throughout the main floor are based on ancient examples.

The tablinum next to the lofty Atrium opens onto the West Porch and the West Garden. The striking columns with their twisted fluting are modeled on those in a villa at Stabiae while the walls and ceiling are decorated with painting appropriate to a garden. Two fountains duplicate originals from Pompeii and Herculaneum.

East garden

14

UPPER FLOOR

The elevator opens onto the large Vestibule (Gallery 201) containing one of the museum's most beautiful marble floors which, unlike most of the others, is curvilinear in design. At the left, bronze doors lead to a terrace with a spectacular view of the gardens below. This panorama reveals the carefully structured nature of the museum's grounds: the gardens in and near the buildings are highly organized and geometric in design but, as one looks beyond toward the sea and the surrounding hills, they become more rustic and natural.

BASEMENT

The conservation and research facilities that support the museum collections are located downstairs. Although the Research Library and Photograph Archives are used mainly by the museum staff, they are open by appointment to anyone involved in specialized research.

West porch and garden with tea room

Antiquities

INTRODUCTION

While the Greek and Roman collection in the Getty Museum covers all aspects of ancient art, the sculpture is the most important part and can, indeed, be ranked among the best in the United States. Classical statuary was Getty's primary interest from the earliest part of his career as a collector. He acquired at the outset several pieces which appear in every handbook on Greek sculpture. One major example is the *Lansdowne Herakles* (illus. p. 38), carved for the Villa of the emperor Hadrian, and purchased, with several other minor pieces, from the collection of the British Marquess of Lansdowne. Other examples will be mentioned in the text.

Getty was acquiring antiquities over a thirty year period, but most of the classical sculptures entered the museum collection only after 1969 when Getty decided to build the new museum. The high point of the collection is, of course, the *Getty Bronze* (illus.), acquired after the founder's death but fulfilling his intentions. It is perhaps the finest classical antiquity in this country. In general, the strongest areas of the sculpture collection are Greek and Roman portraits and fourth century Attic grave reliefs.

The sculpture is mostly on public display, but only a selection of minor arts is visible. Many Greek vases, terracotta figures, and small bronzes are donations that reflect community involvement and love of the fine arts. Part of them are on display, more constitute a study collection available to archaeologists and university students. It should be mentioned that there are several important loans from private collections and, most nota-

The Getty Bronze
Bronze statue of a
victorious athlete by Lysippos
ca. 310 B.C.

bly, from the Los Angeles County Museum of Art which has contributed large statuary from the English Hope and Lansdowne collections and an important ensemble of Greek vases formerly in the Hearst collection.

This guide presents only selected pieces in the galleries, as a handbook of all the displayed material is in preparation. It should be emphasized that most Greek statuary survives only in Roman copies which date largely from the first centuries after Christ. Many of them reproduce the general appearance of the lost Greek originals, although few can claim a comparable artistic level. The copyists were artisans of varying degrees of skill who sometimes achieved true technical virtuosity; rarely, though, did they work with any real understanding of the essence of Greek art. While many, if not the majority, of Greek Classical sculptures were cast in bronze, most surviving copies are in marble, a cheaper material. This change in material has many technical and even artistic consequences. For example, supports for projecting elements had to be added and the style also changed during the translation from the Greek originals to the Roman copies. Nevertheless, without these copies such master sculptors as Myron and Praxiteles would today be empty names.

GALLERY 107:
HALL OF APHRODITE

The display of ancient art begins under the auspices of Aphrodite, the Greek goddess of love whom the Romans called Venus. Entering the gallery, one is attracted to the *Mazarin Venus,* named for the prime minister of Louis XIV, its seventeenth century owner. The Venus is one of the rare cases where the museum has followed the opposite of its usual policy on conservation: here all the seventeenth century restorations – head, arms, breasts – have been kept for their historical value. A free-standing copper statuette is an excellent variant of a Hellenistic Aphrodite tying her sandal of which another small, marble variant is in a wall case. There is also a small replica of Praxiteles' famous *Knidian Aphrodite,* the first Greek sculptural representation of a female nude. Our copy comes from Syria (ex-collection de Clerq) and has still some traces of the original polychromy.

The small alabaster *Getty Venus* tying a fillet around her head (illus.) may be an original from the first century B.C. and shows an extremely sensual treatment of the surfaces. The most impressive items in the gallery are several images of the *Crouching Aphrodite.* An exact replica of the statue usually associated with the Hellenistic sculptor Doidalsas (mid-third century) is in the middle of the room (ex-collections Admiral Lord Anson and Sir Francis Cook). The Aphrodite is carved fully in the round and can be admired from all sides. The voluptuous goddess is interrupted by her divine son Eros in the middle of her toilette. A later variant of the same motif probably from a Roman villa of the second century A.D. is a virtuoso composition executed exclusively for a frontal view, with much of its sensuous appeal derived from the unsurpassed treatment of the marble. The high polish of the flesh contrasted originally with the gilding of the hair. Other variants of the same

subject are in the wall case: one is a small, graceful terracotta of the first century B.C. from Asia Minor and another is a crystal torso (illus.) carved probably in the early imperial period.

The cases house other specimens of minor arts, predominantly objects associated with Aphrodite. There is a rather coarse late first century B.C. terracotta replica of the famous Aphrodite in transparent "wet" drapery, carved in the late fifth century B.C. by Kallimachos, a modeling which emphasizes the forms of the female body. In another case is an extraordinary rare wooden statuette of about 300 B.C. of a nude girl jumping.

There are several bronze statuettes of Aphrodite. One is a small head inspired by Praxiteles' *Knidian Aphrodite,* with an original gold and pearl earring. A charming group shows the goddess punishing her disobedient son. Another statuette with silver eyes reproduces an image of a goddess from the end of the fifth century B.C. Other small bronzes displayed here include a nude youth holding a ram's head, Jason or Phrixos which is a glamorous Greek original probably from about A.D. 100 (illus.) It is a good illustration of the monumentality of Greek art, an effect which comes

The Getty Venus
Alabaster statuette on
limestone base
ca. 50 B.C.

Crouching Aphrodite
Rock crystal statuette,
late first century B.C.

not from absolute size but rather from
the ability to convey a sense of great-
ness. The other youth is a Dionysos from
Alexandria (second century B.C.).

The large tripartite showcase is dominated by a limestone relief of two war-
riors, which originally decorated a
funerary monument, possibly in Sicily.
It still bears traces of polychromy (end
of fourth century B.C.). Around it, the
small limestone herms, combining the

Head of Alexander the Great
Marble
ca. 310 B.C.

heads of a bearded and a female divinity, date from the fourth century B.C. and are from Selinus in Sicily at the time of the Carthaginian occupation of this Greek city and may depict Baalshamin and Tanit, Punic counterparts of Zeus Meilichios and Kore.

GALLERY 108:
GREEK MASTERPIECES

The next gallery houses the master-pieces of Greek sculpture in the museum.

A prestigious ensemble of five marble heads from the late fourth century stands in one corner. They have virtually no rival in any other American collection. From the execution and material it is clear that the five pieces belong together. They must have been part of the sculptural decoration for some memorial dating from the end of the fourth century B.C. involving Alexander the Great. The head of Alexander (illus.), shown in the handsome bloom of youth, is perhaps the finest of the group. The other man, whose face is less imposing, is Alexander's friend Hephaistion. There is also a female head with melon-shaped hairstyle and a fragmentary head of a flute player whose double flute was attached with two pins to his lips with his cheeks distended by playing. The fifth piece is the head of a lion. There are also some twenty-five fragments of the original group in a case to the side. The workmanship without being extremely detailed or elaborate is very powerful, showing the heroic ethos proper to the end of the classical age. A veiled head of a mourning girl (illus.) was found with these fragments in a late antique cache, but her delicate modeling and emo-

tional expressiveness point to a slightly later date towards the end of the second century B.C. A small statuette of Alexander, originally holding a lance, stands nearby; it is a Hellenistic, perhaps second century, creation after a Lysippan original.

Some other important originals are in the other case. A head of a youth (illus.) is associated with the workshop which carved the sculptural decorations of the Parthenon in the third quarter of the fifth century. A bearded head, perhaps Poseidon, may come from a pediment of his temple at Cape Sounion. The head of an Amazon is from a metope of Hera's temple not far from Argos dating from the end of the fifth century. Near her is a head of a goddess from South Italy, about 440–430. Another delightful head of a girl from the Athenian acropolis of

Head of a mourning girl
Marble
ca. 120 B.C.

21

Youth taming a horse
The so-called Cottenham relief
Attic votive marble
ca. 500 B.C.

c. 500 B.C. shows traces of the fire when the Persians burned the city in 480 B.C. From the same sanctuary is a fragment of a horsehead (about 540 B.C.).

Three fine reliefs belong to the very end of the Archaic tradition. The *Cottenham Relief* (illus.) is an Attic votive marble relief from about 500 B.C. representing a beautiful youth taming a young horse. A slightly later relief comes from the island of Thasos (early fifth century B.C.); what remains shows two girls making offerings to a cult image of a goddess seated in a niche. The third relief fragment is later in date. It was carved

in Athens before the middle of the fifth century and shows a runner in armor.

Above the reliefs, three lion's head waterspouts are fixed upon the wall. The largest one is a first century B.C. replacement for an original of a Greek temple of the fifth century B.C. The least well preserved one dates from the fourth century. Both are in marble. The third is in limestone and preserves a good part of the architectural slab. It dates from the late sixth century B.C.

The *Elgin Kore* (illus.) (*kore,* ancient Greek for "girl") is perhaps the finest marble statue in the collection. The sculpture is an original work of about 470 B.C. Its artistic merits are especially evident in comparison to the similar statue of black marble standing in the Hall of Aphrodite. Under an apparent simplicity, the drapery gives an illusion of softness and of movement. From the same collection of the famous English earl comes the so-called *Elgin Throne,* brought to Scotland from Athens in 1817. It may have been carved at the very end of the fourth century in Athens for Demetrios Poliorketes, acclaimed as the liberator of Athens. Thus, on one side, its relief shows the famous early fifth century sculpture group of the *Tyrant Slayers;* on the other, a fourth century statue of *Theseus* (legendary king of Athens) *Slaying the Queen of the Amazons* who supposedly conquered even the Acropolis. Thus two legendary events and two famous monuments are combined to flatter the later "liberator" of the city.

In the center of the room is a fragmentary Attic grave relief from about 520 B.C. (illus.). Two nude youths bend slightly toward each other. The left holds a rolled piece of cloth in his right hand and fastens it as a bandage around the head of the other who is collapsing, his closed eyes indicating imminent death. But the youth keeps smiling, which in archaic art expressed a denial of death; indeed, his passing is interpreted as heroization. The carving is sublime.

Youth bandaging the head
of a dying comrade
Attic marble funerary relief
ca. 520 B.C.

Next to the Elgin throne is the de Bry head (illus.), belonging to Achilles, the central figure from the west pediment of the temple of Athena Alea in Tegea in the central Peloponnesus. After having defeated his adversary, Achilles was looking up to the gods and possibly to Nike who had given him victory. A statue of her probably stood as an akroterion on the temple. Through Pausanias, the second century A.D. guide to Greece, we know that Skopas was in charge of the temple construction. As the carving of our head is much finer than that of most surviving remnants from the site, we must have here an example of the famous mid-fourth century B.C. sculptor at work.

In the corner next to the Skopas head is a Hellenistic marble variant (first half of the second century B.C.) of the famous bronze statue of the *Diadoumenos* which was cast by Polykleitos before 430 B.C.

GALLERY 109:
STUDY COLLECTION

The little room next to the Masterpieces gallery contains provincial Hellenistic (third to first century B.C.) reliefs from Asia Minor, mostly funerary, and Roman reliefs (first to sixth century

Head of Achilles by Skopas
The so-called de Bry head
from the West pediment of
the temple of Athena Alea at Tegea
ca. 350 B.C.

A.D.) from different parts of the Roman Empire. Two tombstones are from Thrace, one from Greece, and two from Asia Minor. The set is completed by an Early Christian Coptic limestone relief from Egypt. Above is a Roman fresco with a frieze of dolphins and swans of the first century A.D.

PASSAGE

Between the hall of Aphrodite and the Atrium, opposite three decorative sculptures, a large case contains other bronzes, including two hydriae used as funerary containers for ashes. One with a female bust above the handle dates ca. 460 B.C.; the other depicts Athena slaying a Giant and is from 350–325 B.C.

GALLERY 110:
ATRIUM

This hall reproduces what would be the atrium or central room in a Roman villa. Several sculptures deserve attention. Near the entrance from the inner peristyle stands a herm as he would have been found in Greek and Roman houses, protecting the doorway. It is a Roman creation in the classical Greek spirit. Above the central basin is a little boy holding a bunch of grapes who must have once decorated a luxurious Roman villa (illus.). His workmanship is similar to that of a neighboring headless statue of Artemis, a reduced version of a fourth century original.

Roman portraits are a strong point in the museum collection and some of them

Boy with grapes
Marble
ca. A.D. 130

are temporarily displayed in the Atrium. While Greek portraits were intended as public monuments, Roman portraits were from the very beginning of a private nature, a quality which brings them close to the modern viewer, giving the illusion of "real people." In their original function, they constituted a kind of family gallery, justifying the inherited claims of the Roman nobility. Portraits of emperors were objects of religious cults presenting the ruler and his family as the protectors of the whole empire. Two fragmentary statues of women from the late first century A.D. were carved by the same workshop, and this common source accounts for the similarity between the two faces. A priest of Sarapis, identified by his star diadem on which traces of original gilding remain, is from third century A.D. Egypt. There is also an impressive bust of the empress Sabina, the wife of the emperor Hadrian. The finest portrait may represent Antonia, daughter of Mark Antony (illus.). The classic style favored in early imperial art moderates a vigorous rendering of individual features, resulting in a harmonious image of a young Roman matron aware of the obligations imposed on her by her rank.

In the tablinum, the passage towards the west porch, are some additional Roman portraits; the most impressive of them is a bust of a bearded aging African man with such an expressive face that one might guess he was an actor (illus.). In the middle stands a great marble vase that once decorated the Villa of the emperor Hadrian. It is carved with Erotes harvesting grapes. Most of the vase is a neoclassical but appropriate restoration

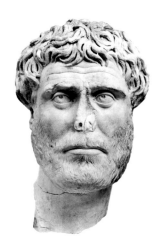

from the end of the eighteenth century designed by J. B. Piranesi. It was loaned to the museum by the Los Angeles County Museum of Art (a Hearst gift), as were the two over life-size statues in the opposite wings of the atrium. Both were found in Ostia late in the eighteenth century and belonged to the Hope collection in England. The *Athena Hope* is a very good replica of an original from the late fifth century B.C. attributed to Agorakritos, a pupil of Pheidias, while the *Hygieia,* of more sophisticated stance, reproduces a statue from the fourth cen-

tury. An artistically superior replica of Hygieia's head stands near the alcove.

Four rooms along the sides of the atrium display frescoes and some small objects from the first centuries B.C. and A.D. In the first cubiculum (113) is a set of black frescoes from an unidentified villa of the first century A.D., together with another set of panels also with painted architectonic elements.

The cubiculum opposite (111) displays a set of bronze vases from the Villa of Popidius Florus at Boscoreale. The small frescoes mounted in the same room include representations of Erotes making flower wreaths and perfumes. Another gives a view of a Nilotic landscape (illus.) with a large villa in the background and a pygmy on a raft menaced by a crocodile.

Portrait bust of Antonia
Marble
ca. A.D. 10

Portrait of a
bearded Roman
Marble
ca. A.D. 250

Nilotic landscape
Roman wall painting
ca. A.D. 70

In the center case there is a piggy bank in the form of a bronze statuette of a beggar girl. A splendid set of silver vases dominates this case: two spherical cups with Erotes and garlands (illus.), another with two Erotes as musicians, a ladle and a jug with a bust of Dionysos must have been executed in the same workshop in Alexandria about 75 B.C. These were found in a grave along with another silver vessel, a gold seal ring with an

engraved stone representing the head of the Polykleitan Doryphoros (illus.) and a funerary diadem cut for the dead man from a thin gold sheet. In the dead man's mouth was placed a gold coin of Mark Antony (31 B.C.); a plastic cast of it is on the same shelf.

In the third cubicle (112) are three black panels from Popidius' villa, one of them depicting an imitation of a painting hung on the wall, representing a woman attending a seated philosopher. (The fourth and best panel from the same room is now in the Virginia Museum of Fine Art, Richmond.) The floor is an original Roman mosaic with the head of Medusa from the second century A.D. A large white-ground fresco of another origin depicts a kitchen scene with rustic vigor; particularly successful is the reproduction of two silver vessels (illus.).

In the last cubicle (114), white walls with small panels containing landscapes and still lifes form a bedroom of the same villa from Boscoreale. The left wall is a reconstruction conforming to the origi-

nal appearance of the room. There are three unfinished ancient sculptures, giving an important insight into ancient carving techniques. In the case opposite them are displayed specimens of Roman glass and some minor sculptures.

PASSAGE
Various terracottas are displayed in the wall case opposite, including two different figures of a drunken old woman and a head of a goddess. Particularly notable is a set of ancient terracotta molds used by the Greeks of what is now modern Taranto in South Italy from the sixth to the fourth century B.C. to produce terracotta figures.

Erotes in garlands
Silver cup
ca. 70 B.C.

Head of Polykleitan Doryphoros
Incised in agate in a gold ring
ca. 70 B.C.

GALLERY 116:
CLASSICAL AND HELLENISTIC SCULPTURE

The most imposing statue in the next gallery is the seated Zeus from Marbury Hall (illus.), a dramatic representation of the father of gods and mortals, reproducing a famous carved cult image which must have been made in the early second century B.C., probably in Pergamon. A really colossal head of Zeus on the opposite wall was part of an impressive cult statue, dating from the late Hellenistic period.

The *Lansdowne Artemis* is on loan from the Los Angeles County Museum of Art, formerly in the Hearst collection. It reproduces an early fourth century Greek statue. The head, which was added in the eighteenth century and removed by our

conservation department, belongs to an Apollo after an original by Kephisodotos, the father of the famous Praxiteles. The nearby head of the Praxitelean *Resting Satyr* is a remarkably well preserved second century A.D. replica, yet the virtuoso carving suggests little of Praxiteles' art.

In the next corner, the most remarkable statue is a late Hellenistic original that represents the youngest son of Niobe falling on his knees as he clutches at the arrow with which Apollo struck him. The modeling is rich and beautiful. Close to him stands a Roman copy of a female figure which may have belonged to a similar group of Niobe's children. A head of Apollo, probably after a late fourth century prototype by Leochares and universally known and admired since the eighteenth century under the name *Apollo Belvedere,* completes the group.

Another famous Hellenistic statuary group consisted of Achilles lifting the dying Penthesilea, the Queen of the Amazons. We have an impressive copy of Achilles' head. The head of Penthesilea from the same copy of this group is in the Basel Museum, Switzerland, where the whole group has been successfully reconstructed from casts of parts dispersed all over the world.

A later Hellenistic statuette presents a satyr in a pose comparable to that of the hanging Marsyas (illus.). This figure was not, however, meant to be actually hanging but served instead as a decorative support for a table or whatever he held above his head.

In the middle of the room is a big marble bear, an appropriate decoration for a Roman villa from the end of the first century A.D. and thus contemporary with our villa. Close by is a marble athlete who was pouring oil from his raised right hand into his left palm. It is a Roman replica after a bronze original by Lysippos, a work of his early career.

Another copy after Lysippos is the next athlete, formerly in the Hearst collection and lent by the Los Angeles County Museum of Art. It is very like Lysippos' famous *Scraper/Apoxyomenos*, showing that the master approached the subject for the first time early in his career. A fragmentary replica of the same statue is in Athens.

Behind both athletes is a small set of

Marbury Hall Zeus
Roman copy after an
original of ca. 180 B.C.

Head of Marsyas
Detail of a marble
furniture support
first century B.C.

Greek and Latin inscriptions. The first one is a decree from the end of the first century B.C., probably from Asia Minor, rewarding a meritorious citizen with honors. Above it is a versified funerary inscription for a nineteen year old youth from the early third century A.D. from Egypt. Next comes statutes and by-laws of an Athenian professional association from about A.D. 100. Under it is a Sicilian funerary inscription from the fifth century B.C. Next to it stands an early fifth century B.C. calendar of festivals and sacrifices taking place in Thorikos on the east coast of Attica. A relief from Asia Minor with a rhetorical funerary text stands in the corner. Three Latin funerary inscriptions are under the window.

Next to the entrance door, three different replicas of the *Ares Ludovisi* show the variety of Roman craftsmanship in copying a famous original, attributed by some archaeologists to Lysippos. The whole statue appears in the *Portrait of John Chetwynd* painted by Pompeo Batoni displayed in the Baroque Painting Gallery (209) (and illus. p. 76 above) upstairs. Since the Hellenistic period this head had been used for various statues, including those of draped men and nude heroes. Our replicas include one on a prismatic base, called a herm, which retains most of its Hellenic vigor. Another, simple head is badly battered but still presents very elegant and rich modeling while showing a slightly academic interpretation, perhaps an idealized portrait. The third, from a standing statue clad in a mantle, is a correct and dry variation with some personal elements in the physiognomy; a portrait was intended.

GALLERY 115: ATTIC MEMORIAL SCULPTURE

The next room contains Attic funerary monuments from the end of the sixth to the end of the fourth centuries B.C. At the end of the fifth century B.C. in Athens, the custom of putting sculptured tombstones on family graves came into fashion again. They were mass-produced, resulting in many good reliefs but with only a few masterpieces. Nevertheless, all of them including the modest examples have the freshness of Greek originals. They breathe an atmosphere of delicate notalgia, underlain by the firm ties of kinship which continue to link the deceased with the living.

Several forms are common. The most usual is a stele, a marble slab, frequently surmounted by a triangular pediment supported by two pilasters. In the field between the two pilasters was a relief or a painting and above it an inscription. The reliefs vary from virtually flat figures to ones that are almost in the round. Free-standing funerary statues are much rarer. The museum has one head which surely belonged to such a monument. Sometimes a marble vase, usually a lekythos, was used as a grave marker. Two such lekythoi are on display. A more elaborate type of vase, a loutrophoros, frequently served as the monument over the grave of an unmarried person. Additional figures, including animals, usually lions, sometimes served as guardians for the grave. Sirens and doves were occasionally used to emphasize the mood of grief.

The Getty Museum collection of Attic memorials is particularly rich and of high quality. Special mention should be made of two pieces which were once in the collection of Lord Elgin. One shows the mother Nikomache mourning her daughter Theogenis and her son Nikodemos. Here the modest craftsman has taken the unusual step of indicating, if only slightly, the advanced age of the mother. The monument dates from the third quarter of the fourth century. The stele of Myttion (illus.), ex-collection Elgin, from the very first years of the fourth century, depicts a young girl wearing a special kind of coat. The name of the deceased and additional decoration including her rolled shroud are painted on the top. A heraldic lion, from the end of the fourth century, was in the nineteenth century in the Van Branteghem collection in Belgium.

Perhaps the best piece is a poorly preserved stele showing a seated woman holding a box of toilet articles and attended by her standing servant. The delicate rendering of the figures, including their drapery, is perfectly suited to the noble and discreet atmosphere of mourning which the artist creates. The upper portion of the servant is a plaster cast from the original fragment now in the Paul Kanellopoulos Museum, Athens.

The magnificent head of a girl near the right window, carved separately for insertion in a big funerary relief, must have been fashioned by a sculptor very close to the school of Praxiteles. Years ago Getty personally acquired this piece, and it remained a favorite of his.

In the other half of the room, three unique terracotta statues are displayed, (illus.). The two sirens, with their bird-like but wingless bodies (they lost their wings in an unsuccessful contest with the

Grave relief of Myttion
Attic marble stele
ca. 390 B.C.

Orpheus and the Sirens
Terracotta funerary group
end of the fourth century B.C.

Muses) stop singing to listen to the legendary musician Orpheus. The lyre which he held on his lap is now missing. Traces of original polychromy are preserved. Orpheus, by his song, rescued his shipmates from the sirens on the expedition after the Golden Fleece and later tried to rescue his wife Eurydice from Hades; the whole group expresses hope for afterlife and must have been made for the subterranean tomb of a Greek in South Italy at the very end of the fourth century B.C.

A small late fourth century gold sheet, with six lines of engraved text of a prayer, is a unique document of an unofficial trend of Greek religion. It accompanied the ashes of a dead man, and the text gives the answer he has to say to his judges:

"Parched with thirst am I and dying."
"Nay, drink of Me, the ever-flowing spring
Where on the right is a fair cypress."
"Who art thou? where art thou?" –
"I am the son
of Earth and star-filled Heaven,
But from Heaven alone is my house."

Two vases complete the Orpheus display. One, a large, pompous krater decorated in southern Italy 340–330 B.C., represents Orpheus performing before Hades and Persephone in his attempt to rescue his wife from the kingdom of shadow. On the other, an Attic calyx krater from the middle of the fifth century, tattooed Thracian women are mercilessly killing Orpheus.

On the opposite wall, next to the window, stands a Klazomenian painted sarcophagus done in western Asia Minor around 480 B.C.

GALLERY 117:
THE ROOM OF COLORED MARBLES

This gallery contains cases for changing displays. On the walls in between are Roman bronze portrait heads, including Lucius Verus, co-emperor of Marcus Aurelius from 161 to 169, a probable head of the emperor Gordianus III, 235–238, on loan from Mr. Hans Cohn, and especially a Roman general from the early first century B.C., possibly L. Cornelius Sulla (illus.). His appearance reflects the aspiration to power and ruthless confidence of the dictator.

A bronze head of an athlete and both feet of the nude statue belong to a torso

L. Cornelius Sulla (?)
Bronze
ca. 90 B.C.

35

in Burdur, Turkey. The whole statue is reconstructed in a modern cast that is displayed in the little temple to the southeast of the elevator entrance to the museum's main garden.

GALLERY 118:
BASILICA
Two bronze portrait statues of youths flank the entrance. The first one, with silver eyes, dates from the second century A.D. and is an anonymous loan. The bronze herm is a first century B.C. cast reproducing a slightly earlier work by Boethos from Chalkedon now preserved in the Bardo Museum in Tunis.

The room is dominated by the *Getty Bronze* (illus. p. 16). The youth has just placed an olive crown on his head; thus he has just won an athletic competition at Olympia. Statues of Olympic victors were erected not only in Olympia itself but also in the native city of the athlete or even in other places, especially religious centers. The easy stance covers an inner tension. He is no longer a boy but not yet a fully mature man. The face shows individual features, and the subject may be a young prince from one of the dynasties established immediately after the death of Alexander the Great. Thus the piece could have been erected in any Greek city just before the end of the fourth century. Besides this, the youth does not conform any longer to the traditional modesty of a young citizen victorious in athletic games but reveals a self-conscious pride on the spiritual model of Alexander himself. It results in the overwhelming presence of a hero who is, in spite of his youth, equal to the gods. In later times, probably in the first cen-

turies of our era, the bronze must have been carried away by Roman collectors on a ship, as it was found in the sea. The style points indisputably to Lysippos, court sculptor of Alexander the Great, who is said to have made over 1500 sculptures. Some of these have been recognized in marble replicas, but the *Getty Bronze* may be the only original to survive. If not by the master himself, the bronze conveys an adequate idea of Lysippos' superb art. The plastic box is necessary to protect the delicate metal from the disastrous effects of humidity.

GALLERY 119:
ETRUSCAN VESTIBULE
This room contains a small selection of Etruscan objects and monuments. Most of them are concentrated in the showcases. These include two bronze helmets and a cuirass found together and dating from the early fifth century B.C.; some terracottas, including an anatomical model used as an ex-voto by an ailing Etruscan; and bronze vessels.

Two bronze statuettes deserve special mention: an exquisite Etruscan figure of Zeus from about 460 B.C. and an archer from Sardinia (illus.) which could be taken for a work of modern art because of its surprising stylization (about 600 B.C.)

Two alabaster urns from the second century B.C. are displayed next to the case. On the first are scenes taken from ancient mythology. This urn is one of the rare instances in ancient sculpture where copious remnants of the original polychromy are still preserved. Only the lid of the second urn survives: it bears a

GALLERY 120: TEMPLE OF HERAKLES

The room itself reproduces a subterranean temple of Herakles in Palestrina, south of Rome. The showcase in the passage leading into the domed hall contains several Herakles statuettes, including two Etruscan, later Hellenistic and Roman examples, and one tiny ivory reproduction of a Lysippan original of Herakles with the apples of the Hesperides. The same statue is also represented with some variations in a pleasant sixteenth century North Italian figure intended as a close imitation of an antique – to the inclusion of artificial breaks. Another marble statuette is a Roman variant of the same type.

Perhaps the most famous piece in our collection, and one to which Mr. Getty devoted some particularly touching pages in his own writings, is the *Lansdowne Herakles* (illus.) found in the Villa of the emperor Hadrian at Tivoli. The youthful hero is shown with his lion skin, the club resting against his left shoulder. It is inspired by a Herakles carved by Skopas around the middle of the fourth century B.C.

Herakles was not only an exemplar of human achievement, he was also the subject of philosophical commentary; he was thus an appropriate model for a Roman emperor, much as he would be for an outstanding American. The statue was restored in early 1977 by Zdravko Barov. Only the aesthetically necessary restorations were retained, clearly indicated in plastic. As the marble of the fragmentary ancient base and feet is weak, the statue is now supported by a stainless steel rod through the eighteenth

reclining male figure with his name inscribed below. The lid of a third urn, with a reclining figure carved in limestone, is on the opposite wall. Next to it is a terracotta slab painted with two heraldic sphinxes dating about 530.

On the other side of the room there are Etruscan sculptures dating from the late sixth century B.C.

Chieftain of yeomen
Sardinian bronze statuette
ca. 600 B.C.

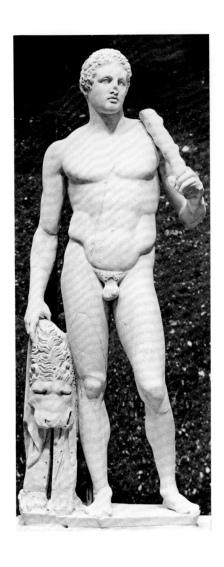

Herakles Lansdowne
Roman marble statue
after Skopas

century restoration holes in the base and right buttock.

Besides the *Lansdowne Herakles,* there are two other statues of the hero in the room. One, from the Hope collection (on loan from the Los Angeles County Museum of Art, Hearst collection), may be a poor but faithful reproduction of another Skopas Herakles. The other is a second century A.D. imitation of the Classical style of the fifth century B.C.

GALLERY 121: MOSAIC GALLERY

Between the Temple of Herakles and the Mosaic Gallery is a small corridor. Several examples of Roman minor arts are displayed in the showcase on the left. Two bronze heads of aquatic birds were made as terminals for furniture or construction beams. The bronze mask dates from the second century A.D. A set of lead fish (second century A.D.), possibly votive offerings from a fisherman, give an interesting insight on maritime fauna of the Eastern Mediterranean in Roman times. We are told by an ichthyologist that many species are represented, some of them now extinct. A military diploma from the reign of the emperor Domitian, giving an honorable discharge from the army with due rewards including citizenship, with the date November 7, A.D. 88, is engraved on two sheets of bronze.

On the front wall of the Mosaic Gallery is an impressive bronze eagle, the official insignia of Roman military power, dating probably from the third century A.D. Standing slightly in front of it is an over life-size portrait of Julius Caesar (100–44 B.C.), probably an early second century copy of an image of the man who was considered the founder of the Roman Empire. On one side of the Getty Caesar are two other images of the same man. One (illus.), formerly in the collection Blücher (the family of the victor at Waterloo), is a posthumous image probably based on Caesar's death mask. Like the colossal Getty Caesar, this head was originally covered by the toga of the statue in which it was inserted. Two small circular holes on the forehead prove that the piece was produced by the three-point technique, confirming, if necessary, that this is a mass-produced image of a very famous man. The third portrait head of Caesar was presented to the museum by Gordon McLendon and reflects the noble image of the father-founder of the Roman Empire current under his immediate successors.

On the far left stands a torso from an imperial cuirassed statue of the late first century A.D. A headless statue of a Roman woman from the early third century stands in the right corner. It was formerly in the Palazzo Sciarra in Rome; at that time it still had its original head which has since been lost.

On the adjoining long wall are an ornamental frieze and two reliefs of African elephants – all of which originally belonged to the same building from the end of the first century A.D. On the floor in front of the heads is a large mosaic on which hunters flush a group of bears into nets. A beautiful floral pattern frames the whole. The mosaic is surely from North Africa and dates from the third century A.D.

Two portrait statues stand next to each other to the right of the reliefs. One from

the mid-second century A.D. represents the empress Faustina the Elder, wife of Antoninus Pius. A seated statue known since the sixteenth century when it was in the Mattei collection in Rome represents Cybele, mother of the gods, with a lion at her side. The head, however, is manifestly a portrait of a specific Roman matron of the second quarter of the first century A.D. (illus.). She must have been a priestess of Cybele, and the type of the goddess was thus used to bear her portrait, a common practice in Roman portraiture.

Blücher Caesar
Marble
late first century B.C.

In the smaller side of the room, under a canopy, is a third century A.D. mosaic from Gaul depicting Orpheus and the beasts. At its corners stand four marble muses from Kremna in southwestern Asia Minor. They date from the early third century. The finest of them, Polyhymnia, is on loan to us from the private collection of Hans Cohn. Against

the wall, at the head of the mosaic, stands a small marble statue of the Good Shepherd from the end of the third century A.D.

Four other mosaics hang on the wall. One with a scene of Achilles and Briseis, is a later Roman variant of a Hellenistic painting (detail illus.). Formerly in the Hearst collection, the second, with two boxers and a bull, represents a scene from Virgil's *Aeneid.* It probably dates to the late second century.

To the left of the Achilles mosaic is a late Republican marble funerary relief from the very end of the first century B.C. and a marble funerary slab for a dog named Helena. On the opposite side of the mosaic is a second century A.D. limestone funerary monument for two Syrian brothers. Below them is a fragmentary triangular marble base representing a procession with a statue of Dionysus borne on a chariot dating from the first century B.C.

Near the exit is an attractive portrait of an unknown Roman lady from the second quarter of the second century.

Finally, on the wall, is a mosaic from Carthage depicting a lion attacking a donkey from the second century A.D. and a marble medallion with the portrait of the emperor Caracalla as heir apparent from the end of the same century. There is also a grave relief of Agrippina, a little girl three years old.

GALLERY 123:
Next to the East Vestibule is a room for temporary exhibitions. From 1981, it will be occupied by the Walter Bareiss collection of Greek vases lent by the owner to the museum.

Priestess of Cybele
Marble
ca. A.D. 50

40

GALLERY 124:
EAST VESTIBULE

Several sculptures reproducing Greek originals of the fifth century are here on display. In the middle of the gallery there is an impressive bust of Athena, formerly in the Lansdowne collection, on loan from the Los Angeles County Museum of Art (Hearst gift). The bust is actually cut from a complete colossal statue reproducing the prototype called the *Athena Velletri,* attributed to Kresilas. Only the head and right third of the bust are ancient. The remainder was restored in the eighteenth century by Bartolomeo Cavaceppi, a late eighteenth century Italian sculptor and highly reputed restorer and imitator, to say the least, of antiquity.

A male torso was inspired by the statuary art of Polykleitos; the original from the late fifth century must have been bronze. It is reminiscent of the famous *Doryphoros* by the master himself. A ruined head of his *Herakles* is also on display. Two statues reproduce the so-called *Narcissus,* a work of the school of Polykleitos at the end of the fifth century. One is a direct copy; the other, much recut in modern times, wears a Phrygian cap and is a Roman adaptation, making the original figure into a statue of Ganymede, the cupbearer of Zeus.

Talthybios,
herald of Agamemnon
Detail of a mosaic
with Achilles and Briseis
ca. A.D. 150

A torso of the satyr Marsyas (illus.), a marble replica of the bronze original by Myron (about 150 B.C.), stands nearby. The satyr is depicted in violent movement – in the act of catching the flute thrown away by the goddess Athena after she invented it. A winged head of Hermes has been traditionally also associated with Myron, but it seems that the original, from the third quarter of the fifth century, was done by another less well known artist of this period. Even though all of these sculptures are copies, they give us at least an idea of the great masterpieces of the fifth century.

UPPER LEVEL GALLERIES

GALLERY 201:
VESTIBULE
The front section of a sarcophagus of the third quarter of the second century A.D. is mounted on the wall facing the elevator. It bears a frieze of garlands and masks, of which the central mask is a head of Gorgon.

GALLERY 229:
MUMMY PORTRAITS
This small passage displays painted wood panels dating from the second to third centuries A.D. (illus.). Beginning in the first century A.D., the Egyptians under Roman rule abandoned their ancient custom of affixing a gilt mask over the faces of their mummies. They replaced those masks with either painted stucco – one such mask is displayed here – or, more frequently, by a painted wood panel set into the wrappings of the mummy and bearing an image of the deceased. To some extent, these images were intended

Torso of the satyr Marsyas
Marble replica of ca. 50 B.C.
of Myron's original
of the fourth century B.C.

Mummy portrait of a boy
Encaustic on panel
ca. A.D. 150

as real portraits of the dead person, sometimes painted long before death. Beginning in the third century, especially toward its end, ready-made paintings with only a superficial resemblance to the deceased became common.

Three of the panels, form a unique ensemble painted about A.D. 230. They are painted in tempera, which began to replace the encaustic technique of heated wax as a medium for the colors in the third century. They are from a box, on the interior panel of which was a portrait of a bearded man. This portrait, which was never actually affixed to the mummy, seems to have served as a kind

Portrait head of Aristotle
Second century A.D.
copy in Haurân basalt

of ancestral image for a family shrine. The two other panels depict the Egyptian gods Isis and Sarapis in the style of Greek art. They probably reproduce a venerated monumental painting of the two divinities dating from around A.D. 200. Here they served as the lids of the box, covering the portrait.

GALLERY 207: GREEK PORTRAITS

While every Roman tried to have portraits of his ancestors for display in his home, Greek portraits were of famous men and were designed for public display. They therefore emphasized the subject's individual characteristics less than his role in society. Because they were designed to be public monuments and were often placed outdoors, Greek portraits were always full-figure statues. Most of those that have survived are Roman copies in which the copyist has adopted the Roman custom of retaining only the head, usually attaching it to a primatic base or herm.

In the middle of the room there is a double herm. It combines portraits of Plato (original from the mid-fourth century B.C.) and his pupil Aristotle – (original from the end of the fourth century). Nearby are another replica of Plato from the very late antiquity and a copy of Artistotle's portrait in basaltic stone from Syria (illus.). Identified portraits of famous men in this room include the historian Thucydides, after an original of the mid-fourth century B.C.; the Athenian statesman Demosthenes, after an original of 280 B.C.; a Stoic philosopher, Zeno; and two Cynic philosophers: Diogenes, original probably dated to the late third century B.C., and Krates, from a late fourth century B.C. prototype.

There are also images of three helmeted Athenian generals (*strategoi*). The original of the first was done by Pheidias about the middle of the fifth century B.C.; it represents Xanthippos, father of Perikles. The second, only the face of which is preserved, is contemporary with Demosthenes from the beginning of the third century; it may be Phokion. The third remains unknown.

There is also an original, colossal third century portrait of Ptolemy II. After the king's death, the areas adjacent to the forehead were slightly cut down and two deep cavities produced. To emphasize the king's military glory, a helmet in the shape of an elephant's head was put over the head, with the holes supporting the tusks. Several other Ptolemaic portraits, including two small heads of his successor Ptolemy III, a very beautiful unidentified youth and an original fourth-century bearded head are in a case.

In the small case is a small bronze bust (illus.). The face of this famous Greek is known from countless life-size Roman copies in marble, two of them on display nearby. The man must have been well-known in ancient times, and modern scholars have worked hard to identify him. Our small bust now settles the problem: the Greek letters engraved on the base give the name MENANDROS, the Athenian poet of the late fourth century B.C. famous for entertaining comedies. The original of the portrait was created for the Athenian marketplace by Kephisodotos the Younger and Timarchos, the sons of Praxiteles.

In the same case is a terracotta male statuette of a rather caricatural appearance. The features of the face point indisputably to the philosopher Socrates, the wisest among all Greeks.

LOWER LEVEL

There are two types of material on display: mosaics which come from modern Syria and date mostly in the sixth century A.D. on the walls, and, under them, Roman sarcophagi. In ancient Rome, inhumation and cremation were parallel burial customs until the second century

Inscribed bust of Menandros
Bronze
first century B.C.
replica of an original of
ca. 270 B.C.

A.D. when inhumation prevailed. For both types of burial, wealthy Romans commissioned marble coffins. The decoration employs Greek myths, but their original meanings have been replaced by symbolic interpretations. For example, Endymion, the sleeping beloved of Selene, is the image of resurrection based on the Roman equation of sleep and death. The story is reproduced on the front of one sarcophagus from the first quarter of the third century from Rome (illus.). Some sarcophagi include portraits of the deceased; one is the fragment of a male head in a shell and another is a female bust between lions.

On the two sarcophagi decorated with Erotes and garlands, one dates from the early third century and was formerly in the Lansdowne collection, while the other, late second century, was reused in the fourth century with new funerary inscriptions added in the middle.

Hanging on the wall to the right is a relief that looks like a sarcophagus at first, but given the height of the carving and the moldings above, it seems rather to have been part of a base. The relief represents the Indian Triumph of Dionysos, but very little besides the lower part of the figures is ancient. The piece, once in the collection of the French cardinal Polignac, was heavily restored in the 1740s by the French sculptor J. Adam and offers an excellent example of eighteenth century taste in antiquities. The eighteenth and nineteenth centuries preferred complete statues, and restorers repaired and refinished sculptures to oblige collectors.

A fragmentary sculpture is part of a late second century A.D. cult image of the god Mithras.

Selene and Endymion
Detail from a Roman
marble sarcophagus
ca. A.D. 220

Warrior in a chariot race
Reverse of a Panathenaic
prize amphora
340/339 B.C.

Athena, Herakles, and Apollo
fighting for the tripod
Attic amphora
by the Troilos Painter
ca. 490 B.C.

AROUND THE CORNER: GREEK VASES

Three of the four showcases in the Room of Greek Vases contain Attic black- and red-figure vases; the fourth, Greek vases made in Southern Italy in the fourth century B.C. Vases provide us with a good illustration of Greek mythological subjects, which served to reflect scenes from everyday life. Detailed descriptions of each piece can be found on their labels, as the pieces on exhibition vary. Several of the vases displayed are on loan from the Los Angeles County Museum of Art. We might close by mentioning a silver statuette of Zeus from the first century B.C. (illus).

GARAGE

Five mosaics contemporary with the sixth century A.D. mosaics displayed in the Basement Gallery are hung at the access to the elevator from the garage. A big fifth century mosaic floor from Antioch with ornamental motifs and animals hangs on the wall of the garage.

Statuette of Zeus
Silver
first century B.C.

Rembrandt van Rijn
(1606–1669)
Bust of an Old Man
ca. 1631
Oil on panel, 66 x 51 cm.

Paintings

INTRODUCTION

Although all major schools of Western Art from the late thirteenth to the early twentieth centuries are represented in the paintings collection, the main emphasis lies in the area of Renaissance and Baroque art, a period spanning the fifteenth to the eighteenth centuries. Mr. Getty's original collection concentrated primarily on Italian paintings of the sixteenth century – the High Renaissance – and Netherlandish – that is, Dutch and Flemish – works of the seventeenth century. The present collection has been developed so that excellent examples can now be seen from all areas of the Renaissance and Baroque.

GALLERY 201:
VESTIBULE

On the ceiling of this room is *Allegory of Divine Knowledge and the Fine Arts* by Paolo de'Matteis (1662–1728), a Neapolitan Baroque artist who was a follower of Luca Giordano. Signed and dated 168?, the painting was originally on the ceiling of the library of SS. Girolamo e Francesco Saverio, a Jesuit church in Genoa. The artist, like his teacher, was said to have been a very rapid painter and supposedly completed this canvas in only five days.

GALLERY 202:
DUTCH PAINTINGS

The paintings in this gallery are from the Netherlands, a small group of provinces including Holland, which in the seventeenth century separated from the Catholic provinces (modern Belgium) to the south. The majority of the population became Protestant, and the volume of

Rembrandt van Rijn
(1606–1669)
St. Bartholomew
1661
Oil on canvas, 86.5 x 75.5 cm.

secular paintings reflects the Calvinist desire to remove religious imagery from places of worship. Landscapes were especially popular, as were still lifes, portraits, and genre subjects (everyday scenes). Many artists still painted religious subjects, but they were made for private use. Paintings could be found in every prosperous household, and this demand was met by hundreds of artists, an astonishingly high number considering the size of the country.

Some of the earliest works from this period are from Utrecht, a city with strong Catholic traditions which still had ties with Italy and the papacy. Most of the artists from Utrecht studied in Italy, and among Dutch schools their style remained closest to that of the Italians. The ceiling painting of *Musicians on a Balcony* by Gerrit van Honthorst (1590–1656) is a good example of the work produced in Utrecht and shows a typically Italian flavor. It was painted in 1622 and is the earliest known illusionistic ceiling from northern Europe, but its inspiration was from Rome where the artist lived until 1620.

The greatest and most well-known of the Dutch artists, Rembrandt van Rijn (1606–1669), is represented by two paintings. The earlier is a *Portrait of an old Man* which was done about 1631 when the artist was still in his mid twenties (illus.). Rembrandt's early works are typified by a dramatic lighting and an intensity that slowly mellows in the course of his career. In this portrait he characteristically throws the light on one side of the sitter's face focusing attention on one frowning eye. The sitter also wears a hat with a feather held on to it with a metal chain and a neck plate from a set of military armor. Such details are meant probably to give a variety of textural surfaces and at the same time to enliven an otherwise simple composition. The sitter has sometimes been thought to have been Rembrandt's father; whoever he was, he must have been close to the artist as he appears in other pictures by him. Rembrandt seems to have "dressed him up" for the pose, making him a vehicle for his youthful exercises.

The other painting by Rembrandt is the *St. Bartholomew* of 1661 (illus.). Again probably using a friend as his model, Rembrandt did not idealize his subject, and this portrait is not a sacred image in the traditional sense. However, it has a kind of melancholy and individualism reminiscent of modern paintings – one reason why Rembrandt is held in such high esteem today.

Jan Lievensz.
(1607–1674)
Eli Instructing Samuel (?)
1631
Oil on canvas, 106 x 96.5 cm.

Aert de Gelder
(1645–1727)
Banquet of Ahasuerus
ca. 1680
Oil on canvas, 112 x 142 cm.

Among his friends and followers should be mentioned Jan Lievensz. (1607–1674), who painted *Eli and Samuel* (illus.), a work very close in spirit to the young Rembrandt. Other Amsterdam artists active in his tradition include Nicolaes Maes (1634–1693), whose *Adoration of the Shepherds* was based on a Dürer engraving, and Jan Victors (1619/20–after 1676), whose *The Angel Leaving the Family of Tobit* dates from 1649. Aert de Gelder (1645–1727), one of Rembrandt's most gifted students who painted in the master's late style, is represented by two paintings, *David Receiving the Sword of Goliath from Ahimelech* and *Banquet of Ahasuerus* (illus.). Both works demonstrate his very personal

interpretation of certain biblical themes, many of which were rarely depicted in the seventeenth century.

Other pictures in the gallery indicate the varied subject matter of Dutch painting. There are two still lifes, one a moralizing *Vanitas Still Life* (illus.) by Pieter Claesz. (1596/7–1660) and the other by Willem Kalf (1619–1693) without an underlying theme. Jan Steen (1625/6–1679) illustrates a story from Aesop's fables in the *Peasant and the Satyr* (illus.), and life in the countryside is recorded in Salomon van Ruysdael's (c. 1600/03–1679) *Landscape with an Inn.*

Pieter Claesz.
(1596/97–1661)
Vanitas Still Life
1634
Oil on panel, 54 x 71.5 cm.

Jan Steen
(1625/6–1679)
The Peasant and the Satyr
Oil on canvas, 51 x 46 cm.

GALLERY 203:
FLEMISH PAINTINGS

This small room is reserved primarily for paintings produced during the fifteenth and sixteenth centuries in the southern provinces of the lowlands (the part now called Belgium and the art is called "Flemish" after the chief province, Flanders). The principal founders of the early Flemish tradition, Jan van Eyck and Robert Campin, developed an extremely sophisticated style rich in detail, color, and liturgical symbolism. This early Northern Renaissance art differed greatly from that of Italy because it contains fewer elements from Roman or pre-Christian art. However, it shared that fascination with the observation of nature, space, and perspective that characterized the Italian Renaissance. In the course of the sixteenth century, northern artists began to travel more regularly to Italy for their training, and the two traditions slowly started to merge. However, a complete affinity did not really occur until the beginning of the seventeenth century and, until then, the two styles remained distinct.

The earliest Flemish painting in the collection is *The Dream of Pope Sergius* by Rogier van der Weyden (1399/1400–1464) or possibly a very close follower (illus.). It is a companion to a painting, now in the National Gallery, London, depicting a scene from the life of St. Hubertus. Both pictures are known to have been painted about 1445 for the church of St. Gudule in Brussels. The wealth of detail that made the Flemish school so famous and that also astounded the Italian artists is particularly evident in the Getty picture. Proportion is still

Rogier van der Weyden
(1399/1400–1464)
Dream of Pope Sergius
ca. 1445
Oil on panel, 89 x 80 cm.

"medieval" in some respects, but it is obvious that the details within the picture are the result of careful observation by the artist of his surroundings.

A picture from the circle of Van der Weyden is the *Portrait of Isabella of Portugal* shown as the Persian sibyl. The sitter has been identified from other portraits which reveal her characteristic features. She was not an exceptionally beautiful woman, and the fashion of shaving her forehead has accentuated her homeliness. But one sees the craftsmanship and almost sculpture-like quality that

Attributed to the
Master of the Parlement de Paris
(active, second half of 15th century)
Crucifixion
ca. 1470–90
Oil on panel, 44 x 71 cm.

typify Van der Weyden's work, especially in her hands and the costume. The sitter does not meet our eyes and retains an imperviousness that was no doubt intentional.

Several artists were influenced by the style of Rogier van der Weyden. An anonymous painter, the Master of the Parlement de Paris, active in the second half of the fifteenth century, carried the Rogierian tradition into France. In his handling of the *Crucifixion* (illus.), the artist included events prior to and following the death of Christ. The figure types and love of narrative detail imply a keen awareness of his Flemish contemporary. The North-Netherlandish artist who painted the *Deposition* (illus.) about 1480/90 was emulating a famous composition by Van der Weyden. It was a very popular work and was copied by several artists throughout northern

Europe. In our version, there is a strong concentration on the pathos of the event as the figures are placed in a shallow space and all attention is diverted to the suffering figure of Christ. This arrangement was also translated into the medium of sculpture.

From the sixteenth century is the small but very delicate *Holy Family* by Bernaert van Orley (c. 1488–1541), one of the best artists working during this period. This painting remains free of the Italian influence that characterizes the so-called Mannerist period, during which an attempt was made to integrate Italian stylistic elements into the earlier tradition.

Somewhat later in the century is the large *Miraculous Draught of Fishes,* signed and dated July 6, 1563 by Joachim Beuckelaer (c. 1530–c. 1573). It is a panoramic example of the transition to Dutch and Flemish genre painting of the seventeenth century. It would be difficult to say whether the main theme of this picture is Christ's miracles at Galilee or the various foreground scenes of peasants. By depicting the apostles' draught of fishes alongside that of the peasants, the artist contrasts the spiritual world of the bible with the materialism of the contemporary. The biblical episodes, however, are already beginning to recede in importance.

North-Netherlandish Master
(active, late fifteenth century)
The Deposition
ca. 1480/90
Oil on panel, 99.5 x 60.5 cm.

The only seventeenth century painting in this gallery is the *Four Studies of a Negro's Head* by Anthony van Dyck (1599–1641) (illus.). Painted about 1617 from a model, these sketches are related to a slightly larger series of sketches – now in the Brussels Museum – which in turn became the model for heads in full-scale finished paintings. The same man appears in at least four such pictures. The author is sometimes thought to have been Rubens, and it is indeed often difficult to distinguish the work of these two painters.

GALLERY 205:
EARLY ITALIAN PAINTINGS

The long and unexcelled tradition of painting in Italy reached its full maturity in the fifteenth century, and as a result the century before is often seen as merely a prelude for what came afterwards. The fourteenth century repre-

Anthony van Dyck
(1599–1641)
Four Studies of a Negro's Head
ca. 1617–20
Oil on panel, 25.4 x 64.8 cm.

sents the end of the Medieval, or Gothic, style but does not demonstrate the wide-ranging ambition and worldliness of the Renaissance. Nonetheless, the art of this period shows a high degree of skill and initiative by individual artists working within the various schools. Because they were commissioned for churches, all the paintings in this gallery are religious in theme.

The present gallery contains paintings from the late thirteenth and early fifteenth centuries as well as a cross section from the fourteenth century. The most important of the early works is probably *The Arrival of St. Ursula* by Bernardo Daddi (active 1312–1344) (illus.), a Florentine who was a close follower of Giotto. This painting was the left wing of a triptych which had a Crucifixion in the center and was done for the church of S. Orsola in Florence in about 1327. It shows all of the color and experimentation that was introduced to Florentine and Tuscan art at this time by Giotto and his school as well as their still developing concern for proper scale, space, and perspective. Another very important picture from this period is the large panel by Donato d'Arezzo show-

ing scenes from the life of St. Catherine. Probably commissioned for a church or a chapel dedicated to her, this painting is an altarpiece, complete examples of which from this period are very rare.

During this time, spatial and anatomical concerns are of less importance to

Bernardo Daddi
(active 1312, died 1348)
The Arrival of St. Ursula in Cologne
ca. 1327
Tempera on panel, 60 x 63 cm.

the artist than are pleasant compositions and delicate, colorful patterns. The *Annunciation,* by an anonymous Florentine artist known as the Master of St. Verdiana, is somewhat more structural and apparently derives from the tradition of Orcagna. The idiosyncrasies of scale and perspective, however, are still very obvious. There is, nonetheless, a certain beauty in works of this kind in which the stylizations correspond to the needs of the theme and its inherent symbolism rather than to some compulsion to render every setting in realistic detail.

Gentile da Fabriano
(ca. 1370–1427)
Coronation of the Virgin
ca. 1420
Tempera and oil on panel, 87.5 x 64 cm.

The most impressive painting in the Getty Museum from this period is the exceptionally large polyptych by the Florentine artist Cenni di Francesco (active 1410–1415). The center panel depicts the *Coronation of the Virgin*, and numerous saints are shown on either wing. We do not know for which church this work was made, but the presence of St. Benedict in two prominent places would indicate that it was for a Benedictine institution. The multitude of colors surrounded by the gold ornamented frame demonstrates the keen sense of decoration and pomp that the Gothic period developed.

The *Coronation of the Virgin* by Gentile da Fabriano (ca. 1370–1427) (illus.) is a rare work by one of the most important and influential artists of the early Renaissance. It is often said to date from the early 1420's but may in fact be somewhat earlier. Gentile worked in various parts of Italy, from northern Italy and Venice to Rome and was one of the principal artists to lead the transition from the Gothic style into the Renaissance. His work combines the color and spiritual qualities of the earlier style with a familiarity with space and naturalistic detail that had previously been lacking. The *Coronation* is not much different in these respects from the *Coronation* by Cenni di Francesco done about the same time, though it is far less stylized. This lack of stylization, however, is already enough to enable us to feel more in touch with the subject because the figures have gained some warmth and individual features.

The change is felt perhaps more strongly in another work by Gentile, the *Nativity* done probably at a later date in his career. Although the pose of the Madonna is completely frontal and symmetrical, the landscape in the background shows the results of a newfound interest in nature. The scene is at night, Joseph is asleep, and the hills are lit from behind. The figures decrease proportionately in size as they recede into the background and in the distance the shepherds are listening to a tiny angel engraved into the golden sky. Such details are a recognizable step in the slow evolution of naturalism in art.

The artist whose work is synonymous with the full development of the early Renaissance style is the Florentine painter Masaccio, whose given name was Tommaso di Giovanni Guidi (1401–1428/9). The *St. Andrew* panel (illus.) can be securely dated to 1426, since it belonged to a much larger altarpiece that was ordered from Masaccio in that year by a wealthy Pisan citizen. In 1568 Vasari saw this polyptych in the Church of the Carmine in Pisa; however, it was subsequently dismembered and is now divided among museums in London, Berlin, Pisa, and Naples. Masaccio was greatly influenced by antique sculpture, and he sought to achieve a more solid and volumetric form in his painting style. The abundant drapery of St. Andrew suggests the presence of his body underneath, and the intensity of the saint's facial expression brings forth an added human quality.

In the same gallery are two Florentine paintings from the sides of wooden chests (called *cassoni*) meant to function as decorated household furniture. Using Greek and Roman themes and already showing an awareness of perspective, these decorative panels suggest the next phase of development in Renaissance style. The fully-realized expression of this movement is seen more completely in Gallery 206.

GALLERY 206:
ITALIAN RENAISSANCE
PAINTINGS

The Italian Renaissance, which took form in the first decades of the fifteenth century, has always been considered one of the high points in the history of art. The word "renaissance" refers to the fact that the Italians revived Greco-Roman culture. Not only classical techniques but also classical themes became popular. Although Italian artists for the most part remained Christians and were patronized by the Church and its various orders, their outlook was increasingly secular. By the sixteenth century their imitations of classical art had become so skilled that it is occasionally difficult to distinguish between old and new. By the end of the century, however, reaction had set in, and the Counter Reformation took hold; the Church asserted itself against artistic heresy, and the Baroque style was born. But the course of art had been changed permanently.

One of the latest tempera paintings in the collection, the large polyptych from Venice, is dated 1490 and is signed by Bartolomeo Vivarini (active 1450–death 1491). It comes from a church near Bergamo and depicts a series of saints in colorful clothing surrounding St. James, the pilgrim saint. He is identified by the scallop shell on his staff, but he may also be Christ dressed as a pilgrim.

Masaccio
(1401–1428/9)
St. Andrew
1426
Tempera on panel, 52.3 x 33.2 cm.

Vittore Carpaccio
(1455/6–1525/6)
Hunting on the Lagoon
ca. 1490–1500
Oil on panel, 75.9 x 63.7 cm.

A decisive movement away from religious subject matter can be seen in the panel by Vittore Carpaccio (1455/6–1525/6) (illus.). It is painted on both sides and this fact, along with the presence of an original hinge, suggests that it served as a door to a cupboard or, more probably, a window cover. One side represents Venetian patricians hunting for cormorants, birds prized for their fine plumage; the reverse depicts a marble niche filled with letters strung over a thin red ribbon. In this unusual work, Carpaccio demonstrates his ability to observe the world around him.

Another Venetian picture of special importance is the *Madonna and Child* by Lorenzo Lotto (active 1504–died 1556) (illus.). Lotto spent most of his life working outside Venice in a variety of widespread places, but his style is completely Venetian in character. This painting, better than any other in the collection, shows the flair for color that typifies Venetian art, with brilliant pigments very subtly modeled. The composition is unusual and very compartmentalized, and the profiles of the donors on the left mark it as a work done when Lotto was still fairly young.

Lorenzo Lotto
(ca. 1480–1556)
Madonna and Child with Donors
ca. 1520s
Oil on canvas, 85.7 x 117.5 cm.

The Getty collection contains a number of other Venetian pictures from the sixteenth century. The finest of these – the large *Portrait* by Paolo Veronese (1528–1588) – may represent the artist himself (illus.). Venetian painters are famous for the rich character of their paint and color. They originated the "painterly" style which came to be imitated for many centuries, and Veronese's portrait is a perfect example of this.

Italian painting executed outside of Venice is represented by several works in this room. In a *Portrait of a Man* (illus.), perhaps painted by Raphael (1483–1520) when he was in Florence, the artist has created a well-balanced composition, using warm colors and careful detailing in the sitter's facial features and in the landscape background. There is a very different quality to the *Portrait of a Lady with a Book of Music,* also painted by an artist active in Florence, who is called Bacchiacca (his given name was Francesco Ubertini, 1495– 1557). His work displays some characteristics of portraits done in a Mannerist style: the sitter is placed within an uncertain perspective setting and the colors are rather cool and dissonant. Finally, from the Piedmont school around Turin there is a large panel depicting the *Adoration of the Magi* by Defendente Ferrari (active 1511–1535). The crowded composition and the emphasis on fine detail work indicate the close artistic relationship between Piedmont and Flemish areas to the north.

Also displayed in this gallery are several early Baroque paintings, primarily those done in the manner identified with Caravaggio whose work was characterized by strongly lit figures against dark backgrounds. This style encouraged stark compositions and heightened realism. It became popular throughout Europe, particularly Rome and Naples. All of these features are visible in the fine work by Pietro Paolini (1603–1681) entitled *Achilles and the Daughters of Lycomedes.* This artist was one of the most talented

Paolo Caliari, called Veronese
(1528–1588)
Portrait of a Man
ca. 1570
Oil on canvas, 193 x 134.5 cm.

Attributed to Raphael
(1483–1520)
Bust Portrait of a Man
ca. 1504
Oil on panel, 67.5 x 53.5 cm.

Giovanni Benedetto Castiglione
(ca. 1600/10–1665)
Shepherds in Arcadia: Allegory of
    Temporal Vanity
ca. 1650s
Oil on canvas, 109.2 x 109.2 cm. (octagonal)

painters who worked in the tradition of
Caravaggio. A popular Baroque theme,
the brevity of earthly life, is illustrated
in a work by Giovanni Benedetto Castiglione (before 1610?–1665) called
Shepherds in Arcadia: Allegory of Tem-
poral Vanity (illus.). The picture also
indicates an increasing nostalgia in the
Italian view of classical antiquity.

GALLERY 209:
BAROQUE PAINTINGS

The largest gallery in the museum, this room contains the more monumental Baroque paintings in the collection. All of the paintings date from the seventeenth and eighteenth centuries, but they come from various countries.

Two of the earliest pictures, *Moses and the Messengers from Canaan* (illus.), and *Elias Fed by the Widow of Sarepta* by Giovanni Lanfranco (1582–1647), were painted about 1622/25 for the Chapel of the Sacraments in the church of S. Paolo fuori le Mura in Rome. These paintings belonged to a series of eight large can-

vases which are now scattered in various museums around the world. Lanfranco was a follower of the Carracci family, one of the principal forces of the Baroque period in Rome; Lanfranco's works were, in turn, also very influential. The present compositions, using a low viewpoint and other daring innovations for that time, were highly original works.

Giovanni Lanfranco
(1582–1647)
Moses and the Messengers from Canaan
ca. 1621–25
Oil on canvas, 218 x 246.3 cm.

73

A somewhat later painting is *Clorinda Rescuing Sofronia and Olindo* by Mattia Preti (1613–1699), an artist who worked in Rome, Naples, and Malta. The story, which comes from the Italian poet Tasso, was apparently a favorite with the artist since he painted it at least three times. Preti, too, worked with strong contrasts of light on dark (chiaroscuro), but he employed a painterly manner reminiscent of Tintoretto and other Venetian artists. This picture was probably commissioned in the 1650s by a private patron.

One of the most interesting paintings from this period is the *Allegory of Fortune* by Salvator Rosa (1615–1673). Rosa was best known as a painter of landscapes, but he did some figure compositions in his very personal way, usually with a high degree of pedantry and a certain cynicism. This work accurately expressed his bitterness about life, showing as it does Fortune, in the form of a woman, pouring wealth and the symbols of high office on a group of stupid animals. One sees the proverbial pearls lying before a swine. This picture, painted in 1658/59, nearly caused the artist's excommunication.

Madonna and the Child with St. Francis by Domenico Piola (1628–1703) was originally installed over an altar in the church of S. Domenico which, before its abandonment in 1798, was the largest church in Genoa. The picture of *St. Sebastian thrown by soldiers into the Cloaca Maxima* by Lodovico Carracci (1555–1619) was painted in 1612 for Cardinal Maffeo Barberini to be placed in the Barberini chapel in the church of San Andrea della Valle in Rome. Instead it

was kept by the Cardinal, later Pope Urban VIII, for his own collection.

The most important Flemish painting in this gallery is the *Portrait of Agostino Pallavicini* by Anthony van Dyck (1599–1641) (illus.). The sitter has been identified by his coat-of-arms which appears on the left side of the canvas. In 1626, when Van Dyck painted this picture, Pallavicini was the Genoese ambassador to the papal court in Rome. Thus, the artist has depicted him in the costume of this office and the bright robes become a stunning *tour de force* in the painter's hands. Nearby, there is a major work by Van Dyck's famous mentor, Peter Paul Rubens (1577–1640). The subject, *Diana and her Nymphs,* was a favorite one of the artist because it enabled him to concentrate on the nude female form. The inventory number included in the painting indicates that it once belonged to the Marquis de Léganès, a Spanish friend of the artist who owned a large number of his works.

Anthony van Dyck
(1599–1641)
Portrait of Agostino Pallavicini
1626
Oil on canvas, 216 x 141 cm.

74

English portrait painters were greatly influenced by the works of Van Dyck and Rubens. In the next century a similar influence was exerted on Pompeo Batoni (1708–87) whose *Portrait of John Chetwynd, First Earl of Talbot* (illus.), is in the same gallery. The inclusion of antique sculptures in this canvas commemorates the sitter's journey to Italy at a time when the "Grand Tour" was fashionable.

The east end of the gallery is dominated by two enormous canvases by François Boucher (1703–1770), *The Fountain of Love* (illus.) and *The Bird Catchers*, both done in 1748. These were cartoons for tapestries which were woven directly over the paintings. Both pictures have been reduced in size but are still among the largest ever made by the artist. The brilliant colors indicate how the tapestries must originally have looked.

GALLERY 223: NINETEENTH AND TWENTIETH CENTURY PAINTINGS

The Getty collections have always emphasized earlier periods, but they do contain some paintings from the nineteenth and early twentieth centuries. This era was dominated by France, and since Napoleonic times the principal avantgarde movements have originated there. In American museums and schools, French art is invariably treated as the forerunner of our own contemporary painting. This is primarily due to the French Impressionists and their revolutionary break from the academic traditions of the mid-nineteenth century. Nonetheless, this gallery includes both non-French and academic paintings as

Pompeo Batoni
(1708–1787)
Portrait of John Chetwynd,
First Earl of Talbot
1773
Oil on canvas, 274.5 x 182 cm.

François Boucher
(1703–1770)
The Fountain of Love
1748
Oil on canvas, 295 x 338 cm.

A similar picture, though not French, is *Spring* by Sir Lawrence Alma-Tadema (1836–1912), painted in 1894 (illus.). It is an important example of the neoclassical movement that flourished in England and Italy at the turn of the century. Artists like Alma-Tadema specialized in scenes of everyday life in Rome; that is, classical genre scenes. This is obviously very different from the neoclassical works of Baroque artists such as Poussin. Alma-Tadema was a painstaking technician and researched his settings very thoroughly in an attempt to render them as authentically as possible. The fashion for this type of work was very strong until the 1910s. It can also be seen in a painting by John William Godward (1861–1922) entitled *Reverie: Greek Woman Seated on a Bench.*

In contrast to these academic paintings are works such as *Landscape Near Rouen,* painted by Paul Gauguin in 1884. It is very much in the impressionistic manner and shows the concern for atmosphere and color that typifies the movement. Although Gauguin is not usually considered as an Impressionist, he worked in that style during his early years. Another painting is *The Wounded Foot* by Joaquin Sorolla y Bastida (1863–1923), a Spaniard who did works in a vaguely impressionistic manner.

well as Impressionist works. One of the earliest is probably *Young Girl Defending Herself Against Eros,* painted by Adolphe Bouguereau (1825–1905) in 1880 (illus.). Bouguereau exemplified perfectly the French academic tradition both in his meticulous technique and in his somewhat superficial themes. In his day Bouguereau was one of the most famous and popular artists in France, a reputation that is beginning to reassert itself today.

Adolphe William Bouguereau
(1825–1905)
Young Girl Defending Herself Against Eros
ca. 1880
Oil on canvas, 79.5 x 55 cm.

Lawrence Alma-Tadema
(1836–1912)
Spring
1894
Oil on canvas, 178.5 x 80 cm.

GALLERIES 226–8: SEVENTEENTH AND EIGHTEENTH CENTURY PAINTINGS

At the end of the hall, the last galleries contain a number of seventeenth and eighteenth century pictures from France, Italy, England, and the Netherlands.

French painting after the Middle Ages borrowed extensively from Flemish and Italian art. Like the Dutch and Flemish, the most prominent French artists studied in Italy, often remaining there for much of their careers and achieving a

Nicolas Poussin (1594–1665)
The Holy Family with Infant St. John
ca. 1650
oil on canvas, 100 x 132 cm.
Owned jointly by the J. Paul Getty Museum and the Norton Simon Museum

level comparable to the Italians. Not until the seventeenth century did French painting fully come into its own; eventually, by the eighteenth century, French artists developed a completely independent style.

The neoclassical art of seventeenth-century France is best represented by the works of Nicolas Poussin (1594–1665). His *Holy Family with Infant St. John the Baptist and St. Elizabeth* is a magnificent example of his mature style. The composition reflects the desire for order and rationality that is associated with classicism. Poussin strongly influenced other artists such as Laurent de la Hyre (1606–1656) who in the 1640s painted the *Landscape with Diana and her Nymphs*. This picture includes not only a neoclassical theme but also the Roman ruins that were such nostalgic souvenirs to the northern artists. A tapestry was eventually woven after this composition.

The brilliantly colorful *Venus and Adonis* by Simon Vouet (1590–1649) was painted at about the same time. Vouet also worked in Italy and, in his youth, painted in the Italian Caravaggesque style. Later, however, he developed a kind of French rococo fully a century before that style would come into popularity. The bright, almost decorative colors of this painting, as well as its graceful composition, are very different from the solemn seriousness of Poussin. In the *Portrait of Madame Bonier de la Mosson,* painted by Jean-Marc Nattier (1685–1766) (illus.), there is a continuation of this decorative style. The sitter, a respected member of the cultural community in Paris, is represented in the guise of Diana, the antique goddess of the hunt.

Nearby, there are a number of eighteenth-century paintings from Italy and other countries. The best of these are the Venetian paintings, including *Arch of Constantine* by Canaletto (1697–1768). Primarily, Canaletto painted views of Venice for tourists, but he occasionally depicted Roman monuments as well. These scenes are generally very accurate and topographically correct, but he does occasionally juxtapose different buildings for compositional reasons. Marco Ricci (1676–1730) is another Venetian whose oeuvre is represented by a *View of Roman Ruins,* in this case monuments on hills resembling the Palatine. Unlike the works of Canaletto, however, the purpose of this painting is clearly not topographical. By composing the elements at will and depicting everything

covered with weeds, Ricci has chosen instead to emphasize their nostalgic character.

One of the most important pictures in the collection is the *Beggars' Brawl* by Georges de La Tour (1593–1652) (illus.). Although his style is similar to that of other northern artists who were influenced by the Caravaggesque manner, La Tour is unique in that he is not known to have traveled outside his native Lorraine. His paintings are both extremely individual and rare. The painting in the Getty collection is not typical of his mature style but shows, instead, his early style which is darker, more solemn, and tends more toward genre: a group of old and ugly peasants

Jean-Marc Nattier
(1685–1766)
Portrait of Madame Bonier de la Mosson as Diana
1742
Oil on canvas, 128.9 x 96.5 cm.

are fighting over a street corner on which to play their instruments.

Another Venetian artist, Giovanni Battista Pittoni (1687–1767), painted the *Sacrifice of Polyxena*. It is one of a series of four works painted by Pittoni in 1733–34 for Marshal Schulenberg, a German who was his principal patron. The paintings in the series had classical themes that illustrated stoic virtues; apparently they were among the artist's most popular works as all were repeated on other occasions. A rather different subject matter was treated by Francesco Zucca-relli (1702–1788) in a painting signed by the artist in 1744. It depicts a pastoral landscape scene filled with mythological figures. Zuccarelli was especially noted for such works and he popularized this theme throughout Europe in the eighteenth century.

A pair of paintings by Alessandro Magnasco (1667–1749) depicting a *Bacchanale* (illus.) and the *Triumph of Venus* are especially striking because of their overwhelming nervous energy. Magnasco was famous for his rapid and energetic style, but these two works epitomize, probably better than any others, the movement and vigor of his pictures. They contain a kind of mannered vitality that gives the sense of a pervasive movement throughout the compositions.

Georges de La Tour
(1593–1652)
The Beggars' Brawl
ca. 1621–30
Oil on canvas, 95 x 142 cm.

Alessandro Magnasco
(1667–1749)
Bacchanale
ca. 1690–1700
Oil on canvas, 118 x 148.5 cm.

Thomas Gainsborough
(1727–1788)
The Earl of Essex and Thomas Clutterbuck
1784–85
Oil on canvas, 148.5 x 174 cm.

The first of the two portraits by
Thomas Gainsborough (1727–1788) in
these galleries, *The Earl of Essex Presenting A Cup to Thomas Clutterbuck,* was
painted soon after 1784 (illus.). Letters
exist that tell of the earl's wish to give
Clutterbuck, who was Sheriff of Hert-
ford County, a cup as a token of esteem
and gratitude. The cup is still in the
possession of the Clutterbuck family. The
second Gainsborough portrait depicts
James Christie, the founder of the famous
and still-existing auction house in London, and the portrait, painted in 1778,
hung for many years in their sale rooms.
Christie is shown leaning on a picture
that may have been there for sale, probably a landscape by Gainsborough.

In the center of this gallery is a large
marble-topped table. The gilt wood base
was made in France about 1740 and is
markedly rococo in style with its twist-
ing lines and asymmetrical design. The
marble top is Roman and was made in
the early seventeenth century. This table
top could well have been bought in Italy
by a young man on the "Grand Tour"
and sent back to Paris where a base would
be made for it. It was the custom in the
eighteenth century for sons of the
nobility to be sent on the "Grand Tour" –
a travel through Europe with a tutor to
complete their education. Mr. Getty's
collection began in this tradition and still
reflects its diverse beginnings. Over the
years, however, the museum has added
to its original treasures to reflect the
variety of western painting.

Panelled room from
the Hôtel Herlaut
French, ca. 1735

Decorative Arts

INTRODUCTION

The term "decorative arts" encompasses furniture, carpets, tapestries, silver, ceramics, clocks, chandeliers, and various small decorative items made of gilt bronze which may be grouped together under the general heading *bronzes d'ameublement.* The museum's collection is almost entirely French and ranges in date from about 1670 to 1790; that is, from the early years of the reign of Louis XIV to the French Revolution. The objects were, for the most part, made in Paris for the French nobility and the Royal Household.

Mr. Getty began to collect French furniture in the late 1930s, continued to acquire in the 50s, and the collection has been expanded greatly in the past ten years. Most of the smaller items, such as the clocks, silver, and ceramics were all acquired in recent years.

The information provided in this guide is purposefully brief, and a more detailed account on each object may be obtained from the labels.

GALLERY 211:
REGENCE PERIOD ROOM

The paneling lining the walls of this room comes from the Hôtel Herlaut, a house that still stands in the Place Vendôme in Paris (illus.). The paneling dates from the 1730s and was removed from its original setting in 1936. Stored in New York after that date, it became extremely damaged and dirty. Prior to its installation, the panels were restored and repainted, but much of the apparently original gilding was left intact. Unfortunately, while in storage the original plaster cornice and central ceiling rosette were

ket Makers. The fourth tapestry shows *Psyche being Abandoned by Cupid* who has returned to his baby-like form.

Most of the furniture in this room dates from approximately 1700 to 1755. The tall gilt wood *torchères* (or candle-stands) support standing candelabra (often known as *girandoles*) decorated with drops of rock crystal. The set of four chairs, also of gilt wood, date to about 1735 (illus.). The gilt wood console table beneath the mirror is a fine example of the curvilinear rococo style, decorated with winged dragons, serpents, lions' heads, and griffins. It dates to about 1730 (illus.).

lost. The present cornice was copied from that in an adjoining room of the Paris house. The parquet floor, though of eighteenth century date, is not part of the original room.

The walls are hung with four tapes-tries depicting scenes from the story of Psyche. The tapestries were woven on the looms at the Beauvais Manufactory which was founded by Louis XIV in 1664. The first set of these tapestries was woven in 1741, and sets were produced intermit-tently until 1770. The designs were made by the famous artist François Boucher (1703–1770). The largest shows *Psyche Arriving at Cupid's Palace Led by a Zephyr.* The painting for this hanging was exhibited by Boucher in the Paris salon of 1739. The two tapestries on the wall facing you show the *Toilet of Psyche* and *Psyche Searching for Cupid among the Bas-*

On the table stands a mantel clock which was probably made in the work-shops of André-Charles Boulle (1642–1732), the most famous royal cabinet-maker at the turn of the eighteenth cen-tury. He perfected the Italian technique of veneering wood with tortoiseshell, brass, and pewter. A drawing by him for this clock exists at the Musée des Arts Décoratifs in Paris. Lying below the dial is Father Time holding the scales, and above is Love, in the form of a child who would have originally held Father Time's scythe; thus showing Love conquering Time. To either side of the clock stands a small Japanese porcelain shell that was mounted in Paris with gilt bronze and transformed into *pot pourri* vases about 1750.

Standing on the commode to the right are a pair of vases made of Chinese *fam-ille verte* porcelain, also decorated in France with gilt bronze mounts. The porcelain dates from about 1700 and the mounts from 1710. The vases are rare, as most Oriental porcelains from this date

One of a set of four chairs
French, ca. 1735

were originally mounted with silver which later was often removed and melted down. The taste for mounting porcelain with gilt bronze did not become fashionable until well into the 1740s. The largest commode, on the right, was made by a fairly obscure cabinetmaker named Doirat, and it dates from the 1730s. Its *bombé* form may be explained by the possibility that it was made for the German market. The pair of vases on the commode are of Chinese porcelain dating from the K'ang Hsi period (1662–1722).

On the wall facing you, on either side of the gilt wood console table, stand two commodes which, at first sight, look very

Console table of gilt wood
French, ca. 1730

similar. The one on the left is inset with panels of Japanese lacquer. Throughout the eighteenth century the French greatly admired this technique, and screens and boxes made of lacquered wood were imported from Japan, via Holland, to be cut up and used to decorate furniture. This commode is not stamped with the maker's name (a guild rule introduced in the 1740s), but the piece is attributed to Joseph Baumhauer (active 1745–1772), a well-known cabinetmaker who provided furniture for the duc d'Aumont and the royal household. The pair of lidded vases on the commode are of Meissen porcelain. They are painted beneath with the mark *AR* for Augustus Rex and can be dated 1735–1740. The commode standing to the right is not by Baumhauer but rather by a cabinetmaker named Adrien Delorme (active 1748–

89

1783). It is a purposefully close copy of the lacquer commode which was a popular model, but it was made a few years later. These two commodes are the latest pieces in the room and date from the 1750s.

The commode nearest to you on the left wall was made by Charles Cressent (1685–1768), cabinetmaker to Philippe, duc d'Orléans, Regent of France. The gilt bronze mount in the center of the top drawer shows two babies: one is rasping tobacco on a snuff rasp and the other gives snuff to a monkey in the center who is putting it on his head. A fine and unusual piece, the commode dates between 1745 and 1749. The commode farthest from you on the same wall is veneered with tulipwood and stamped C. Cochois for Charles-Michel Cochois (d. 1764). However, the commode was probably made in the workshops of André-Charles Boulle (1642–1732) and may have been stamped by Cochois when he restored the piece in the 1740s. Standing on the commode is a pair of lidded bowls made of Chinese porcelain of the early K'ang Hsi period (1662–1722). They were mounted in France with gilt bronze in about 1720 and were considerably altered from their original form. The large table in the center of the room is also attributed to Cressent. It is a fine example of the sturdiness of the baroque style and only hints at the excesses of the coming rococo period. The pair of gilt bronze candlesticks standing on this table can be dated to about 1700. The shafts and bases are decorated with figures of children playing musical instruments. Standing between the candlesticks is an inkstand and a pair of paperweights also of gilt bronze, dating to about 1715. The paperweights are a rare survival.

The only object in this room which we can say with some certainty belonged to Louis XIV is the carpet. In an inventory of the King's possessions, drawn up in the early years of his reign, this carpet is listed and described in detail. It was, at a later date, cut down at each end by about three feet and the shorter borders appear to be nineteenth century replacements. It still retains its bright colors and is one of the few carpets of this date and size still in existence.

GALLERY 212: BAROQUE VESTIBULE

This small gallery, lined with blue silk damask, contains a few pieces of great rarity. The table is veneered with pewter, brass, tortoiseshell, floral wood marquerty, and ivory (illus.). It was probably made at the Royal Manufactory at the Gobelins, a workshop specially set up by Louis XIV to provide furnishings for the royal palaces. Made about 1680, it is extremely beautiful as well as a technical masterpiece. Above the table hangs a large wall clock made of gilt bronze. It shows Love, in the form of two small cupids, conquering Time. One of the cupids holds Time's hourglass and the other his scythe. The clock is attributed to Charles Cressent, who made the commode and the center table in Gallery 211. In a showcase is a terra cotta model of a clock (illus.). Members of the French royal family often commissioned furniture models to be made in terra cotta or wax, but very few have survived. This full-size model, dating from about 1700,

is a sculptural tour-de-force. The scene below the dial shows Pluto abducting Persephone.

On the opposite wall hangs a cartel clock, decorated with a veneer of tortoiseshell and brass, that dates from about 1710.

"Boulle" table top
French (Gobelins?)
ca. 1680

Terracotta model for a clock
French, ca. 1700

GALLERY 213:
ROCOCO PERIOD ROOM

The paneling lining this room dates from about 1755 and was removed from a *hôtel* in the Avenue Henri Martin (now called the Avenue Georges-Mandel) in Paris (illus.). It was installed in that house by the duc de Gramont in 1909 and had been in his *hôtel* on the Left Bank before that date. The panels have been restored, repainted, and re-gilded by the museum. The ceiling cornice and rosette are modern and were carefully modeled after fragments of the original ceiling. The finely painted overdoors are by an unknown artist. The parquet floor, not original to the room, is of eighteenth century date.

This room houses the museum's fine collection of rococo furniture which dates from about 1735 to 1760. With the exception of the small green-stained table, the red lacquer secrétaire, and the two mechanical tables in the window recesses, all the furniture is by Bernard van Risenburgh, the most renowned rococo cabinetmaker of the mid-eighteenth century. The red lacquer of the commode standing between the windows is Japanese; the panels are set into the body of the piece with the gilt bronze framing mounts carefully arranged to hide the seam lines. The central area of the black lacquer commode standing against the opposite wall is also Japanese lacquer, cut from the doors of a cabinet. The rest of the lacquer on this piece is a French imitation. The demand for Oriental lacquer became so great that French craftsmen soon learned how to copy this fine technique very convincingly. Both commodes may be dated to the late 1730s.

Standing on the red lacquer commode is a pair of gilt bronze candelabra mounted with porcelain. The elephants were made in the Meissen Manufactory in about 1741 after models by Peter Reinicke, and the flowers were probably produced at Vincennes after 1745. Standing between the candelabra is a Chinese porcelain vase dating to around 1740; it was decorated in France with gilt bronze mounts about 1755.

A pair of Meissen porcelain vases mounted with porcelain flowers stands on the black lacquer commode. The vases were made about 1730 and were mounted with gilt bronze and flowers in Paris about 1745. Between them stands a Chinese celadon vase also mounted with French gilt bronze.

Panelled room from an hôtel
on the Avenue Georges-Mandel, Paris
French, ca. 1755

One of a pair of commodes
by Bernard van Risenburgh
French, ca. 1750

The pair of commodes on either side of the mantelpiece is reputed to have been made by Van Risenburgh for a hunting lodge belonging to the Elector of Saxony (illus.). They once stood in the Castle of Moritzburg and formed part of a set along with three larger commodes and a pair of corner cupboards. Unfortunately, the corner cupboards and one of the commodes were destroyed in

Clock in the shape of a palm tree attributed to Jean-Pierre Latz, the movement by Julien le Roy French, ca. 1750

the Second World War. Two larger commodes now stand in the Museum für Kunsthandwerk at Dresden. French furniture was extremely popular in the courts of other European countries, and French cabinetmakers often made concessions to the taste of their patrons abroad, as is shown by the extremely florid bronze mounts on these commodes, elaborated to suit the German taste.

On the mantelpiece stands a gilt bronze clock in the form of a palm tree surmounted by a lion's pelt (illus.). The maker of this unique model is not known, but the movement is signed by Julien le Roy. The clock, in the full rococo style, was made about 1750. The gilt bronze firedogs directly below are listed and described in the 1751 sale catalogue of the stock-in-trade of the cabinetmaker Charles Cressent and can be dated to about 1740.

At the center of the entrance wall is a secrétaire decorated with a large panel of Oriental lacquer. The secrétaire is stamped beneath the marble top *I DUBOIS* for Jacques Dubois (born c. 1693, master 1742, died 1763). The lacquer is decorated with European huntsmen. It is likely that these men were members of the Dutch East Indies Company. At this time the Dutch maintained almost sole control of trade with the East, and they were known to the Chinese as "Southern Barbarians." Standing on this secrétaire is a bowl of Chinese export porcelain and a stand of Japanese Imari porcelain, both dating to about 1740. They were mounted in France with gilt bronze in the mid-eighteenth century.

In the window recesses are two mechanical tables made by Jean-François Oeben (born c. 1720, appointed royal cabinetmaker 1754, master 1761,

Mechanical table
by Jean-François Oeben
French, ca. 1754

died 1763). The table nearest you is one of his most elaborate pieces (illus.). In the corners of the top can be seen a lion, a salamander, a swan, and a dove representing the four elements of Earth, Fire, Water, and Air. The top slides back when the drawer in the frieze is pulled out. This drawer is fitted with compartments lined with blue silk. In a painting of Madame

de Pompadour by François Guérin, an identical table can be seen which could indeed be this very piece. The table dates from about 1754. The other table is slightly simpler and a little earlier in date. The holes at the sides are for a winding key which tightens the elaborate spring mechanism that enables the top to slide back when the drawer is unlocked. The folding screen in the far corner of this room is made of Savonnerie knotted pile. The panels were made after designs by the animal painter, Alexandre-François Desportes, and the screen can be dated about 1740.

In the center of the room stands one of the finest pieces in the collection (illus.). The double form of this desk is unique. It was bought in Paris about 1763 by Lady Elizabeth Gunning and remained with the Argyll family till the 1950s. Bearing the stamp of Bernard van Risenburgh, it shows once again his amazing inventiveness and versatility. From the ceiling hangs a fine chandelier, which can be dated to about 1710, made of colored glass and silvered and gilded bronze.

GALLERY 210:
RÉGENCE AND ROCOCO DECORATIVE ARTS
This gallery, lined with pink-brown silk damask, houses furniture that ranges in date from the late seventeenth century to 1750.

Double desk by
Bernard van Risenburgh
French, ca. 1740

The magnificent cabinet, with cream figures is of late seventeenth century date (illus.). It may well have been made at the Gobelins Manufactory, and it was perhaps conceived as a royal gift. A pair to it is in the possession of the Duke of Buccleuch, and tradition holds that it was given to Charles II by Louis XIV. A medallion showing a profile portrait of that King can be seen on the cabinet. The tapestry hanging close by on the same wall was woven at the Gobelins Manufactory between 1728 and 1730. It forms part of a set made for the Chancellor Chauvelin, Keeper of the Seal, and his initials may be seen at the base.

On the opposite wall hangs a large tapestry known as *The Loves of the Gods*. This tapestry was woven at the Beauvais Manufactory after designs by François Boucher. The original conception was a set of tapestries, nine in all, each showing some romantic episode from the lives of the mythological deities. They were first woven in 1749 and were repeated until 1772. This hanging is unusual in that it combines two such episodes, giving it monumental size. To the left is shown Bacchus and Ariadne and, on the right, Jupiter disguised as a satyr surprises Antiope.

The pedestal clock (illus.) in the corner of this gallery is attributed to André-Charles Boulle (1642–1732). This clock dates from about 1720, and identical examples may be seen in the Bibliothèque de l'Arsenal, Paris, the Wallace

Cabinet-on-stand
French (Gobelins?)
ca. 1675–80

Pedestal clock attributed to
André-Charles Boulle,
the movement by
Julien le Roy
French, ca. 1720

Collection, London, and Waddesdon Manor, outside London. Particular note should be taken of the oval dial, with the expanding and contracting hour hand, and the finely modeled figures of the four continents flanking the clock.

On the same wall as the clock, stands a commode of early eighteenth century date. On either side of the keyhole escutcheon, small dolphins appear–the emblem of the heir to the throne. Standing alongside this commode is another of similar form and date. This commode bears, on its back, the stamp of the Château of Maisons-Lafitte and the monogram of the comte d'Artois, the brother of Louis XVI. Standing on the commode to the left is one of a pair of bronzes representing Boreas and Oreithyia. On the commode to the right of the planisphere, the bronze shows Pluto abducting Persephone. They are reductions of the marbles made by the sculptors Gaspard Marsy (1624–1681), Anselme Flamen (1647–1717), and François Girardon (1628–1715) for the gardens of Versailles.

The large clock standing between these two commodes is known as a planisphere. It once contained an extremely elaborate mechanism which enabled the viewer to see the phases of the moon, the times of the eclipse of the first satellite of Jupiter, the times of the tide in various French and English ports, and the time at various parts of the world – including "La Californie" – and other astrological details. The case is attributed to Jean-Pierre Latz and may be dated to 1745–49. Only three complete planispheres are known to exist today. The museum's example apparently was once

in the collection of the Prince de Conti in the 1770s.

The long-case clock standing at the far end of this room dates from about 1725. Judging from the rather prominent crescent moon on the front of the stand, the clock may well have been made for an eastern potentate who would have enjoyed the exuberance of this piece. It is veneered with tortoise shell and brass, and special note should be taken of the finely engraved grill around the face. The mounts, which are fairly crude in quality, are not gilt, which is strange for a piece of such flamboyance. Beneath the clock is a music box which can be set to play one of twelve different tunes.

The *bibliothèque* that faces the planisphere is attributed to the workshop of Antoine-Robert Gaudreau (1680–1751). The mounts on the sides represent Summer and Autumn (Ceres and Bacchus). Standing to the left of the *bibliothèque* is a combined games and writing table. The table is also attributed to Gaudreau who was cabinetmaker to Louis XV from 1726. The leather upholstered desk chair to the right of the *bibliothèque* can be dated to about 1735. The arms contain velvet-lined compartments for the storage of personal items such as snuff boxes, spectacles, etc. Hanging from the center of this room is a gilt bronze chandelier whose design is generally given to André-Charles Boulle (1642–1732). It can be dated to about 1720.

In the center of the other arm of this L-shaped gallery is a large table (known as a *bureau plât*) which is attributed to the hand of Charles Cressent who is also thought to have made the table in the

Corner cabinet by Jacques Dubois,
after a design by Nicolas Pineau
French, ca. 1750

center of the Régence Period Room. This table was made a few years later, about 1735. The large corner cupboard in the corner of the gallery was made by Jacques Dubois (illus.). Together with the double desk by Bernard van Risenburgh, it is one of the masterpieces of the rococo period. It was designed by Nicolas Pineau and was made about 1745. It is not known who ordered this magnificent piece, but it belonged to the Viennese Rothschilds in the nineteenth and early twentieth centuries. The small cartel clock hanging on the wall close by is signed by Jacques Caffiéri (1678–1755). The model is listed in the celebrated *bronzier's* inventories of his models in 1747 and 1755, and it dates to about 1745. The movement is by Julien le Roy who also made the movement of the pedestal clock with an oval face in this gallery.

GALLERY 215:
ROCOCO DECORATIVE ARTS
The corner cupboards in this room were made by Bernard van Risenburgh (active 1730–c. 1765) and are decorated with panels of fine Japanese lacquer. They were made about 1740, and each is stamped beneath the marble top *BVRB* for Bernard van Risenburgh, a great master of the rococo style of furniture. The museum contains ten pieces made by this famous cabinetmaker. On the corner cupboards stand a pair of large celadon vases which have been mounted with gilt bronze to form ewers. The mounts are datable to the mid-eighteenth century.

Standing between these cupboards is a commode veneered with kingwood, tulipwood and other woods and set with gilt bronze mounts. This piece is stamped

One of a pair of ewers
Chinese ceramic ca. 1662–1722;
French mounts ca. 1745–1749

DF which is thought to have been the mark used by the cabinetmaker Jean Desforges (master in 1739). The design of the marquetry is most unusual and shows a total asymmetry. This piece can be dated to around 1740. Standing on this commode is a lidded bowl made of Chinese celadon porcelain mounted in France with gilt bronze. We can accurately date the mounts on the bowl to 1745–1749 because they bear a tax stamp in the form of a very small C surmounted by a crown. This stamp shows that a tax on copper, one of the metals used to form bronze, was paid by the bronze worker. The tax was only levied during those years.

Against the opposite wall stands a pair of commodes made in Southern Germany. They follow closely designs made by François de Cuvilliés (1695–1768), who was the court architect to the Elector of Bavaria and was responsible for the Residenz in Munich and the Amalienburg in the park at Nymphenburg. One of the foremost creators of the rococo style, he published many books of engravings of rococo ornaments. These commodes show a German example of the style, which was often decidedly more exuberant than the French. They were made in about 1745 and were probably carved by Joachim Dietrich.

In the center of the gallery stands a show case containing a pair of Sèvres porcelain vases (illus. p. 104). They originally formed part of a garniture of five pieces that stood on the mantelpiece of Madame de Pompadour's *chambre du lit* at the Hotel Pompadour (now known as the Palais d'Elysée). They also appear in the Sèvres sales records in 1760.

Very few objects can be identified today as having belonged to this famous Royal mistress. The central section was designed to hold *pot-pourri,* while the base held small bulbs such as croci and grape hyacinths.

GALLERY 217: TRANSITIONAL AND NEOCLASSICAL DECORATIVE ARTS

The large L-shaped gallery in front of you contains furniture of the rococo, transitional and neoclassical styles.

To your left and right, as you enter the gallery, are two corner cupboards which are attributed to the cabinetmaker Jean-Pierre Latz (active 1739–1754). The doors are veneered with naturalistic flowers, each composed of many small pieces of wood which once would have been brightly colored but now have faded to a variety of brown hues, only the green stain remaining.

Floral marquetry was popular in the late seventeenth and the early decades of the eighteenth centuries, but it temporarily fell from favor shortly afterwards. It was re-introduced as a decorative motif by the royal cabinetmaker Jean-François Oeben, and it is highly likely that the flowers on these pieces are by his hand. It was not unusual for one cabinetmaker to employ another as a *marqueteur* to decorate his furniture, and these corner cupboards are an example of this type of collaboration. Another pair of corner cupboards by Latz and Oeben can be seen at the other end of this L-shaped gallery. Standing on them is a pair of mounted Chinese porcelain vases. The porcelain dates to the early K'ang Hsi

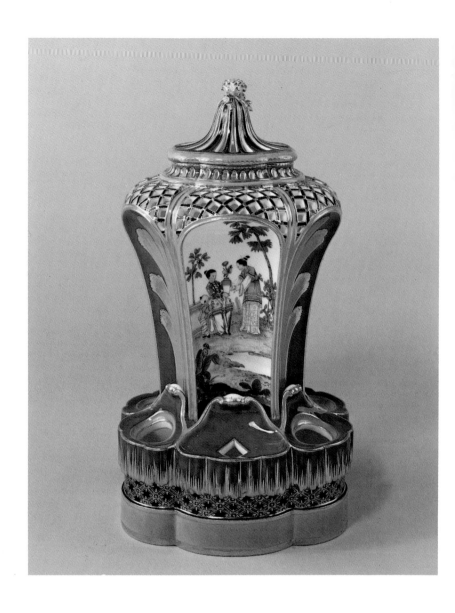

One of a pair of pot pourri vases,
made for Madame de Pompadour
French (Sèvres)
ca. 1760

period (circa 1660), while the elaborate mounts would have been added in Paris about 1745. Porcelain decorated with this design, sometimes referred to as *rouge de fer,* is rarely found mounted.

The large commode standing against the wall to your left was made by the royal cabinetmaker, Gilles Joubert (1689–1775, royal cabinetmaker 1763–1774) (illus.). It was delivered to Versailles in 1769 for Madame Louise, the daughter of Louis XV. Joubert was eighty years old when he made this piece. Trained in the rococo style, he has made a few concessions to the neoclassical style in the design of this commode. Above the commode is a gilt bronze wall clock and bracket decorated with panels of red, green, and cream painted horn (illus. p. 106). The clock case and bracket are stamped *ANT FOVLLET* for Antoine Foullet (1710–1775) and can be dated to about 1760.

Hanging to either side of the clock is a pair of wall lights which can definitely be attributed to the *bronzier* Philippe Caffiéri, the son of Jacques (illus.). The model is found described in detail in an inventory taken of Caffiéri's stock in 1770, and identical lights are in the Lazienski Palace, Warsaw, where Caffiéri worked between 1766 and 1768.

To the left of the commode stands a small table by Bernard van Risenburgh. It is fitted with a writing slide at the front and two more slides at the sides, intended to bear candlesticks. It dates to about 1755.

Standing along the opposite wall is a tripartite cabinet of extraordinary length. Though the piece does not bear the stamp of a cabinetmaker, it is attributed to Bernard van Risenburgh and is a very recent addition to the museum's collection. Above the cabinet hangs a portrait of *Marc de Villiers, secrétaire du roi,* by Jacques-André-Joseph Aved (1702–1766) (illus. p. 108). It is signed and dated 1747.

The gilt bronze clock and barometer which hang on the wall to either side of the painting are attributed to Charles Cressent. They date from about 1735 though the brackets on which they stand are a little later. One of the brackets is signed by St. Germain (active c. 1745–1772), a well-known bronze-maker of the mid-eighteenth century.

The small desk standing in the far left corner is attibuted to Adam Weisweiler. It is known as a *bonheur-du-jour* and is decorated with ceramic plaques made at the Wedgwood factory in England. They were designed by Lady Templeton in the early 1780s. The plaques were modeled by William Hackwood in 1783. Wedg-

Wall clock by Antoine Foullet
French, ca. 1760

wood enjoyed a brisk trade with Paris at this time and supplied that city not only with tableware but also with plaques for mounting on furniture.

Between the two doors to the right of the small desk stands one of the finest pieces of furniture in the collection. This secrétaire was made by Jean-Henri Riesener in the early 1780s (illus. p. 109). The panels of lacquer are Japanese, and the large oval gilt bronze plaque in the center of the fall-front, showing a Sacrifice to Love, is thought to have been modeled after a relief by Clodion. As Riesener was a royal cabinetmaker, he was exempt from the strict Parisian guild rules and was allowed to make his own gilt bronze mounts. They are exceedingly fine and are a technical tour-de-force. The secrétaire has a distinguished provenance. It was probably bought by William Beckford, the famous English collector and dilettante, at the Revolutionary sales in Paris. It passed by inheritance to the Duke of Hamilton. It was sold at the Hamilton Palace sale of 1882 to Cornelius Vanderbilt and was bought by the museum at the sale of his daughter's possessions.

Standing against the opposite wall is a cabinet attributed to Philippe-Claude Montigny (1734–1800). The panels, veneered with brass, tortoise shell, and pewter, would seem to have been taken from a much earlier piece of furniture and then mounted on this neoclassical body. The mounts, too, are in the style of the early eighteenth century. There was a great revival in the taste for furniture veneered with "Boulle" marquetry in the late eighteenth century, and this cabinet shows this trend well. Standing

One of a set of four wall lights
by Philippe Caffiéri
French, ca. 1768–1770

Jacques-André-Joseph Aved
(1702–1766)
Portrait of Marc de Villiers, Secrétaire du Roi
1747
Oil on canvas, 146.5 x 114.5 cm.

Secrétaire by Jean-Henri Riesener
French, ca. 1780

Panelled room
French, ca. 1780

on this cabinet is a bronze group representing Hebe rejuvenating Aeson. It is attributed to the hand of the sculptor Louis-Simon Boizot (1743–1809) and can be dated to around 1785. Boizot directed the sculpture workshops of the Sèvres Manufactory from 1773 to 1800 and also made models for furniture mounts. Flanking the bronze group is a pair of gilt bronze tazzas mounted with marble bowls: they were probably used to contain burning incense.

Above hangs a self portrait of Joseph Ducreux which may have been exhibited in the Paris Salon of 1791. Standing to the right of the cabinet is a small mechanical writing and toilet table which is attributed to Jean-François Leleu (1729–1807). He was an apprentice of Jean-François Oeben and a colleague of Jean-Henri Riesener. The table has deep drawers at the sides to hold cosmetic jars, and it dates from about 1760.

Standing against the opposite wall is a settee and a chair from a set of eleven pieces that is reputed to have belonged to Eugène Beauharnais, the son of Napoleon's wife Josephine. The chairs were bought by Czar Alexander I in 1814 and were sold by the Russian Government in 1928.

GALLERY 218:
NEOCLASSICAL PERIOD ROOM

Unfortunately, the origins of this room are unknown. Since its removal from the former J. Paul Getty Museum, it has been remodeled, painted, and provided with a plaster cornice and ceiling rosette (both modern copies), a mantelpiece from the period, and an eighteenth century parquet floor (illus.). The curtains are modern, but they are copied from an eighteenth century design. The paneling dates from about 1780 and the furniture from about 1760 to 1785. The chandelier was made by the *bronzier* Galle in the early decades of the nineteenth century. The bowl beneath was intended to hold goldfish!

Standing beneath the chandelier is a table made for Louis XVI at the order of Marie Antoinette by the royal cabinetmaker Jean-Henri Riesener (1734–1801). Delivered to the Petit Trianon in 1777, a painted inventory number and the stamp of the *Garde Meuble de la Reine* is still visible beneath the top. The inventory number can be traced to the Royal Accounts which still exist in Paris. Jean-Henri Riesener, a German by birth, was the royal cabinetmaker between 1774 and 1784 and is the most famous of all the craftsmen who supplied objects for the aristocracy. He died in relative poverty after the French Revolution. The gilt bronze candlesticks standing on this table are signed beneath *MARTINCOURT* for Etienne Martincourt and were made about 1780. He was one of the few *bronziers* to sign his works.

On the table also stands a Sèvres porcelain *écuelle*. The cover and plate are painted with the initials *ML* for Madame Louise, the daughter of Louis XV, and with the arms of an unmarried Daughter of France. The piece bears the date letter *L* for 1764 and the letter *S*, the symbol for the painter Merault *l'aîné*.

Standing against the middle of the wall to the right is a commode by Jean-François Oeben (c. 1720–1763) (illus.). Compared to the corner cupboards bearing his marquetry that you saw in the

Commode by Jean-François Oeben
French, ca. 1760

gallery outside, this is a later and more severe piece. Oeben was the master of Jean-Henri Riesener and was the royal cabinetmaker between 1754 and 1763. At Oeben's death, his widow married Riesener who took over his master's workshop. This commode is a fine example of the transitional style, the style that emerged during the transition from the curvaceous rococo to the straighter, more formal neoclassical style. Standing on the commode is a pair of gilt bronze candelabra attributed to Pierre Gouthière (1732–1813/14). The wall lights which flank the painting above are also attributed to his hand. Flanking the com-

Secrétaire by Martin Carlin
French, ca. 1775

mode is a pair of gilt wood chairs stamped *J. BOUCAULT* for Jean Boucault (master 1728, died 1786), and each is branded with the mark of the Château of Versailles.

The secrétaire standing between the two windows facing you is attributed to Adam Weisweiler (c. 1750–1815). He, like Oeben, was a German who emigrated to Paris. The piece is decorated with porcelain plaques made at the Sèvres Manufactory. This decorative technique is thought to have been first used by Bernard van Risenburgh in the late 1750s, and it soon became extremely popular. The porcelain plaques are often signed and dated by symbols on their backs, helping historians to date the construction of the piece. By this means, we are able to date this secrétaire to around 1780. Standing on the secrétaire is a gilt bronze and enamel clock. The dial is signed *Folin l'ainé A PARIS* for Nicolas-Alexandre Folin, and one of the small subsidiary dials is signed by the enameller G. Merlet. This clock dates to the very end of the eighteenth century.

The small circular tables on either side of the mantelpiece also bear Sèvres plaques and were made by Martin Carlin (active c. 1760–1785). There are about nine tables known of this design, and an identical table to that standing on the right can be seen at the Musée du Louvre in Paris. On the mantelpiece stands a gilt bronze clock decorated with female figures which represent sidereal and terrestrial time. The movement is by Charles le Roy (1709–1771), and the clock dates to about 1765. In the fireplace is a pair of gilt bronze firedogs described in the 1781 sale catalogue of the Duchess de Mazarin, where they are stated to be by the *bronzier* Gouthière. Documented works by this master are extremely rare.

Carlin also made the secrétaire standing to the left of the mantelpiece (illus. p. 113). He was a great master of the neoclassical style and provided furniture for Marie Antoinette and Louis XVI's aunts, Mesdames Adelaide and Victoire. As with all secrétaires, the fall-front lets down to form a writing surface, revealing many small drawers and pigeonholes. Standing on the secrétaire is a Vincennes porcelain *jardinière* painted beneath with the date letter *A* for 1753.

The music stand in the far right corner is also by Martin Carlin. The music support can be placed at various angles; it can also be swiveled and raised or lowered. It is a good example of the intricate furniture designed for the idle and pleasure-loving nobility of Paris.

The use of Sèvres plaques is also shown on the secrétaire standing to the right of the entrance door. This piece has lost its original stand and has since been fitted with another, of quite the wrong style, by *F. Durand* in the early twentieth century. The upper part is stamped *C. C. Saunier* for Claude-Charles Saunier (1735–1807), and it is also inscribed beneath *Saunier le jeune 1776*. The Sèvres plaques were painted by Jean-Baptiste Tandart (active 1754–1803) and are all dated 1776.

The cabinet with tambour panels standing to the other side of the door was made by Roger Vandercruse Lacroix (1728–1799), the maternal grandfather of the painter Eugène Delacroix. The tambour panels conceal a marble-lined

Pot pourri vase
French (Sèvres), ca. 1761

shelf above and drawers below. At the side is a drawer that contains an inkwell, sand pot, and sponge box. It was probably made to stand by a bed. The cabinet is in the transitional style and, though relatively plain, is a fine piece.

The folding stools standing in the window bays were once part of a set of sixty-four made by Jean-Baptiste-Claude Sené (1748–1803) for Marie Antoinette's Gaming Rooms at Compiègne and Fontainebleau. They were delivered in 1786. The original fine upholstery has, of course, been worn away, and they have been reupholstered with the same fabric as the curtains as was so often the custom in the eighteenth century. A number of these stools have survived and can be found in major museums and private collections in America and Europe.

The set of three chairs (a fourth is in the gallery outside) is by Georges Jacob who worked mainly for members of the French court. One of the chairs bears the stencil of the *Garde Meuble de la Reine,* showing that the set was originally ordered for Marie Antoinette. An armchair from the set in a French private collection is stamped *G. Jacob* and also bears the brand of the Petit Trianon.

GALLERY 219:
NEOCLASSICAL VESTIBULE
This small room houses three showcases containing part of the museum's collection of silver and Sèvres porcelain. Particular note should be taken of the black Sèvres ice bowls. Black Sèvres is exceedingly rare and was made just prior to the French Revolution. These bowls are dated 1792 and are decorated with *chinoiserie* scenes in platinum and two tones of gold.

All the objects in the showcase to your right are of Sèvres porcelain. The *jardinière,* placed at the top, is painted with a scene taken from a detail of a Teniers painting now in the Hermitage Museum, Leningrad. The *jardinière* is painted beneath with the date letter *I* for 1761. The *rose plateau* below is painted with the date mark for 1758. The pair of cups and saucers are date marked for 1759 and bear the symbol of the painter Charles Buteux.

The showcase on the left contains one of the masterpieces produced by the Sèvres Manufactory, known as a *vase vaisseau à mât* (illus. p. 115). Only ten of these boat-shaped *pot pourri* vases exist today, and they all date from the late 1750s. The pair of Sèvres candelabra standing in this showcase are also rare. Only two other pairs are known, and one may be seen in the Kress Collection in the Metropolitan Museum of Art, New York. All three pieces in this showcase were once in the collection of J. Pierpont Morgan.

Hanging on the walls are six satin panels painted in gouache. The one to the immediate right of the door leading to the Tapestry Gallery bears the monograms of Louis Stanislas Xavier (brother of Louis XVI, who became Louis XVIII in 1814) and Maria-Josephine Louise. They were married on May 14, 1771. These finely painted panels may once have lined the walls of an octagonal room in the Pavillon de Musique that was built for this royal couple at Versailles. Two more panels from the set are in the Musée des Arts Décoratifs, Paris.

GALLERY 220: TAPESTRY ROOM

This gallery is hung with a set of four tapestries made at the order of Louis XVI for Grand Duke Paul of Russia who became Czar Paul I (illus.). The tapestries hung, until the Russian Revolution, in the Palace of Pavlovsk near St. Petersburg. They were woven between 1776 and 1778 from designs by François Boucher and Maurice Jacques. Each depicts some episode in the lives of various mythological deities. Tapestries of this design were particularly popular with the English aristocracy, and a set made for the Earl of Coventry for Croome Court may be seen in the Metropolitan Museum of Art in New York.

Tapestry, one of a set of four
based on cartoons by François Boucher
French (Gobelins)
ca. 1776–1778

Roll-top desk
attributed to David Roentgen
German (Neuwied-on-the-Rhine)
ca. 1785

Standing in the room are two large roll-top desks. The one on the left was made by Bernard Molitor (c. 1730–1812), a German immigrant who first appeared in Paris advertising in a newspaper a secret remedy for killing woodworm. Probably made in the late 1780s, this desk is a fine example of the culmination of the neoclassical style just before the French Revolution. Marquetry is now rarely used, and the gilt bronze mounts have become extremely fine and are confined to small areas. Standing on this desk is a pair of gilt bronze candelabra with blued metal bodies. They may have formed part of a set of *bronzes d'ameublement* delivered by L. F. Feuchères to Mesdames (the aunts of Louis XVI) at the Château of Bellevue in 1784.

The roll-top desk (illus.) standing in the center of the room was made by David Roentgen (1743–1807). Roentgen's workshop was at Neuwied-on-the-Rhine, but he maintained prosperous shops in Berlin, Vienna, and Paris. He is well-known for his elaborate mechanical fittings, and the desk contains many secret drawers. The large plaque on the front is attributed to Pierre Gouthière (1732–1813/14), one of the leading Paris bronze workers. Standing on top of the roll-top desk is a pair of porphyry urns mounted with gilt bronze and made about 1780. The center vase is of the same stone as the urns and can be dated to about 1775.

The secrétaire to the right of the door is stamped *I. DUBOIS* for René Dubois (1737–1799) and is dated to the third quarter of the eighteenth century. He was the son of Jacques Dubois who made the large corner cabinet in Gallery 210.

To the left of the Molitor desk is a toilet and writing table which can be dated to about 1780. Though it is not stamped with a maker's mark, it can be attributed to Louis-Noël Malle. This maker is one of a number of cabinet-makers who specialized in the production of objects veneered with "naïve" marquetry. The card table to the right of the desk is stamped *J. F. OEBEN* for Jean-François Oeben. It is the only known card table produced by this famous maker and dates to about 1760.

Standing between the tapestries on the far wall is one of the latest pieces in the collection. The secrétaire was made by Alexandre Bellangé in about 1824. The ceramic plaques decorating it are obviously quite different in style and execution from those decorating the earlier pieces in the neoclassical paneled room. The mounts, though fine, have lost the crispness that characterizes earlier work. A similar pair of secrétaires is in the British Royal Collection. They were bought by George IV in 1824 for only £53!

The revolving chair upholstered in brown velvet once formed part of a set made for Marie Antoinette's *Chambre à Coucher du Treillage* at the Petit Trianon. The set was delivered in 1787 by the chairmaker Georges Jacob, and part of the set has been returned to the Petit Trianon. It was once painted in polychrome, now unfortunately stripped. The chairs upholstered with tapestry form part of the same set as those in Gallery 217.

GALLERY 221:
NEOCLASSICAL DECORATIVE ARTS

To the right of the entrance stands a cabinet by Guillaume Beneman who was the last important *ébèniste* used by the royal family before the French Revolution. The cabinet is set with *pietre dure* (hardstone) plaques, the one in the center being of late seventeenth century date. The cabinet is reputed to have originally stood in the bedroom of Louis XVI at the château of Saint Cloud. The gilt bronze crossed *L*'s and the cockerel of France decorating the frieze denote a royal provenance. Standing on the cabinet is a pair of Sèvres porcelain *bleu-du-roi pot pourri* bowls, mounted with gilt bronze. They and the cabinet both date to about 1785. Above them hangs a portrait of a young boy by Nicolas de Largillière (1656–1746).

To the left of this piece stands a blue Chinese ceramic vase with fine gilt bronze mounts (illus.). This vase was reputedly bought at the sale of the contents of Versailles at the time of the revolution by the Countess Lubomirska, a Polish aristocrat and a good friend of Marie Antoinette. It descended to Count Potocki, her great-great grandson, from whom it was bought by Mr. Getty. Originally one of a pair, the other vase is in the British Royal Collection and was bought in 1812 by the Prince Regent (later George IV) from Thomire et Cie in Paris.

The small cabinet nearby is stamped *Joseph* for Joseph Baumhauer (active 1745–1778) (illus.). It is set with Japanese lacquer panels and a yellow jasper top. It is in the early neoclassical style, being of rather heavy architectural design with double canted pilasters and capitals.

Standing vase with mounts
attributed to Pierre-Philippe Thomire
French, ca. 1780

120

Cabinet by Joseph Baumhauer
French, ca. 1770

The two cabinets on the opposite wall
were sold from the collection of the Duke
of Hamilton in 1882. The cabinet on the
left is attributed to Adam Weisweiler and
was probably made in the 1780s (illus.).
All the *pietre dure* plaques on this piece
are of late seventeenth century date. The
cabinet on the right is of early nineteenth century date and may have been
made in Weisweiler's post-revolutionary
workshops. The small roundels on the
front are of micro-mosaic and show the
Pyramid of Cestius and the "Doves of
Pliny." They were probably sold in Rome
as souvenirs to tourists at the turn of the
century.

One of a pair of cabinets
attributed to Adam Weisweiler
French, ca. 1785

Chair from a set of seat furniture
by Jean-Baptiste Tilliard
French, ca. 1770

The fine set of seat furniture in the gallery was made by Jean-Baptiste Tilliard and dates to about 1775 (illus.). The oval portraits that hang above two of the chairs are by François-Xavier Fabre (1766–1837) and are of Laurent-Nicolas de Joubert and his wife who were members of a distinguished family from Montpel-lier. The paintings are dated 1785.

In the show case are three Sèvres porcelain cups and saucers and a small tea or chocolate pot. The largest cup, at the bottom of the case, fits into a deeply welled saucer and is of a form known as a "trembleuse," made for old or infirm people with trembling hands.

Cup and saucer
(trembleuse)
French (Sèvres)
1761

Southeast tower and
Roman road

GENERAL INFORMATION

HOURS

The J. Paul Getty Museum is open from 10:00 am until 5:00 pm, either Monday through Friday, June through September, or Tuesday through Sunday, September through June, subject to seasonal change. Visitors are advised to contact the museum for exact information. There is no charge for parking or admission to the museum.

The museum is located at 17985 Pacific Coast Highway, Malibu, California 90265, one mile north of Sunset Boulevard.

RESERVATIONS

Parking reservations are required. They may be made by either telephoning (213) 459-8402 or writing to the museum's reservations' office. Please indicate whether a morning (10–1) or an afternoon (1–5) arrival is preferred. A reservation guarantees parking and admission on a specific day for morning or afternoon arrival. Once a visitor enters, he may stay until the museum closes. Visitors who arrive by car and who do not have a reservation will not be admitted.

Because of limited parking on neighborhood streets, visitors are not permitted to park outside the museum and walk in. Pedestrian traffic is restricted to those arriving by taxi, bicycle (the museum provides racks) or public bus (RTD line 175 stops directly in front of the museum; passengers must request a pass from the driver).

Group organizers must write to the museum in advance to arrange for a bus parking reservation.

TOURS

Free introductory lectures are presented by the museum's Orientation Docents every fifteen minutes at the south end of the Main Peristyle Garden. These informal lectures briefly describe the history and design of the museum building and give a general introduction to the collections.

Visitors who wish to have a guided tour of the museum can rent a cassette unit at the Bookshop for a nominal fee. Visitors should allow at least 90 minutes for the tour. It covers the building, gardens and galleries. Self-conducted tours are possible through a variety of museum guidebooks, brochures and catalogues. Tours of the collection by staff members for a minimum of five people may be arranged by calling the Public Information Department at (213) 459-2306.

THE BOOKSTORE

Located in the entrance vestibule, the Museum Bookshop is open from 10:00 am to 5:00 pm. A wide spectrum of interests and subjects is represented, from general survey books on art to specialized treatises. Gift items include lithographed reproductions of paintings, postcards, appointment calendars, notecards, bookmarks, slides and exact replicas of selected museum pieces. Publication lists are available.

GARDEN TEA ROOM

The Garden Tea Room offers a cafeteria-style lunch from 10:30 am until 2:30 pm and beverages and snacks until 4:30 pm. Located in the West Garden, the Tea Room can be reached through the

Atrium. Special buffet luncheons can be served for groups in a private dining room by prior reservation. Arrangements can be made by telephoning (213) 454-7569.

PHOTOGRAPHY

Visitors are permitted to take photographs in the building and galleries. Tripods and open flashbulbs are not allowed, but visitors may use flashcubes and electronic units. Photographers may be asked to sign a photography-permission form; the museum does not permit commercial filming at any time.

MUSEUM MAILING LIST

Subscribers to the Mailing List receive the museum's monthly *Calendar* and advance notification of all lectures, study groups, exhibits, and special events.

Subscribers also receive a 10% discount in the museum bookstore at Christmas.

There is a $5. charge to cover postage and handling. Please do not combine Mailing List fee with any other payment. Separate check for Mailing List should be directed to Administration, The J. Paul Getty Museum.

I would like to subscribe to the J. Paul Getty Museum Mailing List:

$5 each subscription: Total enclosed:

Name

Address

City   Phone

State   Zip

Please send additional information about

☐ Postcards & notecards, posters, slides, and the J. Paul Getty Museum Appointment Calendar.

☐ Other publications

SOME TITLES FROM THE J. PAUL GETTY MUSEUM:

Masterpieces of Painting in The J. Paul Getty Museum
by Burton B. Fredericksen, 1980
51 full-page color plates illustrate the riches of the painting collection; many of the works are recent acquisitions and have never been reproduced in color.
$16.00 softcover; $24.00 hardcover

The J. Paul Getty Museum Guidebook
Sixth edition, 1982.
Softcover, $4.50

Herculaneum to Malibu: A Companion to the Visit to The J. Paul Getty Museum Building
by Norman Neuerburg, historical consultant for the design of the new museum building, 1975
Softcover, 80¢

Alma-Tadema's Spring
by Burton B. Fredericksen, 1978
Discussion of one of the most popular paintings in the museum.
Softcover, $3.50

Clocks: French 18th Century Clocks in the J. Paul Getty Museum
by Gillian Wilson, 1976
Catalogue of the fourteen French clocks in the museum's decorative arts collection.
Softcover, $6.00

Decorative Arts in the J. Paul Getty Museum
by Gillian Wilson, 1977
Pictorial checklist of all the decorative arts pieces in the museum up to 1977.
Softcover, $7.50

Catalogue of the Ancient Art in the J. Paul Getty Museum
by Cornelius C. Vermeule and Norman Neuerburg, 1973
Catalogue of the major antiquities – sculpture, frescoes, and mosaics – acquired by 1972. Packaged together with
Recent Acquisitions: Ancient Art
by Jiří Frel, 1974
Softcover, $15.00

The Getty Bronze, 1982 2nd Edition
by Jiří Frel, 1978
The first account of the museum's fourth century B.C. lifesize statue of a victorious athlete.
Softcover, $5.00 ; Cloth, $10.00

Skopas in Malibu
by Andrew Stewart
Commentary on the museum's marble head of a warrior from the west pediment of the temple of Athena Alea at Tegea and related works of art.
Softcover, $8.00 ; Cloth, $16.00

Greek Portraits in the J. Paul Getty Museum
by Jiří Frel
Roman Portraits in the J. Paul Getty Museum
by Jiří Frel
Mummy Portraits in the J. Paul Getty Museum
by David L. Thompson
Three books with popularly written catalogues and essays on portraiture in the classical world.
Each: Softcover, $16.95

Ancient Herbs in the J. Paul Getty Museum Garden
by Jeanne D'Andrea
Discussion of ancient Greek and Roman use of herbs for color, flavor, medicine, and religion. Illustrations of 21 herbs by Martha Bredemeyer.
Softcover, $10.00

Yes, please send me the following titles:

_____

_____

_____

_____

Please send to:

_____
Name

_____
Address*

_____
City   State   Zip

*If a P.O. Box is used, please give a daytime telephone number.

☐ Please bill me. We prefer to bill you with the shipment. Invoices are payable upon receipt.

☐ I enclose payment. If prepayment is desired, enclose amount for books (plus sales tax, if applicable) and we will ship COD on the shipping and handling costs.

All shipments made via UPS (domestic) and surface rate (overseas).

Prices subject to change without notice.

Please send additional information about

☐ Postcards & notecards, posters, slides, and the J. Paul Getty Museum Appointment Calendar.

☐ Other publications

The J. Paul Getty Museum
17985 Pacific Coast Highway
Malibu, California 90265

Mailing address:
P.O. Box 2112
Santa Monica, California 90406

GARDEN LEVEL

■ STAIRS
▲ ELEVATOR
● RESTROOMS

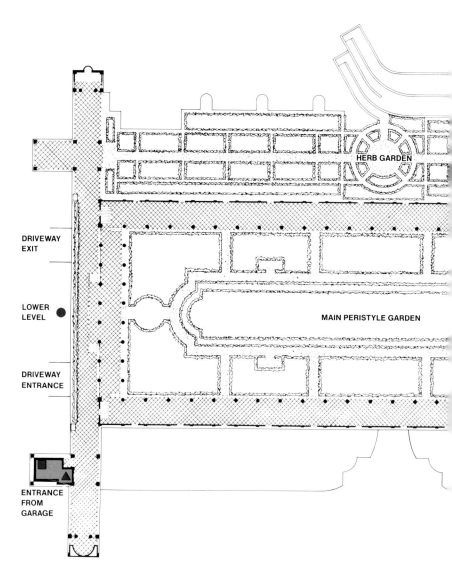

DRIVEWAY
EXIT

LOWER
LEVEL ●

DRIVEWAY
ENTRANCE

ENTRANCE
FROM
GARAGE

HERB GARDEN

MAIN PERISTYLE GARDEN

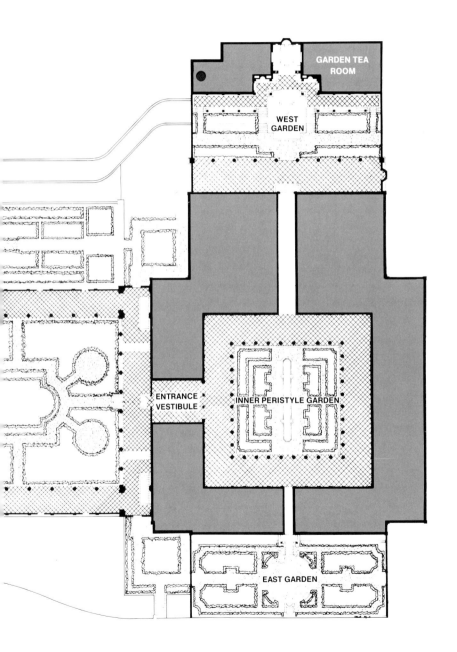

GARDEN TEA ROOM

WEST GARDEN

ENTRANCE VESTIBULE

INNER PERISTYLE GARDEN

EAST GARDEN

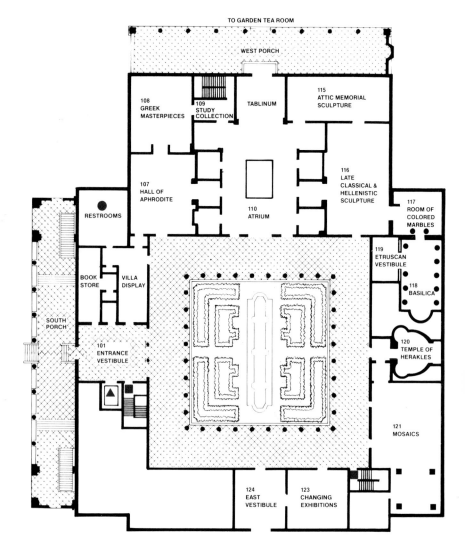

MAIN
LEVEL

■ STAIRS
▲ ELEVATOR
● RESTROOMS

TO GARDEN TEA ROOM

WEST PORCH

108
GREEK
MASTERPIECES

109
STUDY
COLLECTION

TABLINUM

115
ATTIC MEMORIAL
SCULPTURE

107
HALL OF
APHRODITE

116
LATE
CLASSICAL &
HELLENISTIC
SCULPTURE

● RESTROOMS

110
ATRIUM

117
ROOM OF
COLORED
MARBLES

119
ETRUSCAN
VESTIBULE

BOOK
STORE

VILLA
DISPLAY

118
BASILICA

SOUTH
PORCH

101
ENTRANCE
VESTIBULE

120
TEMPLE OF
HERAKLES

▲ ■

121
MOSAICS

124
EAST
VESTIBULE

123
CHANGING
EXHIBITIONS

132

UPPER
LEVEL

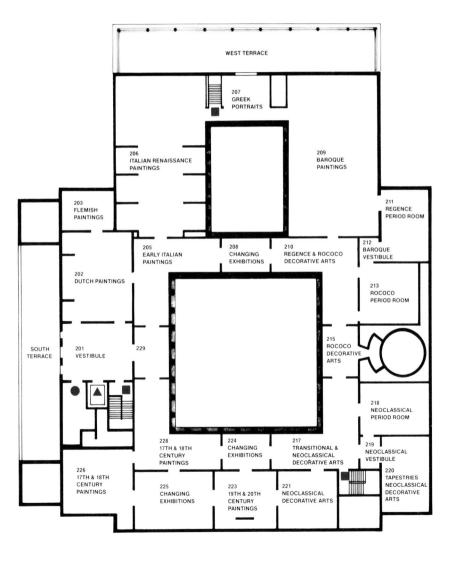

WEST TERRACE

207
GREEK
PORTRAITS

206
ITALIAN RENAISSANCE
PAINTINGS

209
BAROQUE
PAINTINGS

203
FLEMISH
PAINTINGS

211
REGENCE
PERIOD ROOM

205
EARLY ITALIAN
PAINTINGS

208
CHANGING
EXHIBITIONS

210
REGENCE & ROCOCO
DECORATIVE ARTS

212
BAROQUE
VESTIBULE

202
DUTCH PAINTINGS

213
ROCOCO
PERIOD ROOM

SOUTH
TERRACE

201
VESTIBULE

229

215
ROCOCO
DECORATIVE
ARTS

218
NEOCLASSICAL
PERIOD ROOM

228
17TH & 18TH
CENTURY
PAINTINGS

224
CHANGING
EXHIBITIONS

217
TRANSITIONAL &
NEOCLASSICAL
DECORATIVE ARTS

219
NEOCLASSICAL
VESTIBULE

226
17TH & 18TH
CENTURY
PAINTINGS

225
CHANGING
EXHIBITIONS

223
19TH & 20TH
CENTURY
PAINTINGS

221
NEOCLASSICAL
DECORATIVE ARTS

220
TAPESTRIES
NEOCLASSICAL
DECORATIVE
ARTS

© 1982 The J. Paul Getty Museum
17985 Pacific Coast Highway
Malibu, California 90265
Mailing address:
P.O. Box 2112
Santa Monica, California 90406
(213) 459-8402 reservations
All rights reserved
Sixth edition

Designed in Los Angeles by
John Anselmo Design Associates, Inc.
Text set in Garamond by
Typographic Service Co.
Lithographed on Quintessence Dull by
Alan Lithograph Inc.

Text on the collections by
Burton Fredericksen, *Curator of Paintings,*
Jiří Frel, *Curator of Antiquities,*
Gillian Wilson, *Curator of Decorative Arts.*

Photography by
Donald Hull,
Les Nakashima
(aerial, fac. p.1), and
Julius Shulman
(building and grounds)

Museum plans by
Pamela Palmer and Marti Kyrk.